Banking and Financial Systems in the Arab World

Also by Philip Molyneux and Munawar Iqbal

THIRTY YEARS OF ISLAMIC BANKING

Banking and Financial Systems in the Arab World

Philip Molyneux
Professor of Banking and Finance
University of Wales Bangor

and

Munawar Iqbal
Chief, Islamic Banking and Finance Division
Islamic Research and Training Institute
Islamic Development Bank
Jeddah

palgrave
macmillan

First published 2005 by
PALGRAVE MACMILLAN
Houndmills, Basingstoke, Hampshire RG21 6XS and
175 Fifth Avenue, New York, N.Y. 10010
Companies and representatives throughout the world

PALGRAVE MACMILLAN is the global academic imprint of the Palgrave Macmillan division of St. Martin's Press, LLC and of Palgrave Macmillan Ltd. Macmillan® is a registered trademark in the United States, United Kingdom and other countries. Palgrave is a registered trademark in the European Union and other countries.

ISBN 1–4039–4131–9

This book is printed on paper suitable for recycling and made from fully managed and sustained forest sources.

A catalogue record for this book is available from the British Library.

Library of Congress Cataloging-in-Publication Data
Molyneux, Philip.
   Banking and financial systems in the Arab world / Philip Molyneux & Munawar Iqbal.
      p.   cm.
   Includes bibliographical references and index.
   ISBN 1–4039–4131–9
   1. Banks and banking, Arab countries.   2. Financial institutions—Arab countries.   3. Banks and banking—Religious aspects—Islam.
   4. Finance—Arab countries.   5. Banking law (Islamic law)   I. Iqbal, Munawar.   II. Title.
   HG3366.A6M65 2004
   332.1′0917′4927—dc22   2004052107

10   9   8   7   6
14   13   12   11   10   09   08   07   06

Printed and bound in Great Britain by
Antony Rowe Ltd, Chippenham and Eastbourne

Contents

List of Tables

List of Figures

Preface

This text provides state-of-the-art analysis of banking and financial systems in the Arab world. The early chapters of the text present an overview of Arab economies, linking this to banking and financial sector trends in the Arab world over the last twenty years. Major contemporary themes relating to the structure and performance of Arab and Gulf Cooperation Council (GCC) banking systems including financial liberalization and the efficiency features of banking systems are analyzed in detail. Specific attention is paid to the recent empirical work on banking sector efficiency in various countries including Egypt, Jordan, the Gulf and Maghreb banking systems. Developments in retail, corporate and investment banking as well as the growth of Islamic banking are also noted throughout the text. In addition, regulatory developments impacting on banks in the Arab world, including the impact of Basel 2 and the OECD's Financial Action Task Force initiatives, are also discussed.

We believe that this text will be the first to provide a rigorous analytical evaluation of banking sector developments in the Arab world. Throughout the text, particular attention is paid to the changing performance features of Arab banking and financial systems in the light of global, regional and local economic developments. An attempt is also made to provide insights into comparative banking sector developments in the main GCC and non-GCC banking markets.

This text could not have been completed without the support and work of many individuals. It is not possible to list all involved but particular thanks go to Idries Al-Jarrah, Khalid Shams Mohamed, Sari Al-Shammari and Abderazak Bakhouche, all excellent PhD students at the University of Wales, Bangor, who provided outstanding research support without which this text could never have been completed. Thanks also go to Hessa Al-Khalifa, Abdulla Khaled Al-Attiya and Mohamed Hamid for the insights they provided to us. Thanks also due to Ali Almmari, Yener Altunbas, Ted Gardener, Jon Williams and Keith Williams who have also made helpful comments on various aspects of Arab banking issues.

We are thankful to Dr Umar Chapra, Senior Adviser, Islamic Research and Training Institute of the Islamic Development Bank, for providing useful insights on the subject. We are grateful to all who gave useful comments on earlier drafts of each chapter. Thanks are due to Mr Aman al-Hoque for secretarial assistance for preparing some chapters of this book.

Finally, thanks to our families and loved ones for their usual forbearance with projects of this kind.

The authors and publishers are grateful to Abderazak Bakhouche, Idries Al-Jarrah and Khalid Shams Mohamed for permission to the material from their Phd theses. Every effort has been made to contact all copyright-holders for copyright material in this book. If any have been inadvertently omitted, the publishers will be pleased to make the necessary arrangement at the earliest opportunity.

PHILIP MOLYNEUX
MUNAWAR IQBAL

About the Authors

Philip Molyneux is Professor in Banking and Finance and Director of the Institute of European Finance at the University of Wales, Bangor. He also has a chair at Erasmus University, Rotterdam, Netherlands. His main area of research is on the economics of the banking and financial services industry and he has published widely in this area including recent publications in the *Journal of Banking and Finance* and *Journal of Money, Credit and Banking*. Recent texts include: *Efficiency in European Banking* (Wiley 1998), *Private Banking* (Euromoney) and the latest, *European Banking: Efficiency, Growth & Technology* (Wiley, 2001). Professor Molyneux has acted as a consultant to New York Federal Reserve Bank, World Bank, European Commission, UK Treasury, Citibank Private Bank, Bermuda Commercial Bank, McKinsey's and various other international banks and consulting firms. In November 2001 he was the Visiting Bertill Daniellson Research Fellow at the Stockholm School of Economics and University of Gothenburg. Professor Molyneux has recently been appointed as one of eight expert financial sector advisers to the European Union's Economic and Monetary Affairs Committee that implements financial services regulations for the European Community.

Munawar Iqbal is Chief of Research in Islamic Banking and Finance at the Islamic Research and Training Institute of the Islamic Development Bank, Jeddah, Saudi Arabia (the largest Islamic financial institution in the world with an authorized capital of US dollars 20.5 billion). Professor Iqbal has also served as Economic Adviser to Al-Rajhi Banking and Investment Corporation, Saudi Arabia (the largest Islamic commercial bank in the world). Earlier, he served as the Director, International Institute of Islamic Economics, Islamic University, Islamabad, Pakistan. He has taught at the International Islamic University, Islamabad, McMaster University, Canada, and Simon Fraser University, Canada. He has published/edited more than ten books and published more than thirty papers in the field of Islamic Banking and Finance. Recent publications include *Islamic Banking and Finance: New Perspectives on Profit-Sharing Risk* (Edward Elgar, 2002) and *Islamic Banking and Finance: Current Developments in Theory and Practice* (The Islamic Foundation, UK, 2001). He was the founding Editor of the *Review of Islamic Economics*, the Professional Journal of the International Association for Islamic Economics, and also founding Editor (and continues to date) of the *Islamic Economic Studies*, the professional journal of the Islamic Development Bank. He has lectured extensively in the field of Islamic Banking and Finance throughout the world.

1
Introduction

Over the last 40 years Arab countries have made significant progress in laying down the foundations of modern economies and financial systems. Gulf economies have been boosted largely by oil export revenues resulting in among the highest rates of economic growth and per capita income in the world. Other Arab countries, such as those of North Africa, have experienced less rapid and more variable development although major reforms have been implemented at various stages aimed at introducing more market-based economic and financial systems. Typically, the energy-rich Gulf economies are characterized by low domestic income diversification, low inflation rates, stable exchange rate policies, high dependence on foreign labour, and a major role played by governments in the economic growth process. Those outside the Gulf have a high dependence on primary sectors and the government. The service sector throughout the Arab world tends to be modest in size compared with Western counterparts.

Certain policies have been undertaken aimed at restructuring these economies. Such reforms have aimed at economic diversification, privatization of public enterprises, encouragement of greater participation of endogenous labour (in Gulf States) and the relaxation and reformation of investment rules aimed at encouraging foreign direct investment. With regard to financial system development, countries have made significant progress in building the infrastructure of their financial systems, resulting in higher rates of financial deepening that fulfil the growing financial needs of the real sector of the economy. Before the existence of domestic banks, the presence of foreign banks helped in shaping the banking and financial systems of most Arab countries, and induced them to set out or establish a more modern financial sector architecture.

Nowadays Arab financial systems are characterized by relatively high levels of financial deepening, capitalization, and deposit bases, and most have experienced increasing levels of profitability in the latter part of the 1990s and early 2000s. Financial systems have also adopted reform policies aimed at unleashing competitive forces and improving the regulatory structure of

1

the respective markets. Progress has been made in many systems towards increasing the openness within the banking and financial system, monetary policy has become more market-based, and systems are increasingly regulated according to international standards. All these features help enhance the competitive environment in which banks and financial firms operate. Arab banks are also emulating the strategic behaviour of their Western counterparts by adopting new technology, implementing more-advanced risk management systems, developing new distribution channels and diversifying their product mix. Offering non-traditional commercial banking services such as private banking, insurance, leasing and Islamic financial products is becoming commonplace. Banks are also putting greater emphasis on generating appropriate returns to shareholders (and stakeholders) and standards of prudential control and corporate governance are being strengthened. Overall, there continues to be increasing pressure on banks to improve their cost of operation and to use more sophisticated technologies that increase productivity with the ultimate goal of improving overall efficiency and revenue generation by the financial system.

This book is the first, as far as we are aware, to provide a detailed insight into the banking and financial features of Arab systems. It brings together an extensive practical and academic literature on the economies and financial features of Arab systems and analyzes contemporary trends and developments impacting on bank strategy and performance. The main features of the text are outlined below.

Chapter 2 provides an overview of the main socio-economic characteristics of Arabian countries over the last twenty years or so. The aim is to outline the nature of economic development that has taken place in the region as well as highlighting various broad financial sector developments and other reforms that have taken place. The Arabic region comprises 21 countries whose people speak the Arabic language (called Arabia in this text). These countries can be classified economically into oil- and non-oil-exporting countries. Four major Arabian blocs have appeared over the past years. These blocs include the Council of Arab Economic Unity, the Arab Maghreb Union, the Gulf Cooperation Council (GCC) and the Council of Arab Mashreq countries. These blocs share similar objectives; integrating and enforcing the economic and cultural ties between member countries. The area and population of individual Arabian countries vary considerably. The living standards for individual countries also vary widely particularly in terms of per capita GDP. Many Arabian countries, for instance, suffer in terms of high poverty levels, high rates of illiteracy and low levels of human development. Despite the variations in the economic resources of individual countries, Arabia is rich in natural resources. Especially, its oil reserves account for two-thirds of the world's crude oil. The financial systems in the Arab world are primarily bank-based. Capital markets are relatively underdeveloped. In addition, the state has traditionally played a major role in the banking and financial sector.

In Chapter 3 we discuss the economic performance of Arabian countries over the last two decades or so. The economic growth of Arabian countries (as measured by real GDP) slowed over 1982–91, averaging 1.6 per cent compared to 4 per cent for other developing countries over the same period. This slowness led to low levels of investment and high levels of unemployment. This was also associated with rising levels of external indebtedness and fiscal deficits, especially for non-oil-exporting countries. This led many Arabian countries to undertake macroeconomic reforms to promote economic growth. During the 1990s, Arabia's economic performance improved compared to the 1980s and the gap of economic growth compared to other developing countries reduced despite the difficult situation faced by some individual economies. Real GDP growth averaged 3.9 per cent between 1992 and 1999 compared to 5.6 per cent for all developing countries over the same period. The trade balance of Arab oil countries witnessed surplus during the 1990s while those of the non-oil Arab countries witnessed deficits, but these deficits as a percent of GDP have been falling. Inflation rates have been reduced in many Arabian countries, especially in comparison with 1980s levels. While the external debts of some Arabian countries are still high, external debt as a percentage of GDP appears to be following a declining trend. The total foreign exchange reserves of the Arabian countries increased sharply during the 1990s, especially the reserves of the non-oil exporting countries. Investment levels have also witnessed improvement, especially foreign investment. The final part of the chapter introduces various issues concerning financial sector development in the Arab world.

Chapter 4 reviews the main features of the financial systems of Jordan, Egypt and the main Maghreb countries (Algeria, Morocco and Tunisia). All these countries have experienced various financial reforms aimed at liberalizing their financial systems. Jordan and Egypt, in particular, have witnessed major financial reforms over the last decade, aimed at replacing financial repression and excessive regulation with a more competitive environment. The reform procedures in the countries have included deregulation of interest and credit controls, privatization of banks and the gradual opening up to foreign banks, improving bank capitalization in accordance with Basel standards and introducing new prudential guidelines. In general, stock markets have been upgraded and they have begun to play a wider role in financing various economic sectors within their respective countries. However, commercial banks still dominate financial systems and the state still plays a major role in most systems. Financial indicators reveal an enhanced role for financial intermediaries in the process of economic growth and exhibit the positive impact of economic and financial reforms undertaken in these countries. Furthermore, financial systems have deepened and the proportion of credit allocated to the private sector as a percent of GDP has generally increased, suggesting that the financial institutions are gradually becoming more efficient in allocating financial resources to the most efficient users.

Chapter 5 discusses financial systems of the Gulf Cooperation Council countries: Saudi Arabia, United Arab Emirates, Bahrain, Kuwait, Oman and Qatar. It covers the development of individual GCC countries' banking systems and financial markets, an analysis of the performance of Gulf banks, and briefly outlines recent moves to create a GCC economic and financial union. In general these countries have experienced various financial reforms aimed at strengthening their financial systems and these have mainly included moves to deregulate as well as to improve prudential standards. Stock markets have been upgraded and they have begun to play a wider role in financing various economic sectors within their respective countries, although their importance still remains limited. Commercial banks still dominate GCC financial systems and banking systems are highly concentrated. Gulf banking systems show favourable improvement in terms of their asset quality, capital adequacy and profitability during the 1990s. Such indicators reveal an enhanced role for financial intermediaries in the process of economic growth and exhibit the positive impact of economic and financial reforms undertaken in these countries. Furthermore, from earlier analysis we know that financial systems have deepened in these countries and the proportion of credit allocated to the private sector as a percent of GDP has increased, suggesting that banks have become more efficient in allocating financial resources within the respective countries. Taken together, this suggests that the performance and efficiency of financial and banking systems under study is likely to have improved during the 1990s. Although it is difficult to say specifically whether this improvement is a result of reforms or improvements in the general macroeconomic environment, perhaps one can at least suggest that the reform process has had some positive influence.

In Chapter 6 we discuss the features and developments in Islamic banking. Islamic banking practice which started in the early 1970s on a modest scale has shown tremendous progress during the last 30 years. A number of Islamic banks and other Islamic financial institutions have been established under heterogeneous, social and economic milieu. Now there are around a hundred Islamic banks and financial institutions working in the private sector, with the largest number being located in the Gulf Cooperation Council (GCC) countries followed by other Middle Eastern countries. The Arab world accounts for over 58 per cent of the number and over 80 per cent of Islamic bank assets. Recently, many conventional banks, including some major multinational Western banks, have also started using Islamic banking techniques. Various components of the Islamic financial system are now available in different parts of the world in varying depth and quality.

A detailed and integrated system of Islamic banking and finance is gradually evolving. While Islamic banking fulfils the religious requirements for Muslims, it also broadens the choice-set available to others by offering sales-finance, low-risk products (i.e. buying and selling) as well as products based on sharing risks and returns. In addition to providing more choices to clients, this mix of fixed and variable return modes has a number of healthy effects for the efficiency and stability of the system. Islamic banking should not be seen as a religious movement but rather viewed as another way of performing the financial intermediation function.

Chapter 7 examines issues concerning the study of financial system efficiency. Early chapters point out that a major objective of various financial liberalization programmes undertaken in many Arab countries is to promote more competitive, stable and better performing operating environments for banks and other financial firms. Inextricably linked to these objectives is the improvement in the efficiency of banks and the financial system overall. Among the many functions the financial system performs, there are two that are essential for any economy: one is the administration of the payments mechanism, and the other is intermediation between ultimate savers and borrowers. However, undertaking these functions may not be sufficient for the financial system to maintain its well-being and performance. The experience of many financial systems that have experienced financial crises suggests an essential element in the functioning of the financial system is the extent of its efficient operation. This is extensively linked to the soundness and safety of the financial system overall. The first part of the chapter discusses why an efficient banking and financial system is desirable from a policy perspective and shows how financial sector deregulation is inextricably linked to various efficiency concepts. The remainder of the chapter examines how one can measure banking system efficiency and the main results from the empirical literature.

Chapter 8 discusses recent empirical evidence on Arab banking sector efficiency. Overall, the literature suggests that profit inefficiencies appear to be greater than cost inefficiencies in most Arab banking systems, a finding similar to that found for US and European banking systems. This means that there is greater variation in bank profit performance compared with cost differences across systems. Banks therefore need to focus more on revenue generation coupled with appropriate risk management practices if they are to boost performance and emulate best practice. X-inefficiencies also typically exceed scale economies although with regard to bank size the largest institutions appear to realize substantial economies perhaps creating further incentive for merger activity. The findings for Gulf banks also reveal that foreign banks are less cost efficient, but more profit efficient than national banks. This suggests that foreign banks focus more on revenue generating than do their domestic counterparts. As foreign banks tend to have a different business mix (high end retail clients, large corporate banking services, and so on), it is perhaps not surprising that they are found to be less cost efficient but more profit efficient. The literature also finds that Islamic banks appear, on average, to be more efficient than their traditional banking competitors and this may be another reason why this type of banking business is gaining popularity in the region. While substantial variations in the cost and profit features of Arab banks exist, the main findings generally concur with the results on banking sector efficiency in the US and Europe. What is surprising is that there is little evidence to suggest that the major financial reforms had a noticeable impact in improving banking sector efficiency during the 1990s. This may be because the efficiency gains associated with liberalization programmes are counterbalanced by changes in the economic environment and/or other operating conditions faced by Arab banks. The high degree of concentration and role of the government in Arab banking systems may also mitigate financial liberalization effects. Nevertheless, there does appear to be consensus that Arab banking markets are becoming more competitive and this is highlighted in the following chapter where we discuss contemporary developments and expected future trends in Arab banking systems.

Chapter 9 provides insights into contemporary banking sector developments and strategy. Since the late 1990s, banks throughout the Arab world have been generating strong returns to their shareholders. This performance has resulted mainly from banks' emphasis on improving their cost and revenue efficiency during the 1990s and also managing their risk exposures more effectively. Shareholder (or stakeholder) value has become a critical driver of bank strategy. Much greater attention is nowadays placed on the efficient allocation of capital throughout the banking firms. Risk and return features of banks' operations are managed more effectively and this has also encouraged the trend to more performance-enhancing balance sheet and risk management practices, such as the growing use of sophisticated securitization and credit risk management techniques. Arab banks now place much more emphasis on boosting their non-margin income from off-balance-sheet activities such as from trading, underwriting, private banking and asset management business. The banking industry has also been transformed by consolidation and profits strengthened by buoyant domestic economies. Banking markets have become more concentrated and at the same time more competitive as new financial and non-financial entrants make the banking business more contestable. In addition, universal banking continues to be the dominant form of bank operational model. Similar to their counterparts in the West, Arab banks aim to maintain their performance by developing long-term customer relationships and capturing an increased range of clients' (both retail and corporate) financial activity. Given this strategic direction, many banks are focusing on developing their non-traditional business in areas like insurance, private banking, asset management, pensions and other investment services. The focus on developing a wider array of retail financial services is driven by the rapidly changing demographics and client demand in the region. Corporate and investment banking business is increasingly overlapping with traditional lending business being supplemented with a growing array of more specialized and capital market based services.

The operating environment for Arab banks is also being influenced by various international regulatory developments. Bank for International Settlements' initiatives aimed at enhancing bank supervision and corporate governance have generally been taken on-board, as have the OECD's Financial Action Task Force's (FATF) recommendations on anti-money-laundering and terrorist-financing. Introduction of Basel 2 capital adequacy rules and the formation of a single GCC banking market will also impact on the strategies of many banks.

2
An Overview of Arabian Economies

Introduction

This chapter provides an overview of the main socio-economic features of Arabian countries over the last twenty years or so. The aim is to describe the nature of economic development that has taken place in the region as well highlighting the various broad financial sector developments and other reforms that have taken place. The Arabic region comprises 21 countries whose people speak the Arabic language and these countries can be classified economically into oil- and non-oil-exporting countries. Many Arabian blocs have appeared over the past years. These blocs share similar objectives; integrating and enforcing the economic and cultural ties between member countries. These blocs include the Council of Arab Economic Unity, the Arab Maghreb Union, the Gulf Cooperation Council (GCC) and the Council of Arab Mashreq countries.

The area and population of individual Arabian countries vary considerably. The living standards for individual countries also vary widely particularly in terms of per capita GDP. Various Arabian countries, for instance, suffer poverty, high rates of illiteracy and low levels of human resource/development. Despite the variations in the economic resources of individual countries, Arabia is rich in natural resources, especially oil reserves that account for two-thirds of the world's crude oil. The financial systems in the Arab world are primarily bank-based. Capital markets are relatively underdeveloped. In addition, the state has traditionally played a major role in the banking and financial sector.

Economic, social and demographic trends

Arabia comprises 21 countries whose people speak the Arabic language. Geographically, Arabia covers the largest part of the Middle East and North Africa; its borders extend from Iraq in the East to the North Atlantic Ocean in the West, and from Turkey in the North to the Arabian Sea in the South (see Figure 2.1).

Regionally, four major Arabian blocs have emerged over the last fifty years (see Table 2.1). The first is the Council of Arab Economic Unity that was established in Cairo in 1957. This bloc aimed to achieve closer economic integration among its members through free movement of goods, persons and capital. The second bloc is the Arab Maghreb Union, established in

Northern Africa and the Middle East

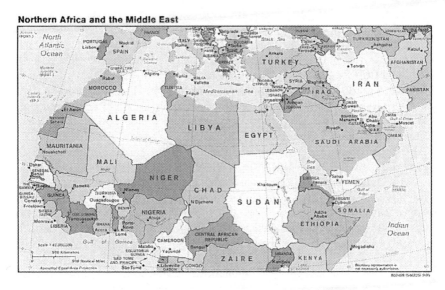

Figure 2.1 Geographical map of Arabian countries
Source: UTLibrary(http://www.lib.utexas.edu/maps/middle_east_and_asia/n_africa_mid_east_pol_95.jpg – used by permission of The General Libraries, The University of Texas at Austin

Table 2.1 Members of Arabian countries

Council of Arab Economic Unity	Arab Maghreb Union	The states of Gulf	Arab Mashreq	Other Arabian Countries
Egypt	Algeria	Bahrain	Egypt	Comoros
Iraq	Libya	Iraq	Jordan	Djibouti
Jordan	Mauritania	Kuwait	Lebanon	Somalia
Lebanon	Morocco	Oman	Palestine	Sudan
Palestine	Tunisia	Qatar	Syria	
Syria		Saudi Arabia		
		The UAE		

Sources: Adapted from El-Erian *et al.* 1996, p. 2; and Bayomi, 1995.

1989, with the aim of strengthening economic and cultural ties, ensuring regional stability and promoting trade among its members. The third bloc, the Gulf Cooperation Council (GCC), was established in 1981. This bloc includes all the Arabian Gulf states and has as its main objective to secure stability in the Gulf region through economic and political cooperation, and the coordination of commercial, monetary, financial, and economic policies among member states. The fourth bloc is known as the Arab Mashreq (Mashreq translates as 'the East') that also aims to promote economic and political integration between its members.

In addition to the above classification based on regional and trading blocs, Table 2.2 shows that Arabian countries can also be classified into oil and non-oil producing countries.

The area of individual Arabian countries varies considerably (Table 2.3). The area of the largest three (Sudan, Algeria and Saudi Arabia) is more than 7 million square kilometres comprising about 64 per cent of the total Arabia area. On the other hand, the area of each of the smallest six countries (Kuwait, Qatar, Bahrain, Djibouti, Lebanon and Comoros) does not exceed 25 thousand square kilometres.

The population of Arabian countries was around 275 million in 1999; nearly the same size as the USA. The smallest countries, in terms of population, are Bahrain, Djibouti and Qatar, where each has less than one million persons, while the largest are Egypt, Algeria, Morocco and Iraq, each with a population of over 20 millions persons (Table 2.4). Population density in Arabia also varies considerably. While Bahrain, Lebanon and Comoros have the densest

Table 2.2   Oil and non-oil Arabian countries

Oil producing countries	Non-oil producing countries*
Algeria	Comoros
Bahrain	Djibouti
Iraq	Egypt
Kuwait	Jordan
Libya	Lebanon
Oman	Mauritania
Qatar	Morocco
Saudi Arabia	Palestine
UAE	Somalia
	Sudan
	Syria
	Tunisia

Source: Adapted from El-Erian *et al.*, 1996, p. 2.
* Although other countries such as Egypt, Syria, Tunisia and the Republic of Yemen export oil, the role of oil in their economies is relatively limited.

Table 2.3   Area of Arabian countries (sq. km, thousands)

Arab states	Area
Oil-exporter (total)	7,055
Algeria	2,382
Saudi Arabia	2,150
Libya	1,760
Iraq	438
Oman	212
UAE	84
Kuwait	18
Qatar	11
Bahrain	1
Non-oil exporter (total)	6,619
Sudan	2,506
Mauritania	1,026
Egypt, Arab Rep.	1,001
Somalia	638
Yemen, Rep.	528
Morocco	447
Syria	185
Tunisia	164
Jordan	89
Djibouti	23
Lebanon	10
Comoros	2
Middle East & North Africa	11,024

Source: The World Bank, 1999/2000, pp. 230–1.

populations, Mauritania, Libya, Saudi Arabia and United Arab Emirates are the least populated.

Arabian countries possess abundant natural resources. Nevertheless, the living standards in the individual countries exhibit a broad diversity of characteristics. While some Arabian countries are classified among high-income countries with per capita income of more than $7,000 (United Arab Emirates, Kuwait, Bahrain, and Libya), some others have per capita income less than $1,000 and are classified among the poorest in the world (Morocco, Comoros and Mauritania). The dispersion in prosperity across the region is reflected in various indicators such as those shown in Table 2.5. For instance, around 10 per cent of the population of Bahrain, Lebanon and Jordan live in poverty compared to about half the population of Yemen, Djibouti and Mauritania.

Furthermore, other human development indicators (i.e. adult literacy, educational attainment and life expectancy) show that only four Arabian countries, out of the 21, rank as highly developed countries (Table 2.6).

Table 2.4   Population and population density of Arabian countries over 1970–99 (in millions, figures rounded to nearest digit)

	1970	1980	1990	1999	*Population density/1999*
*Arab oil-exporter (total)**	29	39	70	87	130
Algeria	15	20	25	30	3
Iraq	10	13	17	22	10
Saudi Arabia	...	...	16	21	10
Libya	2	3	4	5	13
UAE	0	1	2	3	35
Oman	1	1	2	2	45
Kuwait	1	1	2	2	50
Qatar	...	...	1	1	100
Bahrain	...	...	1	1	900
*Arab non-oil-exporter (total)**	82	105	151	188	100
Egypt	35	40	50	62	2
Sudan	15	20	25	30	12
Morocco	15	20	25	30	15
Yemen, Republic of	...	...	13	15	30
Syria	6	9	12	18	30
Tunisia	5	6	8	10	50
Somalia	3	5	9	9	60
Jordan	2	3	4	5	60
Lebanon	...	...	3	4	60
Mauritania	1	2	2	3	83
Djibouti	...	...	...	1	300
Comoros	...	...	...	1	400
Arabian countries (total)*	111	144	221	275	...
Middle East & North Africa	...	...	...	290	...

* For countries that have available data; ... = not available
Source: World Bank, 1991, various pages; and Arab Monetary Fund, 2002 (www.amf.org.ae) for 1990 and 1999 data.

These include Bahrain, Qatar, Kuwait, and the Untied Arab Emirates, while at the other extreme are Djibouti, Mauritania, Sudan and Yemen. Adult illiteracy is high in Arabia especially in the non-oil exporting countries. In the least developed countries, it is slightly less than 50 per cent (for instance in Djibouti, Morocco and Yemen).

The above indicators provide a snapshot of various demographic and economic characteristics across the Arab world and highlight the diversity in the region. Differences in the human development characteristics in these countries are attributed mainly to the variations in the distribution of natural resource in these countries. About two-thirds of the world's crude-oil reserves lie in these countries, with one-quarter located in Saudi Arabia. Arabia also possesses various non-fuel mineral and non-mineral

Table 2.5   Poverty in Arabian countries (mid-1997)

	Population suffering from poverty (million)	Poverty (%) of population
Oil-exporter	10.4	19
Algeria	8.4	29
Saudi Arabia	. . .	. . .
Libya	1.0	16
Iraq	. . .	. . .
Oman	0.6	24
UAE	0.5	18
Kuwait	. . .	. . .
Qatar	. . .	. . .
Bahrain	0.1	10
Non-oil exporter	57.2	31
Sudan	10.3	37
Mauritania	1.1	48
Egypt, Arab Rep.	20.5	33
Somalia	. . .	. . .
Yemen, Rep.	8.1	49
Morocco	10.7	39
Syria	3.0	20
Tunisia	2.1	23
Jordan	0.6	10
Djibouti	0.3	41
Lebanon	0.4	11
Comoros	0.2	34
Arabian countries	67.6	28

Source: UNDP, *Human Development Report 1999*, pp. 146–50.

resources. Algeria, Morocco, Tunisia, Jordan and Syria account for about one-third of the world's phosphate production. Arabia is also endowed with other natural resources like potash (Jordan), iron (Mauritania), ammonia and urea (Qatar), copper and gypsum (Mauritania), cotton (Egypt and Sudan), tobacco (Syria) and coffee (Yemen) (El-Erian *et al.*, 1996).

During the 1960s and 1970s, several Arabian economies experienced favourable economic performance (Bisat *et al.*, 1997). The discovery of natural resources, especially oil, contributed tremendously to their economic growth during this period. Increases in the price of oil, especially between 1973 and 1979, enhanced economic performance especially in the oil exporting countries. The other Arabian countries experienced a positive secondary effect, primarily because of remittance flows and the availability of greater financial assistance from the rich oil countries.

During the 1980s, the economic performance of Arabia lagged especially in comparison with the higher rates of economic growth achieved in other

Table 2.6   Trends in human development of Arabian countries for 1997

Arab states	Life expectancy at birth	Adult literacy	HD rank*
Oil-exporter (average)	71	73	
Bahrain	73	86	High
Kuwait	76	80	High
Qatar	72	80	High
Libya	70	77	Medium
UAE	75	75	High
Saudi Arabia	71	73	Medium
Oman	71	67	Medium
Algeria	69	60	Medium
Iraq	62	58	Medium
Non-oil-exporter (average)	62	59	
Jordan	70	87	Medium
Lebanon	70	84	Medium
Syria	69	72	Medium
Tunisia	70	67	Medium
Comoros	59	55	Medium
Sudan	55	53	Low
Egypt	66	53	Medium
Djibouti	50	48	Low
Morocco	67	46	Medium
Yemen	58	43	Low
Mauritania	54	38	Low
Somalia	N/A	N/A	

* The HD rank, according to the UNDP, is based on longevity as measured by life expectancy at birth; educational attainment as measured by a combination of adult literacy (two-thirds weight) and the combined gross primary, secondary and tertiary enrolment ratio (one-third weight); and standard of living, as measured by real GDP per capita.
Source: UNDP, 1999, pp. 135–40.

developing regions of the world (Alonso-Gamo *et al.*, 1997a and b). The economic growth of the Arabic countries (as measured by real GDP growth) averaged about 1.6 per cent over 1982–91. This growth rate was much lower than that of other developing countries and Asian industrialized countries that achieved more than 4 per cent annualized growth over the same period. The slowness in economic growth was attributed mainly to the vulnerability of sources of income in Arabia that relied heavily on exports of natural resources.

Moreover, during the 1980s, the investment performance of Arabian countries weakened markedly (Bisat *et al.*, 1997). Investment levels stayed at about 20 per cent of GDP from the mid-1980s until the mid-1990s; a level lower than the average for developing countries as a whole, reaching nearly 26 per cent by 1996. In addition to low levels of domestic investment, Arabia attracted only modest amounts of foreign direct investment, a significant share of which was concentrated in the energy sector. From the mid-1980s until 1995, the ratio of foreign direct investment to GDP amounted to only 0.5 per cent annually. In comparison, the Asian region attracted foreign direct investment flows equivalent to more than 1 per cent of GDP per year over the same period.

Since the mid-1990s there has been a renewed emphasis on economic and financial reforms across the region that has helped foster increased levels of FDI. This, combined with improvements in oil prices has boosted the oil-exporting economies, particularly towards the end of the decade.

Role of the state

Before the 1980s, various Arabian countries relied on the public sector as a mechanism for their economic growth (Zeinelabdin, 1997). Governments invested in areas considered important to development, especially in projects where the private sector was either unwilling or unable to invest because of perceived risks or excessive capital requirements. Fulfilling major social objectives was often behind decisions to establish various government enterprises in 'strategic' sectors of the economy.

Economic policy in Arabia, especially in non-oil countries, started to change during the 1980s as a result of increases in foreign indebtedness and the rise in fiscal deficits (El-Erian and Fennell, 1997). Arabic governments were forced to re-examine their policy stance. As a consequence, various Arabian countries initiated widespread macroeconomic reforms, especially since the early 1990s, involving substantial privatization programmes. The largest moves in this respect have occurred in Morocco, Tunisia, Egypt and Jordan.

Privatization in Arabia has been viewed as a means of reducing public indebtedness as well as a way to attract foreign technology and management; the latter is supposed to improve economic efficiency. The objectives of privatization enumerated by the governments of the respective countries varied although they had identical objectives. These were to develop a stronger private sector, improve the performance and profitability of public enterprises, strengthen performance of financial market institutions and improve the climate for increased private investment.

Constraints to growth

In addition to decline in oil price that heavily affected the economic performance of Arabian countries during the 1980s and early 1990s, other important structural constraints have been suggested as contributory factors to dampening economic growth. The dominance of the public sector in most countries has, some suggest, undermined the productivity of the private sector (Alonso-Gamo *et al.*, 1997 a and b, and Bisat *et al.*, 1997). The existence of large public sectors has crowded-out private sector initiatives resulting in a lack of investment opportunities for foreign and domestic private capital.

The large revenues derived from oil and other natural resources have allowed various Arabian countries to finance their external account deficits. This has however contributed to the postponement of needed internal reforms including trade liberalization. Moreover, the excessive reliance on volatile oil export receipts in various Arabian countries has increased the vulnerability of such revenues to external shocks.

The financial systems of many Arabic countries are also underdeveloped. Only a few Arabic countries have well-established stock markets (namely Morocco, Tunisia, Egypt, Jordan, Oman, Kuwait, Lebanon and Bahrain), making it difficult for domestic firms in many activities to raise equity and non-bank finance (Alonso-Gamo *et al.*, 1997b). (Though it should be noted that all the Gulf economies had established exchanges by 2003.) Furthermore, the existence of restrictions on the establishment of foreign banks has also limited competition and hindered transfer of knowledge and technology for local institutions (Alonso-Gamo *et al.*, 1997b). In most Arabian countries no more than 49 per cent of a domestic bank can be held by foreigners. In Lebanon, a foreign bank can open only one branch; and in Morocco, offshore branches are allowed but can only deal with non-residents.

Finally, lack of adequate institutional and legal frameworks for investment in many Arabian countries has resulted in lack of transparency in the regulatory environment. However, since the mid-1990s, many Arabian countries have become members of the World Trade Organization (WTO) which has enhanced transparency and increased credibility of these countries in terms of their trading performance.

Economic reforms and the globalization process

During the 1980s and early 1990s, many Arabian governments faced unfavourable economic conditions, represented by rising rates of unemployment and increasing social demands associated with sluggish economic growth. In response, governments initiated structural reforms aimed at facilitating a more efficient allocation of resources and achieving higher rates of growth.

Various Arabian countries have undertaken steps to expand the role of their private sectors through deregulation, opening their economies to greater foreign participation, adopting transparent commercial procedures and harmonizing tax provisions. The countries that initiated substantial privatization programmes since the 1990s or earlier include: Egypt, Algeria, Kuwait, Yemen and Jordan (El-Erian *et al.*, 1996). Other countries that have undertaken major reform programmes include Morocco, Tunisia and Mauritania (see, for example, Alonso-Gamo *et al.*, 1997b; El-Erian and Fennell, 1997; Bisat *et al.*, 1997). On the other hand, oil-exporting economies have intensified adjustment efforts by focusing on expenditure reduction in the face of lower oil revenues and a reduced flow of investment.

Several Arabian countries also introduced new legislation in the second half of the 1990s aimed at simplifying investment procedures (particularly Mauritania, Lebanon, Egypt, Morocco and Jordan). Further steps have also been undertaken by several Arabian countries including Egypt, Morocco, Sudan, Yemen, Algeria and Syria to remove price distortions (such as administered prices, interest rate ceilings and restrictions on foreign exchange) (El-Erian *et al.*, 1996; El-Erian and Fennell, 1997).

The aforementioned policies have, in general, enhanced foreign investment and increased non-oil exports. El-Erian and Fennell (1997), for instance, note that various Arabic countries including Egypt, Jordan, Lebanon, Morocco and Tunisia have renewed their access capabilities to international capital markets. Furthermore, many Arabian countries have joined the World Trade Organization (WTO): Bahrain, Djibouti, Egypt, Jordan, Kuwait, Mauritania, Morocco, Qatar, Tunisia and United Arab Emirates. Other countries have requested WTO membership: Saudi Arabia, Algeria and Sudan. (Alonso-Gamo *et al.*, 1997b).

In addition, various Arabian countries have undertaken substantial financial sector reforms to enhance the role of financial institutions and to improve the investment climate (Alonso-Gamo *et al.*, 1997b, and El-Erian and Fennell, 1997). Such reforms have helped a number of Arabian countries obtain relatively high sovereign credit ratings from the international credit rating agencies as shown in Table 2.7.

Table 2.7   Credit ratings of Arabian countries for 1997*

Country	Moody's	Standard & Poor's
Bahrain	Ba1	
Egypt	Ba2	BBB–
Jordan	B1	BB–
Kuwait	Baa1	
Lebanon	Ba1	BB–
Oman	Baa2	BBB–
Qatar	Baa2	BBB
Saudi Arabia	Baa3	
Tunisia	Baa3	
The UAE	Baa1	

* Moody's ratings rank long-term foreign currency bonds and notes (from D, C, Ca, and Caa: default rate; B and Ba: non-investment grade; and Baa, A, Aa, and Aaa: investment grade.) Intermediate rankings range from 1 (highest) to 3 (lowest). S&P's ratings rank long-term foreign currency credit (from C to CCC+: default rate; B– to BB+: non-investment grade; and BBB– to AAA: investment grade).
Source: Adapted from Alonso-Gamo *et al.*, 1997, p. 32.

A large number of Arabian countries have also embarked on comprehensive reforms of their financial and banking sectors to promote savings and to obtain better allocation of funds. Others have or are considering taking steps to open their banking sectors and stock markets to greater foreign participation. According to El-Erian and Fennell (1997), the Arabian countries that initiated comprehensive financial sector reforms during the 1990s include Jordan, Lebanon, Morocco, Tunisia and Egypt.

To sum up, Arabia possesses valuable natural resources that have helped enhance living standards in these countries. However, many Arabian countries suffered from sluggish economic growth (along with higher levels of population growth) during the 1980s. This has forced the authorities to initiate economic reforms aimed at adoption of a more market-oriented environment.

Oil and non-oil economies – a comparison of Jordan, Egypt, Saudi Arabia and Bahrain

So as to get a more detailed feel for the differences between oil and no-oil Arab economies this section provides a brief comparison of the economies of four major Arab systems. We chose to look at these economies as they have relatively larger and well-developed banking and financial systems. For instance, apart from Jordan, the banking and financial systems in the countries under study are the largest in the Arab region. This contrasts with the banking systems operating in other Arabian countries such as Iraq, Libya and Syria which are primarily government owned, and those in the Comoros, Djibouti and Somalia where they are substantially underdeveloped. Moreover, the banking systems in Kuwait and Lebanon have undergone extreme economic conditions as a result of wars during the 1990s and therefore are less amenable to comparative study.

As noted in the case of Arab countries in general, Jordan, Egypt, Saudi Arabia and Bahrain differ widely in terms of their socio-economic make-up. Table 2.8 shows some of these differences. Bahrain is the smallest in terms of both the country's area and population but is the most developed in terms of GDP per capita. At the opposite end of the scale is Egypt, with a population larger than any other Arabian country but with GDP per capita around US$ 1,010 over 1990–9. Both Saudi Arabia and Bahrain are oil-exporting countries and their people enjoy relatively high living standards, while those in Jordan and Egypt are considerably less prosperous.

Historically, Jordan's population experienced three sharp increases due to immigration resulting from Middle East wars. Following the 1948 and 1967 wars, about 700,000 people moved from Palestine to Jordan, and after the Gulf War in 1990, about 400,000 Palestinians left Kuwait to Jordan (Mohammed, 1994). Such events contributed largely to the high levels of unemployment experienced in this country, especially during the 1990s.

Table 2.8   General indicators for Jordan, Egypt, Saudi Arabia and Bahrain

Indicators	Jordan	Egypt	Saudi Arabia	Bahrain
Area (000, sq. km)	90	1,000	2,150	1
Population (millions)/1999	5	60	20	1
Population density (persons/sq. km)/1998	50	60	10	900
Population growth (average 1995–9)	12	7	13	15
Human poverty (% of population)/ mid-1997	10	30		10
Life expectancy at birth	70	65	70	70
Adult literacy %	85	55	75	85
Human development rank	Medium	Medium	Medium	High
GDP per capita (US$, average 1990–9)	1,410	1,010	6,880	9,700
Rates of inflation (consumer prices, annual % change) (average 1992–8)	4	10	1	1
Unemployment rate (average 1992–9)	16	9	. . .	15

Egypt is a non-oil country and has the largest population in the Arabian world. It has experienced high levels of poverty, illiteracy and unemployment despite the conducted structural reforms undertaken to mitigate the impacts of such factors over the last decade. The population of Saudi Arabia experienced substantial growth at around 3.5 per cent per annum during the 1990s. This high growth rate makes around 50 per cent of Saudi population under the age of 18. While recent unemployment data are unavailable, Saudi Arabia is facing serious pressures for job creation in the long run. In response, the Saudi government has pursued a programme of 'Saudization' whereby private companies are to increase the percentage of Saudi Arabian employees among their workforce by 5 per cent per annum. In Bahrain, non-Bahrainis constitute about 35 per cent of the population. Bahrain's government reported that unemployment was 2.35 per cent in 1999 but the United Nations Development Programme (UNDP) estimates unemployment to be over 15 per cent. Referring to the report of the World Trade Organization (2000), Bahrain's authorities launched in early 1996 a Bahrainization policy that defines the percent of Bahraini employees to be employed by firms of varying sizes across varying sectors of economy.

The human development indicators shown in Table 2.8 illustrate other significant differences between the four countries. While Jordan and Bahrain have the lowest illiteracy ratios (at about 15 per cent), Egypt has the highest illiteracy rate, affecting slightly less than half of its population. Poverty levels in both Bahrain and Jordan are around 10 per cent of the population, compared with around 33 per cent in Egypt. There is little evidence of such hardship in Saudi Arabia. Whilst inflation has not been an economic problem in Saudi Arabia and Bahrain over the last decade, inflation rates are still relatively high in Egypt, averaging around 10 per cent over the last decade.

In general, the people of Arab oil countries (like Saudi Arabia and Bahrain) enjoy relatively high standards of living while those of the non-oil countries (such as Jordan and Egypt) have much lower living standards, as indicated by various economic and social indicators (not least, by the much lower per capita GDP levels experienced in these countries).

Jordan

Jordan was established in 1921 on the East Bank of the Jordan River. It is defined by the UNDP (1999) as a middle-income country with a per capita GDP of about $1,400 over 1990–9. It has a small, open and mixed economy where the government performs a key role in basic economic activities (i.e. transportation, communications, electricity, large-scale manufacturing, and the tourism sector). The size of the public sector in Jordan is large in relation to the level of domestic economic activity. According to the report of the Bureau of Economic and Business Affairs/Jordan (1998), Jordan's government remains the country's largest single employer; for instance, its expenditure accounted for about 37 per cent of GDP in 1999.

Historically, Jordan's economic performance was robust during the 1970s to the mid-1980s. Domestic prices were generally stable, with inflation averaging 5 per cent until the mid-1980s. McDermott (1996) notes that real GDP rose by 9.5 per cent a year between 1976 and 1980, and investment averaged 35 per cent of GDP. However, the economic performance has slowed since the mid-1980s and Jordan's government started to face imbalances between economic growth and population growth. Over this period, the flow of foreign grants from Arabian countries, and inflow of workers' remittances, started to decline after a fall in oil prices. By the mid-1980s, Jordan's debt servicing reached 45 per cent of exports and the country's fiscal deficit (excluding foreign grants) increased to 20 per cent of GDP. During 1988–90, the cost of living index rose by 56 per cent, the domestic currency lost 51 per cent of its value against the dollar and the country's reserves declined sharply. The growth in budget deficits forced the authorities to borrow from domestic and foreign banks.

In addition to the aforementioned problems, Jordan's economic performance was impeded by its limited resources as well as by policy-induced structural weaknesses in various sectors. Jordan's trade regime was characterized by high tariff and non-tariff barriers and by institutional inefficiencies that severely hindered its exports and restricted the performance of the industrial sector (Alonso-Gamo *et al.*, 1997a). Maciejewski and Mansur (1996) indicate that Jordan's budget was affected by high military expenditures and extensive subsidy programmes (including those on basic foods, energy, agricultural production and transportation). In the agriculture sector, subsidized water and support of producers' prices contributed to an inefficient use of resources. The energy sector also suffered from inadequate pricing policies for oil products and electricity.

To face pressing social needs, Jordan's government initiated various economic reforms in the 1990s aimed at increasing economic growth, reducing unemployment, enhancing financial stability and promoting the role of the private sector in the process of economic development (Bureau of Economic and Business Affairs/Jordan, 1998). Over the 1991–2 period, many economic indicators improved. Inflation fell to 3.5 per cent, averaging less than 5 per cent during 1989–94. The fiscal deficit (excluding foreign grants) declined from about 18 per cent of GDP in 1991 to less than 4 per cent in 1992 (Maciejewski and Mansur, 1996). These improvements were associated with a revival in investment (from 22 per cent of GDP in 1989 to 29 per cent in 1994) and real GDP grew by more than 7 per cent a year (McDermott, 1996).

However, the decision of the Arab Gulf States to limit economic ties with Jordan after the Gulf War in 1991–2 deprived it of the remittances of Jordanian workers in the Gulf. This action also limited access to traditional export markets, a secure supply of oil and substantial foreign aid. Moreover, absorbing up to 300,000 returnees from the Gulf countries exacerbated unemployment and strained the government's ability to provide essential services. Maciejewski and Mansur (1996) indicate that various structural measures were introduced after the Gulf crisis in 1991, including tariff reforms, interest rate liberalization and introduction of flexible exchange rate policies.

As part of its public sector reforms, Jordan's government sold a large part of its shares in the company of Jordan Hotels and Tourism and completed the commercialization of the Alia Gateway Hotels and duty-free shops at Amman International Airport in 1992. According to IMF reports (1996 and 2000), Jordan's real GDP grew by 16 per cent in 1992 but the growth momentum slowed to 6 per cent per annum during 1993–5. Inflation fell to 4–5 per cent during this period, and unemployment declined to 12–15 per cent from about 25 per cent in 1990, despite a high labour force growth. However, the economic performance during the period 1996–8 deteriorated. While the country maintained low inflation and started to build up its official foreign exchange reserves, the real GDP growth slowed to about 1 per cent.

In 1998, Jordan's government reactivated its privatization programme started in the early 1990s by selling parts of the Jordan Cement Factories Company and the Jordan Telecommunications Company to foreign investors. The Aqaba Railway Corporation was leased to an American consortium, and Jordan's first independent power project (IPP) was awarded to a Belgian firm (US Commercial Service/Jordan, 2001). In addition, the government sought a strategic foreign partner for 49 per cent of Royal Jordanian (RJ) Airlines. Aqaba, a major Jordanian city, was designated as a Special Economic Zone (SEZ). Apart from the mining sector (Phosphate and Potash), Jordan's authorities plan to privatize most of the remaining government-owned enterprises.

In 1999, the Jordanian authorities introduced a further series of structural reforms (see Table 2.9 for details). In the fiscal area, income tax reforms were

Table 2.9   Major economic reforms in Jordan over the last decade

Date	Major economic reforms
1993	The Jordanian government signed an agreement with the IMF for an investment plan of $7.8 billion that relied on the Jordanian private sector to contribute between 61 per cent and 67 per cent of the required funding throughout the five-year period 1993–7. The aim was to enhance domestic investment and the role of the private sector in the process of economic growth.
1994	The government enacted a general sales tax to replace a previously imposed consumption tax. The tax applies to all durable and consumer goods except food staples and health care and education-related products.
1996	Three main tariff reductions occurred: the tariffs on commodities fell by 5 per cent and 50 per cent; the tariffs on tobacco and alcohol were reduced by 60 per cent and 120 per cent; and on automobiles between 70 per cent and 200 per cent. The aim was to provide greater incentives for foreign investment in these areas.
1996	The government left importing basic foodstuffs (such as cereals, sugar, milk and frozen meat) tariff free. The aim was to remove possible price distortions and to widen the role of the private sector.
1996	The Jordanian government issued a new income tax law; imposing a 35 per cent maximum marginal rate. Taxes on individual incomes are between 5 per cent (for annual incomes less than $3,000) and 30 per cent (for annual incomes exceeding $22,500). Taxes are set at 35 per cent for banks and financial institutions and 25 per cent for companies engaged in brokerage and agency activities. The law exempts re-invested profits from income tax.
1997	The Jordanian government partially privatized the state-owned Jordan Cement Company and took steps to privatize the Aqaba Railway.
1998	The government privatized the Aqaba Railway and partially privatized the state-owned cement company. Significant progress was made towards privatizing the Jordan Telecommunications Company and Royal Jordanian, the national airline.
1999	Income tax reforms were introduced; this included the simplification of personal income tax and tax treatment of dividends and interest income and the rationalization of investment incentives.

Sources: Adapted from the Bureau of Economic and Business Affairs, 1993–1998; International Monetary Fund, 2000; and Central Bank of Jordan, 1997.

introduced including the simplification of personal income tax, treatment of dividends and interest income and the offering of more investment incentives. Jordan also became a member of the WTO. As part of the membership process, several reforms were undertaken to harmonize the general sales tax (GST) on domestic and imported goods along with amendments to customs law (International Monetary Fund/Jordan, 2000). These reforms aimed at motivating foreign and private investment. The authorities also modified Investment Law in 2000, to allow equal treatment for foreign and local investors. Both Jordanian and foreign investors are permitted to invest in trade, services and industrial projects in the free zones. Investment incentives take the form of income tax and custom-duties exemptions, both of which are granted to Jordanian and foreign investors. The ceiling on all duties was brought down to 30 per cent as of March 2000, with a 10 per cent ceiling on materials used as industrial inputs (US Commercial Service/ Jordan, 2001).

According to the report by US Commercial Service/Jordan (2001), Jordan's authorities have undertaken further steps to encourage investment in less-developed areas. These include dividing the country into three development areas: zones A, B and C. Investments in Zone C, the least developed areas of Jordan, receive the highest tax and custom-duties exemptions. Here profits are exempt from income and services taxes for a period of 12 years and the goods imported to and/or exported from free zones are exempt from import taxes and custom duties.

Overall, the Jordanian authorities undertook various economic reforms including widening the role of the private sector (by allowing more participation in various governmental utilities and projects) during the 1990s. Furthermore, many market-oriented regulations have been introduced to encourage external trade and foreign investment. Despite the difficulties faced by Jordan's economic performance during the 1990s (lack of natural resources and the increase in population resulting from the resettlement of Palestinians in Jordan), the authorities have succeeded in improving various macroeconomic features of the economy.

Egypt

Egypt is a low-income country and its economic structure consists of a state sector (estimated at 30 per cent of GDP) and a private sector. The country's economic performance was sluggish during the 1980s and early 1990s. The annual real GDP growth averaged 3 per cent during 1985/86 through 1992/ 93, inflation exceeded 20 per cent and the budget deficit was about 15 per cent of GDP. The country also suffered from a heavy burden of debt and weak exports. The fall of oil prices during 1980s had a further negative effect on Egypt, including lower remittances and aid (Handy *et al.*, 1998). During this period, the Egyptian economy suffered from significant administrative restrictions including administered prices, interest rate ceilings, multiple official exchange rates and various restrictions on the private and foreign sectors. The financial sector suffered from segmentation, limits to competition, subsidized credit allocations and negative real interest rates.

Following the unfavourable economic conditions during the late 1980s and early 1990s, Egypt initiated an extensive structural reform programme in 1991/92. The programme aimed at privatizing a substantial proportion of public entities, liberalizing trade as well as strengthening the financial sector. Handy *et al*. (1998) indicate that the reform procedures were enhanced by substantial capital inflows after the Gulf War in 1991. National reserves rose to over $11 billion for the three years beginning 1991/92. The reduction in interest rates between 1990 and 1992 helped mobilizing capital to seek profitable investments. Tightening of credit conditions also played a role, as high interest rates created strong incentives for capital inflows. In 1991/92, the interest differential between Egypt and US rose to 14.2 per cent, before declining to 10.5 per cent by 1993/94. During 1994–6, capital inflows slowed, mainly because of the decline in the interest-rate differential, but accelerated again in 1996.

The Egyptian government reduced tariff and non-tariff restrictions during 1990–6 to enhance transparency of the trade regime. In 1991, the government instituted a general sales tax (GST) and adopted value-added tax. Varieties of non-tariff barriers that discriminated against foreign firms were eliminated in 1992. In 1997, the Egyptian government enacted legislation aimed at promoting foreign investment through packages of incentives to enhance transparency of government regulations and strengthening intellectual property rights (Handy *et al.*, 1998). By 1996/97, the structural reforms had resulted in a decline in inflation to 6.2 per cent (from 21 per cent in 1990/91), and the country experienced current and capital account surpluses. The authorities also started to privatize large parts of the public sector that encompassed a wide variety of economic activities (estimated at about one-third of economic output and employment). By 1998, the government divested its shares in 42 industrial, agricultural, construction and tourism sectors (accounting for more than one-quarter of state-owned enterprises). The privatization involved the sale of interests in 84 companies with a market value of about LE 17.7 billion (representing about 7 per cent of Egypt's GDP) (Subramanian, 1997; Handy *et al.*, 1998).

According to the report of US Commercial Service/Egypt (2001), the Egyptian reforms yielded an increase in real GDP growth (at 4–5 per cent in the latter part of the 1990s), low inflation (3.8 per cent by 1998/99) and enhanced foreign currency reserves. The country's debt rating in the international markets also increased (Moody's upgraded Egypt's sovereign rating from the speculative grade of Ba-1 to the investment grade of Baa-1, and Standard and Poor's rated Egypt's investment rating as BBB– but reduced its economic performance rating from stable to negative in July 2000.)

Egypt's privatization programme broadened in 1999 when the government opened maritime, telecommunications and infrastructure sectors to the private sector on a build–own–operate–transfer basis. In addition to awarding three contracts for power generation in 1998 and 1999, the Egyptian Electrical Authority named a consortium, led by Merrill Lynch and the Egyptian Investment Bank, to evaluate the country's seven state-owned power generation and distribution companies for privatization. The estimated assets value of these is around $14 billion (US Commercial Service/Egypt,

2001). Over the period 1993 through February 2002, 190 companies and utilities were privatized (for LE 16.9 billion), out of an aggregate of 314 companies that were held by the public sector. Now only 181 companies are in the possession of the public sector.

Privatization and other economic reforms (i.e. trade liberalization, deregulation of the financial system and updating various commercial laws and regulations) improved Egypt's overall economic performance during the 1990s. According to the report by the Ministry of Planning & CAPMAS (Central Agency for Public Mobilization and Statistics) of Egypt (1999), the reforms helped reduce inflation from about 20 per cent during 1986–92 to less than 10 per cent in 1993–4 and to about 4 per cent by 1997–9. Furthermore, unemployment rates that had ranged between 10 and 22 per cent during the 1980s fell to 9.8 per cent in 1993 and to less than 8 per cent by 1998–9.

Saudi Arabia

Saudi Arabia's history dates back to its establishment in 1932 and it is known as a country that takes care of Muslim pilgrims who visit the two holy cities of Mecca and Medina. Saudi Arabia is one of the wealthiest countries in the world. It has 261 billion barrels of proven oil reserves (more than one-quarter of the world total) and up to 1 trillion barrels of ultimately recoverable oil. It is the world's largest oil producer (at eight million barrels per day), and the country has enormous untapped gas potential.

Saudi Arabia's economy is based primarily on market principles and consists of a mix of private ownership and a large state sector. The government maintains price controls for basic utilities, energy and agricultural products. The oil and government sectors have played major roles in developing different sectors of the economy. Since its boom in 1973, oil helped the government to maintain an annual budget surplus until 1982 when there was a sharp decline in oil prices. Oil revenues fell from about SR 320 billion in 1980 to SR 76 billion by 1990, but recovered to SR 160 billion by 1997 (Al-Sahlawi, 1997; Saudi Arabia Monetary Agency, 1999).

Parastatal corporations have dominated the economic output of Saudi Arabia since the early 1970s. These firms include the oil firm of Saudi Arabia (ARAMCO), the Saudi Arabia Basic Industries Corporation (SABIC), the Saudi Arabia Telephone Company, the Saudi Arabia Electricity Company and the Saline Water Conversion Corporation. The Saudi Arabian Monetary Agency (SAMA) (1999) indicate that prior to the oil boom in the 1970s, parts or all of these firms, including ARAMCO, were in private hands.

The Saudi Arabian government imposes few taxes, relying on oil revenues, customs duties, and licensing fees for most government revenue. Saudi people do not pay income tax but are obliged to pay 'zakah', a compulsory religious levy on all Muslims set by Islamic law at 2.5 per cent of net wealth. Business income tax rates range from 25 per cent (on annual profits of less than $26,667) to a maximum rate of 45 per cent (for profits of more than

$266,667). Import tariffs are generally 12 per cent ad valorem, but certain specified essential commodities (e.g. defence purchases) are not subject to customs duties (Bureau of Economic and Business Affairs/Saudi Arabia, 1998).

Oil and its derivative products account for 90–95 per cent of Saudi Arabian export earnings, and about 35–40 per cent of GDP. The lack of diversity in sources of GDP, some have argued, has delayed Saudi Arabia's economic development. Based on the report of US Embassy Riyadh (2001), Saudi Arabia's real GDP grew by only 0.5 per cent in 1999 despite the recovery in oil prices. Saudi Arabian per capita GDP (current dollars) peaked in 1981 at about US$ 28,600 and declined thereafter due to a fall in oil prices. In 2001 it was US$ 8,460. As a result of rising public debt, declining capital expenditures, and sluggish economic growth, the Saudi government announced, in 1999, its intention to offer the private sector the opportunity to take a wider role in economic development. In Saudi Arabia, the oil sector and government services sector are the major sources of GDP, accounting for about 55 per cent during the 1990 to 1999 period. Reviewing the changes in contribution of different economic activities in Saudi Arabia's GDP, the share of the oil sector fell from 36 per cent in 1990 to around 31 per cent in 1999. On the other hand, the contribution of the government sector increased from around 18 per cent of GDP in 1990 to 20 per cent by 1999. The banking and finance sector accounted for around 7 per cent of the Saudi GDP throughout the 1990s. The Saudi Arabian government has also begun to consider a series of structural reform measures aimed at boosting capital investment. These reforms include liberalizing trade and investment regimes, diversifying the economy, privatizing parts of the (dominant) state sector and diversifying tax revenues away from the over-reliance on volatile oil prices.

The Saudi government approved a new foreign investment law in 1999 to enhance investment. The law permits foreign investment in all sectors and relaxes rules restricting foreign ownership in local businesses. The law allows foreign investors to transfer money freely from their enterprises outside the country and allows joint-venture companies to sponsor their foreign investors as well as their foreign employees. It also permits foreign investors to own real property for company activities. The Saudi government has also undertaken legal reforms to provide increased transparency regarding such issues as the resolution of commercial disputes, clearer guarantees for the protection of intellectual property rights and improved guidance to potential investors regarding projects in which they cannot participate.

Saudi has applied for membership of the WTO. This has required Saudi Arabia to remove protection barriers, place ceilings on tariffs, open key services sectors to foreign participation, and improve intellectual property rights protection. These changes resulted in a more open, transparent and rules-based trade regime. Such procedures are expected to stimulate improved efficiency levels and higher economic growth prospects, and improve the investment climate for foreign and domestic investors.

Up to 1999, Saudi privatization had been largely limited through allowing private firms to take on certain service functions, such as the management of seaports and airports, and the provision of some postal collection, health and education services. The Saudi government declared, in 1999, its intention to sell its stake in the Saudi Arabian Telephone Company to a foreign strategic partner. Privatizing the ownership of Saudi Arabian Basic Industries Corporation has not progressed beyond 30 per cent for many years despite a mandate in the firm's constitution to become private. Other privatization possibilities include Saudi Arabian Airlines, hotels, municipal services, and grain mills and silos, as well as large minority stakes in banks.

Overall, the Saudi Arabian economy is still dependent on oil revenues that account for about one-third of the country's GDP and more than 90 per cent of its export earnings. However, the continued volatility in oil prices and the adverse consequences of the 1990 Gulf War has encouraged Saudi authorities to diversify the economy by encouraging the private sector to play a wider role. This process is on-going.

Bahrain

Bahrain's history starts from its establishment in 1932. The country is an archipelago of 36 low-lying islands situated midway down the Arabian Gulf. The three main islands are Bahrain (on which the capital Manama is located), Sitra, and Muharraq. These are joined by causeways and make up about 95 per cent of the 707 square kilometres land area. Bahrain is a member of the Gulf Cooperation Council and works actively towards economic integration with the other members.

Prior to the discovery of oil in 1932, the people of Bahrain earned their livelihood from three main sources: pearl fishing, agriculture and trade. The first two were the industries largest employers but trade provided the major source of revenue to the state. Wilkenson and Atti (1997) indicate that there were many other smaller industries with less potential for employment; the most notable of these were weaving and embroidery, pottery, copper work and metalworking.

Throughout the oil boom years of the 1950s and 1960s, the country developed a solid modern infrastructure; the electricity and water utilities are well developed, telecommunications facilities are of a high standard and the financial sector offers a broad range of products and services. After independence in 1971, Bahrain has pursued a liberal trade and investment policy, and has integrated its economy closely with those of other countries in the region. In addition, well-developed and highly competitive trade encouraged expansion of the merchant sector where duties and tariffs on imports contributed effectively to the national budget.

Bahrain's oil reserves are limited as compared to other Gulf countries but still constitute the main pillar of the economy. The oil and gas sectors have contributed around 50 per cent of government revenues (at about 52 per cent of its export and around 14 per cent of its GDP) over the last decade (Arab Chamber of Commerce, 2001). The existence of natural gas in Bahrain has also opened the way to set up related industries. As Bahrain's oil reserves are expected to last for a decade or so, efforts are being made to reduce the size of the public sector which dominates key economic activities and remains an important source of employment for Bahrain (public sector activities comprise petroleum, aluminium and telecommunications).

The government sector, oil industry and other industrial activities constituted around 50 per cent of its GDP over 1990–9 (the contribution of the oil and natural gas industry has fallen over the past decade and accounted for around 55 per cent of the industrial sector over the 1997–9 period). The manufacturing sector is mainly based on energy-intensive products, including aluminium, metal industries, and chemicals. The service sector also accounts for a substantial proportion of the Bahraini economy. The contribution of the banking and financial sector to GDP increased from around 8 per cent in 1990 to 9 per cent in 1999. It had increased to around 13 per cent by 2003.

The need to encourage private investment has led to a liberal economic policy relating to trade. Bahraini government has partially or fully privatized a number of state-owned companies, especially in the industrial sector during the 1990s. Private investment was allowed in petroleum refining, and in petroleum extraction, through production-sharing agreements with the government of Bahrain. Liberalization is proceeding in other service sectors including telecommunications, maritime and air transport, and tourism. In maritime transport, the authorities aim to develop Bahrain as a competitive regional distribution centre. In this regard, a new port is being developed to add to the existing capacity of port facilities at Mina Salman. Nowadays, Bahrain has one of the most diversified economies in the Gulf and has the largest collection of manufacturing industries and the biggest community of international bank branches in the region.

Monetary competence is apparent in Bahraini policy management. The convertible currency has been fixed at US $2.66 to the Bahraini dinar since 1986. The Bahrain Monetary Agency has held the country's inflation rate at less than 3 per cent for many years, thus encouraging stability and fair spreads in market-based interest rates. There have been no bank failures. Interest rates were partially decontrolled in 1988 and fully decontrolled in 1994 (Wilkenson and Atti, 1997).

Finance and banking is one of the largest sectors in the economy. The sector consists of a number of investment, commercial and specialized banks, offshore banking units and money-changing companies. The growth of Bahrain as an international financial centre is partially attributed to the disappearance of Beirut as a major banking centre during the 1980s as well as its stable macroeconomic climate. In 1989, the Bahrain Stock Exchange commenced operation and since then it has sought to extend its services to local and international companies and helped in strengthening the economic ties with other GCC countries (Arab Chamber of Commerce, 2001).

Bahrain offers several advantages to foreign investors, including no personal or corporate taxation and no restriction on capital and profit repatriation. The Bahrain Development Bank was established in 1991, followed by the Bahrain Marketing and Promotion Office in 1992. Both are geared to attract international private-sector investment. An office of the UN Industrial Development Organization was opened in Bahrain in 1996 aimed at attracting foreign investment to realize joint ventures with local entrepreneurs (Arab Chamber of Commerce, 2000). Regulations now allow 100 per cent foreign ownership in new industrial ventures or in service companies if their regional headquarters are located in Bahrain. The government also allows the establishment of representative offices or branches of foreign companies without local sponsors. Joint ventures allow for up to 49 per cent foreign ownership.

Since 1999, additional reforms have taken place; foreign equity ownership limits on firms listed on the Bahrain Stock Exchange have been raised from 24 per cent to 49 per cent. In addition, efforts are being made to simplify the procedures of foreign investment projects (World Trade Organization, 2000). Foreign firms receive the same investment incentives available to Bahraini companies, including corporate tax exemption, no restriction on capital and profit repatriation, and duty-free access to GCC member states for products manufactured in Bahrain (Arab Chamber of Commerce, 2000).

According to the report of the Arab Chamber of Commerce (2001), two free-trade zones exist in Bahrain, used for temporary storage of imported goods set for re-export. Mina Salman, Bahrain's major port, provides a free transit zone to facilitate the duty-free import of equipment and machinery. The government of Bahrain continues to offer incentives to international firms to establish light and heavy industries and to deal freely on the island.

To sum up, the Bahraini authorities have undertaken various reforms aimed at further diversifying its economy. In particular, the country has taken the initiative to become a major finance centre in the Gulf region. The transition of the country from its dependency on oil can be noted by comparing the components of GDP in the 1980s, when oil accounted for about 35 per cent of its GDP, to the current situation when oil contributes around 15 to 16 per cent. In addition, the financial sector has contributed more than 10 per cent towards its GDP (on average) over the last decade. Bahrain's success is attributed mainly to liberal trade policies being pursued and the development of appropriate infrastructure services to foreign investors.

Select comparative analysis

The following provides a brief comparative analysis of the economic performance of the four main Arab economies covered above during the 1990s. Of the four economies, the real GDP of Jordan and Egypt experienced annual growth of around 8.5 and 14.8 per cent, respectively, between 1990 and 1999 (see Table 2.10). These rates of growth were higher than the average rate of growth for the non-oil Arab countries (5.1 per annum) over the period 1992–9. The real GDP growth of both countries was higher at the beginning of the 1990s but experienced a slowdown towards the end of the decade. As compared to this, Saudi Arabia and Bahrain experienced lower growth rates at 5.8 and 6.3 per cent respectively during 1990–9. These growth rates were slightly higher than the average rate for Arab oil countries at 5.6 per cent over the period 1992–9.

Looking at the contribution of different economic activities to the GDP of the four countries under study, Table 2.11 shows that, apart from Jordan where the distributive sector (commerce, transport, banking and finance) dominates economic activity, commodity sectors predominate in other countries, especially in Saudi Arabia and Egypt.

In Jordan, government services, finance and banking and the industrial sectors are the main economic sectors, providing about one-half of GDP during 1990–9. Reviewing the major changes that have taken place in the contribution of different economic activities in Jordan, we note that the contribution of agriculture has fallen over time from around 7 per cent in 1990 to 2 per cent by 1999. On the other hand, the contribution of mining has grown substantially. Mineral production in Jordan is dominated by two industries: phosphate and potash. The contribution of other economic sectors in Jordan's GDP has not shown noticeable changes since the early

Table 2.10   GDP indictors for Jordan, Egypt, Saudi Arabia and Bahrain over the last decade

Indicators	Jordan	Egypt	Saudi Arabia	Bahrain
Real GDP growth, annual % change, average 1990–9	8.5	14.8	5.8	6.3
GDP per capita (1987 US$), average 1990–7	1,410	1,020	6,880	9,700
Composition of GDP – current prices (US$, avg. 1990–9)	5,990	58,510	126,280	6,620
Commodity sector (%)	28	47	59	37
Distribution sector (%)	38	31	18	24
Services sector (%)	20	17	21	35

Source: Adapted from the Arab Monetary Fund (2002) (www.amf.org.ae).

Table 2.11 Distribution of GDP (current prices) to economic sectors for Jordan, Egypt, Saudi Arabia and Bahrain (average 1990–9) (%)

Sector	Jordan	Egypt	Saudi Arabia	Bahrain
Agriculture, Fishing & Forestry	5	16	6	1
Mining, Quarrying & Fuel	4	7	35	17
Manufacturing Industries	12	17	9	13
Electricity, Water and Gas	2	2	0	3
Construction	5	5	9	5
Total commodity sector	28	47	59	38
Commerce, Rest. and Hotels	9	1	7	10
Transport, Commercial and Storage	13	9	6	8
Finance, Insurance and Banking	16	20	4	8
Total distributive sector	38	31	18	25
Housing	. . .	2	2	9
Government services	17	7	18	18
Other services	3	8	2	7
Total service sector	20	17	21	34
GDP at factor cost	85	94	98	97
Net indirect taxes	15	6	2	3
GDP at purchaser' values (US$ million)	5,990	58,508	126,780	5,577

Source: Adapted from the Arab Monetary Fund, 2002 (www.amf.org.ae).

1990s. Banking and finance industry has also not increased in economic importance over the last decade.

In Egypt, the banking and finance sector, the industrial sector and agriculture are the main economic activities, contributing about 60 per cent of GDP over the period 1990–9. The share of these economic areas has not shown noticeable changes during 1990–9. The tourism and the Suez Canal revenues dominate Egypt's services sector (tourism revenues were $US 2.2 billion through the second quarter of 1999). As a result of the privatization programme, the private sector's role has steadily expanded in key sectors such as metals (aluminium, iron, and steel), petrochemicals, cement, automobiles, textiles, consumer electronics, and pharmaceuticals (US Commercial Service/Egypt, 2001). The banking and finance sector accounts for around 20 per cent of the overall economy and this remained stable over the 1990s.

In Saudi Arabia, the oil sector and government services sector are the major sources of GDP, accounting for about 55 per cent between 1990 and 1999. Reviewing the changes in the contribution of different economic activities in Saudi GDP, the share of the oil sector fell from 36 per cent in 1990 to around 31 per cent in 1999. On the other hand, the contribution of the government sector increased from around 18 per cent of GDP in 1990 to 20 per cent by 1999. The banking and finance sector accounted for around 7 per cent of the Saudi GDP throughout the 1990s.

In Bahrain, the government sector, oil industry and other industrial activities constituted around 50 per cent of its GDP over 1990–9. Within the industrial sector, the contribution of the oil and natural gas industry has fallen over the past decade and accounted for around 55 per cent of the industrial sector over the 1997–9 period. The manufacturing sector is mainly based on energy-intensive products, including aluminium, metal industries, and chemicals. The service sector also accounts for a substantial proportion of the Bahraini economy. The contribution of the banking and financial sector to GDP increased from around 8 per cent in 1990 to 9 per cent in 1999.

In addition to various GDP indicators one can examine another dimension of economic performance by viewing trade patterns. Trade activity indicators for the four countries under study are shown in Table 2.12. Over the last decade, Jordan has suffered from permanent trade deficits. However, the annual growth in exports, at about 8 per cent, has exceeded the 5 per cent growth in imports. This has resulted in a fall in Jordan's trade deficits over the last decade. The trade deficit as a per cent of GDP decreased from around 38 per cent in 1990 to around 25 per cent in 1999. It should be noted that Jordan's exports were dominated by traditional goods (raw materials such as potash and phosphates). Other important exports are pharmaceuticals, detergents and fertilizers. As the production base in Jordan's economy is narrow, the economy is highly dependent on imports. In Egypt, both exports and imports have increased over the last decade but the annual increase in imports, at around 8 per cent, has been twice the annual growth in exports. While the trade deficit has grown, it fell as a percentage of GDP from 19 per cent in 1990 to around 14 per cent in 1999, an indication that Egypt's GDP has increased over the last decade. In Saudi Arabia, the trade surplus averaged around 16 per cent of the GDP over the period 1990–9. However, Saudi exports increased annually at around 1 per cent over the period 1990–9 while its imports increased at around 2 per cent over the same period. Bahrain's exports have experienced an annual increase of around 1 per cent and imports fell by around 0.5 per cent per annum. This resulted in Bahrain experiencing both trade deficits and surpluses during the 1990s (running a balanced trade budget for the 1990s period overall). The trade indicators reveal improved trade balances in the four countries toward the second part of the 1990s.

The external indebtedness of both Jordan and Egypt has been reduced over the last decade (see Table 2.13). However, Jordan still carries a big external debt, at about $7 billion at the end of April 2000 (about 92 per cent of GDP). The Jordanian government has stated its plan to use some of the proceeds from privatization to reduce this debt. On the other hand, while the absolute figure of Egyptian's debt has not shown significant changes over the last decade (at around $29 billion over 1990–8), debt as a per cent of GDP fell from around 80 per cent in 1990 to 33 per cent in 1998.

Table 2.12 Trade indicators for Jordan, Egypt, Saudi Arabia and Bahrain over the last decade

Country	1990	1991	1992	1993	1994	1995	1996	1997	1998	1999	Average 1990–9	Annual growth % (avg.)
Jordan												
Export	1,064	1,132	1,220	1,248	1,425	1,771	1,817	1,836	1,802	1,832	1,515	8.02
Import	2,601	2,513	3,257	3,542	3,381	3,696	4,293	4,102	3,828	3,717	3,493	4.77
Trade balance	−1,537	−1,381	−2,037	−2,293	−1,957	−1,925	−2,476	−2,266	−2,026	−1,885	−1,978	2.52
Trade bal. % of GDP	−38	−33	−40	−41	−32	−30	−37	−32	−28	−25	−33	
Egypt												
Export	2,569	3,620	3,054	3,121	3,472	3,451	3,539	3,919	3,206	3,546	3,350	4.23
Import	9,169	7,759	8,304	8,216	9,584	11,764	13,036	13,245	16,537	16,009	11,362	8.29
Trade balance	−6,601	−4,139	−5,250	−5,095	−6,113	−8,312	−9,497	−9,326	−13,330	−12,463	−8,013	9.87
Trade bal. % of GDP	−19	−12	−13	−11	−12	−14	−14	−12	−16	−14	−14	
Saudi Arabia												
Export	44,416	47,697	50,287	42,395	42,614	50,041	60,728	60,732	38,822	48,482	48,622	1.02
Import	24,069	29,085	33,273	28,202	23,364	28,087	27,765	28,743	30,013	28,032	28,063	1.83
Trade balance	20,347	18,611	17,014	14,193	19,250	21,954	32,963	31,989	8,809	20,450	20,558	0.06
Trade bal. % of GDP	19	16	14	12	16	17	23	22	7	15	16	
Bahrain												
Export	3,760	3,513	3,464	3,723	3,617	4,113	4,700	4,384	3,270	4,088	3,863	0.97
Import	3,712	4,115	4,263	3,858	3,748	3,716	4,273	4,026	3,566	3,588	3,886	−0.37
Trade balance	49	−602	−799	−135	−131	397	427	358	−296	500	−23	103.04
Trade bal. % of GDP	1	−13	−17	−3	−2	7	7	6	−5	8	0	

Source: Adapted from Arab Monetary Fund, 2002 (www.amf.org.ae).

Table 2.13 External debt indicators for Jordan and Egypt over the last decade

	1990	1991	1992	1993	1994	1995	1996	1997	1998	1990–8 average
Jordan										
External debt	7,043	7,458	6,922	6,770	6,883	7,023	7,091	6,960	7,388	7,060
External debt as % of GDP	175	178	135	122	113	108	107	100	101	126
Egypt										
External debt	28,372	29,317	28,348	28,303	30,189	30,792	28,810	26,804	27,670	28,734
External debt as % of GDP	80	86	68	60	58	51	43	35	33	47

Source: Adapted from Arab Monetary Fund, 2002 (www.amf.org.ae).

In contrast to Jordan and Egypt, Saudi Arabia[1] is considered to be one of the world's largest international creditors. The Saudi's average aid-to-GDP ratio averaged 4 per cent of GDP per annum during the past three decades. Bahrain is also an oil exporter country and used to have insignificant external debt.

The external reserves of these countries, especially Jordan and Egypt, have witnessed favourable growth over the last decade (Table 2.14). The external reserves of Jordan and Egypt grew at around 15 per cent and 49 per cent over the period 1990–9. On the other hand, the reserves of both Saudi Arabia and Bahrain have experienced modest growth. The external reserves of Saudi Arabia and Bahrain, and perhaps their debts, were significantly impacted by the consequences of the Gulf War in 1991–2. Overall, the external debt and reserves for the countries under study (especially those of Jordan and Egypt) have shown significant improvement during the last decade.

Domestic investment in Jordan also grew noticeably during 1995–9, averaging about 29 per cent per annum compared to 22 per cent in the Middle East and other Arabian countries (Table 2.15). However, domestic investment in Jordan has shown decreasing rates of growth after 1995; falling from about 34 per cent, as a percentage of GDP, in 1995 to about 27 per cent in 1999. The domestic investment in both Saudi Arabia and Egypt averaged slightly less than 20 per cent of GDP over 1995–9. (There is no available data regarding the size of domestic investment as a per cent of GDP for Bahrain.) Direct foreign investments to both Jordan and Egypt have witnessed significant increases over the last decade. In Jordan, foreign investment increased from about US$ 13 million in 1995 to more than US$ 300 million in 1998, averaging about US$ 175 million over the whole period. However, there is no recent data available for Saudi Arabia and Bahrain.

To summarize, this section of the chapter provides an insight into the economic features of four Arab economies – two oil and two non-oil producers. While major differences exist between these countries it can be seen that they all experienced robust economic growth, but in terms of GDP per capita there are big differences, and pressures of rapidly growing populations have adversely impacted on various systems. Oil revenues certainly make a big difference in the oil producing countries, although all the countries have embarked on industrial policies aimed at diversifying their industrial and service sectors. Not least has been the recent move to deregulate their financial systems. The following section outlines the main features of financial sector liberalization, details of which will be covered in the following chapters.

Financial liberalization and intermediation processes

So far, we have outlined the main economic features of the Arab world, highlighting various trends. A major theme of policy action in recent years

Table 2.14 International reserves (excluding gold) of Jordan, Egypt, Saudi Arabia and Bahrain over 1990–9 (US$, millions)

Country	1990	1991	1992	1993	1994	1995	1996	1997	1998	1999	Average	Annual increase per cent
Jordan	849	825	769	595	431	427	697	1,693	1,170	1,991	945	15
Bahrain	1,235	1,515	1,259	1,149	1,104	1,274	1,265	1,362	1,349	1,371	1,288	1
Saudi Arabia	11,668	11,673	5,935	7,428	7,378	8,622	14,321	14,876	14,220	16,997	11,312	5
Egypt	2,684	5,325	10,936	13,040	13,476	16,192	17,400	18,667	18,114	14,481	13,031	49

Source: Adapted from Arab Monetary Fund, 2002 (www.amf.org.ae).

Table 2.15 Investment activity in Jordan, Egypt, Saudi Arabia and Bahrain over 1995–9

Indicators	Jordan	Egypt	Saudi Arabia	Bahrain	Arab oil countries (avg.)	Arab non-oil countries (avg.)
Gross domestic investment as %, average 1995–9	29	N/A	20	10	19	23
Foreign direct investment, current US$ millions, average 1995–8	175	800	N/A	N/A	8	92

has been for countries to engage in substantial reform programmes based on developing private sector involvement within the respective economies and also liberalizing the financial sector. Many of these issues will be touched upon throughout this text. Before we provide more details on economic and financial sector performance in the Arab world it is important to be aware of the main role performed by financial intermediaries and why they are so heavily regulated. This will lead on to the arguments that are used to support financial sector liberalization.

The main functions of a financial system are to intermediate between saving and investing economic units. This includes selecting investment projects and the final users of financial resources according to their creditworthiness and monitoring the use of these resources. In particular, financial systems transform the maturity, liquidity, risk and return characteristics of the liabilities issued by borrowing units to meet the preferences of lenders.

The financial system ensures that citizens have the incentive to save and that savings are employed efficiently. Herring and Santomero (2000) argue that a well-functioning financial system makes a critical contribution to economic performance by facilitating transactions, mobilizing savings and allocating capital across time and space. Financial institutions provide payment services and a variety of financial products that enable the corporate sector and households to cope with economic uncertainties by hedging, pooling, sharing and pricing risks. A stable and efficient financial sector reduces the cost and risk of investment. Financial markets also provide a crucial source of information that helps coordinate decentralized decisions throughout the economy. Rates of return in financial markets guide households in allocating income between consumption and savings, and in allocating their stock of wealth. Merton (1995) summarizes that the overall objective of regulating the financial sector should be to ensure that the system functions efficiently, helping to deploy, transfer and allocate resources across time and space under conditions of uncertainty.

In both developed and developing economies, banks are the principal source of non-market finance to the economy. In the Arab world, banks dominate the financial sector. Banks gather and assess information about prospective borrowers and their investment opportunities. The second function performed by banks is to serve as the principal repository for liquidity in the economy. By pooling the transaction balances of many different transactors, banks can acquire large, diversified portfolios of direct claims on borrowers that enable them to meet liquidity demands while still holding substantial amounts of illiquid assets. Furthermore, banks offer longer-term deposits that must compete directly with other instruments available in the financial markets. The return on deposits must be sufficient to compensate for the risk and delayed consumption associated with accepting deposit claims on the bank. Furthermore, banks transform the longer-term, risky, illiquid claims that borrowers prefer to issue into safer, shorter-term, more liquid demand

and the savings deposits that savers prefer. This asset transformation often involves maturity transformation as well.

Financial intermediaries enhance economic efficiency by overcoming frictions through channelling resources toward the most efficient investment, giving households access to economies of scale in processing information that enables the identification of investment projects and ensures that businesses act in ways that do not conflict with savers' interests. Intermediaries help individual savers by providing access to large investment projects via fund-pooling mechanisms. Thus, financial intermediaries improve the efficiency of the economy by letting savers invest in large projects. Furthermore, intermediaries benefit small savers by making riskier investments available to them through the risk-pooling mechanism. The intermediary can offer this service at a lower cost than savers can manage individually. Savers therefore have access to economies of scale. Intermediaries can also help investors by providing access to long-term projects through liquidity management. The pooling mechanism provides financial economies of scale by reducing the cost of illiquid investments. In addition, intermediaries can improve investors' access to worthwhile investments by means of a screening mechanism. Financial intermediaries can therefore help capital move to its highest value, thus improving allocative efficiency.

Financial intermediaries can help reduce problems associated with asymmetric information or moral hazard by offering financial contracts that are not available in markets and by providing economies of scale in monitoring and control. Therefore, financial intermediaries perform a major role in mediating conflicting incentives between lenders and borrowers that arise from imperfect information and incomplete contracts.

In banking, the perceived riskiness of the intermediation process, the importance of banks as suppliers of credit in the economy and the special role of banks in operating the payments system are among the main reasons for the special regulatory attention paid to this business area. Prudential regulations in banking aim mainly to protect individual investors and to enhance the stability and soundness of the financial system.

Herring and Santomero (2000) consider the rationale for regulating the financial system. Financial regulation aims to protect financial markets and institutions from shocks that might pose a systemic risk. Regulatory measures that might be taken to reduce systemic risk include asset restrictions, capital adequacy standards, deposit insurance and disclosure standards. Some measures, such as interest rate ceilings on deposits, were intended to prevent excessive competition. Other measures, however, such as geographic restrictions, may increase exposure to systemic risk by impeding diversification. Second, protecting consumers is the second rationale for financial regulation. Such regulation is put in place to protect consumers from excessive pricing or opportunistic behaviour by participants in financial markets. Competition policy also aims to protect monopolistic pricing and therefore to enhance the efficiency of the allocation of financial assets within the financial sector, and between the financial sector and the rest of the economy. As consumers face the problem of asymmetric information in their evaluation of financial service providers, they are vulnerable to adverse selection as well as to moral hazards, where agents put their own interests above those of the customers. To ease such problems, regulators often establish fit and proper tests for financial firms. Such enforcement of conduct provides firms with incentives to adopt procedures that ensure consumers are honestly served. The provision of insurance is another response to the asymmetric information problem. Reserve requirements, capital requirements and liquidity requirements are designed to ensure that a financial services firm will be able to honour its liabilities to its customers, and are also built into the system so as to safeguard against systemic risk.

The establishment of safe and sound banking systems across the Arab world is therefore important because it minimizes the likelihood of economic downturns resulting from financial panics. The avoidance of such events can limit the exposure of governments that often may have to bear a significant part of the costs of the bailout. Prudential regulation is meant to protect the banking system from these problems by inducing banks to invest prudently. One form of prudential regulation relates to capital requirements, typically related to international guidelines set by the Bank for International Settlements (BIS) (for example the Basel Accord). Capital requirements force banks to have more of their own capital at risk so that they internalize the inefficiency of investing in high-risk assets. Regulatory policies that can be used to generate improvements over using capital requirements alone include such things as portfolio restrictions, enhanced supervision of management and systems and the design of incentive-compatible safety nets. The goal of these policies is to limit the scope of banks to engage in excessive risk-taking and moral hazard behaviour while creating (franchise value) incentives for prudential bank behaviour (El-Shazly, 2001).

The central role of an economic system (including both the private and public sectors) is to coordinate economic activity across the various agents in the economy. Analysts of economic growth have long discussed the proper role of the government in promoting economic growth. There have been many arguments about whether the regulated or market-based financial system is better in promoting development, and most economists agree that each system has its own benefits and drawbacks.

The market approach presumes that in the absence of inefficient government intervention the market generally functions efficiently, and so the government should act to ensure secure property rights and competition. In contrast, the government approach presumes that market failure is pervasive and thus government intervention is necessary to mobilize savings, allocate resources efficiently and promote technological catch-up.

Many developing countries' financial systems are characterized by financial repression. Financial repression characterizes excessive government intervention in the financial sector, resulting in non-market real rates of interest, thus suppressing the role of the market for banking sector deposits and the intermediation process in general. Government intervention in the regulation of financial and economic sectors can take many forms. For instance, there may be selective or directed credit policies to implement planned sectoral investment programmes. Selective credit policies use interest rate ceilings and subsidies to direct funds through a non-price-rationing system to priority investment projects. Brownbridge and Gayi (1999) argue that improved credit allocation can be attained by reducing government intervention in directing credit or setting interest rates so that banks allocate credit according to commercial criteria. More efficient and higher quality financial services can be attained through increased competition that comes from liberalized entry and/or the removal of regulations that restrict competition.

A substantial body of literature initiated by the seminal work of McKinnon (1973) and Shaw (1973) has argued that financial liberalization (market-based system) increases savings, improves the efficiency with which resources are allocated among alternative investment projects and therefore raises the rate of economic growth. Financial liberalization defines the process of freeing up interest rate controls, exchange rates and capital controls, the entry of foreign banks, deregulation of financial services and the enhancing of the supervisory re-regulation that accompanies deregulation.

McKinnon (1973) notes that the higher the returns on financial assets, the greater the accumulation of money balances will be and the stronger the incentive for investment. Thus, liberalizing interest rates encourages economic growth through the positive impact of complementarity of financial assets and physical capital. Shaw (1973), on the other hand, emphasizes the benefits of an efficient and well-functioning system to improve a country's per capita income. He proposed that efficiency gains in the intermediation process would be attained if more individuals held their assets with banks. The increased institutionalization of savings could increase the real return to savers and at the same time reduce the costs of lending to investors, improving efficiency of investment and hence economic growth. Put another way, higher real interest rates can improve the intermediation role of financial institutions (Fry, 1995, p. 29).

Many commentators have argued that deregulation and liberalization in the financial sector can lead to more efficient allocation and higher economic growth. According to Hellmann *et al.* (1997), this is because market-based systems rely on stock markets that can generate efficient information about the real performance of firms. Thus, the stock market can play the role of effective monitoring, because firms' stock prices will fall with bad performances. However, various failures of market-based financial liberalization, like those experienced by various South East Asian and Latin American countries throughout the 1990s, dictate that, in practice, a balanced view concerning the impact of financial liberalization needs to be taken.

That is, financial sector liberalization needs to focus on either markets or intermediaries (or both) and also should be accompanied by the relevant regulatory and legal framework if it is to be effective. Recent empirical evidence, by Levine and Demirgüc-Kunt (2000), indicates that financial deepening itself, regardless of whether in a regulated or market-based system, can lead to higher economic growth.

According to Fry (1995 and 1997), there are prerequisites for successful financial liberalization. First, adequate prudential regulation is needed to enhance the stability of the financial system by constraining excessive risk-taking by financial institutions. Second, there needs to be successful monetary policy resulting in a reasonable degree of price stability. Third, governments should conduct fiscal policy in a disciplined manner in order to reduce their borrowing requirements. Fourth, banking institutions need to be competitive and efficient to increase savings and investment, and this ultimately should promote economic growth. Finally, the authorities need to reduce or abolish discriminatory taxes on the financial system, such as excessive reserve requirement in order to enhance competition within the financial system.

Furthermore, the timing and sequencing of liberalization programmes need to be considered so as to avoid adverse consequences of macroeconomic instability. There is growing agreement that policy should first seek to create macroeconomic and financial sector stability before financial liberalization programmes are undertaken (Galbis, 1994; Alawode and Ikhide, 1997). Specifically, there should be substantial reductions in the size of fiscal deficits to lessen inflationary pressures and a strengthening of bank and financial sector supervision to reduce the possibilities of excessive risk-taking by financial institutions. Finally, liberalization of the domestic financial sector should precede the liberalization of external sectors to ensure that domestic banks can adapt quickly to compete with international financial institutions.

In general, the main rationale for planned financial sector deregulation is to enhance the stability of this sector and to present favourable consequences of deregulation and market-based policies as a means for mobilizing economic resources to their most efficient uses. The main issues discussed above are particularly pertinent in the case of Arab economies as many have financial sectors that are primarily bank-based where the state plays a major role.

Conclusion

This chapter introduces the Arab world, highlighting the main economic, demographic and various other features of the region. The Arab world comprises 21 countries whose people speak the Arabic language and these can be classified economically into oil and non-oil exporting countries. The region has a population of some 275 million inhabitants with great differences in per capita GDP and other socio-economic indicators across countries. Four major Arabian trading blocs have appeared over the past years and these share similar objectives; integrating and enforcing the economic and cultural ties between member countries. These blocs include the Council of Arab Economic Unity, the Arab Maghreb union, the Gulf Cooperation Council (GCC) and the Council of Arab Mashreq countries. Arabia is rich in natural resources, especially oil reserves that account for two-thirds of the world's reserves. A comparison is given of oil and non-oil producing Arab economies just to provide a flavour of the differences in the recent economic performance of contrasting countries and also to highlight various deregulation trends. The latter part of the chapter discusses various issues concerning financial sector development and regulation that are particularly relevant in the case of the Arab world where financial systems are primarily bank-based and capital markets are relatively underdeveloped. In addition, the state has traditionally played a major role in the banking and financial sector.

3
Economic Performance of Arabian Countries during the 1990s

Introduction

This chapter outlines the economic performance of Arabian countries over the last decade. The economic growth of Arabian countries (as measured by real GDP) slowed over 1982–91, averaging 1.6 per cent compared to 4 per cent for other developing countries over the same period. This slowness led to low levels of investment and high levels of unemployment. This was also associated with rising levels of external indebtedness and fiscal deficits, especially for non-oil exporting countries forcing many Arabian countries to undertake macroeconomic reforms to promote economic growth.

During the 1990s, Arabia's economic performance improved compared to the 1980s, and the gap of economic growth compared to other developing countries reduced despite the difficult situation faced by some individual economies. Real GDP growth averaged 3.9 per cent between 1992 and 1999 compared to 5.6 per cent for all developing countries over the same period. The trade balance of Arab oil countries witnessed surplus during the 1990s while those of the non-oil Arab countries witnessed deficits, but these deficits as a percent of GDP have been falling. Inflation rates have been reduced in many Arabian countries, especially in comparison with 1980s levels. While the external debts of some Arabian countries are still high, external debt as a percentage of GDP appears to be following a declining trend. The total external reserves of the Arabian countries increased sharply during the 1990s, especially the reserves of the non-oil exporting countries. Investment levels have also witnessed improvement, especially foreign investment. The final part of the chapter introduces various issues concerning financial sector development in the Arab world.

Drivers of economic growth in the Arab world

The growth in economic performance of Arabian countries, as measured by real GDP, has shown substantial improvement over the period 1992–9.

During this period, growth rate exceeded 4 per cent per annum compared to around 2 per cent during 1982–91. However, while annual real GDP growth hit a high of around 8 per cent in 1992, it has slowed since, although the growth gap compared to other developing countries has been narrowed, as shown in Table 3.1.

The economic growth of Arab oil countries has improved from about 1 per cent over the period 1982–91 to around 6 per cent during 1992–9. The fastest growing economies include those of Kuwait, Qatar and the United Arab Emirates (UAE) while the slowest include those of Iraq, Algeria and Libya. The real GDP of non-oil Arab countries has grown from around 2 per cent annually during the period 1982–91 to more than 5 per cent over the period 1992–9. The fastest growing non-oil countries include Lebanon, Egypt and Jordan while those experiencing the slowest growth included Djibouti, Mauritania and Comoros. The enhanced real GDP growth of the former countries is perhaps attributed to the economic reforms undertaken and the adoption of more market-oriented policies in these systems.

In terms of real GDP per capita, Arabian countries have not witnessed significant changes over the last two decades, as shown in Table 3.2. The lack of growth in per capita GDP, especially in the oil exporting countries, is attributed mainly to the negative consequences of the Gulf War in 1991 because countries in the region were burdened with significant war expenses.

Concerning the composition of GDP, Table 3.3 shows that the commodity sector (that includes mainly agriculture, fuel, manufacturing and construction activities) dominates the other economic sectors in all countries comprising about half of the total GDP of Arabian economies over 1990–9. The distributive sector that reflects trade in goods accounted for about 27 per cent of total GDP and the services sector around 21 per cent. The service sector includes mainly banking, insurance, finance, hotel, transport, government and other services.

Surprisingly, both the oil and non-oil exporting economies rely just as heavily on commodity exports. The oil economy that has the largest service sector is Bahrain, reflecting the role of its petroleum-related and offshore financial services sectors. In addition, both Kuwait and Oman also appear to have sizeable service sectors. In contrast, Algeria, the poorest oil-exporting country (in terms of GDP per capita) has the smallest service sector that accounts for just under 13 per cent of GDP. Of the non-oil exporting countries, Lebanon and Morocco have the largest service sectors. Economies that have limited natural resource endowments tend to depend more heavily on trade – as in Jordan.

International trade and the liberalization process

Exports of Arabian countries have increased from about $135 billion in 1990 to more than $155 billion in 1999 and averaged about $140 billion

Table 3.1 Real GDP growth, annual percentage change of Arabian countries, 1982–99 (US$, million)

Real GDP (annual per cent change)	1982–91 (average)*	1992	1993	1994	1995	1996	1997	1998	1999	1992–9 (average)*
Oil-exporter (average)*	1	16.9	3.3	1.4	5.8	9.9	5.1	–7.1	9.5	5.6
Kuwait	–6	83.5	20.8	3.3	7.1	17.0	–3.4	–15.7	17.2	16.2
Qatar	–2	11.1	–6.4	3.0	10.4	11.3	24.7	–9.2	18.9	8.0
Emirates	0	4.4	0.9	7.1	11.9	12.1	5.0	–6.0	10.1	5.7
Bahrain	2	2.9	9.5	7.0	5.1	4.3	4.1	–2.6	7.1	4.7
Oman	8	9.8	0.3	3.4	6.8	10.7	3.7	–10.6	10.4	4.3
Iraq	...	14.2	1.5	1.5	0.3	0.0	1.0	0.9	3.0	2.8
Saudi Arabia	1	4.4	–3.8	1.4	6.4	10.6	3.7	–12.4	8.4	2.3
Algeria	2	4.7	4.0	–15.7	–1.7	13.5	2.2	–1.1	1.1	0.9
Libya	1	–3.0	–20.3	–14.0	11.8	13.8	7.2	–7.6	–0.5	–1.6
Non-oil exporter (average)*	2	4.4	1.3	4.6	12.0	5.9	7.1	3.4	2.3	5.1
Lebanon	–3	24.6	35.9	21.5	21.4	16.9	14.4	8.8	2.0	18.2
Egypt	6	22.0	12.3	10.2	17.0	11.3	12.3	9.4	7.6	12.8
Jordan	2	22.5	8.4	9.1	7.1	2.1	5.0	4.7	2.2	7.6
Tunisia		19.1	–5.7	7.0	15.3	8.7	–3.5	5.9	3.8	6.3
Sudan	3	–52.0	–3.0	7.7	58.0	–13.2	28.4	18.2	–8.0	4.5
Syria	2	5.2	4.7	11.4	8.4	5.9	–5.6	–3.4	4.8	3.9
Morocco	5	2.2	–5.8	13.2	8.7	11.1	–8.8	6.4	–1.2	3.2
Yemen	...	–1.4	–10.8	–8.1	–7.7	12.1	21.0	–9.6	13.0	1.1
Comoros	1	9	3	–5	–4	0	...	...	1	1
Djibouti	0	0	–4	–3	–4	–4	1	1	1	–1
Mauritania	4	1.3	–18.6	7.4	5.0	3.5	–1.7	–8.6	–4.4	–2.0
Somalia	–47.9	...	...	...	...	...	...	...	...	...
Arabian countries	2	7.8	0.0	1.7	7.9	9.3	3.9	–3.1	5.8	4.2
Industrial countries	2	1	1	2	2	2	3	2	2	2
Developing countries	4	6	6	7	6	7	6	3	4	6
Middle East and North Africa	3	5	2	2	2	5	3	3	3	3

* For countries that have available data; ... = Not available.
Source: Arab Monetary Fund, 2002 (www.amf.org.ae) for 1992–9 values of Arabian countries; IMF, World Economic Outlook, May 2000, for other data (pp. 203–12).

Table 3.2 Per capita GDP for Arabian countries (US$), (figures for 1975 to 1990 adjusted using 1987 prices)

	1975	1980	1985	1990	1995	1999
Oil-exporter (average)*	12,057	11,825	7,950	9,074	9,158	9,686
UAE	29,200	29,900	20,000	18,250	17,755	17,745
Kuwait	24,400	18,400	11,400	8,610	13,553	13,160
Libya	10,500	13,200	6,900	7,758	5,772	5,859
Bahrain	...	10,000	7,300	9,004	10,103	9,956
Saudi Arabia	9,000	10,200	5,700	6,662	6,798	6,525
Oman	3,800	3,600	5,700	7,182	6,477	6,724
Iraq	5,200	6,600	3,600	4,145	3,834	3,674
Algeria	2,300	2,700	3,000	2,449	1,484	1,633
Qatar	...	...	...	17,609	16,642	21,898
Non-oil exporter (average)*	843	1,000	1,013	815	1,226	1,371
Jordan	1,200	2,100	2,200	1,159	1,517	1,524
Tunisia	1,000	1,200	1,300	1,520	2,013	2,201
Syria	1,000	1,200	1,100	1,147	1,171	1,044
Sudan	1,100	1,000	900	512	351	381
Morocco	600	800	800	1,055	1,216	1,197
Egypt	500	700	800	690	1,060	1,435
Mauritania	500	500	500	530	462	365
Comoros	...	500	500	500	500	500
Djibouti	...	...	...	...	...	...
Lebanon	...	...	...	1,124	3,656	4,676
Somalia	...	...	...	44	...	...
Yemen	...	...	...	682	318	383
All developing countries	600	700	700	800	900	1030
Arabian countries	6,450	6,413	4,481	4,532	4,983	5,309
Industrialized countries	12,600	14,200	15,500	17,600	19,300	19,300

* For countries that have available data; ... = Not available.
Source: UNDP (1999), *Human Development Report* (for years 1975–85), and Arab Monetary Fund, 2002 (www.amf.org.ae) for other data.

Table 3.3   Composition of GDP in Arabian countries (average 1990–9) (in per cent)

	Commodity	*Distributive*	*Services*
Arabian countries (average)	48.5	26.6	21.0
Arab oil-exporter (average)	51.3	23.7	24.5
Saudi Arabia	59.0	17.7	21.5
UAE	57.6	21.5	21.3
Algeria	56.4	22.9	12.6
Kuwait	48.7	19.6	31.9
Oman	50.1	20.6	28.4
Qatar	54.6	20.8	24.1
Bahrain	37.6	24.8	34.1
Iraq	47.3	41.7	21.4
Libya	50.7	24.0	25.3
Arab non-oil exporter (average)	46.0	29.2	17.9
Egypt	46.5	30.6	17.0
Morocco	48.4	26.0	25.6
Tunisia	42.7	25.7	18.9
Syria	53.1	27.7	11.1
Lebanon	27.7	38.7	33.6
Sudan	46.3	36.4	15.3
Jordan	27.7	38.1	19.5
Yemen, Republic of	53.5	24.2	18.9
Mauritania	50.2	25.2	14.0
Djibouti	...	...	...
Comoros	...	...	...
Somalia	63.9	19.1	5.6

... = Not available

Note: The commodity sector includes mainly agriculture, fuel, manufacturing and construction activities; the distribution sector includes mainly traded goods; and the service sector includes mainly banking, insurance, finance, hotel, transport activities, government, other services activities and housing.

Source: Arab Monetary Fund, 2002 (www.amf.org.ae).

over this period, as shown in Table 3.3. The exports of Arab oil countries comprised more than 85 per cent of the total value of exports over this period. The exports of Saudi Arabia and the United Arab Emirates in particular comprised about 63 per cent of the total oil countries' exports. In terms of annual export growth, those of Algeria, Yemen and Qatar have grown the fastest. On the other hand, imports to Arabian countries increased from about $100 billion in 1990 to more than $140 billion in 1999 (Table 3.4). Imports of Arab oil countries comprise about 70 per cent of total Arabian imports. In particular, the imports to Saudi Arabia and the United Arab Emirates comprise around 60 per cent of imports of Arab oil countries while the imports of Egypt comprise around one-third of those of

Table 3.4 Exports of Arabian countries, 1990–9 (millions of US dollars)

	1990	1991	1992	1993	1994	1995	1996	1997	1998	1999	Average* 1990–9	Average annual growth
Arabian countries (total)*	136,290	119,620	130,710	121,380	127,590	145,290	168,530	169,060	132,320	156,420	140,720	2
*Arab oil-exporter**	120,380	103,420	115,570	106,910	111,150	125,850	147,620	147,820	110,430	132,710	122190	1
Saudi Arabia	37	46	44	40	38	40	41	41	35	37	40	0
UAE	18	22	21	22	25	23	23	23	28	27	23	6
Algeria	9	9	10	9	8	8	9	9	10	7	9	-2
Kuwait	6	1	6	10	10	10	10	10	9	9	8	6
Libya	11	10	9	7	8	7	6	6	6	6	8	-5
Bahrain	3	3	3	3	3	3	3	3	3	3	3	0
Oman	5	5	5	5	5	5	5	5	5	5	5	0
Qatar	3	3	3	3	3	3	3	3	5	5	3	7
Iraq	9	0	1	0	0	0	...	...	...	...	2	...
*Arab non-oil-exporter**	15,910	16,200	15,140	14,470	16,440	19,440	20,910	21,240	21,890	23,710	18,540	5
Tunisia	22	23	26	26	28	28	26	26	26	25	26	2
Morocco	27	26	26	26	24	24	23	22	33	31	26	2
Syria	15	10	8	8	7	7	5	5	3	3	7	-9
Egypt	16	22	20	22	21	18	17	18	15	15	18	-1
Yemen, Republic of	4	2	1	1	1	4	9	12	7	10	6	17
Jordan	7	7	8	9	9	9	9	9	8	8	8	2
Lebanon	3	3	4	3	3	4	5	3	3	3	4	0
Mauritania	3	3	3	3	3	3	3	2	3	2	3	-4
Sudan	2	2	2	3	3	3	3	3	3	3	3	6
Somalia	1	1	1	...	...	...	...	...	...	...	1	...
Djibouti	...	...	...	...	...	...	...	...	...	...	...	...
Comoros	...	...	...	...	...	...	...	...	...	...	...	...

*For countries that have available data; ... = Not available.
Source: Arab Monetary Fund, 2002 (www.amf.org.ae).

the non-oil countries. In terms of annual growth, imports to the United Arab Emirates have grown noticeably over the last decade.

Overall, the trade balance for Arabian countries decreased from around $36 billion in 1990 to around $14 billion in 1999. As to be expected, the trade balances of Arab oil countries were in surplus, while those of the non-oil countries have experienced continued deficits over the last decade (See Tables 3.5 and 3.6).

Inflation trends during the 1990s

Inflation rates in Arabia, as measured by changes in the consumer price index, witnessed improvement during the 1990s, especially in comparison with the high levels experienced during the 1980s. Inflation averaged about 8 per cent during 1992–8 compared to 12 per cent during 1982–91 (See Table 3.7). The lower levels of inflation are similar to those experienced in other developing countries over the same period. Despite the decline in general inflation, some Arabian economies still suffer from relatively high rates of inflation (i.e. Algeria, Yemen, Sudan and Lebanon). The ability of various Arabian countries to reduce their inflation rates over the last decade is perhaps indicative of their adoption of more appropriate macroeconomic policies and the gradual structural reforms that have taken place.

External indebtedness and reserves of Arab countries

The external debt of the Arabian countries averaged about $130 billion over 1990–8, with insignificant changes during this period (Table 3.8). The debt of non-oil Arabian countries accounts for around 77 per cent of the total debt over the whole period. The most indebted countries include Egypt, Morocco, Algeria and Syria.

Despite insignificant changes in absolute levels, the external indebtedness as a percent of GDP (Table 3.9) has witnessed noticeable falls especially for the non-oil countries; declining from about 6.7 per cent to 5.7 per cent over the period 1990–8. As a percentage of GDP, the most indebted countries are Jordan, Mauritania, Morocco and Algeria.

While total external indebtedness remained at a similar level throughout the 1990s, Arabian country's reserves have witnessed an increase especially the non-oil countries (Table 3.10). The non-oil Arab countries reserves increased from about $7.7 billion in 1990 to more than $36 billion in 1999. On the other hand, the reserves of Arab oil countries increased from about $28 billion in 1990 to reach around $48 billion by the end of the decade. This increase in the reserves of Arab oil countries came mainly from the recovery that followed the Gulf War. In particular, the total reserves of Saudi Arabia and Bahrain comprise more than 50 per cent of the total Arab oil country reserves, while those of Egypt comprise more than

Table 3.5 Imports of Arabian countries, 1990–9 (millions of US dollars)

	1990	1991	1992	1993	1994	1995	1996	1997	1998	1999	Average* 1990–9	Average annual growth
Arabian countries (total)*	100,600	101,910	115,470	110,080	110,070	127,220	134,110	136,220	149,130	142,450	122,730	5
*Arab oil-exporter**	69,720	71,980	81,910	79,320	76,490	86,310	88,070	90,380	97,480	92,450	83,410	4
Saudi Arabia	35	40	41	36	31	33	32	32	31	30	34	–2
UAE	17	19	21	25	30	27	29	29	31	35	26	12
Algeria	14	9	10	11	13	12	10	10	10	10	11	–3
Kuwait	6	7	9	9	9	9	10	9	9	8	8	4
Libya	11	11	6	7	5	6	6	6	6	5	7	–6
Bahrain	5	6	5	5	5	4	5	4	4	4	5	–2
Oman	4	4	5	5	5	5	5	6	6	5	5	3
Qatar	2	2	2	2	3	4	3	4	3	3	3	3
Iraq	7	1	1	1	1	1	...	...	...	...	2	...
*Arab non-oil-exporter**	30,880	29,930	33,560	30,760	33,580	40,910	46,040	45,840	51,650	50,000	39,315	7
Tunisia	18	17	19	20	20	19	17	17	16	17	18	–1
Morocco	22	23	22	22	21	21	18	17	20	22	21	0
Syria	5	4	4	5	6	4	3	2	2	2	4	–7
Egypt	30	26	25	27	29	29	28	29	32	32	29	1
Yemen, Republic of	4	4	3	3	1	2	3	4	4	4	3	0
Jordan	8	8	10	12	10	9	9	9	7	7	9	–1
Lebanon	8	13	12	7	8	12	16	16	14	12	12	6
Mauritania	1	2	2	2	2	2	1	1	1	1	1	0
Sudan	2	3	2	3	3	3	3	3	4	3	3	6
Somalia	1	1	1	...	...	...	...	...	...	...	1	...
Djibouti	...	...	...	...	...	...	...	...	...	...	...	...
Comoros	...	...	...	...	...	...	...	...	...	...	...	...

* For countries that have available data; ... = Not available.
Source: Arab Monetary Fund, 2002 (www.amf.org.ae).

Table 3.6 Balance of trade of Arabian countries, 1990–9 (millions of US dollars)

	1990	1991	1992	1993	1994	1995	1996	1997	1998	1999	Average* 1990–9
Arabian countries (total)*	35,680	17,690	15,230	11,290	17,520	18,080	34,430	32,840	−16,820	13,960	17,990
*Arab oil-exporter**	50,640	31,440	33,640	27,580	34,650	39,550	59,550	57,440	12,960	40,260	38,770
Saudi Arabia	20,350	18,610	17,010	14,190	19,250	21,950	32,960	31,990	8,810	20,450	20,560
UAE	10,080	8,830	6,840	4,030	4,700	5,850	7,760	7,400	550	3,380	5,940
Algeria	1,160	2,590	2,580	1,340	−980	360	3,490	5,070	1,020	−240	1,640
Kuwait	2,990	−3,620	−710	3,230	4,580	5,050	6,570	6,040	1,000	4,660	2,980
Libya	5,650	2,400	5,100	2,380	4,510	4,220	4,610	3,450	380	4,220	3,690
Bahrain	50	−600	−800	−130	−130	400	430	360	−300	500	−20
Oman	2,830	1,680	1,790	1,250	1,630	1,820	2,760	2,600	−170	2,560	1,870
Qatar	1,950	1,490	1,830	1,350	1,220	80	960	530	1,670	4,710	1,580
Iraq	5,590	60	10	−60	−110	−190	…	…	…	…	880
*Arab non-oil-exporter**	−14,960	−13,740	−18,420	−16,300	−17,140	−21,470	−25,120	−24,600	−29,780	−26,300	−20780
Tunisia	−1,980	−1,400	−2,420	−2,400	−1,930	−2,420	−2,190	−2,390	−2,600	−2,580	−2230
Morocco	−2,690	−2,580	−3,380	−2,960	−3,200	−3,820	−3,510	−3,200	−3,130	−3,430	−3190
Syria	1,050	300	−160	−370	−650	−240	−390	−30	−230	−80	−80
Egypt	−6,600	−4,140	−5,250	−5,100	−6,110	−8,310	−9,500	−9,330	−13,330	−12,460	−8010
Yemen, Republic of	−760	−720	−890	−670	−250	150	470	490	−670	380	−250
Jordan	−1,540	−1,380	−2,040	−2,290	−1,960	−1,930	−2,480	−2,270	−2,030	−1,880	−1980
Lebanon	−2,030	−3,200	−3,530	−1,820	−2,280	−4,180	−6,560	−6,820	−6,410	−5,530	−4240
Mauritania	80	40	−150	−150	−120	−70	−80	−80	−60	−70	−70
Sudan	−240	−590	−500	−530	−640	−630	−880	−990	−1,330	−630	−700
Somalia	−250	−90	−100	…	…	…	…	…	…	…	−150
Djibouti	…	…	…	…	…	…	…	…	…	…	…
Comoros	…	…	…	…	…	…	…	…	…	…	…

* For countries that have available data; … = Not available.
Source: Arab Monetary Fund, 2002 (www.amf.org.ae).

51

Table 3.7 Inflation in Arabian countries over 1982–98 (per cent)

Consumer Prices (annual percent change)	1982–91 (average)	1989	1992	1995	1998	1992–8 average*
Arab oil-exporter (average)*	5	4	5	4	2	4
Oman	2	3	1	−1	−1	0
Saudi Arabia	...	1	0	5	0	2
Bahrain	1	2	...	3	0	2
Kuwait	4	3	−1	3	1	1
Qatar	3	4	3	3	3	3
UAE	4	7	6	5	2	4
Libya	8	...	18	11	7	12
Algeria	11	10	...	...	6	6
Iraq	...	...	...	...	...	...
Arab non-oil (average)*	19	23	11	6	4	12
Djibouti	5	...	3	5	2	4
Jordan	7	6	4	2	5	4
Morocco	7	4	6	6	3	4
Comoros	3	...	1	7	1	6
Syria	22	60	3	1	0	6
Mauritania	8	4	10	7	8	7
Egypt	18	13	21	9	5	10
Lebanon	80	50	40	11	5	24
Yemen, Republic of	...	...	...	...	11	44
Sudan	...	...	...	...	...	...
Somalia	...	...	...	...	...	...
Arabian countries (Average)*	12	13	8	5	3	8
Developing Countries	10	62	10	10	6	8
Middle East and North Africa	14.6	21.9	18	24.5	9.3	15.7

* For countries that have available data; . . . = Not available.
Sources: Arab Monetary Fund, 2002 (www.amf.org.ae) for Arabian countries over 1992–8; Zeinelabdin, 1990, for data prior to 1992.

50 per cent of those of non-oil countries. The Arabian countries that have witnessed a significant increase in their reserves over the last decade include the United Arab Emirates and Lebanon.

In general, the fall in external indebtedness as a percentage of GDP over the last decade, in addition to increases in external reserves, probably reflects the adoption of more prudential fiscal policies in various Arabian countries, as well as the benefits accruing due to higher energy prices.

Domestic investment and FDI in the Arab world

The proportion of GNP allocated to capital formation should enhance economic growth, as the bulk of domestic investment is usually provided from national savings.[1] As such, domestic and foreign investment patterns

Table 3.8 External debt of Arabian countries (US$, millions)

	1990	1991	1992	1993	1994	1995	1996	1997	1998	1990–8 average*
Total Arabian countries*	127,293	128,048	125,504	125,068	133,493	140,354	137,871	128,361	132,031	130,891
*Oil-exporter (total)**	28,816	28,443	27,829	27,162	30,786	33,679	33,708	31,277	30,697	30,266
Iraq	...	...	...	...	...	...	...	...	...	...
Algeria	26,416	25,969	25,489	24,847	28,178	31,042	31,062	28,710	28,469	27,798
UAE	...	...	...	...	...	...	...	...	...	...
Qatar	...	...	...	...	...	...	...	...	...	...
Kuwait	...	...	...	...	...	...	...	...	...	...
Libya	...	...	...	...	...	...	...	...	...	...
Oman	2,400	2,474	2,340	2,315	2,608	2,637	2,646	2,567	2,228	2,468
Bahrain	...	...	...	...	...	...	...	...	...	...
Saudi Arabia countries	...	...	...	...	...	...	...	...	...	...
*Non-oil-exporter (total)**	98,477	99,605	97,675	97,906	102,707	106,675	104,163	97,084	101,334	100,625
Egypt	28,372	29,317	28,348	28,303	30,189	30,792	28,810	26,804	27,670	28,734
Syria	14,917	16,353	15,913	16,235	16,540	16,757	16,698	16,254	16,328	16,222
Morocco	23,101	20,792	21,030	20,680	21,530	22,085	21,134	18,978	19,325	20,962
Sudan	9,155	9,220	8,984	8,994	9,400	9,779	9,369	8,998	9,226	9,236
Tunisia	6,662	7,109	7,201	7,415	8,002	9,118	9,463	9,426	9,727	8,236
Jordan	7,043	7,458	6,922	6,770	6,883	7,023	7,091	6,960	7,388	7,060
Somalia	1,926	1,945	1,898	1,897	1,935	1,961	1,918	1,853	1,886	1,913
Yemen, Republic of	5,154	5,256	5,253	5,341	5,460	5,528	5,622	3,418	3,590	4,958
Lebanon	358	336	301	368	778	1,551	1,933	2,353	3,980	1,329
Mauritania	1,789	1,819	1,825	1,903	1,990	2,081	2,125	2,040	2,214	1,976
Djibouti	...	...	...	...	...	...	...	...	...	...
Comoros	...	...	...	...	...	...	...	...	...	...

* For countries that have available data; . . . = Not available.
Source: Arab Monetary Fund, 2002 (www.amf.org.ae).

Table 3.9 External debt of Arabia as a per cent of GDP

	1990	1991	1992	1993	1994	1995	1996	1997	1998	1990–8 average*
Arabian countries* (average)	6.71	6.30	6.01	6.52	5.56	5.21	5.35	5.26	5.00	5.77
*Oil-exporter (avg.)**	9.95	12.29	11.25	11.03	7.81	6.47	6.57	5.50	6.85	8.63
Iraq	..	..	..	..	..	..	..	..	..	..
Algeria	13.80	19.70	18.54	17.40	11.55	9.55	8.43	8.28	9.69	12.99
UAE	..	..	..	..	..	..	..	..	..	..
Qatar	..	..	..	..	..	..	..	..	..	..
Kuwait	..	..	..	..	..	..	..	..	..	..
Libya	..	..	..	..	..	..	..	..	..	..
Oman	6.11	4.87	3.96	4.67	4.06	3.38	4.71	2.72	4.00	4.27
Bahrain	..	..	..	..	..	..	..	..	..	..
Saudi Arabia countries	..	..	..	..	..	..	..	..	..	..
*Non-oil-exporter (avg.)**	6.06	5.10	4.97	5.52	5.06	4.93	5.08	5.20	4.58	5.17
Egypt	7.01	6.70	5.19	3.93	3.60	3.40	2.77	2.08	1.87	4.06
Syria	8.57	3.06	1.57	1.26	1.49	0.93	0.70	2.56	1.08	2.36
Morocco	5.66	7.63	12.92	11.52	11.39	10.92	8.88	9.21	7.60	9.52
Sudan	0.19	0.18	0.43	0.30	0.05	0.18	0.00	0.00	0.02	0.15
Tunisia	9.91	8.69	7.83	8.36	8.62	7.58	6.76	6.66	6.22	7.85
Jordan	13.63	14.83	12.69	9.10	7.95	8.36	14.16	11.83	11.33	11.54
Somalia	1.85	0.00	0.00	..	..	..	..	..	..	0.62
Yemen, Republic of	1.23	2.31	1.60	1.72	1.53	1.86	1.44	1.30	1.97	1.66
Lebanon	1.36	1.06	1.17	0.90	1.33	1.42	1.66	4.05	1.58	1.61
Mauritania	11.24	6.52	6.26	12.61	9.55	9.67	9.34	9.14	9.58	9.32
Djibouti	..	..	..	..	..	..	..	..	..	..
Comoros	..	..	..	..	..	..	..	..	..	..

* For countries that have available data; . . . = Not available.
Source: Arab Monetary Fund, 2002 (www.amf.org.ae).

Table 3.10 Monetary reserves (excluding gold) of Arabian countries, 1990–9

Country (% of total)	1990	1991	1992	1993	1994	1995	1996	1997	1998	1999	Avg. 1990–9
Oil-countries (US$, mil.)	28,210	31,470	26,990	25,330	26,430	30,440	40,240	46,080	44,660	47,910	34,780
Saudi Arabia	41	37	22	29	28	28	36	32	32	35	33
Emirates	16	17	21	24	25	25	20	18	21	23	21
Libya	20	18	18	13	13	19	17	16	15	13	16
Kuwait	7	11	19	17	13	12	9	7	9	10	11
Algeria	3	5	5	6	10	7	11	17	15	9	10
Oman	6	5	7	4	4	4	3	3	2	3	4
Bahrain	4	5	5	5	4	4	3	3	3	3	4
Qatar	2	2	3	3	3	2	2	2	3	3	2
Iraq	..	..	..	..	..	..	..	..	..	..	..
Non-oil countries (US$, mil.)	7,720	12,690	18,630	21,260	25,160	29,190	32,760	35,420	35,240	36,180	25,440
Egypt	35	42	59	61	54	55	53	53	51	40	51
Lebanon	9	10	8	11	15	16	18	17	19	21	16
Morocco	27	24	19	17	17	12	12	11	13	16	15
Tunisia	10	6	5	4	6	6	6	6	5	6	6
Syria	2	5	3	3	4	7	5	5	5	6	5
Jordan	11	7	4	3	2	1	2	5	3	6	4
Yemen	5	5	2	1	1	2	3	3	3	4	3
Mauritania	1	1	0	0	0	0	0	1	1	1	0
Sudan	0	0	0	0	0	1	0	0	0	0	0
Somalia	0	..	..	..	..	..	..	..	..	0	0
Total (US$, mil)	35,930	44,160	45,610	46,590	51,590	59,630	73,010	81,500	79,910	84,090	60,210

* For countries that have available data; . . . = Not available.

Source: Arab Monetary Fund, 2002 (www.amf.org.ae).

can strongly influence growth potential. Domestic investment in Arabia (as a proportion of GDP) has increased but showed some volatility over the 1995–9 period. For instance, domestic investment as a percentage of GDP in oil countries ranged from about 17 per cent in 1996 to about 22 per cent in 1998. The domestic investment in non-oil countries has stayed at a level of around 20 per cent over the same period, as shown in Table 3.11. Countries that enjoyed high rates of domestic investment include Lebanon, Jordan, Syria, Tunisia and Algeria. These investment rates along with their improved growth over the last decade should have helped enhance overall economic performance in their economies.

Regarding foreign investment, the available indicators suggest that there was an increase in foreign direct investment to oil and non-oil Arabian countries during the 1990s. Table 3.12 shows that foreign investment almost tripled between 1982 and 1998 in the non-oil exporting countries. Unfortunately, there is only limited information about foreign direct

Table 3.11   Gross domestic investment of Arabian countries as percentage of GDP

	1995	1996	1997	1998	1999	1995–9 average*
*Oil-exporter (average)**	20	17	16	22	21	19
Algeria	32	25	24	27	27	27
Saudi Arabia	21	18	20	21		20
Egypt, Arab Rep.	17	17	18	22	23	19
Kuwait	15	15	14	16	12	15
Bahrain	13	9	6	. . .	. . .	10
Iraq	. . .	. . .	. . .	. . .	. . .	. . .
Libya	. . .	. . .	. . .	. . .	. . .	. . .
Oman	. . .	. . .	. . .	. . .	. . .	. . .
Qatar	. . .	. . .	. . .	. . .	. . .	. . .
UAE	. . .	. . .	. . .	. . .	. . .	. . .
*Non-oil exporter (average)**	23	22	22	25	24	23
Lebanon	33	30	27	28	. . .	29
Jordan	34	32	27	25	27	29
Syria	27	26	29	30	30	28
Tunisia	25	25	27	28	28	26
Yemen, Rep.	22	22	21	29	21	23
Morocco	21	20	21	23	23	21
Comoros	20	19	21	20	19	20
Mauritania	19	19	18	20	22	20
Djibouti	9	9	10	. . .	. . .	9
Somalia	. . .	. . .	. . .	. . .	. . .	. . .
Sudan	. . .	. . .	. . .	. . .	. . .	. . .
All Arabian countries (Average)*	22	20	20	24	23	22
Middle East & North Africa	24	21	21	22	. . .	22
World	22	22	22	. . .	. . .	22

* For countries that have available data; . . . = Not available.
Source: World Bank, 2000.

Table 3.12   Foreign direct investment in Arabian countries (US$, millions)

	Annual average		1995	1996	1997	1998	1995–8 average*
	1982–7	1987–92					
Oil-exporter (total)*	16	15	6	24	3	9	8
Kuwait	0	0	1	19	1	3	5
Oman	11	6	5	4	2	5	3
Algeria	–1	. . .	1	0	0	0	0
Bahrain	3	3	. . .	. . .	. . .	. . .	. . .
Iraq	0	0	. . .	. . .	. . .	. . .	. . .
Libya	–12	3	. . .	. . .	. . .	. . .	. . .
Qatar	0	1	. . .	. . .	. . .	. . .	. . .
Saudi Arabia	11	–2	. . .	. . .	. . .	. . .	. . .
UAE	3	3	. . .	. . .	. . .	. . .	. . .
Non-oil exporter (total)*	84	86	93	76	97	142	92
Egypt, Arab Rep.	62	47	62	35	30	54	37
Morocco	3	12	10	20	37	16	21
Tunisia	12	9	28	13	11	33	17
Jordan	3	1	1	1	12	16	8
Yemen, Rep.	1	12	23	3	5	11	7
Sudan	0	0	0	0	3	19	5
Lebanon	0	0	4	4	5	10	5
Syria	1	4	10	5	3	4	4
Mauritania	0	0	1	0	0	0	0
Djibouti	. . .	. . .	0	0	0	0	0
Comoros	0	0	0	0	0	0	0
Somalia	1	0	0	0	0	0	0
Total Arabian countries	1,300	1,700	960	1,800	2,950	1,980	2,170
Middle East & North Africa	. . .	. . .	200	3,600	5,900	5,000	3,700

* For countries that have available data; . . . = Not available.
Source: World Bank, 2000.

investment to oil-exporting Arabian countries. Based on available data, the top non-oil countries acquiring external investment are Egypt, Morocco, Tunisia and Jordan.

Recent economic performance in the Gulf region

This section looks at the economic performance of Gulf economies, focusing particularly on the countries that are members of the Gulf Cooperation Council (GCC). The GCC was founded in 1981 with the aim of coordinating policies in various political, economic, and social matters across the Gulf region.[2] GCC countries consist of six Arab Gulf states: the Kingdom of Saudi Arabia, the United Arab Emirates (UAE), the Kingdom of

Bahrain, the Sultanate of Oman, the State of Qatar, and the State of Kuwait (see Figure 3.1).

The Gulf countries stand out as one of the most important economic regions of the world. In particular, the capability of the region to meet the world demand for hydrocarbon consumption has driven the region's strategic economic significance in the global economy. GCC countries were responsible for about 18 per cent of total world oil production in 1999, and they account for around 45 per cent of the world's proven crude oil reserves and 15 per cent of world's total proven natural gas reserves.[3] The consequent importance of the Gulf region to the global oil market and economy lies in the fact that any interruption in Gulf oil production can destabilize the world economy, especially through deliberate limiting of the supply of oil. GCC countries (and Saudi Arabia in particular) can also make up any shortages in the world oil supply when oil production is interrupted elsewhere.

Table 3.13 shows the amount of oil and gas production and reserves in each GCC as well as each country's share in the total GCC production and reserves of these products. The largest oil producer in the GCC is Saudi Arabia

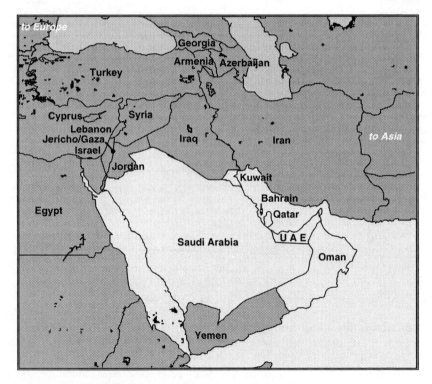

Figure 3.1   Gulf Cooperation Council (GCC) countries
Source: http://www.lib.utexas.edu/maps/middle_east_and_asia/middle_east_pol_2003.jpg

Table 3.13 Oil and gas production and reserves of the GCC in 1999

	Oil production (1,000 barrel per day)		Oil reserve (billion barrel)		Natural gas production** (million cubic metres/year)		Natural gas reserves (million cubic metres/year)	
	Country total	% in GCC total	Country total	% in GCC total	Country total	% in GCC total	Country total	% in GCC total
Kuwait	1882.9	14.3%	96.5	21%	10860	6.9%	1480	6.5%
Qatar	632.5	4.8%	4.5	1%	26200	16.5%	8500	37.5%
Oman	895	6.8%	5.7	1%	11565	7.3%	805	3.6%
Saudi Arabia	7560	57.2%	263.5	56%	49780	31.4%	5777	25.5%
Bahrain	179.8	1.4%	0.15	0%	11030	7.0%	110	0.5%
UAE	2060	15.6%	98.1	21%	48980	30.9%	6003	26.5%

** Data for this item correspond to the year 1998.
Source: Secretariat General's Economic Bulletin, 2001. Percentages are the authors' calculations based on this source.

with a share of 57 per cent in 2000. Saudi Arabia also has the largest proportion of oil reserves (56 per cent). Although Saudi Arabia's natural gas production comprises the largest share among GCC countries, Qatar's natural gas reserves are the largest.

GCC countries achieved significant economic development throughout the 1990s. According to the GCC Secretariat General's report (2001, pp. 15–16), the GDP of GCC countries grew by 78 per cent from $180 billion in 1990 to $321 billion in 2000. The size of the GCC economy as of 2000 ranged between the largest, Saudi Arabia, accounting for 54 per cent of total GCC GDP, and the smallest, Bahrain (see Figure 3.2). In 2000, Saudi Arabia's GDP amounted to some $173.3 billion, followed by $66.1 billion for the UAE, $37.7 billion for Kuwait, $19.7 billion for Oman, $16.4 billion for Qatar, and $7.9 billion for Bahrain. In fact, the differences in oil production quantities (and their revenues) are the main determinant of the respective economies' sizes.

The significant income generated from the wealth of the hydrocarbon resources, accompanied by relatively small populations in GCC countries, has led to high levels of per capita income. For instance, the average per capita income in the GCC countries stood at around $10,362 in 2000, up from $8,144 in 1990 and $8,653 in 1995. Individually, Qatar had the highest per capita income in the GCC region in 2000, standing at around $29,000, followed by the UAE with a per capita income of around $21,500 (GCC Secretariat General's Economic Bulletin, 2001).

In addition, over the period 1995–2000, most GCC countries achieved positive nominal GDP average annual growth rates (see Table 3.14). This

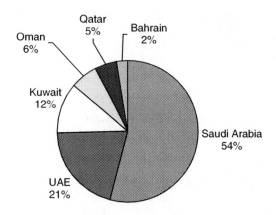

Figure 3.2   Distribution of GCC GDP at current prices, 2000
Source: Percentages are the authors' calculations based on the GCC Secretariat General's Economic Bulletin, 2001.

Table 3.14   GCC GDP annual growth over the period 1995–2000 (current prices) (%)

	1995	1996	1997	1998	1999	2000	avg.	Real GDP growth in 2001 (%)
Saudi Arabia	6.4	10.6	3.7	–12.4	8.4	21.8	6.4	1.6
UAE	11.9	12.1	5.0	–6.0	10.1	20.4	8.9	5.6
Kuwait	7.1	17.0	–3.4	–15.7	17.2	26.9	8.2	4
Oman	6.8	10.7	3.7	–10.6	10.4	20.8	7.0	7.4
Qatar	10.4	11.3	24.7	–9.2	18.9	33.3	14.9	5.6
Bahrain	5.1	4.3	4.1	–2.6	7.1	20.3	6.4	4
GCC	8.0	11.0	6.3	–9.4	12.0	23.9	8.6	4.7
World								2.2

Sources: GCC Secretariat General's Economic Bulletin, 2001; and *The World Factbook*, 2002 (various pages and authors' own calculations).

indicator averaged 6.4 per cent in Saudi Arabia and Bahrain and reached 14.9 per cent in Qatar, the latter being mainly explained by the fact that this country undertook substantial capital expenditure on developing its gas sector during this period (*Gulf Business*, July 2002). In real terms, GCC economic rates of growth exceeded world levels in 2001.

Generally, the GCC economies are vulnerable to international price conditions surrounding their primary export product, oil. For instance, during 1995–2000, GCC GDP performance fluctuated mainly on account of the vulnerability of the oil sector. Thus, as Figure 3.3 shows, both GDP and oil sector growth rates exhibit similar patterns. Figure 3.3 also indicates that all GCC countries experienced negative GDP growth in 1998 because of the crash in oil prices, so that the average oil price stood at $12.60 a barrel for

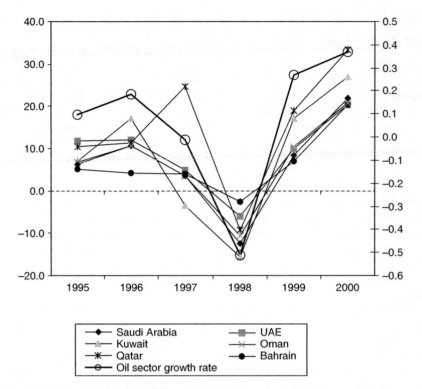

Figure 3.3 GDP and oil growth rates of individual GCC countries over the period 1995–2000
Source: Adapted from the GCC Secretariat General's Economic Bulletin, 2001.

Brent in that year compared with \$19.12 in 1997 (*MEED*, 25 June 1999). The decrease in the oil price came after a huge excess supply in the oil market, mainly due to reduction in oil demand by the countries affected by the Asian financial crisis.[4] The recovery in oil demand and the success of the OPEC cartel to limit oil supply resulted in an increase in economic growth after 1998. Figure 3.3 also shows that the least affected country in the GCC during 1998 was Bahrain, mainly because of the more diversified nature of its economy and the country's lower dependence on oil income. As mentioned earlier, the strong growth of the Qatari economy shown in Figure 3.3 was mainly due to the large capital expenditures on gas projects that were undertaken over the period.

Another characteristic of GCC countries' economies is that all experienced low levels of inflation (generally less than 5 per cent) throughout the 1990s.[5] For example, in 2001, the inflation rate ranged from 1 per cent in Oman to 4.4 per cent in the UAE. These inflation rates are similar to those experienced in the developed countries, which range between 1 and 4 percent for the same year.[6] The most significant source of GCC countries' inflation levels is due to imports, as more than 90 per cent of GCC countries' imports are supplied by non-GCC countries.[7] Nevertheless, increased competition and substitutes for imported goods probably helped moderate the inflation level. Moreover, since most of the imports of GCC economies are dollar denominated, GCC economies can face price inflation due to unstable exchange rates against the US dollar. However, on average, the dollar was relatively stable over the 1990s against major international currencies and this helped dampen potential inflationary pressures (Qatar Central Bank, 2000).

In addition, the use of appropriate monetary and fiscal policies to control liquidity and finance budget deficits helped, to some extent, in keeping pace with changes in oil prices and achieving stability in average general prices. The low interest rate/inflation climate in the global economy throughout the 1990s must also have been an important factor in limiting inflationary forces. The broad effect of this low-inflation environment has clearly been seen in the maintenance of a stable macroeconomic climate.

Most of the GCC countries were able to settle the high levels of external debt that were generated from the financial burden associated with the military operation that terminated the Iraqi invasion of Kuwait. The current external indebtedness of GCC economies reflects, more or less, the extent to which they have financed their development projects as well as public deficits. For example, governments like Qatar and Oman have tapped international markets and sold bonds to finance government projects in the gas and petrochemicals area. Budget deficits have also been run to bolster domestic government policy (*Gulf Business*, January and February 2000). Because of low oil prices in 1998, GCC countries were downgraded by the international credit rating agencies, compelling them to offer more attractive payment of interest (or in certain cases to postpone bonds debuts) until improved oil prices prevailed. However, oil prices had increased by mid-1999 and these countries gained improved ratings allowing them to make various successful international bond issues.

As we noted earlier in this chapter, Saudi Arabia has the highest external debt, amounting to $28.8 billion in 2000, followed by the UAE ($14.1 billion), Qatar ($10.1 billion), Kuwait ($7.9 billion), and Oman ($4.4 billion). Relative to GDP, most Gulf countries' external debts are modest, except for those of Qatar whose external debts in 2000 amounted to 60 per cent of GDP (see Figure 3.4), having actually declined from about 80 per cent of GDP in 1998. The large Qatari external debt was mainly due to the country's determined plan to complete the construction of its huge gas field project. Repayments of these debts are expected to be arranged from the sales of gas (*Gulf Business*, July 2002).

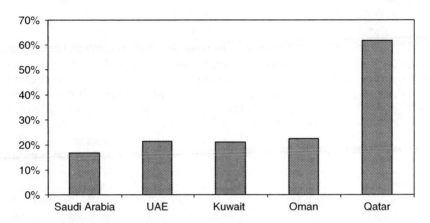

Figure 3.4 External debts as a share of GDP, 2000
Source: Adapted from Bank for International Settlements, 2002 (http://www.bis.org).

GCC countries' exchange rate policies aim at providing stability and convertibility, and maintaining the value of the national currencies against major international currencies. This goal has been pursued for some time given that the majority of GCC countries have maintained fixed exchange rates against the US dollar since the early 1970s. Kuwait is the main exception as it has tied its currency with a basket of major international currencies, although in January 2003 it started to peg its currency to the US dollar as part of the GCC policy to introduce a single currency by 2010.

The adoption of the fixed exchange regime, as well as the choice of the US dollar to which most GCC currencies have been pegged, is a result of the fact that most GCC income is in US dollars generated from oil exports, in addition to the fact that the US currency is an internationally accepted medium of payment in world trade. In essence, GCC economies might be more exposed to the risk of currency fluctuation if they floated against non-US dollar currencies. GCC countries back their pegged currencies to the dollar by using dollar reserves generated from oil revenues. However, in certain cases, it has cost these countries their reserves in order to keep their exchange rates as officially specified at the pegged rate. For example, during the first days of the Iraqi invasion of Kuwait, most GCC governments intervened with their reserves in order to maintain their exchange rates. Moreover, in late 1998 and early 1999, the Saudi authorities strengthened the position of the riyal against speculation activities in the international currency market, especially in the wake of the Asian financial crisis (*Gulf Business*, August 1999).

Although GCC countries are believed to run surpluses because of their abundant wealth of hydrocarbon resources, most of these countries actually ran fiscal deficits in the 1990s. This was mainly because their governments shouldered the burden of huge expenditures associated with maintaining and providing public services as well as financing various state projects in the petrochemical industry, expansions in water and electricity facilities and in oil and gas field developments. The deficits are also due to low diversification of government income, mainly derived from oil revenues that amount to no less than 70 per cent of total government revenues. Although none of the GCC governments levy personal income taxes, many of the GCC countries have introduced varieties of indirect taxes. These include fees on expatriates' visa extensions and renewals, fees on medical services, airport tax, fuel price increases, and electricity tariffs. Many of these were introduced with the aim of diversifying government income but are subject to increase or decrease according to oil market conditions and government financial status.

From a record 30 per cent of GDP in 1991, the fiscal deficits of GCC countries have been dramatically reduced over time to around 5 per cent in 1999. In that year, the GCC countries operated with deficits amounting to $15.5 billion. The GCC budgets, however, returned a surplus of $0.94 billion in 2000 owing to sustained strong oil prices and the continuation of tight fiscal policies.[8] In fact, the adverse impact of the 1998 economic downturn is believed to have had some positive outcomes. It has accelerated financial and economic reforms and privatization policies, and paved the way for the private sector to play a greater role in economic development. This subsequently may have helped reduce the burden of government finance in various areas.

The GCC economies' dependence on oil has reached substantial levels, as can be seen from the contribution of the oil sector to GDP, government revenues, and export earnings (see Figure 3.5 a and b). For example, across the GCC countries, the oil sector's contribution to GDP ranges between about 28 per cent in the UAE to 58 per cent in Qatar. Revenues of oil sales in total government revenues were no less than 70 per cent for each of the GCC countries (excluding Qatar). Moreover, oil exports comprised no less than 80 per cent of total GCC exports. Hence, the vulnerability of the overall economy to international oil prices should not be understated.

In order to develop a more diversified economic environment, the GCC countries have adopted certain strategies. The first of these is the development of the gas industry. GCC countries hold 15 per cent of the world's proven natural gas reserves, and those endowed with huge reserves, such as Qatar, Saudi Arabia, and Oman, are rapidly developing this sector. Establishing a more diversified industrial base (in gas and heavy industries, for example), of course, requires intensive capital investment. Such investment is typically arranged through joint ventures, the supply of expertise, and other measures aimed at attracting foreign capital, such as the provision of facilities and various tax exemptions. The second main type of diversification strategy relates to the development of industries that produce oil and gas derivatives, such as petrochemicals. The establishment of these industries

(a)

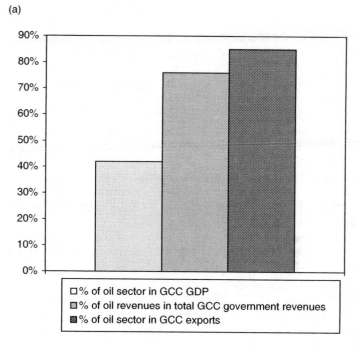

□ % of oil sector in GCC GDP
▣ % of oil revenues in total GCC government revenues
▓ % of oil sector in GCC exports

Note: Data on Qatar's oil revenues are not available.
Source: Percentage calculations are based on GCC Secretariat General's Economic Bulletin, 2001 (various pages).

(b)

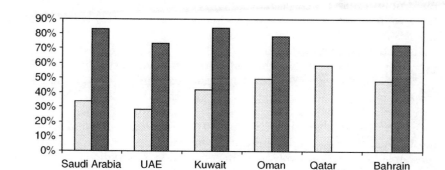

□ % of oil sector in GDP   ▓ % of oil revenues in total government revenues

Note: Oil revenues as a share in total government revenues for Qatar are not available.
Source: Percentage calculations are based on GCC Secretariat General's Economic Bulletin, 2001.

Figure 3.5 (a and b)   Share of oil revenues in GCC GDP, exports, and total government revenues, 2000

has been motivated by the perceived substantial advantage deriving from abundant hydrocarbon reserves. Moreover, abundant hydrocarbon wealth has also permitted the development of industries such as aluminium and steel projects that rely heavily on hydrocarbon inputs into the production process.

The third strategy relates to promoting import substitution and, with the aim of promoting import substitution industries, many small to medium-size light manufacturing firms have been established in the Gulf (*Gulf Business*, August 2002). These firms have been encouraged by the provision of various facilities (such as water and power) as well as reduced tariffs. However, import substitution policies have not been so successful because the current manufacturing base (which typically depends on government support) has not been set to compete internationally. Moreover, accession to the WTO exposes these firms to greater competition, as GCC countries will be committed to trade barrier removal.[9]

The final diversification strategy relates to the development of service sectors such as tourism and finance. The service sector has been growing and making a larger contribution to GCC GDP. For example, the service sector in the GCC countries grew by more than 63 per cent over the period 1990–2000.[10] Some GCC countries have undertaken substantial service sector development in various areas, including tourism, the financial sector, information technology, education, and promoting exhibition and conference activities. For example, the UAE (in particular, the Emirate of Dubai) has a well-established and a premier re-export centre equipped with modern facilities that attract local and international firms. Further, Bahrain has focused on developing banking services that are mainly aimed at attracting offshore banking units. Moreover, Bahrain announced the establishment of an International Islamic Financial Market in August 2002. Dubai has a well-developed 'Internet City' and is competing hard with Bahrain to develop a major offshore financial sector. It also has the most developed tourism industry in the Gulf. Qatar is aiming to follow such steps by promoting tourism and conferencing. These developments in the service sector are aimed at achieving greater economic diversification and creating opportunities for the private sector that result in greater foreign investment.

Overall, the GCC countries' economies have been growing and powered mostly by their main source of income from oil production. However, these economies still remain exposed to fluctuations in international oil prices. This indeed suggests an increased need for reforms and greater economic diversification.

The above provides a broad insight into the main economic features of the GCC countries' economies. The following sections present the main features of financial and banking system developments in the region.

Evidence on financial sector development in Arab economies

The issue of financial sector development is inextricably linked to the growth process occurring in an economy and causality is expected to be bi-directional. Meltzer (1998) refers to an early study of Bagehot (1873) who argued that financial intermediation was critical for the rapid industrialization of England in the early nineteenth century, and stressed the importance of financial intermediation in pooling funds, that were sufficiently large to fund risky and large-scale projects.

Goldsmith (1969) argued that financial superstructure accelerates economic growth and improves economic performance as it facilitates the migration of funds to the best users. Thus, economic and financial reforms might promote the growth of the financial system, and financial developments can be traced by linking the relationship between infrastructure and superstructure. Furthermore, changes in a country's financial structure can be noted by reviewing the sequence in which different types of financial institutions have appeared over time, and the relative importance of different financial instruments in the balance sheets of financial institutions.

Financial infrastructure is usually measured by national wealth and national product while financial superstructure is described by the presence, nature and relative size of financial instruments and financial institutions. The quantitative aspects of financial structure include the distribution of total financial assets and liabilities among financial institutions and non-financial economic units. In particular, change in the ratio of the financial assets of the financial sector to the total volume of total financial assets outstanding may reflect the institutionalization of the process of savings and investment. Similarly, changes in the distribution of the total financial assets of financial institutions reveal the changes in the role of the banking system in the process of promoting saving (Al-Sahlawi, 1997).

Goldsmith (1969) analysed data from thirty-five countries over the period 1860 to 1963 and found that financial growth and economic development are positively correlated over periods for several decades. He measured financial development by the financial intermediation ratio (the ratio of financial intermediary assets divided by gross national product). King and Levine (1992, 1993a,b) consider financial development over various periods starting in 1960 for a comprehensive cross-section of countries. They expand the set of financial development measures to capture the various services provided by financial intermediaries. One measure approximates the liquidity-providing role of financial intermediaries through liquid liabilities (currency plus demand and interest-bearing deposits, or M2) as a percentage of a country's GDP. Another measure is the ratio of credit provision to private firms to GDP (to capture monitoring, screening and control activities as well as the pooling of funds and diversification of risks). The first measure approximates the intermediaries' role in overcoming technological frictions, while the second approximates their role in overcoming incentive frictions. King and Levine (1993b) find that these measures are positively correlated with real GDP growth rates, even after controlling for initial conditions, government spending, inflation, political stability and some other policy measures. They also show that subsequent growth rates are positively correlated with initial liquidity ratios. This finding may suggest that financial development causes growth.

The following text and tables present a similar set of economic and financial indicators for four major Arabic countries (Saudi Arabia, Bahrain, Jordan and Egypt). Table 3.15 shows the financial sector development ratios that are typically used to measure financial sector development.

Referring to Table 3.16, the currency ratios in the four countries under study fell especially in Saudi Arabia and Bahrain over 1990–9. This suggests that the financial systems in these countries are not in the early stages of

Table 3.15 Summary of financial deepening ratios

Currency ratios	Include currency outside banks as % of money supply (M1) and as % of broader money supply (M2).
	When the ratios rise at the early stages of development, the real economy is expected to grow due to monetization (because of the safety of holding currency instead of tangible assets). However, these ratios are expected to decline as more financial instruments are created by financial institutions with more attractive attributes.
Monetary ratios	Include narrow money supply (M1), broader money supply (M2), demand deposits, time and savings deposits, and total deposits as a percentage of GDP.
	These ratios capture the evolution of the financial system. These ratios are also used as an indication of the velocity of circulation. The ratios increase gradually as the financial system and economy develop and progress ahead. Furthermore, the general increase in these ratios reflects higher confidence in the financial system.
Financial ratios	Include the ratios of total financial system assets and the commercial banks' total assets as a percent of GDP; and the ratio of commercial banks' assets as percent of total financial assets.
	The first two ratios are used to measure the importance of the financial institutions in the financing process, while the last ratio reflects the importance of the banking system relative to the rest of the financial system.
% of credit to private sector	Total credit of the private sector as a percent of total credit of the financial system.
	The volume of credit to the private sector is used as a proxy to examine whether reforms have actually led to a more efficient allocation of credit, because it is assumed that the private sector uses resources more efficiently than the public sector.

Table 3.16 Currency ratios in Jordan, Egypt, Saudi Arabia and Bahrain over 1990–9 (%)

	1990	1991	1992	1993	1994	1995	1996	1997	1998	1999
Jordan										
Currency outside banks/M1	70	62	58	61	61	60	62	60	59	62
Currency outside banks/M2	32	27	24	23	22	20	18	18	16	16
Egypt										
Currency outside banks/M1	68	68	68	69	102	68	67	67	69	71
Currency outside banks/M2	15	14	13	14	14	14	14	14	14	14
Saudi Arabia										
Currency outside banks/M1	44	37	35	35	36	35	32	32	32	35
Currency outside banks/M2	24	21	20	19	12	11	10	10	16	18
Bahrain										
Currency outside banks/M1	41	32	28	28	31	31	31	30	26	27
Currency outside banks/M2	11	9	8	8	8	7	7	6	5	6

Sources: Adapted from Arab Monetary Fund, 2002; and authors' estimates.

financial development and these financial systems already provided various and more attractive financial instruments for savers and investors than merely holding funds at financial institutions.

On the other hand, monetary ratios, which measure the velocity of currency circulation (M1 and M2 as a percent of GDP), have shown little movement over the last decade (Table 3.17). The other monetary ratios (deposit ratios as a percent of GDP) suggest some increases in Jordan, Saudi Arabia and Bahrain, indicating an increase in financial deepness in these countries.

Commercial banks' assets as a percent of GDP increased in Jordan, Saudi Arabia and Bahrain during the 1990s, as illustrated in Table 3.18. The other financial ratios which measure the assets of commercial banks as a percentage of financial system assets have also indicated noticeable increases in the four countries over the 1990–9 period. Taken together, these indicators suggest a growing role for financial institutions in the financing process and a wider role for commercial banks relative to the rest of players in these systems.

Concerning the growth of credit to the private sector, Table 3.19 shows that lending to the private sector as a proportion of total credit (and as a percentage of GDP) has increased in the four countries. This suggests that the financial institutions are more efficient in employing their sources of funds, as the private sector is assumed to be more efficient than the public

Table 3.17 Monetary ratios in Jordan, Egypt, Saudi Arabia and Bahrain over 1990–9

	1990	1991	1992	1993	1994	1995	1996	1997	1998	1999
Jordan										
M1/GDP	54	57	48	44	41	38	33	33	31	34
M2/GDP	117	131	118	114	114	112	110	113	116	127
Demand dep./GDP	16	21	20	17	16	15	12	13	13	13
Time and Saving dep./GDP	63	75	70	70	73	74	77	80	85	94
Egypt										
M1/GDP	25	17	16	16	11	16	16	16	16	16
M2/GDP	114	85	82	82	83	78	78	79	79	80
Demand dep./GDP	8	5	5	5	5	5	5	5	5	5
Time and Saving dep./GDP	88	67	66	66	66	61	62	62	63	64
Saudi Arabia										
M1/GDP	26	27	27	27	28	26	25	26	29	30
M2/GDP	48	49	47	51	87	81	79	83	59	58
Demand dep./GDP	15	17	18	18	18	17	17	17	20	19
Time and Saving dep./GDP	22	22	20	24	24	24	24	24	29	28
Bahrain										
M1/GDP	15	18	20	19	16	15	15	15	16	17
M2/GDP	55	66	67	65	64	66	65	67	81	79
Demand dep./GDP	9	12	14	13	11	10	10	10	12	13
Time and Saving dep./GDP	39	49	48	46	48	51	50	53	65	61

Sources: Adapted from Arab Monetary Fund, 2002; and authors' estimates.

sector. As such ratios capture the efficiency of financial intermediaries in monitoring, screening and controlling for credit risks these figures suggest that the four countries have become more efficient in the intermediation process.

In sum, all the financial development ratios discussed above suggest that the four financial systems under study have deepened during the 1990s. It is also clear that banks operating in these countries play a major role in mobilizing financial assets and directing investment to supposedly efficient uses. These trends are likely to be common to many Arab banking systems over the last decade or so.

Other factors that may have contributed to promoting financial deepness in the countries under study include the globalization of financial services that one would expect to increase competition and lead to improvements in the quality of financial services' provision. A number of innovations have occurred and new products have been introduced, such as credit and debit cards. Other feature that may explain the improvement in financial

Table 3.18 Financial development indicators for Jordan, Egypt, Saudi Arabia and Bahrain over 1990–9

	1990	1991	1992	1993	1994	1995	1996	1997	1998	1999
Jordan										
Total financial assets/GDP	141	154	135	131	133	134	134	139	148	144
Commercial banks' assets/GDP	153	198	178	172	177	183	188	196	202	218
Commercial banks' assets/T. assets	109	129	132	131	133	136	140	141	136	152
Egypt										
Total financial assets/GDP	126	102	99	99	101	96	98	97	98	100
Commercial banks' assets/GDP	138	110	104	100	100	95	96	96	94	93
Commercial banks' assets/T. assets	110	108	106	102	100	99	98	98	96	93
Saudi Arabia										
Total financial assets/GDP	105	93	86	89	89	83	80	83	9	31
Commercial banks' assets/GDP	59	58	60	72	74	71	68	70	84	80
Commercial banks' assets/T. assets	56	63	70	81	83	86	84	84	924	258
Bahrain										
Total financial assets/GDP	65	70	77	75	70	75	71	72	86	81
Commercial banks' assets/GDP	110	116	115	116	125	119	117	131	141	150
Commercial banks' assets/T. assets	168	165	149	155	180	159	165	182	164	186

Sources: Adapted from Arab Monetary Fund, 2002; and authors' estimates.

sector developments in Saudi Arabia and Bahrain (in particular) is the greater macroeconomic stability experienced by these two countries during the 1990s.

Conclusion

This chapter highlights the main economic features of the Arab world. One can see that many Arabian countries improved their economic stance during the 1990s, although there remain substantial differences across individual economies. Real GDP grew at around 4 per cent annually over 1992–9 compared to 2 per cent during 1982–91. Inflation rates were

Table 3.19 Growth of credit to the private sector in Jordan, Egypt, Saudi Arabia and Bahrain (US$, millions) over the last decade

	Credit to private sector	Total credit	GDP (current prices)	Credit to private/T. credit	Credit to private/T. GDP
Jordan					
1990	2,487	4,219	4,021	59	62
1991	2,673	3,939	4,194	68	64
1992	2,933	4,430	5,139	66	57
1993	3,290	4,957	5,570	66	59
1994	3,951	5,633	6,078	70	65
1995	4,514	6,166	6,508	73	69
1996	4,743	6,298	6,645	75	71
1997	4,986	6,474	6,976	77	71
1998	5,462	7,473	7,306	73	75
1999	5,729	6,496	7,465	88	77
Egypt					
1990	14,701	36,302	35,489	40	41
1991	9,080	30,235	34,228	30	27
1992	10,913	31,617	41,755	35	26
1993	12,823	33,245	46,896	39	27
1994	16,575	37,629	51,661	44	32
1995	22,287	43,835	60,457	51	37
1996	28,080	50,432	67,305	56	42
1997	35,204	59,604	75,617	59	47
1998	44,676	70,522	82,710	63	54
1999	53,029	81,812	88,964	65	60
Saudi Arabia					
1990	17,437	10,254	104,671	170	17
1991	19,653	11,535	118,034	170	17
1992	22,991	28,491	123,204	81	19
1993	27,210	33,511	118,516	81	23
1994	30,227	41,282	120,167	73	25
1995	32,363	43,605	127,811	74	25
1996	33,004	42,724	141,322	77	23
1997	35,701	50,547	146,494	71	24
1998	42,911	60,053	128,377	71	33
1999	43,311	43,000	139,206	101	31
Bahrain					
1990	1,283	−23	4,529		28
1991	1,628	511	4,616	319	35
1992	1,799	1,147	4,751	157	38
1993	2,177	1,316	5,201	165	42
1994	2,434	1,374	5,566	177	44
1995	2,521	1,620	5,849	156	43
1996	2,539	1,499	6,102	169	42
1997	2,857	1,811	6,349	158	45
1998	3,096	2,234	6,184	139	50
1999	3,464	2,848	6,621	122	52

Sources: Adapted from Arab Monetary Fund, 2002.

significantly reduced in many countries. External debt as a percentage of GDP fell, and reserves, especially of the non-oil exporting countries, were significantly enhanced. Domestic and foreign investments within the Arab region have also improved. However, despite improvements in the trade balances of various Arabian countries many non-oil countries are still suffering from substantial trade deficits. In addition, the economic structure of Arab economies also indicates that the services sector is relatively underdeveloped (compared with Western economies at least) and the state accounts for a major share of GDP in most economies. The latter part of the chapter introduced various issues concerning financial sector development and regulation that are particularly relevant in the case of the Arab world where financial systems are primarily bank-based and capital markets are relatively underdeveloped. Nevertheless, the indicators of financial sector development for four Arabic countries (Saudi Arabia, Egypt, Bahrain and Jordan) suggest that these financial systems deepened during the 1990s. It is also clear that banks operating in these countries play a major role in mobilizing financial assets. The following chapter continues on the theme of financial sector development by examining the evolution of banking and financial systems outside the Gulf.

4

Banking and Financial Systems in Non-Gulf Arab Countries

Introduction

This chapter outlines the main characteristics of the financial systems of non-Gulf Arab countries. The aim is to outline factors that have impacted on the performance and structure of financial institutions operating in these countries. The following presents an overview of the financial systems of Egypt, Jordan, the Maghreb countries and other Arab countries. We also examine briefly the financial reforms that have taken place in these countries. Particular attention is paid to reforms that have taken place over the last decade. The chapter examines changes in the financial structure of non-Gulf Arab countries over the last decade and covers issues relating to issues such as the relative importance of the commercial banks, changes in banking sector market concentration and credit distribution to the main economic sectors.

An overview of the financial systems in non-Gulf Arab countries

Financial system of Egypt

Between 1957 and 1973, the Egyptian authorities implemented a comprehensive wave of nationalization of all 27 commercial and specialized banks of the country, closed its stock market and consolidated the banking system into four non-competing state banks; each focusing on separate economic sectors. However, since 1970, high population growth and relatively poor economic performance has led to pressure for domestic investment on a larger scale and therefore steps were taken to permit foreign banks to re-establish in the country (in partnership with Egyptian banks). The Egyptian banking sector expanded markedly in the mid-1970s spurred by the country's outward-looking growth policies and greater policy emphasis on private sector development (Handy *et al.*, 1998). To promote economic reform within the country, the government enacted an Investment Law in 1974, allowing for the establishment of commercial and investment banks, with a minimum 51 per cent domestic ownership. Furthermore, a banking law enacted in 1975 defined what constituted banking businesses. This legislation identified three main types of banks operating in the Egyptian system: commercial banks that accepted deposits and provided finance for a wide variety of transactions; business and investment banks that performed medium- and long-term (lending) business and finance operations (these banks can also accept deposits and finance foreign-trade operations); and specialized banks which offered specific types of economic activities and accepted demand deposits.

All specialized banks are state-owned and are assigned the task of providing long-term finance for priority sectors like real estate and agricultural and industrial development. There are also public sector commercial banks, private and joint-venture banks and foreign banks (operating through branches). Foreign banks were all registered as business and investment banks, as their role was mainly to raise long-term funds. They were restricted from dealing in foreign currency business until 1993 when the banking law was modified to allow existing foreign banks to engage in such operations. Since 1993, foreign banks operating in Egypt have received equal treatment to domestic banks.

Although the banking system has been opened to private sector banks since 1975, the four state-owned commercial banks have continued to dominate the market. They account for around 50 per cent of total banking sector assets. They have a significant market share in retail and corporate banking services through large branch networks and a close relationship with state-owned companies. They are also major participants in the equity capital of most joint-venture banks. Furthermore, during the 1970s and 1980s, the securities markets remained underdeveloped and hampered by the absence of a governing securities law and inadequate regulation. According to Handy *et al.* (1998), financial intermediaries such as mutual funds, finance companies, leasing companies, brokers, moneychangers, and market makers were lacking. In addition, the insurance sector was underdeveloped and largely state-owned.

At the beginning of the economic stabilization programme in 1990/91, Egypt's financial system suffered heavily from long-standing structural weaknesses resulting from the unstable economic environment and over-regulated financial system. The imposed interest rate limits on bank deposits and loans were well below the rate of inflation. Furthermore, preferential interest rates were mandated for loans to public enterprises and to industrial and agricultural enterprises. The Central Bank of Egypt (CBE) also attempted to manage credit expansion to public and private sector companies using maximum loan-to-deposit ratios and bank-specific ceilings for certain types of credits. According to Subramanian (1997), these financial repression practices resulted in heavy losses and substantial non-performing loans for commercial banks in the early 1990s, when provisioning levels exceeded

18 per cent of the total loans booked at the end of 1992. These losses contributed to a sharp deterioration in the capital–asset ratio of the banking system from 3.5 per cent in 1985 to 2.4 per cent in 1990.

In 1991, the Egyptian authorities undertook a series of financial reforms aimed at enhancing the efficiency of the financial system (see Table 4.1). In 1991, the CBE established a capital adequacy ratio equivalent to 8 per cent of risk-weighted assets, in accordance with the Basel guidelines. In 1992, minimum capital requirements for Egyptian banks were LE 100 million for authorized capital and LE 50 million for paid-up capital; branches of foreign banks were required to show a minimum capital base of not less than $15 million.

The new capital requirements of 1991, indicated earlier, produced a sharp recovery in the banks' capitalization to 4.3 per cent. On a risk-adjusted basis, the capital adequacy ratio for the banking system reached 10.6 per cent by the end of 1996. Subsequently, a gradual decline in provisioning appears to have signalled a parallel decline in non-performing loans (or vice versa). The level of non-performing loans fell from around 14.7 per cent of total loans in June 1996 to 13.4 per cent in June 1997 and total provisions were equivalent to about 80 per cent of non-performing loans by the end of June 1997.

To increase reliance on indirect monetary policy instruments, the Central Bank of Egypt introduced, from January 1991, weekly auctions of three-month Treasury bills which helped to maintain the banks' viability (Subramanian, 1997). When the Treasury bill issues were initiated, the bulk of these were held by the commercial banks. Banks' holdings of securities as a share of their total assets increased from 13 per cent at the end of 1991 to 23 per cent by 1993, before easing to 16 per cent at the end of 1995. Moreover, the income from this source was tax exempt. Over time, the supply of debt to the market was increased and longer maturities were introduced.

To strengthen the banking system, new prudential guidelines (as already mentioned) were introduced in 1991 for foreign currency exposures, capital adequacy levels, asset classification and provisioning, bank liquidity and auditing rules. This was followed in 1992 by guidelines covering investment abroad and in 1993 by regulations on credit concentration. Regulations that discriminated against private banks and inhibited a level playing field for all participants were removed. Branches of foreign-owned banks were allowed to operate in local currency and full entry of foreign banks through the establishment of local subsidiaries was authorized. Foreign partners were allowed majority equity-holdings in joint venture banks. Bank fees and charges, creditor and debtor rates, and transactions on the foreign exchange market were liberalized. Administrative credit allocations were phased out and Treasury bill auctions were used to manage liquidity and indirectly provide a reference interest rate to the financial markets.

Table 4.1 Measures undertaken to enhance bank competition and performance in the Egyptian banking market since 1991

Measure	Details
Reserve and liquidity requirements	To reduce the implicit tax on banking activity, the non-interest-bearing reserves held by banks at the Central Bank of Egypt (CBE) were reduced (from 25 per cent) to 15 per cent of total Egyptian pound deposits. Alternatively, banks continued to hold with the CBE 15 per cent of total foreign currency deposits as a reserve earning interest equivalent to LIBOR. Meanwhile, the liquidity ratio was reduced to 20 per cent (down from 30 per cent) and 25 per cent for local- and foreign-currency balances, respectively.
Capital adequacy ratio	The banks' minimum capital requirements were increased in 1991 to 8 per cent along the lines of the Basel Committee on Banking Supervision. Capital was defined to consist of two components: primary capital, which includes paid-up capital, and reserves. Other capital includes provisions for general banking risks.
Foreign-exchange exposure	The banks' foreign-exchange exposures were limited; the ratio of foreign currency liabilities to foreign currency assets became subject to a maximum limit of 105 per cent, and the open position for a single currency, for all currencies combined, became subject to limits of 10 per cent and 20 per cent, respectively, of bank capital.
Investment concentration abroad	Investment abroad by banks is subject to a limit of 40 per cent of the bank capital. In addition, the banks' deposits held with single foreign correspondents should not exceed 10 per cent of total investments abroad (or US$ 3 million, whichever is higher).
Credit concentration	Since 1991, the CBE limit banks' single customer exposure of credit facilities to 30 per cent of bank capital (and the exposure should not exceed 25 per cent of a bank's paid-up capital and reserves). There is also surveillance by the CBE on geographical and sectoral concentrations of bank lending so as to diversify portfolio risk. For equity holdings, bank participation in the share capital of joint-stock companies is limited to 40 per cent of the company's capital.
Loan classification and provisioning	Stricter loan classification and provisioning criteria were issued to ensure that individual banks act prudently. Non-performing loans are classified as substandard, doubtful or bad according to the delay in debt repayment.

Source: Adapted from El-Shazly, 2001, various pages.

In 1993, the monetary authority liberalized rates of interest on demand deposits and subsequently removed ceilings on bank lending to the private sector and bank-specific ceilings on lending to the public sector in the same year. Following the liberalization of interest rates that were initiated in 1991, nominal deposit rates reached 16 per cent in 1991/92, but declined to 10 per cent in 1995/96 and lending rates declined from 19 per cent to 14 per cent, reflecting improved intermediation.

During the period 1993 to 1994, the authorities mandated public banks to divest their shares in the joint-venture banks with a maximum ownership of 20 per cent to reduce market concentration and enhance competition. Furthermore, the government divested public holdings in two joint-venture insurance companies. By 1997, the state banks had limited their holdings to three joint-venture banks and reduced their holdings to below 20 per cent in the majority of other institutions (Handy *et al.*, 1998; El-Shazly, 2001). Steps were also taken to reduce the competitive advantages of the public sector banks by allowing public sector companies to deal with all banks without prior permission from the central bank. By the end of June 2000, the public banks' ownership was above 20 per cent in eight (out of twenty-three) joint venture banks, whose privatization had been planned to be completed by the end of the same year. The authorities also plan to privatize the four public sector commercial banks and the necessary legislation was passed by the parliament in 1998, but none has so far been offered for sale.

On the market transparency front, public disclosure of financial information was generally poor. Before 1998, banks used to publish their financial statements only at the end of the fiscal year. Meanwhile, the income statements of some banks, especially the state-owned banks, were brief, with a couple of lines on revenues and expenditures that did not even show the amount of provisions. The public had better financial information only for banks which were listed on the stock exchange. These banks were mandated by the capital market law (Law 95/1992) to submit quarterly statements regarding their financial position to the Capital Market Authority, which made the information publicly available.

The evolution of the banking system during the past decade has been associated with changing patterns of credit allocation, both in terms of the economic sector and the type of borrower. Prior to financial liberalization in the 1990s, credit was focused mainly on the industrial and services sectors. From 1991/92 onwards credit to the agriculture and trade sectors increased substantially. The share of lending to the private sector has also grown sharply. As of January 1996, the share of credit to the private sector stood at 43 per cent, compared with 29 per cent in the early 1990s.

According to the 1999 report of the National Bank of Egypt, Egypt's banking sector consists of 7 public sector banks (3 specialized and 4 commercial), 31 investment and merchant banks (11 joint venture and 20 foreign bank branches) and 24 commercial banks, as well as 2 offshore registered

Table 4.2 Structure of the Egyptian banking system as at 31 December 1999

		Number	*Branches*
Commercial banks	Public sector	4	918
	Private & joint venture	24	330
Business and investment banks	Private & joint venture	11	105
	Foreign banks (branches)	20	46
Specialized banks	Industrial	1	14
	Real estate	1	26
	Agriculture	1	1,005
Total		62	2,444

Source: El-Shazly, 2001; http://www.mafhoum.com/press/49E2b.htm

banks (Table 4.2). Despite the emergence of new banking institutions, the big four state banks continued to account for over 75 per cent of commercial bank deposits based on their extensive branch network, with a similar share of total lending. The new commercial banks focused on lending to the private sector and multinationals.

Egypt's capital market

While banks are the main source of finance for projects in Egypt, Egyptian investors have begun considering the stock or bond markets to obtain capital. The Cairo and Alexandria stock exchanges, dormant since 1956, started gaining momentum in late 1992. The authorities have made considerable progress in modernizing its capital markets since the passage of Law 95 in 1992 which aimed at finding alternative sources of financing to private and public firms. In addition, the privatization programme, particularly between 1995 and 1997, was a major spur for development of the capital markets and foreign investor interest.

As of May 2000, the market capitalization of the Cairo and Alexandria Stock Exchange was approximately US$ 38 billion with 1,051 companies listed. Trading value for 1999 was $12.4 billion, of which US$ 10.5 billion were in listed securities. This represents a trading volume of about 1.1 billion shares, largely confined to a few heavily traded companies. The capital markets sector, as of March 2000, consisted of 30 mutual funds (23 managed and traded in Egypt and 7 offshore), 24 portfolio investment management companies, 20 underwriters, 9 venture capital firms, 140 brokerage firms and one central depository for clearing and settlement. The recent development of the Egyptian stock market reflects its growing role in providing financing and promoting savings in the domestic economy.

To conclude, the Egyptian financial sector has witnessed many major reforms over the last decade. These include liberalizing interest rates, enhancing bank capital requirements and prudential regulations in accordance with international standards; the introduction of new banking laws giving a wider role for foreign banks that boosted competition and promoted privatization of the public banks. The new reforms have led to a stronger financial position for Egyptian banks.

Financial system of Jordan

The introduction of banking into Jordan dates back to the early 1920s when a British entity, the Ottoman Bank, opened in Amman and acted as a fiscal agent to the government in the absence of a central bank at that time. In 1936, the Arab Bank, which had its head office in Jerusalem, opened a branch in Amman and the Bank moved its head office from Jerusalem to Amman in 1949. The next foreign bank to open a branch in Amman was the British Bank of the Middle East in 1949. By 1949, the number of banks' offices operating in Jordan was five, located in the two largest cities (Amman and Irbid), and in that year steps were taken to create a local national currency (by establishing a Currency Board) that replaced the Palestinian Pound (Mohammed, 1994). The process developed and led to the establishment of the Central Bank in 1964. The next Jordanian bank to start operating, after the Arab Bank, was the National Bank in 1955. In 1960, two additional commercial banks were established, the Cairo Amman Bank and the Bank of Jordan.

Between 1959 and 1968, four specialized credit institutions were established to enhance economic development and to fill the gap in financing the main economic activities like agriculture, industry and housing. The government took the initiative of establishing these institutions to create a channel for collecting funds from a broad range of sources and to help investors benefit from the specialized services provided. In 1970, the Jordanian banking system was underdeveloped and comprised eight commercial banks (four of them were branches of foreign banks). Thirty years later the number of banks has increased threefold; the total number of branches has risen from 41 to more than 300 and are spread all over the country (El-Erian *et al.*, 1996).

The Jordanian banking sector was heavily regulated until the end of the 1980s and entry into the industry was restricted (Karasneh *et al.*, 1997). Jordan also experienced various banking crises, associated with one or more of its major banks in the late 1980s and/or beginning of the 1990s (Petra Bank, Islamic National Bank and Amman Bank). The deficiency of prudential regulation and supervisory capacities was among the reasons for these crises. Pre-reform weaknesses included insufficient minimum capital requirements, and the fact that classification and provisioning criteria of loans were not in agreement with international standards. Bank supervision that did take place focused on compliance with allocative controls on interest rates and foreign exchange rather than on prudential requirements.

To promote competitiveness of the banking system and enhance investment in local economic activities, the Jordanian authorities have undertaken various financial reforms including the restructuring and addition of new products to the Amman financial markets. The banking system that dominates the financial sector has been the major focus of these reforms. During the 1990s, the supervisory framework was strengthened by increasing staff numbers and promoting technical qualifications (El-Erian *et al.*, 1996). Furthermore, the Central Bank of Jordan (CBJ) engaged in various reforms concerning the foreign exchange market from 1988 onwards, as shown in Table 4.3

Interest rate ceilings were applied in Jordan on deposit and loan rates during the 1980s. These ceilings aimed to enhance the stability of the Jordanian dinar and to enhance international foreign reserves. The ceilings were amended several times and the first step toward freeing interest rates was taken in 1988 when those on deposit rates were abolished. The decision to

Table 4.3 Liberalization of foreign exchange in Jordan during the 1990s

Date	The event
1992	Moneychangers were licensed to deal with foreign currency but the exchange rate for moneychangers was to be determined by the Central Bank of Jordan (CBJ).
1996	The CBJ liberalized the foreign exchange system. Under the new measures: • The mandatory reserve requirement for foreign currency deposits held by banks was reduced from 35 per cent to 14 per cent; • Banks must keep 80 per cent of their mandatory reserves at the Central Bank but can use the remaining 20 per cent in the inter-bank market; • Foreign currency holders may engage in asset swap deals with banks on the spot (dinars-for-dollars) and on a forward (dollars-back-for-dinars) basis, with rollover options.
1997	The CBJ issued new measures to further liberalize the foreign exchange system. Under the new measures, a licensed bank may: • Open non-resident accounts in dinars and/or in foreign currencies; • Allow resident account holders to maintain up to one million dollars in foreign currency accounts. • Transfer the value of imports to foreign beneficiaries without CBJ approval; • Allow residents to take Jordanian dinar-denominated banknotes and payment instruments in and out of the Kingdom without restrictions and take out or transfer cash notes in foreign currencies up to the equivalent of JD 35,000 (approximately $US 50,000) to cover payments.
1997	All restrictions pertaining to the inflow and outflow of foreign currency (including gold) were rescinded. Banks may buy or sell an unlimited amount of foreign currency on a forward basis. Banks are permitted to engage in reverse operations involving the selling of foreign currency in exchange for JD on a forward basis for covering the value of imports. Ceilings related to amounts residents are permitted to transfer abroad have been scrapped.

Sources: Adapted from Bureau of Economic and Business Affairs, 1993–1998; International Monetary Fund, 2000; Central Bank of Jordan, 1997.

complete the freeing of interest rates on loans was taken in 1990. After that, lending limits to the private and public sectors were eliminated in 1992 and 1993, respectively.

Jordan has also applied required reserve ratios on commercial banks, initially introduced in 1967 at 7 per cent of banks' liabilities. This ratio was raised in subsequent years as a tool for inflation control and reached 13 per cent by 1979. During the early 1980s, the reserve requirement ratio was reduced in order to encourage bank lending during a recession period. The ratio was further reduced by the Central Bank of Jordan to 6 per cent in 1984. However, because of inflationary pressures in 1988, the ratio was increased to 9 per cent and had further rises reaching 15 per cent by the end of 1993. In 1996, the Central Bank of Jordan changed the reserve requirement scheme by offering banks more flexibility to maintain a daily minimum balance of 80 per cent of their reserve requirements with the central bank during a one-month maintenance period (the remaining 20 per cent could be held on a period-average basis during the maintenance period) (El-Erian and Fennel, 1997). Moreover, to eliminate discrimination against intermediation in the Jordan dinar, reserve requirements on foreign currency deposits were lowered from 35 per cent (remunerated) to 14 per cent (non-remunerated).

In 1991, Treasury bill auctions were introduced in order to bring about a wider role for market forces to influence treasury bills rates and to facilitate the use of indirect techniques of monetary control (Central Bank of Jordan, 1997). These procedures were aimed at encouraging new entrants to mobilize deposits from the public and to reassure depositors that their deposits were safe through the enforcement of a set of prudential guidelines. Furthermore, in 1996 the Central Bank of Jordan abolished the distinction between resident and non-resident accounts. This resulted in identical treatment of resident and non-resident foreign currency deposits (FCDs) with respect to current payments, elimination of the ceiling on residents' FCDs, permission being granted to the banks to manage investments in foreign currencies for both residents and non-residents, and the application of similar regulations governing margin foreign exchange transactions.

Moreover, the Central Bank of Jordan, in November 1996, permitted Swap operations in foreign exchange to enhance the efficiency of the foreign exchange markets by allowing bank clients to sell foreign exchange at the spot rate and repurchase it at a forward rate for any period of time. Further, in June 1996, the central bank liberalized all transactions on foreign exchange. In an effort by the government to promote competition between banks and reduce lending rates, the central bank also required banks to publish their prime lending rates and deregulated commissions, and reserve requirements were reduced from 14 per cent to 12 per cent.

A new banking law aimed at improving the industry's efficiency and enhancing bank regulation and supervision was approved by the Jordanian

Parliament in June 2000. This law is aimed at protecting depositors' interests while encouraging free market forces in the development of the financial market. The Deposit Insurance Corporation was established in September 2000.

Jordanian banks rely heavily on traditional banking activities, namely, the extension of direct credit facilities, as a main source of income. Credit facilities offered by banks include loans, discounted bills and overdraft facilities. Investment banks are not permitted to extend overdraft facilities. The corporate bond market remains under-developed, and continues to be overshadowed by traditional direct lending. Some banks, however, have started adopting modern banking practices such as automated cheque clearing, and the use of magnetic check processors, unified reporting forms and electronic data-transmission networks. The Central Bank of Jordan has adopted policies aimed at stimulating the local capital market, particularly where long-term project finance is required. A number of banks have established mutual funds. In addition to long-term instruments, e-banking, securitization, short-selling, and treasury stocks are being introduced in some banks.

Jordan's banking system now comprises 13 commercial banks (of which five are branches of foreign banks), five investment banks, two Islamic banks, one industrial development bank, six specialized credit institutions and a number of financial institutions that do not accept deposits (including the Social Security Corporations). There are also 18 insurance companies operating in the country (Central Bank of Jordan, 2001). Although the Central Bank distinguishes between 'investment banks' and 'commercial banks', there are no significant differences in their operations. The number of operating branches of these banks rose to 457 in 1999 compared with 451 in 1997. Despite the increase in the number of operating branches, density remained at the same level around ten thousand people per branch. The number of Jordanian banks' branches operating abroad, including representative offices, rose to 115 by the end of 1998, of which 49 operated in Palestinian territories.

Jordan's capital market

The Amman Stock Exchange (ASE) is one of the leading capital markets in the Middle East. The stock exchange in Jordan commenced its operations in 1978 and deals mainly with securities, stocks, government and corporate bonds. The ratio of Jordan's market capitalization to GDP, which stood at about 74 per cent in 1994, exceeds that of most emerging markets and is similar to that of many industrial countries. Market capitalization remained at around $4.7 billion between 1992 and 1994 (El-Erian *et al.*, 1996) but exceeded $ 6 billion by the end of 2000.

The Amman Stock Exchange (ASE) was reorganized as a privately managed institution in 1999. In 2000, the ASE completed the transition to an electronic trading system. Listing requirements are being reviewed and updated, while an automated depository centre will be established as a custodian for all transaction contracts. Currently, there are 34 brokerage firms and 158 listed public-shareholding companies on the exchange. Forty-three per cent of ownership is by non-Jordanian investors (37 per cent by Arabs and six per cent by non-Arabs).

With respect to ownership and participation in the major economic sectors in Jordan, there is no noticeable discrimination against foreign participation. In fact, many Jordanian businesses seek foreign partners, perceived as the key to increased competitiveness and providing entry into international markets.

To conclude, Jordan's financial system has witnessed major developments and reforms especially over the last decade. This includes the liberalization of interest and exchange rates, the introduction of new financial regulations that are consistent with international standards and the modernization of Jordan's capital market. The number of banks and branches in Jordan has increased over the last two decades leading to a more competitive environment. In addition, government policy continues to focus on deregulation aimed at promoting greater efficiency in the overall financial sector.

Comparison of Jordan and Egypt's banking system

This section provides a brief comparison of the structural and financial features of the Jordanian and Egyptian banking systems. Table 4.4 shows that the commercial banks in Jordan and Egypt dominate other financial institutions, and their shares in the financial market have not changed significantly over the last decade. The next important type of financial institution in the four countries are the central banks. On this basis, the commercial banks are clearly the most important constituents of the financial system in these countries. The table also shows that Jordan's banking system is rather concentrated.

Table 4.4 Market share of commercial banks in Jordan and Egypt (average 1992–2000) (%)

Country	Total assets	Total loans	Total customer deposits
Commercial banks' share			
Jordan	75	88	90
Egypt	62	85	90
Share of the top 3 banks			
Jordan	79	82	78
Egypt	52	48	54

Source: Authors' estimates.

To illustrate the growth features of respective countries' financial systems, we evaluate changes in the consolidated balance sheet of the banking systems over the period 1992–2000. Table 4.5 shows that the two banking sectors witnessed considerable growth in the size of their assets, deposits, equity and loans (in terms of nominal values) during the 1990s. However, there were significant increases in the size of problem loans and loan loss reserves in Jordan, although this perhaps could be attributed mainly to the change in classification of the debts according to international standards. The favourable growth in the size of equity in Jordan and Egypt outlines the move to strengthen the financial position of the banking sector in these countries.

Concerning the profitability of banking business, Jordanian banks appear to have experienced a decline over the last decade or so in contrast to the more favourable performance of Egyptian banks. In general, there has been positive progress in the financial structure indicators of the countries under study over the last decade, which reflects greater financial intermediation and a more sound financial position for the financial system. The profitability indicators, at least for Egypt, also indicate improvements that reflect the ability of banks to better utilize their assets and improve their competitive advantage.

Table 4.6 shows the distribution of credit by the banking systems. It can be seen that slightly less than half of the credit facilities granted by Jordanian banks are granted to the trade sector. The shares of the other economic sectors remained relatively stable during the 1990s. In Egypt more than

Table 4.5 Average annual growth (%) of the main banking sector indicators (nominal values) for Jordan and Egypt over 1992–2000

	Jordan	Egypt
Asset quality indicators		
Total assets	18.00	10.00
Loans (net)	14.00	20.00
Problem loans	15613.00	–13.00
Loan loss reserves	90.00	107.00
Capital adequacy indicators		
Total equity	25.00	23.00
Profitability indicators		
Net interest revenue	6.79	65.34
Net income	8.87	14.17
Average return on assets	–2.59	13.92
Average return on equity	–2.53	13.32
Other indicators		
Customer deposits	15.00	18.00
Off-balance-sheet items	–5.32	17.41

Source: Calculated from Bancscope (2003).

Table 4.6   Distribution of credit to economic sectors in Jordan and Egypt

Jordan	Trade (%)	Industry (%)	Construction (%)	Others (%)	Total (JD, mil.)
1994	45	13	21	21	3,250
1995	46	13	20	18	3,710
1996	46	13	20	20	3,920
1997	47	13	19	21	3,980
1998	46	14	18	22	4,290
1999	46	15	17	21	4,470
Average	46	14	19	21	3,940

Egypt	Trade (%)	Industry (%)	Households (%)	Services (%)	Agriculture (%)	Average (LE, mil.)
1989/90–90/91	15	53	7	23	3	2,340
1992/93–94/95	29	28	23	19	1	8,270
1995/96–96/97	34	27	12	24	3	12,510
Average	26	36	14	22	2	7,710

Source: Various annual Central Bank reports from Jordan and Egypt 1994 to 2000.

one-third of banking credit facilities were granted to the industrial sector in the early 1990s although this declined at the expense of the trade sector throughout the decade.

Banking and finance in Maghreb countries

The section reviews the main developments in the banking and financial systems of Maghreb countries since independence in the mid-1950s and early 1960s. Over this era, interest rates were administratively determined, and the supply of credit and money was controlled directly by the state through the old French style *encadrement* system. Having no autonomy, every bank was forced to lend to a (public-owned) specific economic sector compatible with its own pre-defined specialization. In more recent times, Algeria, Morocco and Tunisia have undertaken financial liberalization measures including the abandonment of the aforementioned interventionist practices by relaxing the role of the state in the financial system and transfer of the management of some state-owned banks to the central bank. Interest rates and credit allocation are currently freely set in the market and private and foreign capital is permitted in the local banking markets.

White (2001) asserts that in the broader context of comparison with other countries and regions, Algeria, Morocco and Tunisia exhibit similar, historical, social and political characteristics. A vast majority of the people follow Islam and speak Arabic. Arabs and Berbers, the original population of North Africa, are the main ethnic components of the population in the three countries. These similarities have created a sense of unity and community,[1] widely and remarkably seen during the independence war in Algeria. In addition, historically imposed unification has further linked the three countries particularly under the rule of the Romans and Islamic dynasties. One major event in the post-independence[2] era of Algeria, Morocco and Tunisia is the formation of the Arab Maghreb Union (AMU). For the first time in modern history, the heads of state of Algeria, Libya, Mauritania, Morocco and Tunisia met in June 1988 in Ziralda, Algeria, to discuss potential economic and political cooperation. In February 1989, the same five heads of state met again in Marrakech, Morocco, and signed the 'Traité de Marrakech' announcing the creation of the Arab Maghreb Union (AMU). The AMU aimed at achieving objectives similar to those of the European Union (EU) and North American Free-Trade Agreement (NAFTA), including coordinating economic policy between the state members and strengthening economic and financial linkages across all economic sectors.

According to the 'Traité de Marrakech', the AMU has three main objectives: first, strengthening the fraternal relations between the member states and people and defending their rights; second, progressive adoption of free movement of people, goods and capital between the members; and finally, the implementation of common and coherent policies in economic and political affairs in order to drive the member countries to a fully integrated single market. The AMU intended to follow the example of the European Union (EU) to bring the five countries together with full economic and institutional political integration. One practical measure implemented by the Union was the free movement of people and goods by removing visa requirements, which has resulted in more than three million people having moved between Algeria, Morocco and Tunisia over the period from 1989 to 1994. Since 1994, the integration process has been slow and often static. The present situation (2004) is still a long way from an integrated single Maghrebi market. Political disputes between the countries, in particular Algeria and Morocco, can explain this lack of movement towards further integration. Overall, although a number of agreements have since been signed, Vermeren (2002) contends that security and political instability in Algeria and the dispute over Western Sahara between Algeria and Morocco remain the main obstacles to developing further integration in the Arab Maghreb Union (AMU).

Brief history of the Maghreb financial systems

Algeria

Goumiri (1993) and Naas (2003) analyze the main characteristics of monetary policy and the emergence of the banking sector in Algeria from the post-colonial to the liberalization period. Over the 1962–85, they categorize the evolution of the Algerian banking sector into three major phases: the sovereignty phase (1962–3), the nationalization and socialization phase (1966–80), and the organic restructuring phase (1982–5). These phases were compatible with the dominance of the centrally planned system characterized by substantial public, priority and strategic sectors, administratively designed investment and development plans, and full state intervention in the process of development and industrialization. In the late 1980s, the banking sector was oriented towards market-based regulations.

First, the phase of sovereignty started just after independence in 1962. This phase witnessed the creation of four major financial institutions: the Treasury (August 1962), the Central Bank (December 1962), the Caisse Algérienne de Développement[3] (CAD, May 1963), and the Caisse Nationale d'Épargne et de Prévoyance (CNEP, August 1963). First, the Treasury was in charge of allocating financial resources to investments, particularly those in favour of the agricultural sector. Second, the creation of the Banque Centrale d'Algérie established the Algerian Dinar as the country moved out of the Franc Zone. The central bank was granted traditional functions including money issue, credit control and reserves and state external debt management. In addition to these functions, in 1964, the central bank was in charge of granting loans and advances in favour of the state-managed agricultural sector. Finally, the CAD and CNEP were created to collect savings and finance planned investments, as well as to play the role of a payment instruments provider. Second, the phase of 'Algerianization and socialization' started in 1966, and this consisted of the construction of the core of the Algerian commercial banking system. Naas (2003) indicates that the government needed the creation of its commercial banking fabric, mainly in order to channel more financing into its socialist plans. The government, headed by President Boumédienne, nationalized foreign banks that had operated in the country since the colonial era. BenHalima (1987) looks at the nationalization process that created the major three Algerian commercial banks, which were Banque Nationale d'Algérie (BNA,[4] June 1966), Crédit Populaire d'Algérie (CPA, December 1966), and Banque Extérieure d'Algérie (BEA, October 1967). BNA was principally, and since 1968 exclusively, in charge of lending money to the agricultural sector, whereas CPA and BEA were primarily in charge of lending money to other sectors, including hotels, trade and construction, and to export and import-oriented industries.

The financial policy applied along with the nationalization and socialization process was passive, as reflected by the central planning and administrative regulation in place. The government kept prices constant for prolonged periods and heavily subsidized basic commodities, which resulted in generating repressed inflation, and excess in the consumer goods market. Also, the financial policy encouraged the government to allocate financing and investment centrally using administrative schemes or periodic development plans. The Treasury used the Algerian Bank for Development to allocate investment and finance provided externally through hydrocarbon exports revenues and substantial external borrowings.

In the phase of nationalization and socialization, the Algerian government imposed four major principles on its financial and banking institutions. These principles were adopted to ensure the administratively planned exploitation of the banking sector to channel financial resources towards state-planned investments rather than autonomously shaping investing and financing decisions. These principles related to unique banking domiciliation, bank specialization, the outlawing of self-financing and the illegality of inter-enterprise lending.

First, the principle of unique banking domiciliation, which was introduced in the Budget Law of 1970, reflects the mono-bank principle. According to this principle, enterprises were obliged to concentrate their banking accounts and their banking operations at one bank only. Second, the bank specialization principle, as a result of the mono-banking principle, stated that banks were allowed to open banking accounts[5] to enterprises that were operating in an economic sector that matched their sector specialization. For instance, while BNA, and Banque de l'Agriculture et du Développement Rural (BADR), were specialized in the agricultural sector, and BEA was primarily specialized in lending money to substantial industrial firms such as in hydrocarbons and steel, CPA was in charge of lending to industries in the service and construction sectors.

Thirdly the principle of outlawing self-financing prohibited enterprises from engaging in profit accumulation and self-financing of their investments, unless the planning authorities (Ministry of Planning) approved these activities. Banks did not have autonomy to decide upon their investment and financing decisions. Every investment required the approval of the Ministry of Planning, then the approval of Comité Directeur de la Banque Algérienne de Développement (BAD) to allocate financial resources; the final approval came from the Ministry of Finance. Finally, the illegality of the inter-enterprise lending principle outlawed profit and net cash accumulation and their use for inter-enterprise financial operations. Instead, following the principle of financial resource centralization at the Treasury, enterprises were required to centralize their unexploited credits, loans and profits at their mono-bank, which, in turn, reported to the Treasury and Ministry of Finance to decide upon their future exploitation according to the objectives of the various state plans.

Even though the central bank was heavily involved in the economy, Goumiri (1993) and BenBitour (1998) point out that the Treasury was the most important institution in the financial system of Algeria over the period of central planning. The Treasury managed the government revenues and payments, and allocated all the financial resources of the government to the financial and banking institutions. The Treasury was responsible for lending more than two-thirds of total investments between 1970 and 1980. The banking and financial system had a limited intermediary role and was regarded as a tool to be used to finance planned investments.

The third phase of the Algerian banking system's evolution was the organic restructuring phase that started in 1984. This phase was part of a major organic restructuring operation of government-owned enterprises launched in 1982 in almost all sectors of the economy. The banking sector witnessed the creation of two new banks: Banque de l'Agriculture et du Développement Rural (BADR, 1984) and Banque du Développement Local (BDL, 1985). These two banks were established by taking over a number of structures and branches belonging to the BNA and CPA, respectively. Following the principle of banking specialization, BADR was required to lend money to the agricultural sector and agro-industrial industries, whereas the BDL was forced to lend money to local government-owned enterprises, which were operating under the authority of local government departments. Thus, from the 1960s to the 1980s, the Algerian financial system was compulsorily exploited by the government to bridge government finance and government investment, with the objective of building a large government-owned sector.

Morocco

When Morocco obtained its independence from France in 1956, the Moroccan banking system consisted of structures that were primarily branches of French banks headquartered either in Paris or Algiers. The new government of Morocco focused on establishing a banking system that would serve its economic and political objectives, within the framework of reclaiming sovereignty over the economic and financial sectors. Over the period 1956–9, the Central Bank of Morocco[6] was created along with the new national currency, the *Moroccan Dirham*. The sovereignty-reclaiming programme also required existing banking structures to apply for new licensing agreements from the newly independent government. This measure resulted mainly in a restructuring of the financial sector through reduction in the number of approved banks from sixty-nine in 1954 to twenty-six by 1961.

The phase of bank creation started in 1959, when the government created its first bank, Banque Marocaine du Commerce Extérieur (BMCE). This bank was required to provide foreign trade financing to Moroccan companies. Other development banks were created, including Caisse de Dépôt et de Gestion (CDG), Fonds d'Equipement Communal (FEC), Banque Nationale pour le Développement Economique (BNDE), and Caisse d'epargne Nationale (CEN). The setting up of the Moroccan banking system continued between 1961 and 1967, as new banks were created. This included Crédit Agricole (CA), Crédit Populaire (CP) and Crédit Immobilier et Hôtelier (CIH). Achy (2000) notes that, in the 1960s, the primary role of the banking system was to collect savings, finance government budget, public enterprises and priority and strategic sectors through the mandatory holding of government securities, and bonds issued by development banks on behalf of the government.

The second significant phase of the evolution of the Moroccan banking system was launched with the Royal order number 1-67-66 of 21 April 1967 enacting law relating to the banking industry and credit. The main contributions of this law consisted of a more precise definition of a bank's activity, the demarcation of duties of Central Authorities as well as the establishment of a new regulatory structure. The articles of the order were applied to money deposit banking, and were extended to the Crédit Populaire in 1970. In 1986, the regulations of title III of the enacting law relating to bank and credit control were extended to the Banque Nationale pour le Développement Économique and to the Crédit Immobilier et Hôtelier, which were, in other aspects, allowed to collect deposits. In 1987, La Caisse Nationale du Crédit Agricole was permitted to finance other activities in rural areas. In addition, and in order to promote investment projects initiated by the Moroccans residing abroad, two institutions were created in 1989. These were the Bank Al-Amal, which was charged, in particular, with granting participative loans or subordinated loans, and Dar ad-Damane, which aimed to offer guarantee services on the loans authorised by the Bank Al-Amal.

In 1973, the process of *Morocconization* was launched which included the banking sector. Hamdouche (1997) notes that the nationalization process that had taken place, unlike in Algeria, permitted the Moroccan private sector to invest in banking firms. Zamiti (1998) discusses the credit policy in Morocco over the period 1976–90. The policy included dividing financial institutions into deposit money banks and specialized financial institutions. Deposit money banks were allowed to open branches and collect deposits. However, specialized financial institutions were not permitted to deal with the public and open branches. Specialized banks were required to provide finance to projects of a development character and with governmental clients. As in Algeria, the French-style system of 'l'encadrement du crédit' was adopted with the aim of controlling the supply of funds, and to ensure these were allocated according to government instructions outlined in the periodic plans. The government coerced its commercial banking structure to invest in government bonds, which were either issued by the Treasury or by government-owned specialized development banks on behalf of the government. In the early 1980s, banks were required to retain 30 per cent of their deposits as treasury bonds. In addition, commercial banks were also required to hold 15 per cent of their deposits as bonds issued by specialized banks.[7]

As part of the structural adjustment reform programme, which was designed with the assistance of the IMF in the mid-1980s, the Moroccan government implemented measures with the objective of liberalizing the financial and banking industry. One measure was the adoption of universal banking. Specialized financial institutions became able to collect deposits and savings from the public and open branches across the Kingdom. The financial sector in Morocco underwent a process of profound financial liberalization in the early 1990s, as part of the structural adjustment reform programme. The liberalization measures included the elimination of credit ceilings, the deregulation of interest rates, the gradual removing of mandatory holdings of government securities, and the strengthening of prudential regulation of banks in accordance with international standards. Financial liberalization was reflected in the new banking law of 1993[8] relating to credit institutions' activity and their supervision, which represented a significant change in the Moroccan banking system. The new law allowed for the unification of the legal framework applicable to credit institutions including banks and other specialized financing institutions, and the strengthening of the central bank authority, Bank Al-Maghrib, over supervisory functions. For instance, Bank Al-Maghrib required financial and banking institutions that received funds from the public to undertake a compulsory annual audit and publish their financial statements. The law also imposed measures to protect customers and depositors such as the establishment of a Depositors' Guarantee Fund as well as a support mechanism for credit institutions in difficulty.

Tunisia

As in Morocco prior to independence, banking structures operating in Tunisia were branches and affiliates of banks based in France or Algiers. These banking structures primarily served the financial needs of French settlers and French-friendly community in Tunisia. Shortly after independence in 1956, the new government headed by Président Bourguiba, decided to nationalize all banking structures and to link these to the public sector. In 1958, Banque Centrale de Tunisie was established, and a month later, the currency unit, the Tunisian Dinar, was created. The central bank was primarily attributed the duties of money issue and money supply to the public-owned enterprises. At the same time, the government terminated the foreign exchange system under which the Tunisian Dinar was pegged to the French Franc.

Hall (2001) notes that since independence, the state realized the non-existence of a strong private sector, and has pursued an economic development strategy based on the interventionist role of the government and its control and ownership over 'strategic' sectors including foreign exchange and the financial sector. However, the nationalization process was not accomplished until 1966. By this year, the process of *'Tunisification'* targeted seven banks out of the thirteen operating by then. The remaining six remained under French jurisdiction until 1966,[9] when the government headed by Ben Salah nationalized all these banks.

In the 1960s and 1970s, the Tunisian government restructured the financial and banking sector by establishing new banking and financial government-owned firms. The primary role of the newly established nation-alized banking sector was to collect savings and channel these to the treasury and government-owned enterprises. That is, the government exploited the structure of the banking industry within the framework of state intervention and regulation. Financial regulation in Tunisia consisted of the administrative allocation of credit, and the central determination of interest rates, in addition to the prohibition of foreign banks from operating in local markets. The financial regulation also included the centralization of bank credit decision-making.[10] Banks were compelled to hold up to one-fifth of their assets in government bonds and to allocate a fixed percentage of their deposits for lending at preferential interest rates to priority sectors.

Financial liberalization in Algeria, Morocco and Tunisia

Algeria, Morocco and Tunisia all experienced substantial financial reforms during the 1980s and 1990s that had the impact of creating new monetary and financial markets, brought about the adoption of indirect monetary instruments, deregulated interest rates and gave autonomy to banks in their credit allocation decisions. The reform process also dismantled various entry barriers by allowing private and foreign capital to operate in the respective banking sectors. The primary objective of financial reforms was to move towards the use of indirect instruments of monetary control, the adoption of internationally accepted methods of supervision and prudential regulation, and the modernization of the legal and institutional structures of the respective banking systems. Another objective of the financial liberalization programmes was to break down financial repression practices, as reflected by both the administratively determined interest rates and the quantitative controls on credit allocation based on the *Encadrement du Crédit* system. In addition, the financial liberalization programme envisioned reducing the dependence of the economy on local banking capital and aimed to encourage foreign capital through the chartering and licensing of new foreign-owned banks.

Enders *et al.* (1997) review the steps of interest rates liberalization in Algeria, Morocco and Tunisia, and notes that the process of deregulation in the three countries was gradual. Overall, as Table 4.7 indicates, interest rates in Algeria, Morocco and Tunisia maintained a decreasing trend from the mid-1990s onwards.

The passing of the Algerian Money and Credit Law (April 1990) terminated the determination of interest rates by the Treasury. According to this law, the central bank was responsible for the monetary policy of the country and, therefore, interest rates determination. In 1990, the measures relating to discriminatory and preferential interest rates for certain sectors, considered as priority, were abolished. Interest rates for the private and public sector became unified and commercial paper from both sectors became subject

Table 4.7 Selected interest rates in Algeria, Morocco and Tunisia from 1990 to 2001 (per cent)

Rates	Deposits rates			Lending rates**			Money market rates*		
Countries	Algeria	Morocco	Tunisia	Algeria	Morocco	Tunisia	Algeria***	Morocco	Tunisia
1990	7.67–14.67	10.65–11.19	9.6	13.75–20.00	10.75–14.30	14.81		8.31	11.81
1991	15.67	11.84	9.6	15.00–20.00	10.9–15.2	14.81		10.00	11.81
1992	9.75–12.16	10.10–12.38	9.6	15.00–20.00	11.04–15.59	14.81		8.80	11.31
1993	12.16	11.25–12.38	7.4	15.00–20.00	10.0–14.0	11.81		7.04	8.81
1994	15.38–17.50	7.17–11.50	6.9	17.63–22.63	10.0–13.00	11.81	19.5–20.0	–	8.81
1995	16.00–18.00	7.00	6.9	22.83	10.0–12.50	11.81	19.4–23.0	–	8.81
1996	16.50–18.00	7.00	6.1	14.00–18.50	8.00–15.00	10.81	17.2–19.0	6.60	7.81
1997	8.50–17.00	7.00	5.0	8.63–10.44	8.00–13.75	9.87	11.8–14.55	–	6.87
1998	8.50–12.00	6.25–5.50	5.0	8.50–12.50	7.00–13.00	9.87	10.0–13.0	6.5	6.87
1999	8.50–10.00	3.30–5.05	3.9	8.50–11.3	7.00–13.00	8.87	10.4–12.0	5.21	5.87
2000	7.00–8.50	3.30–5.05	3.9	8.5–11.2	7.50–13.00	8.87	6.8–8.3	5.53	5.87
2001	6.57		4.0	7.5			3.4		

*End of Period rates.
**Lending rates in Tunisia were set within a spread of 3 per cent iof the money market rate.
***Naas, 2003, p. 237.
Source: Various, including IMF country reports.

to the same eligibility criteria of refinancing. Also, in 1990, controls on interest rates on deposits were discontinued and became fully deregulated. In 1994, the central bank replaced ceilings on lending rates by limits on banking spreads. However, in 1995, limits on banking spreads were annulled. Eltony (2000) reports that in Algeria, real deposit rates were negative before 1999, and reached the highest level in 1992, at 15 per cent. In 1999 and 2000, these rates became positive, at 5.5 per cent and 4 per cent respectively. Interest rates increased over 1990–5, but declined thereafter.

In Morocco the first attempt to deregulate interest rates was in the mid-1980s, when interest rate subsidies for priority sectors were eliminated. Between 1989 and 1991, interest rates on lending and for time deposits were further liberalized, and ceilings on lending rates for all types of credits, except for export and small and medium-sized companies, were replaced by limits on banking spreads. In 1996, the process of interest rate liberalization was continued by terminating the use of limits on banking spreads, and all the remaining aspects of control on lending and deposits rates. For instance, lending interest rates became freely negotiable between banks and their clients.[11] Also, credits of less than one year must have fixed interest, whereas credit of more than one year can have either fixed or variable interest rates indexed to the money market rate. In Morocco before implementing the financial liberalization in the mid-1980s, interest rates were administratively set and were negative in real terms, due to high inflation. For instance, real interest rates were –7 per cent in 1980, but increased to 4.9 per cent by 1987. In the 1990s, although inflation picked up, nominal interest rates were sufficiently high, between 14 per cent and 16 per cent, and real interest rates maintained their positive sign, but a steady decline of nominal interest rate has been accruing since 1995.

In Tunisia, the creation of the money market in 1987 was the first step to the gradual process of interest rate liberalization. Interest rates on special savings accounts became pegged to the money market rate (MMR) in the proceeding month. The liberalization process was furthered by deregulating interest rates on term deposits of at least three months. In the late 1980s and early 1990s, lending rates, except for those to priority sectors, were allowed to be freely moving with a spread of 3 per cent above the money market rate. Over 1994–6, the gradual liberalization of interest rates was completed by lifting all controls on lending rates for both priority and non-priority sectors. However, Boughrara (2001) mentions that, even though interest rates have been liberalized in Tunisia, a number of deposit rates remained regulated. For instance, interest rates on sight deposits (up to three months) must not exceed a ceiling of 2 per cent, interest rates on special savings deposits[12] are set at 2 per cent below the money market rate, and savings accounts dedicated to housing finance had a fixed rate of 5.25 per cent.

As discussed earlier, in the pre-liberalization period, Algeria, Morocco and Tunisia controlled the money supply and influenced banking sector liquidity and credit allocation by the adoption of the French-style *'l'encadrement du Crédit'*. During the mid-1990s, the three countries deregulated the credit allocation process and gave greater autonomy to government-owned banks. Besson (1993) asserts that the *'l'encadrement du Crédit'* was effectively a form of credit ceilings and directed credits, which consisted of fixing, for every bank, a monthly progression of norms and ceilings on credits. Any supply that exceeded the set norms generated certain sanctions. For the case of Algeria, Morocco and Tunisia, *'l'encadrement du Crédit'* involved the requirement of banks to use the money channelled from the Treasury to provide state-owned banks and priority sectors with credits. The process of financial sector liberalization required the abandonment of the *'l'encadrement du Crédit'* principle.

In Algeria, the gradual reduction in directed credits was initiated in 1987, when the Treasury decided to withdraw from directed investment in state-owned enterprises. The emergence of the Law of Money and Credit in 1990 resulted in the disassociation of the Treasury from monetary policy responsibilities, which were transferred to the central bank. Also, this law terminated the adoption of the unique banking domiciliation and specialization principles, under which banking transactions of a government-owned enterprise were forced to be lodged with specific banks, which were uniquely involved in financing projects in the sector in which the enterprise operated. Consequently, all economic sectors were opened to all banks, including specialized banks. In addition, Iradian *et al.* (2000) indicate that in 1994–5, the central bank of Algeria introduced remunerated reserve requirements on commercial banks. Iradian *et al.* (2000) also indicate that Algerian banks have been granted greater autonomy, particularly concerning the forced allocation of credit to high-risk state-owned firms and the holding of treasury bills. The mandatory holding of treasury bills was phased out in 1994. However, commercial banks still hold significant amounts of treasury paper from past re-capitalization exercises. Abed and Fischer (2003) report that by the period 2000–2 the Treasury identified the remaining non-performing loans of banks, and re-capitalized three government-owned banks through infusions of cash and the issuance of treasury securities.

Enders *et al.* (1997) review the abandonment of credit rationing in Morocco. During 1991–3, the obligatory holdings of bonds and paper issued by specialized governmental banks[13] were gradually reduced from a peak of 15 per cent. In 1994, while the requirement of holding bonds issued by BNDE and CIA was discontinued, the requirement to hold bonds issued by other government bodies remained in place, and was equivalent to 2 per cent of deposits. In addition, the requirement for compulsory holdings by commercial banks of government paper was reduced from 35 per cent of short-term deposits in 1986 to 10 per cent of short-term liabilities by 1994.

Further, all the preferential access to refinancing and credit provided to smaller and export-related companies was terminated by 1996.

Tunisian deregulation of credits started in 1988, when the central bank terminated the procedure by which banks had to obtain central bank authorization for credits and loans decisions. In 1990, the central bank discontinued the requirement on banks to supply loans and credit to certain government-owned enterprises and economic sectors at preferential interest rates. In 1994, the deregulation of credits continued as banks were no longer obliged to hold treasury bills, and in 1996, obligatory sectoral lending ratios were abandoned.

In addition to interest rate and credit allocation deregulation, another feature of the financial liberalization programme related to the dismantling of entry barriers and the disengagement of the state from the financial sector, in terms of ownership and management. These measures have been implemented through the process of privatization and the lifting of constraints on private and foreign capital to invest in local markets, aimed at increasing competition in the financial sector and improving the performance of banks. In all three countries, privatization has been preceded by permitting national and foreign investors to set up financial and banking firms, and also, in the case of Morocco and Tunisia, through transferring government-owned banks to the private sector using the capital market or by negotiating sales to private institutions.

In Algeria, the new law of Money and Credit of 1990 permitted setting up private and foreign banks. Since 1994, the privatization of the financial sector has been preceded by allowing private and foreign banks to operate in the local market. No major transfer of management and ownership concerning public banks has been made to date.[14] As a result of the indicated Law, in 2003, there are more than fifteen non-government commercial banks (three privately-owned and eight foreign-owned) and six government-owned commercial banks (Naas, 2003). The recently established private and foreign banks tend to be small and have limited networks.[15] The entry of new foreign and private banks has intensified since 1997, as the Bank of Algeria authorized more than twenty new banks with different forms of ownership: fully foreign, fully national private, and national private-foreign. One major obstacle that has significantly hindered the rapid privatization of large government-owned banking firms is their under-capitalization, which was caused by the large amounts of non-performing loans granted to government-owned enterprises. The government implemented re-capitalization processes in the 1990s either in the form of cash or bond-loan swaps. The first major re-capitalization operation occurred between 1992 and 1993 when the Treasury substituted government bonds for non-performing loans. As a first step, this operation was substantial as the government bonds accounted for approximately a quarter of GDP (these bonds were paid off by 1996). The second major re-capitalization operation in the form of bonds-loans swaps occurred in 1997, in favour of three main public banks (BADR, BNA, and CNEP[16]). The cost of this operation was about 8.5 per cent of GDP.

During 1989, the Moroccan government cancelled the procedures of the *Morocconization decree* of 1973, which imposed a 49 per cent limit on foreign ownership in strategic sectors, including the financial sector. The new Banking Law of 1993 allowed private and foreign capital to invest and create banking and financial institutions. Morocco has used its main stock exchange – the Bourse de Casablanca – to process the privatization of its banking sector. Currently, there are seven commercial banks listed in the market representing a third of total market capitalization. The privatization of banks started over 1995–7, and as of the end of 2000, there were only three major government-owned banks.[17] A new law approved in 2000 allowed Morocco's largest bank (Banque Centrale Populaire) to float about a fifth of its shares on the Bourse de Casablanca.

In Tunisia, financial liberalization involved the abolition of entry constraints on non-government-owned banks to enter the market. This has been done by opening banks' capital to foreign and private participation, by permitting foreign and private capital to open branches and operate onshore, and by allowing offshore banks to collect deposits in Tunisia Dinar from residents, but with some restrictions. The programme to restructure the banking system and enhance the presence of foreign capital continued in 2002 with the privatization of the International Banking Union (UIB) and transformation of joint-venture development banks into full service banks. The transaction for privatizing the UIB was finalized in November 2002 with the sale of 3,640,000 public shares, representing 52 per cent of capital to the French bank 'la Société Générale' for TD 102.7 million. This transaction, in the context of the privatization programme, is a major event in that it was the first sale of a controlling share in a Tunisian bank to foreign interests.

Structural and financial features of Maghreb banking systems

Banking sector structure

In the three countries under study, commercial banks represent the core of the financial system. Table 4.8 shows their main characteristics.

Table 4.8 shows that, in 2001, the banking sector of Morocco is the largest. Commercial banks' assets represent more than 95 per cent, 93 per cent, and 65 per cent of Algeria, Morocco and Tunisia's total banking assets, respectively. The size of the banking sectors in the three countries has significantly increased due to entry of new banks into the system, the growth of activities of banks, and the conversion of non-commercial banks into commercial banks.[18] According to the respective banking laws, the main activities of commercial banks consist of collecting deposits of any term and form, from

Table 4.8 Comparative size characteristics in commercial banking in Algeria, Morocco and Tunisia

	Assets size of commercial banking sector (in billions of dollars)			Size of commercial banking sector to GDP (%)		
	Algeria	Morocco	Tunisia	Algeria	Morocco	Tunisia
2001	28.072	30.372	13.939	51.34	90.69	69.55
2000	25.947	30.683	13.480	47.89	93.25	69.26
1999	27.772	29.085	12.156	57.57	83.10	58.44
1998	26.720	29.608	13.053	55.85	83.01	65.82
1997	25.490	25.843	11.098	53.25	77.34	58.73
1996	24.831	20.103	11.010	53.00	54.87	56.20
1995	23.376	19.451	10.853	56.66	58.97	60.20
1994	24.510	17.236	9.967	58.40	56.79	63.76
1993	35.641	14.046	8.786	71.62	52.41	60.14
1992	33.118	13.691	9.062	69.18	48.12	58.48
1991	33.703	14.026	9.151	73.72	50.39	70.34
1990	52.711	11.530	8.860	84.92	44.64	63.19

	Size of financial sector (in billions of dollars)			Size of financial sector to GDP (%)		
	Algeria	Morocco	Tunisia	Algeria	Morocco	Tunisia
2001	32.431	37.533	14.118	59.31	112.07	70.44
2000	27.326	35.853	13.661	50.44	108.97	70.19
1999	25.440	34.923	12.431	52.73	99.78	59.77
1998	26.907	35.531	13.316	56.24	99.62	67.15
1997	25.169	31.296	11.092	52.58	93.66	58.70
1996	21.204	24.181	10.913	45.26	66.00	55.71
1995	19.042	23.643	11.140	46.15	71.67	61.79
1994	19.462	20.699	10.048	46.37	68.20	64.28
1993	31.824	17.387	8.702	63.95	64.88	59.57
1992	29.073	16.599	9.099	60.73	58.34	58.71
1991	23.842	16.169	9.085	52.15	58.09	69.83

Source: Adapted from the Arab Monetary Fund, 2002.

different economic agents, providing various forms of loans and credit of any maturity and ensuring the normal work of payment and exchange.

Only two 'Islamic' banking firms are operating according to the rules of 'Islamic Shariah', one in Algeria, and one in Tunisia. There is none in Morocco. The Islamic investment bank 'Beit Ettamouil Saoudi Tounsi' was created in the early 1980s, while the Algerian commercial bank Al-Baraka Bank was established in 1991. Both of these banks hold less than one per cent of total bank deposits and assets in the respective countries.

Overall, the number of banks and banking branches has considerably increased in the three countries over the period 1990–2002. This is primarily due to the expansion of the existing banks, and the entry of new banks. Table 4.9 exhibits the main banking characteristics of Algeria, Morocco and Tunisia according to bank number, network and penetration.

Table 4.9 shows that the number of banks and bank branches has developed significantly in the last few years. Overall, even though the number of banks and branches has increased, the Algerian and Moroccan banking systems still have a relatively low penetration rate compared to Tunisia. In Algeria, the number of bank branches has doubled over the period 1995–2002, from less than 650 to more than 1,120 branches by 2000–2. The table also shows that the density of banking branches is far lower in Algeria, compared to Morocco and Tunisia, where banking density in 2002 was nearly 26,000 inhabitants per branch .

In Morocco, the number of branches rose from less than a thousand in 1990 to about 1,800 in 2000–2. Similarly, the average value of assets per branch increased from DH 174 mn in 1990 to about DH 230 mn in 2000–2. Banking density in Morocco has fallen over 1990–2002, with less than 20 thousand inhabitants per branch. Achy (2000) notes that the banking system in Morocco is rather limited. Only one-fifth of the Moroccan population has access to banking services, and less than two-fifths of the labour force has a bank account. The branch concentration is dominated by six banks, three of them local and three of them subsidiaries of the major French banks. Tunisian commercial banks' networks have significantly increased in recent

Table 4.9 Comparative commercial banking characteristics in Algeria, Morocco and Tunisia

	Number of banks			Number of branches			Penetration measures as branches number to population		
	Algeria	*Morocco*	*Tunisia*	*Algeria*	*Morocco*	*Tunisia*	*Algeria*	*Morocco*	*Tunisia*
2002	26	18	14	1197	1884	868	25,898	15,484	11,150
2001	26	19	14	1129	1810	868	29,150	16,143	11,145
2000	21	21	14	1077	1707	857	27,316	16,801	11,155
1999	17	21	14	1064	1618	828	28,000	17,460	11,401
1998	12	21	14	1061	1523	817	27,787	18,240	11,420
1997	8	20	13	1043	1450	792	27,289	18,834	11,641
1996	7	16	13	1008	1414	786	27,877	18,989	11,565
1995	7	15	13	963	1386	770	28,858	19,040	11,636
1994	6	14	13	954		753	28,595	–	11,660
1993	6	14	13			738	–	–	11,653
1992	5	14	12			701	–	–	12,026
1991	5	14	12			674	–	–	12,255
1990	5	14	12			626	–	27,000	12,939

Source: Adapted from Naas, 2003, p. 280.

Table 4.10   Banks in Algeria

Bank name	Symbol	Specialization	Year of establishment	Ownership
Al-Ryan Banque-Algérie		Commercial	2000	Foreign
Arab Bank		Commercial	2000	Foreign
Arab Banking Corporation-Algérie[1]	ABC-A	Commercial	2000	Foreign
Banque Algériènne de Développement Rural	BADR	Commercial	1982	Public
Banque de Développement Local	BDL	Commercial	1985	Public
Banque El-Baraka-Algérie	El-Baraka	Commercial	1991[2]	Foreign-public
Banque Éxtérieur d'Algérie	BEA	Commercial	1967	Public
Banque Générale Meditérraniénne	BGM	Commercial		Private
Banque Nationale d'Algérie	BNA	Commercial	1966	Public
BNP/Paribas		Commercial		Foreign
Caisse Nationale d'Épargne et de Prévoyance[3]	CNEP	Commercial	1964	Public
CitiBank-Algérie		Commercial	1998	Foreign
Compagnie Algériénne de Banques	CAB	Commercial	1999	Private
Crédit Populaire d'Algérie	CPA	Commercial	1967	Public
Natexis Banque[4]	Natexis	Commercial	2000	Foreign
Société Générale d'Algérie		Commercial	2000	Foreign
Algerian International Bank		Merchant	2000	Private
So-Finance		Merchant		Private
Union Bank		Merchant	1995	Private
El-Mouna Bank		Offshore	1998	Foreign
Banque Algériénne de Développement	BAD	Specialized	1963	Public
FINLEP		Investment		Private
Société de Refinancement		Specialized	1998	Private

Notes:
1. 70% of this bank is owned by the parent banks based in Bahrain.
2. This bank is equally owned by the Saudi-based bank Al-Baraka and the Algerian Bank BADR.
3. The country's biggest saving bank transformed into a commercial bank in 1997.
4. 80% of is owned by the parent banks, and the remaining by small Algerian investors.

Table 4.11 Banks in Morocco

Bank name	Symbol	Specialization	Year est.	Ownership
Banque Commerciale du Maroc[1]	BCM	Commercial	1911	Listed
Banque Marocaine du Commerce Extérieur[2]	BMCE	Commercial	Sep 1959	Listed
Banque Marocaine pour l'Afrique et l'Orient	BMAO	Commercial		
Banque Marocaine du Commerce et l'Industrie[3]	BMCI	Commercial	1964	Listed
Banque Nationale de Crédit Agricole	BNCA	Commercial		
Crédit du Maroc	CM	Commercial	1963	Private (Crédit Lyonnais 51%)
Crédit Immobilier et l'Hôtelier[4]	CIH	Commercial	1920	Public
Banque Centrale Populaire	BCP	Commercial	Feb 1961	51% public, 49% private
Société Générale Marocaine de Banques[5]	SGMB	Commercial		
Société Marocaine de Dépôt et Crédit	SMDC	Commercial		
WafaBank[6]	Wafabank	Commercial	1985	Listed
ABN-Amro Bank-Maroc		Foreign		
Arab Bank- Maroc				
Citibank- Maroc				
Caisse Marocaine des Marchés	CMM			
Caisse de Dépôt et de Gestion	CDG			
Bank Al-Amal				Public
Banque Marocaine				
Banque Nationale pour le Développement Économique	BNDE	Specialized		Public

Notes:
1. In 1992, Banque Commerciale du Maroc acquired Société de Banque et de Crédit.
2. This bank was the first to be privatized.
3. In 2001 the BNP Paribas's 51.5% subsidiary BMCI acquired the ABN Amro's local arm for US$ 30 mn.
4. Previously a real-estate/mortgage bank.
5. SGMB is the only major non-Casablanca bourse listed bank, 50%-owned by Société Générale France.
6. Established in 1964, but renamed to Compagnie Marocaine de Credit et de Banque in 1985, then to Wafabank in 19 April 1997, after absorbing Union Bancaire Hispano-Marroqi. Wafabank increased its share of total bank deposits from 8.8% in 1994 to 12% to 2000.

Table 4.12   Banks in Tunisia

Bank name	Symbol	Specialization	Year of establishment	Ownership
Amen Bank[1]	AM	Commercial	1971-Listed	
Arab Banking Corporation-Tunisia	ABC-T	Commercial		
Arab Tunisian Bank	ATB	Commercial	1982-Listed	Private 64% Arab bank
Banque de l'Habitat	BH	Commercial	1989-Listed	32% gov.
Banque de Tunisie	BT	Commercial	1984-Listed	Private
Banque du Sud	BS	Commercial	1968-Listed	State 2.6% privatized in 1997
Banque Franco-Tunisienne	BFT	Commercial		
Banque Internationale Arabe de Tunisie	BIAT	Commercial	1976-Listed	Private local (73%)
Banque Nationale Agricole	BNA	Commercial	1959-Listed	Gov. (18%)
Banque Tunisienne de Solidarité	BTS	Commercial		
CitiBank	Citibank	Commercial		
Société Tunisiénne de Banques[2]	STB	Commercial	1957	Gov. 21%
Union Bancaire pour le Commerce et l'Industrie	UBCI	Commercial	1961-Listed	Private
Union Internationale de Banque[3]	UIB	Commercial	1963-Listed	
Union Tunisienne de Banques	UTB	Commercial		
Banque Arabe Tuniso-Libyenne de Developpment et du Commerce Éxtérieur	BATLDCE	Merchant, development and commercial	August 1983	50% Gov. 50% Libyan Arab Foreign Bank, Tripoli (50%)
Banque de Coopération du Maghreb Arab	BCMA	Development		
Societé Tuniso-Saoudienne d'Investissement et de Developpement	STUSID	Investment	1981	
Banque de Tunisie et des Émirates d'Investissment	BTEI	Development		
Banque Tuniso-Kuweitienne de Developpement	BTKD	Development		
Banque Tuniso-Qataui d'Investissment	BTQI	Merchant		
Amen Lease	AL	Leasing		
Arab International Leasing	AIL	Leasing		
Arab Tunisian Lease	ATL	Leasing	1996	

Table 4.12   (Continued)

Bank name	Symbol	Specialization	Year of establishment	Ownership
Comapagnie Internationale de Leasing	CIL	Leasing		
General Leasing	GL	Leasing		
Tunisie Leasing	TL	Leasing		
Union Tunisiénne de Leasing	UTL	Leasing		
Banque d'Affaire de Tunisie	BAT	Merchant		
International Maghreb Merchant Bank	IMMB	Merchant		
Alubaf Investment Bank	Alubaf	Commercial		
Beit Ettamouil Saoudi Tounsi	BTST	Islamic	1983	
CitiBank-Offshore		Offshore		
North Africa International Bank	NAIB	Commercial	1984	
Tunis International Bank	TIB	Merchant	1982	

Notes:
1. The first bank created fully by domestic private capital.
2. In 2000, this bank absorbed the Banque Nationale de Développement Touristique (1959) and Banque de Developpement Économique de Tunisie (1959).
3. Acquired by France's Société Générale who purchased a 52% stake.

years, from less than 600 in 1990 to more than 8,000 by 2000–2. This expansion has increased the availability of banking services to the population as the ratio of inhabitants per branch has fallen from more than 14 thousand in 1990 to less than 12 thousand by 2000–2.

In Algeria, by 2000–2, in terms of branch concentration, more than 60 per cent of total branches are owned by four banks. In 2000, BADR, CNEP, and BDL and BNA had 305, 182 and 182 branches, respectively. BADR, CNEP, BDL, BNA and CPA lead in terms of country average, as they own an estimated three-quarters of the banking sector assets. The three-firm concentration ratio (BADR, CNEP, BDL) is around half of total banking sector assets. The Moroccan banking system is characterized by the predominance of the three leading banking groups (BCM, BMCE, Banque Populaire), which have approximately two-thirds share of total banking sector assets. Most of their activity is located in urban area: the six largest cities account for approximately half of the banking network. The top four banks control about three-quarters of the country's deposits and two-thirds of all loans. In addition, the three largest banks in terms of stock market capitalization are BCM,[19] BMCE, and Wafabank.[20] These banks account for about three-quarters of total banking market capitalization and a fifth of total market capitalization. In Tunisia, the three-firm and five-firm asset concentration ratios were about 55 per cent and 75 per cent by 2000–2. The first five banks own more than half of the country's bank branches. The eleven commercial banks quoted on the Tunis stock exchange represent about a quarter of total market capitalization. The Société Tunisiénne de Banques (STB) is the largest bank in terms of market capitalization and accounts for about a quarter of total banking market capitalization and 6 per cent of total stock market capitalization. The three largest Tunisian banks in terms of market capitalization represent about 60 per cent and 15 per cent of total banking capitalization and total stock market capitalization, respectively.[21]

Bank ownership features

In the Maghreb countries, like other Arab economies, three main agents own banking institutions. These are the government, domestic private capital and foreign capital. Lee (2002) discusses bank ownership in Arab countries, and finds that domestically owned capital (private and public) accounts for about 84 per cent of total bank equity capital, whereas foreign investors own the rest. The private sector is the main owner with approximately three-fifths of total equity capital, then the government with about a quarter of equity capital. Lee (2002) elaborates that in countries such as Iran (100 per cent), Syria (100 per cent), Libya (100 per cent) and Algeria (95 per cent), state ownership of the banking sector is dominant. In countries such as Lebanon (25 per cent) and Morocco (23 per cent), foreign capital appears to be more significant and is above the average of foreign equity capital of Arab countries (16 per cent). Saudi Arabia has the lowest level of foreign capital ownership in the banking sector at about 1.1 per cent, then Algeria at 2 per cent. Similarly, Henry and Boone (2001) find a significant relationship between high bank concentration and high government ownership, particularly in the case of Algeria, as well as other countries such as Libya and Syria. The aforementioned authors find that Tunisia and Morocco have relatively lower government ownership-concentration ratios than in Algeria.

As of the end of 2002, the Algerian banking sector comprised six major state-owned banks,[22] a number of small private commercial and investment banks, a few foreign branches,[23] and other types of financial institutions such as leasing companies and public banks. The government has not yet opened the capital of public banks for privatization. Even though the presence of private and foreign banks is increasing, it is still considered insignificant compared to Morocco and Tunisia. Private and foreign-owned banks own approximately 5 per cent of total assets, deposits and capital of total banking sector. As of late 2001, in Algeria, the French bank, Société Générale, started negotiations to buy the third-largest public sector bank, Crédit Populaire d'Algérie – described as the least bad state-owned bank – but nothing had been achieved by early 2004. In the meanwhile, Société Générale is in the process of upgrading its existing small branch network to four in the country's four major cities. BNP Paribas has upgraded to a full branch while Crédit Agricole Indosuez has a representative office. The HSBC has a representative office through its British Arab Commercial Bank subsidiary, and Citibank has a full branch in Algiers.

The presence of government ownership in the Moroccan banking sector has fallen over the 1990–2002 period, to a third of total banking assets, and a quarter of total banking equity capital. The government still has majority shares in four banks, which used to be specialized banks[24] The presence of foreign and private capital in the Moroccan banking system has increased and reached about a quarter of total banking assets and equity capital by the late 1990s. Unlike in Algeria, foreign banks benefited from the Moroccan bank privatization programmes launched since the early 1990s. Chaput *et al.* (2000) note that in Morocco there is an oligopoly run by a number of Moroccan capitalists (families) in collaboration with foreign partners, who hold about a quarter of banks' capital. A number of international banks, such as Société Générale, bought and gradually increased their stakes in the capital of a number of major Moroccan banks. French banks are the main shareholders and management position holders in BMCE, and CM and SGMB.[25] Société Générale has its own-branded subsidiary in Morocco with about 150 branches. BNP Paribas and Crédit Lyonnais also operate subsidiaries under different brands in alliance with powerful local families: Banque Marocaine du Commerce et de l'Industrie (BMCI) in the case of BNP-Paribas and Crédit du Maroc in the case of Crédit Lyonnais. The German-based bank Commerzbank has also stakes in Banque Marocaine du Commerce Extérieur, while the Spanish bank (Santander Central Hispanohas) has a stake in Banque Commerciale du Maroc.[26] Banco Bilbao Vizcaya Argentaria also has a minority position in Wafabank, alongside Crédit Agricole Indosuez. The American bank Citibank also has a branch in Morocco.[27] Thus, it can be noted that French banks are in a position of building up controlling interests in Moroccan banks, similar to their non-financial French companies counterparts in other sectors of the Moroccan economy. Other international banks hold only minority positions. Besides, it has been reported[28] that Banque Commerciale du Maroc (BCM) and Wafabank have agreed to merge into one entity effectively from the first quarter of 2004. This deal is a takeover bid for 100 per cent of Wafabank's capital, following the BCM purchasing 36.4 per cent of capital share in Wafabank for about two billion Moroccan Dirhams, US$ 218 million in late November 2003. This merger will posit the new entity VCM-Wafabank as the largest bank in Morocco in terms of assets, deposits and branches.

In Tunisia, Chabrier and Ingves (2002) note that although the share of government ownership in the banking sector has fallen over 1990–2002, it still has considerable ownership. The Tunisian government still has the majority stakes in three of the largest commercial banks and owns approximately half of development banks' capital.[29] This represents approximately a third of total banking sector assets. The aforementioned authors note that government-owned banks in Tunisia tend to be characterized by greater exposure to credit risk due to their previous policies of directed lending to strategic sectors. In addition, the economic and financial liberalization programme provides the primary explanation for the increasing presence of private and foreign capital in the Tunisian banking sector. Domestic private capital owns about half of total commercial banking sector assets. Amen Bank is the first Tunisian bank created and owned by domestic private capital. Foreign capital owns approximately half of total assets and capital of development banks, and about a third of total commercial banks' assets and capital. Middle East based banks are present through Arab Bank and Bahrain-based Arab Banking Corporation. French banks include BNP Paribas, which has an affiliate in Union Bancaire pour le Commerce et l'Industrie (UBCI), while Société Générale owns 52 per cent in the Union Internationale de Banque (UIB). Société Générale also has representative offices in Tunis.

One observation about the role of foreign and private capital is the manner in which it enters the banking industry. In Algeria, private and foreign financiers chose to establish their own operations rather than waiting for the launching of the bank privatization process. In Morocco and Tunisia, foreign financiers mostly preferred to purchase stakes in existing banks rather than establish new operations. Iradian *et al.* (2000) present two main explanations that may support this inclination in Morocco and Tunisia. First, the number of banks might seem sufficient to satisfy the demand for banking services in the short term. Second, there is potential for raising efficiency in domestic banks through the use of modern technology and improved management. Thus, while government ownership is still predominant in the Algerian banking system, private and foreign ownerships of the banking sector is higher than government ownership in Morocco and Tunisia. We expect Tunisian and Moroccan banks to have more independence in terms of making loan decisions than Algerian banks. Also, based on studies that find a positive relationship between private and foreign bank ownership and perfomance we might expect banks in Morocco and Tunisia to be more efficient than in Algeria.

Balance sheet characteristics

Lee (2002) studies the average balance sheet structure of the banking systems of Algeria, Morocco and Tunisia with other Middle Eastern and North African (MENA) countries over the period 1989–2001. He reports significant increases in the size of assets, deposits, capital, and credits for all the countries under study. In the three countries under study, the balance sheet structure appears to accommodate mainly credits to the economy, credits to the government, security portfolios, and credits to the central bank, on the assets side, and short, time and saving deposits, and other funds on the liabilities side.

On the assets side, Algerian banks provide fewer credits to the economy than in Morocco and Tunisia, with an average of 46 per cent, 53 per cent, and 85 per cent of total assets, respectively. Credits to the economy by the banking system were around a third of GDP compared to a half in Morocco and Tunisia. Chaput *et al.* (2000) report that the level of bank credits to the economy as a percentage of GDP remains low in the three countries under study, compared to other more developed markets such as Singapore, where credits were 110 per cent of GDP in 1999. Lee (2002) also finds that Tunisian banks allocate fewer credits to the government than in Algeria and Morocco, with on average approximately 6 per cent, 15 per cent, and 30 per cent, respectively. This reflects that the government budget in Tunisia and Algeria experienced relatively more favourable balance than in Morocco. In addition, the portfolio of securities investments account for approximately 30 per cent, 25 per cent and 12 per cent on total banking assets in the three countries, respectively. Although Algerian banks have invested in the three shares listed on Algiers Stock Exchange, the majority of their securities portfolio represents the stakes of Algerian banks in other government-owned enterprises.

Overall, bank credits to the economy tend to be of low maturity. There are three main factors that can explain this. First, banks may seem unable to transform efficiently and profitably their short-term liquid deposits into medium and long-term illiquid assets. Second, banks seem to suffer from the lack of accurate and reliable information on enterprises and projects that may encourage them to extend credits for longer terms. Third, banks might have realized the existence of legal and regulatory weaknesses that prevent them from playing fully their role in financing projects, such as lengthy legal processes to collect overdue loans, and long delays in judicial procedures.

On the liabilities side Moroccan banks have received more short-term demand deposits than savings deposits, with 50 per cent and 25 per cent of total liabilities and equity, respectively. In contrast, Tunisian banks are less dependent on demand deposits (20 per cent) than time deposits (40 per cent) in their sources of funding. Algerian banks have approximately the same level of short-term deposits and time deposits, with each at a quarter of liabilities and equity. Finally, capital accounts show that over 1990–9, Algerian banks had equity to assets ratios of less than 4 per cent, but this improved from 1999 onwards to about 6 per cent, due to the various operations of re-capitalization, compared to 12 per cent in Morocco and 14 per cent in Tunisia.

Profitability

Studies that have investigated the profitability and solvency of the banking sector in Algeria have typically found poor performance and soundness according to international and regional comparisons over the period 1990–2001. Chabrier and Kabur (2000) found that the return on assets of Algerian banks was very low, compared to banks in Morocco and Tunisia, at less than half a percent. The aforementioned study refers to some characteristics of Algerian banks' balance sheet structure as the reasons for this low level of returns. Algerian banks sustained relatively high levels of non-performing claims on loss-making government-owned enterprises. Due to the influence of (past) governments on banks,[30] and despite the autonomy of decision-making granted to bank managers regarding credit allocation, Algerian banks had to continue providing funds to public enterprises to support their working capital, especially wages and salaries. Banks might have liquidity constraints created by the large amounts of government bonds swapped within the framework of the bank-recapitalization programme, currency devaluation losses, and non-performing claims on government-owned enterprises. These bonds might have also yielded lower interest income than expected. In addition, Algerian banks have found it difficult to enlarge their net interest revenue or interest spread. Over the period 1990–2001, the fall in deposit interest rates was larger than the decrease in lending rates, leading to lower profitability in lending business (particularly in sectors outside the upstream hydrocarbon sector).

Unlike in Algeria, Moroccan banks experienced relatively large (but overall stable) net interest revenues of up to 8 per cent despite the larger decrease of lending interest rates compared to interest rates on deposits. Banks benefited from the abolishment of mandatory credits for priority sectors over the period 1990–5. Also banks benefited from the discontinuation of the forced holding of government securities at administratively low-interest rates, and subsequently, banks have substituted these securities for debt instruments yielding market interest rates (as well as Treasury bills). Chaput *et al.* (2000) report that Moroccan banks' income from treasury securities increased by 50 per cent between 1993 and 1998. In addition, large and relatively stable net interest margins imply that financial liberalization measures did not significantly influence the degree of competition among banks. High levels of interest spread may reflect the fact that the Moroccan banking sector is still highly concentrated, and banks are not strongly competing on interest rate business.

In Tunisia, Chabrier and Ingves (2002) report that commercial banks increased their return on assets (ROA) from 0.6 in 1996 to 0.8 per cent in 1997 and 1.2 per cent by 1998–2001. However, return on equity (ROE) fell from 28 per cent in 1990 to 14 per cent by 1999–2001. The aforementioned study suggests that the level of profitability of Tunisian banks is relatively high. One possible explanation for this phenomenon is a large interest spread driven by the absence of competition (due to the high levels of industry concentration). In terms of costs, the operating costs to average assets ratio experienced a relatively stable trend at approximately 2.3 per cent over the

1990–2002 period compared to 2.2 per cent in Morocco and 2 per cent in the Euro area. Enders *et al*. (1998) note that Tunisian banks were experiencing ROA rates in the range of those experienced in the OECD countries, with privately-owned banks persistently outperforming government-owned banks. The aforementioned study suggests that the high level of ROA was driven mainly by the large net interest revenues. Tunisian banks were lending, on average, 2.7 per cent above the money market rate while deposits were remunerated at approximately 0.5 per cent below the money market rate. Overall, Moroccan and Tunisian banks are more profitable and efficient than banks in Algeria.

Financial markets

The establishment and development of stock exchanges in Algeria, Morocco and Tunisia can be regarded as a major step towards market-based financing of the economy and reducing the dependence of enterprises on bank lending. The Bourse de Casablanca is the oldest in the region, established in 1929, followed by Bourse de Tunis (1969), and more recently Bourse d'Alger (1999). While only three shares are listed on the Algiers exchange, the market capitalization and number of listed companies in Casablanca and Tunis increased considerably due to privatization programmes executed in the 1990s. However, all three stock exchanges are still small and have not developed in line with the respective banking systems. In Algeria, the Algiers Stock exchange (ASC) is the smallest in the region with only three still-dominantly government-owned shares listed.[31] Currently, there is no financial and banking firm quoted on the market. The Casablanca Stock exchange (CSE) is the largest in the region with a market capitalization of DH 115 bn (US$ 14 bn) and fifty-eight listed companies, in 2000, accounting for about two-fifths of Morocco's GDP. The CSE witnessed considerable development in the 1990s, as market capitalization increased from DH 7.8 bn in 1993 to DH 145 bn in 2000, and market capitalization to GDP ratio from 5 per cent in 1990 to 40 per cent in 2000. Since 1993, the programme of privatization contributed considerably to the development of the Casablanca exchange. The number of listed firms increased from 44 in 1995 to 58 in 2000. In terms of market concentration, the share of the first ten securities quoted as a proportion of total market capitalization declined from 88 per cent in 1994 to 65 per cent in 2000. The financial sector accounts for about half of total market capitalization. The capitalization of the seven quoted commercial banks represents a third of total market capitalization. The Tunis Stock Exchange (TSE) capitalization stood at DT 3.9 bn (US$ 2.6 bn) in 2000 with forty-four quoted companies, representing around 14 per cent of the country's GDP. Similarly, the number of quoted firms increased from thirteen in 1990 to forty-six in 2002. Over the period 1990–2000, the capitalization of the Tunis market increased nearly eight times. However, over 2000–2, the capitalization of the market decreased from

3.8 to 2.8 billion Tunisian Dinar. Interestingly, foreign capital is strongly present in Tunis. It is estimated to be 60 per cent of quoted firms, holding around a fifth of total market capitalization. Currently, there are a number of leasing firms, three insurance companies and fourteen commercial and development banks listed on the Tunis exchange that account for around a half of total market capitalization.

Despite these developments, the exchanges in Morocco and Tunisia are relatively underdeveloped compared to other Arab stock markets, such as in Egypt and Jordan. First, the number of listed shares in Cairo and Amman is greater than that in Morocco and Tunisia. Second, as of the end of 2000, the capitalization of the Casablanca and Tunis stock exchanges reached US$ 14 bn and US$ 2.6 bn, respectively, compared to US$ 21 bn and US$ 5 bn in Cairo and Amman, respectively. Also, in 2000, the ratio of market capitalization to GDP was higher in Morocco (40 per cent) than in Egypt (23 per cent) and Tunisia (13 per cent), but lower than that of Jordan (70 per cent). Nevertheless, share dealings on the Casablanca and Tunis exchanges were greater than in Cairo and Amman exchanges. For instance, in 2000, the value of shares traded in Casablanca and Tunis amounted to US$ 1.8 bn, compared to US$ 0.7 bn for Egypt and US$ 0.9 bn for Jordan.

Other non-Gulf financial systems

So far we have examined the features of the main non-Gulf financial systems, namely the largest in the Arab region. It would be inappropriate not to mention other financial systems such as Iraq, Libya and Syria that are primarily government banking systems. Furthermore, the banking systems in Comoros, Djibouti and Somalia are substantially underdeveloped and few data are available. Moreover, the banking systems in Lebanon and Iraq have experienced extreme economic conditions as a result of wars and so are problematic to study. Typically, the lack of relevant information about banking systems in other Arab countries is the main reason for excluding them from detailed study in this book.

Conclusion

This chapter reviews the main features of the financial systems of Jordan, Egypt and the main Mahgreb countries (Algeria, Morocco and Tunisia). All these countries have experienced various financial reforms aimed at liberalizing their financial systems. Jordan and Egypt, in particular, have witnessed major financial reforms over the last decade, aimed at replacing financial repression and excessive regulation with a more competitive environment. The reforms procedures in the countries have included deregulation of interest and credit controls, privatization of banks and the gradual opening up to foreign banks, improving bank capitalization in accordance with Basel standards and introducing new prudential guidelines. In general, stock markets have been upgraded and they have begun to play a wider role in financing various economic sectors within their respective countries. However, commercial banks still dominate financial systems and the state still plays a major role in most systems. Such indicators reflect an enhanced role for financial intermediaries in the process of economic growth and exhibit the positive impact of economic and financial reforms undertaken in these countries. Furthermore, financial systems have deepened and the proportion of credit allocated to the private sector as a percent of GDP has generally increased, suggesting that the financial institutions are gradually becoming more efficient in allocating the financial resources to the most efficient users.

5

Banking and Financial Systems in Gulf Cooperation Council (GCC) Countries

Introduction

This chapter provides an overview of the financial systems of the Gulf Cooperation Council countries: Saudi Arabia, United Arab Emirates, Bahrain, Kuwait, Oman and Qatar. It covers the development of individual GCC countries' banking systems and financial markets, an analysis of the performance of Gulf banks, and briefly outlines recent moves to create a GCC economic and financial union. In general these countries have experienced various financial reforms aimed at strengthening their financial systems. These have mainly included moves to deregulate as well as to improve prudential standards. Stock markets have been upgraded and they have begun to play a wider role in financing various economic sectors within their respective countries, although their importance remains limited. Commercial banks still dominate GCC financial systems and banking systems are highly concentrated. Gulf banking systems show favourable improvement in terms of their asset quality, capital adequacy and profitability during the 1990s. Such indicators reflect an enhanced role for financial intermediaries in the process of economic growth and exhibit the positive impact of economic and financial reforms undertaken in these countries. Furthermore, from earlier analysis we know that financial systems have deepened in these countries and the proportion of credit allocated to the private sector as a percentage of GDP has increased, suggesting that banks have become more efficient in allocating financial resources within the respective countries.

Taken together, this suggests that the performance and efficiency of the financial and banking systems under study is likely to have improved during the 1990s. Although it is difficult to say specifically whether this improvement is a result of various reforms or improvements in the general macroeconomic environment, one can at least suggest that the reform process has had some positive influence.

Banking sector development in Saudi Arabia

Early banking activities in Saudi Arabia were limited to the presence of a handful of foreign-based trading houses, such as the branch of Algemene Bank Nederland, and of various money changers. Their main business was to provide financial services for locals and pilgrims. The more formal and organized form of banking system emerged after the exploration of oil in 1939 and, as soon as World War II ended, the Saudi market attracted leading foreign banks to open branches. Hence, the French Banque de l'Indochine and Arab Bank Limited opened their branches in Jeddah in 1948; while in 1950, three international banks opened their branches, namely the British Bank of the Middle East, the National Bank of Pakistan, and Bank Misr (of Egypt).

Saudi Arabia did not have a national currency until 1952, a year that witnessed the establishment of the Saudi Arabia Monetary Agency (SAMA). During 1950–6, SAMA introduced a paper money in the form of pilgrim receipts, which was covered by foreign currencies and precious metals. The introduction of the Saudi national currency, called Riyal, came in 1960.

SAMA was (and continues to be) responsible for issuing and preserving the value of the Saudi Riyal, and for supervising and setting regulations governing the banking sector. At the time of SAMA's establishment, the Saudi government continued to use the Al-Kaki and Bin Mahfouz Money Changer Company as its agent to undertake its payment services. In 1953, this company was permitted by the government to be transformed into a bank known as the National Commercial Bank, the first Saudi bank. By 1960, the Saudi banking system witnessed opening of an additional three foreign banks and two domestic banks. However, the two newly established Saudi banks, namely the Riyadh Bank and Al-Watani Bank that started in 1957 and 1959 respectively, faced financial difficulties due to various liquidity problems. These were mainly caused by poor governance as board members of the two banks borrowed heavily, exposing the banks to various default problems. Being unable to meet depositors' claims, Al-Watani Bank became insolvent and was liquidated and merged with the Riyadh Bank (Al-Suhaimi, 2001). In 1966, a banking law provided SAMA with broader supervisory powers that made banks subject to various liquidity, capital adequacy, lending, and reserve requirements.

By the early 1970s, other banks had entered the Saudi banking system, attracted by the opportunities brought about by the boom in the economy resulting from the increased oil revenues, especially from 1973 onwards. The strong presence of foreign banks, of which there were ten by the mid-1970s, encouraged the Saudi authorities to introduce a policy encouraging foreign banks to be converted into publicly traded companies with the participation of Saudi nationals. The legislation introduced in 1975 aimed to preserve the rights and interests of foreign banks' positions as partners in the newly incorporated banks. In order to maintain the performance and stability of the banking sector, foreign banks were allowed to hold up to 50 per cent ownership and include the name of their origins in the bank title.[1] They could also maintain management responsibilities and were allowed to enjoy treatment equal to that of national banks.

During the 1970s, five major specialized lending institutions were also established: namely, the Saudi Credit Bank, Saudi Agricultural Bank, Public Investment Funds, Saudi Industrial Development Fund, and the Real Estate Fund (Al-Sahlawi, 1997). These banks were established by the government to provide funds for specific sectors. The loans offered by these banks typically financed mid- to long-term development projects at subsidized rates.

In the 1980s, the Saudi economy experienced two major incidents. One was the sharp rise in oil prices during 1979–81 due to the Iran–Iraq war, and the second was the severe decline in oil prices in 1986 (Al-Suhaimi, 2001). These incidents affected the Saudi banking system in that Saudi banks substantially extended their lending in the early 1980s, backed by the increase in their balance sheets after the oil price hike. Many of these loans were made without adequate assessment and monitoring procedures. Consequently, when oil prices fell in 1986, many banks faced difficulties recovering their loans owing to the severe contraction in the domestic economy, mainly because of declining government revenues. (For instance government revenues fell from SR333 billion in 1981 to SR74 billion by 1987.) As a result, non-performing loans in the banking system increased sharply, amounting to 20 per cent of total loans by 1986. This, understandably, depressed bank profits on account of the substantial rise in loan loss provisions. However, these incidents helped discipline banks' lending activities and, by 1988, most banks had adequate provisions for doubtful loans, with average loan provisions increasing to more than 12 per cent of total lending (Bank for International Settlements, 2001).

Another noteworthy event during the 1980s was the near failure of the Saudi Cairo Bank resulting from unauthorized bullion trading during 1979 and 1981. Accumulated losses exceeded the bank's capital, forcing the authorities to intervene. SAMA directed the bank to issue new shares and double its capital by 1986, and the increase in capital was undertaken by the Saudi Public Investment Fund.

During the 1980s, various other national banks were established, including Al-Rajhi Banking and Investment Corporation (the largest money exchanger licensed as a full commercial bank), Saudi Investment Bank (authorized as a full commercial bank with foreign ownership reduced to 25 per cent and the remaining shares sold to the public), and the United Saudi Bank (formed after the take-over of three foreign banks). These banks contributed to the restructuring of the Saudi banking sector. Meanwhile, SAMA encouraged banks to strengthen their capital positions so as to improve the soundness of the system.

Another major development during the 1980s was the introduction of government bonds that helped strengthen banks' investment portfolios. In addition, automated teller machines were introduced in order to advance the quality of banks' services to the public, and debit and credit card services became more widely available.

The decade of the 1990s commenced with a serious test to the Saudi banking system after the Iraqi invasion of Kuwait. Banks faced substantial deposit withdrawals in August 1990, accounting for 11 per cent of total banking sector deposits and these were exchanged into foreign currencies. By the end of 1990 the withdrawals eased (declining to 1.1 per cent of total deposits) owing to the intervention by SAMA. The authorities provided the banking system with substantial liquidity in Saudi Riyal and foreign currencies through greater use of repo arrangements. This helped to stabilize the system and maintain a healthy banking system during these turbulent times.

From 1991 to 1995, domestic loans and advances increased by 90 per cent, and profitability indicators continued to show sustained improvement. The second half of the 1990s witnessed a merger between the United Saudi Commercial Bank and the Saudi Cairo Bank, to form the United Saudi Bank. The United Bank also merged with the Saudi American Bank in 1998. Moreover, Saudi banks continued to embrace operational development by investing in new technologies such as electronic funds transfer systems and by setting up widespread point-of-sale terminals.

The Saudi banking sector expanded during the 1990s. Banking credit grew by 147 per cent with an annual average growth rate of 11 per cent, and reaching $46.2 billion by 2000. Also, deposits rose by 73 per cent, reaching some $71.2 billion.[2] Moreover, the level of financial capital and reserves of the banking system reached $11.6 billion, mirroring an annual growth of 10 per cent over the 1990–2000 period. By 2000, total banking assets amounted to some $121.1 billion. There were eleven commercial banks operating in Saudi Arabia, of which four were joint ventures with foreign banks. From mid 1975, no new foreign bank entities have been allowed to enter the Saudi banking system. However, in the move towards GCC financial sector integration, the International Gulf Bank of Bahrain and the Abu Dhabi National Bank of the UAE have been lately granted licences to open branches on Saudi soil.

Saudi Arabian financial markets

According to Azzam (1998), Saudi financial markets are relatively under-developed given the size of the country's economy and banking system. This is a reflection of the historical importance of cash and liquidity in the banking system, and the fact that until the early 1990s the banks had no difficulty in attracting funds and borrowers had no difficulty in finding willing lenders. This situation started to change in 1993 when there was a slowdown in deposit growth, resulting from reduced repatriation of capital from abroad and a reduction in government oil revenues, combined with increasing demand for credit on the part of the government, and, to a lesser extent, the private sector. According to Al-Sahlawi (1997), the main gap in Saudi financial markets is the lack of medium-term liability instruments. The vast bulk of Saudi banks' deposits, both from customers and banks, is in short-term money. No Saudi bank has issued medium-term notes or bonds as part of its funding programme. Historically, Saudi banks have had large amounts of assets placed with banks abroad and these could be repatriated to cover any short-term liquidity requirements.

There has been some development of products on the asset side, although these have arisen mainly in the form of government debt (Cunningham, 1995). In 1988 SAMA began to issue government development bonds (GDBs) on behalf of the Ministry of Finance and National Economy. The stated intention was to cover the government deficit (Presley, 1992). Yields on the bonds are theoretically linked to profits on unspecified development projects. In practice they are directly linked to the returns on US treasury bonds (Wilson and Presley, 1992). The GDBs give a premium of 0.2 per cent over US treasuries on the two-year bonds, rising to a premium of 0.5 per cent over five years on the five-year bonds. By the end of 1993 it was estimated that outstanding bonds totalled around $46 bn of which about half were taken up by governmental institutions. Bonds may be bought on the secondary market by GCC institutions or individuals, Bahrain offshore banks and the overseas-based branches of Saudi companies. The GDBs proved popular with the banks when interest rates were falling in the early 1990s but when rates started to rise again in early 1994 purchases quickly tailed off (Azzam, 1998). The secondary market in bonds is thin, not least because all the banks are using the same criteria in determining whether to buy or not to buy (Al-Sahlawi, 1997). SAMA does, however, offer a repurchase facility for up to 25 per cent of banks' holdings of the bonds. In November 1991 SAMA started to issue treasury bills with maturities up to one year. Repurchase facilities (for up to 75 per cent of holdings) and reverse repurchase facilities exist (Presley, 1992).

Activity on the Saudi stock market started to increase towards the end of the 1980s with a series of public share issues. This trend accelerated after the Gulf War and in the two and a half years to the middle of 1994 eleven institutions (10 commercial banks and one Islamic bank) raised a total of $4.7 bn in capital in response to the new capital adequacy policy imposed by SAMA (Cunningham, 1995). Moreover, new publicly traded firms were established. However, after that the pace slackened reflecting a decline in the Saudi stock index and tightening liquidity in the economy (Azzam, 1998). From a peak of 1233 in April 1992 the Saudi stock index sank to around 1135 in July 1994 and hovered around that level until the end of the year. In fact, in the early 1990s the Saudi share market witnessed a systematic transformation, represented by the introduction of the Electronic Share Information System (ESIS). ESIS has contributed to the regulation and development of the operation of the market and restricted trading only through the central trading units at commercial banks, which are continually supervised and monitored by SAMA (Al-Suhaimi, 2001). At present SAMA undertakes the responsibility of developing, regulating and directly supervising the Saudi share market and its day-to-day operations (SAMA Annual Report, 2001). The Saudi share market recorded a marked improvement during 2000 due to increased economic activity and the ongoing policy of restructuring aimed at partially privatizing state sectors. The share price index stood at 2258.29 at the end of 2000, rising by 11.5 per cent over the end of the preceding year, and the total value of shares traded went up by 15.5 per cent from US$ 15,078 million in the preceding year to US$ 17,411 million in 2000 (see Table 5.1).

Furthermore, the total number of shares traded increased to 555 million from 528 million in the preceding year, recording a rise of 5.1 per cent, and market capitalization stood at US$ 68,000 million at the end of 2000 as against US$ 61,045 in the preceding year, rising by 11.5 per cent, (SAMA, Annual Report, 2001). Despite the downturn in the domestic economy resulting from the instability in oil prices and the Gulf War, the Saudi financial system has witnessed substantial progress over the past decade. Many banks have increased their capitalization, and the number of publicly traded firms has also increased. Further, the stock market has witnessed substantial expansion. Overall, the Saudi financial system, the largest in the Gulf region, has experienced a remarkable expansion in banking accompanied by ongoing updating and revision of its regulatory framework to ensure increased soundness and prudence in the financial system.

Table 5.1   Saudi share market indicators over the period from 1990 to 2000

Year	No. of shares traded (1000s)	Value of shares traded (US$, million)	Market value of shares (US$ million)	Number of transactions	General index (national stock indicator) (points)
1990	17,000	1,173	25,866	85,298	979.80
1991	31,000	2,275	48,266	90,559	1765.24
1992	35,000	3,651	54,933	272,075	1888.65
1993	60,000	4,629	52,800	319,582	1793.30
1994	152,000	6,632	38,600	357,180	1282.90
1995	117,000	6,191	40,800	291,742	1367.60
1996	138,000	6,770	45,780	283,759	1531.00
1997	312,000	16549	59,456	460,056	1957.80
1998	293,000	13,736	42,650	376,617	1413.10
1999	528,000	15,078	61,045	438,226	2028.53
2000	555,000	17,411	68,000	498,135	2258.29

Source: Saudi Monetary Agency Annual Report, 2001, p. 331.

Banking in the UAE

The British Bank of the Middle East was the first bank to be established in the region now known as the UAE in 1946, located in Dubai. This bank opened its second branch in Abu Dhabi following the discovery of oil. Later, the Eastern Bank and the Ottoman Bank opened their branches in Abu Dhabi in 1961 and 1962 respectively. The year 1963 witnessed the establishment of the first national bank, the National Bank of Dubai, followed by the opening of Abu Dhabi National Bank in 1968. Obviously, the attractiveness of these two cities in the UAE derives mainly from the concentration of trade activities (primarily in Dubai) and oil exports (largely in Abu Dhabi).

The UAE Central Bank (2001a) notes that after the formation of the federation which resulted in the establishment of the state of UAE in 1972 (consisting of seven emirates), the rush to open national and foreign branches accelerated. In 1972, the Currency Board was established to issue the UAE national currency, the Dirham, and to supervise and regulate the banking system. In the same year, the number of commercial banks increased to six domestic and fifteen foreign banks, most of them concentrated in Abu-Dhabi and Dubai and a few in the third largest emirate, Sharjah. Following the dramatic increase in international oil prices, the number of banks reached thirteen national and twenty-eight foreign banks by 1975. After 1975, the Currency Board realized that the economy needed more banking institutions to help with financing associated with the economic boom. Therefore, more bank licences were issued and by 1977 there were twenty national and thirty-four foreign banks operating throughout the Emirates. In 1980, the UAE issued a Federal Law establishing the Central Bank of the UAE, with extensive powers to operate as the country's central bank. The central bank was formally in charge of issuing and controlling the supply of the Dirham and maintaining gold and foreign currencies to support its value. In 1981, the UAE Central briefly lifted the freeze on new bank establishments but imposed it again specifically on the licensing of new foreign banks. It also instructed the existing foreign banks that from 1984 they would not be allowed to have more than eight branches throughout the UAE.

In the early 1980s, the UAE Central Bank adopted several measures to strengthen the banking system (UAE Central Bank, 2001b). It set minimum capital requirements, enhanced audit and reporting requirements, increased inspection, established a department dedicated to oversee bank loan risks, and set regulations that limited the amount of loans that could be given to the board of directors. In 1983 one bank failure resulted from the violation of the loan limit to the Board of Directors. This caused the UAE Central Bank to appoint administrators to this bank and, in essence, the central bank and the government of Dubai bailed out the bank with an amount of $380 million. The oil price fell below $10 per barrel in 1986. This led to a sharp decline in federal revenues. Consequently, contractions in government expenditure slowed down economic activities and, as a result, the banking sector experienced loan problems arising from accelerated loan losses. This led to a restructuring of the banking sector when three banks in Dubai merged, as did another three in Abu Dhabi. This resulted in banking sector numbers falling to nineteen national and twenty-nine foreign banks. Another threat emerged in the wake of Iraq's 1990 invasion of Kuwait, when between 15 and 30 per cent of customer bank deposits were transferred out of the UAE. At this time, the UAE Central Bank injected funds into at least two banks in order to strengthen their liquidity and restore confidence in the banking system as a whole.[3]

During the 1990s, the UAE Central Bank introduced various regulations aimed at improving banking sector soundness. By 1993, banks were subjected to a capital to assets ratio of 10 per cent. Moreover, banks were required to accumulate reserves by shifting 10 per cent of their annual net profits to the reserve accounts until the latter equalled 50 per cent of their paid-up capital. In 1994, banks were urged to move toward adopting International Accounting Standards. These directions enhanced, to some extent, the capitalization of the UAE banking system. For example, in 1997, the average ratio of capital to risk-weighted assets for all banks was 21 per cent, which was well above the Basel 1988 recommendations. Recently, the UAE Central Bank has raised the capital reserve ratio to 14 per cent.

At present, there are 19 local banks comprising four based in Abu Dhabi, six in Dubai, four in Sharjah, two in Ras al-Kheimah, and one each in Fujeirah, Umm al-Quwain and Ajman. Abu Dhabian interests control three of the four banks based in Abu Dhabi: National Bank, Commercial Bank and Union National Bank (this last being the new name for the local operations of Bank of Credit and Commerce International – BCCI). The Arab Bank for Investment and Foreign Trade (known as Arbift) is owned by Libyan Arab Foreign Bank. The six Dubai banks include two which are state owned: National Bank and Emirates Bank International. Commercial Bank of Dubai and Mashreq Bank (which was formerly known as Bank of Oman) and Dubai Islamic Bank are partially owned by the government. The Middle East Bank is owned by Emirates Bank International. The United Arab Bank has its head office and general manager in Abu Dhabi, but qualifies as a Sharjah bank because that is where its shareholders come from and because it is treated as a Sharjah bank by the Central Bank of the UAE. The other two Sharjah banks are Bank of Sharjah, which is managed by Banque Paribas, and Investbank. The national banks of the other Emirates are controlled by their respective ruling families.

Commercial banks' assets totalled $54.532 bn at the end of 2000, representing 25 per cent of all banking assets in the GCC. (Saudi Arabia accounted for around 45 per cent of GCC assets and Kuwait for about 16 per cent.) Assets in the banking system grew at an average rate of 7 per cent per annum in the four years to the end of 2000. Five banks dominate the UAE banking scene in terms of market share: National Bank of Abu Dhabi, National Bank of Dubai, Abu Dhabi Commercial Bank, Emirates Bank International and Mashreq Bank. The first two had assets just in excess of $26 billion at the end of 2000, while the other three had assets of around $15.3 billion. At the other end of the scale, five banks had assets of less than $1.3 billion.

Commercial banks in the UAE have made significant developments over the last decade or so. Commercial credit to different economic sectors grew by 169 per cent over the period 1990–9, with an average annual growth of 12 per cent.[4] These credits amounted to $37.6 billion in 2000. Deposits in the commercial banks grew by 72 per cent with an annual growth of 8 per cent. Total deposits reached $36.8 billion in 2000. Moreover, bank capital and reserves amounted to some $9.3 billion in 2000, having experienced annual average growth of 9 per cent throughout the 1990s. Total banking sector assets amounted to $75.5 billion in 2000. Over the decade of the 1990s, only small changes in the number of banks occurred, and by the end of 2003 the number of national banks had reached 19 while foreign banks stood at 26 banks.

Overall, UAE banks operate in a relatively healthy financial system. The banking system development over the last twenty years or so reflects the system's ability to cope with minor crises as well as the changing demands of clients and the economy.

UAE financial markets

Financial markets in the UAE are not sophisticated; lending to local companies and financing trade (particularly in Dubai, which acts as a re-export centre to the region) are the mainstays of local banking business (Al-Awad, 2001). Portfolio management is important, particularly in Abu Dhabi, although in this the foreign branches have a clear advantage over the local banks (Al-Owain, 2001). As in other Gulf countries, the banking market is so liquid that there has been no need to develop medium-term debt liability instruments. The shortage of local assets is seen in the fact that foreign assets accounted for 55 per cent of all commercial bank assets in the UAE at the end of 2000. The government of the UAE does not issue treasury bills or bonds. In April 1999 the Central Bank initiated a new certificates of deposit programme with maturities ranging from one to eighteen months. They are priced slightly below US dollar interbank rates and may be bought by local banks.

The official stock market in the UAE opened at the start of 1999 in Dubai. Before that, most trading was conducted informally on the telephone through brokers located mainly in Abu Dhabi and Dubai. At the end of 1998, there were 40 shares traded and 10 brokerage companies licensed by the central bank. Share prices are published in newspapers and price movements are monitored by the unofficial index set up by the National Bank of Abu Dhabi in 1989 with a base of 1,000 points.

In 1995 the central bank issued new regulations imposing minimum capital adequacy requirements for brokers and placing them under its direct control. The minimum capital requirement was set at Dh 1 million ($272,000) for brokerage houses dealing in domestic shares and Dh 2 million ($545,000) for those trading internationally. The central bank made it necessary for brokers to obtain a licence and prohibited dealers from operating in the market without authorization. The new regulations also made it mandatory for brokerage houses to be audited and their personnel to be qualified and reliable. The new rules were designed to end confusion in the market as several brokers were practising without central bank permission, while others were not qualified to deal in shares.

Critics would say that the UAE Stock Market in its present form lacks rules and regulations. There is uncertainty about fair pricing and reluctance among joint-stock companies to publish regular, timely and complete financial information. Furthermore, pricing methodologies are not transparent and very little information is available on the companies whose shares are traded (Al-Amri, 2000). Shareholding companies are not required to publish half-yearly results and the market is not open to international investors. Moreover, there is heavy concentration of share ownership with the government. Abu Dhabi has a majority stake in the Emirates Telecommunications Corporation (Etisalat), the largest listed company with a market capitalization of Dh 17.8 billion ($4.85 billion) in 1999 (Al-Mannai, 2001). At the end of 1999, total capitalization of listed companies reached Dh 85.6 billion (US$ 22.75 billion), making the UAE market the second largest in the Gulf after Saudi Arabia (National Bank of Abu Dhabi, Economic and Financial Report, January 2000).

Banking business in Bahrain

According to the Bahrain Monetary Agency (1994), banking business in Bahrain started when a branch of the Eastern Bank opened in 1921. This bank was the only one operating in Bahrain until the British Bank of the Middle East opened its branch two decades later in 1944. The National Bank of Bahrain, the first local bank, opened its doors in 1957 followed by the establishment of a Jordanian bank, the Arab Bank Limited in 1960.

Within this emerging financial system, the Gulf Rupee was the main currency enjoying locally a common acceptance.[5] In the meantime Bahrain engaged in negotiations with neighbouring emirates (Qatar, Dubai, and Abu Dhabi) to issue a common Gulf currency. However, because the negotiations failed, Bahrain continued to deal with the Gulf Rupee until it replaced it with the Bahraini Dinar, which was introduced in 1965 (Bahrain Monetary Agency, 1994). The Bahrain Currency Board was in charge of issuing and managing the supply of the Bahraini Dinar. The expansion of the financial system, powered by the rapid increase in oil revenues, brought to the surface the need to direct, supervise, and control the financial system by a well-equipped institution. Consequently, the Bahrain Monetary Agency (BMA) was created in 1973 to take over the work of the Currency Board and practise extensive central banking powers. The Bahraini Dinar was linked to the British Pound Sterling and then to the US Dollar. The devaluation of these two currencies (the Pound Sterling in 1967 and the US Dollar in 1971 and then in 1973) created losses to the value of the Dinar held by the Currency Board, banks, and the public. As a result, the Dinar was linked to the SDR and, in the meantime, the reserves of the US Dollar were used as an interventional currency serving to stabilize the international value of the Dinar with a margin set at certain limits. The establishment of the BMA, the issuance of the national currency, and the progressive strengthening of the economy after the 1973 oil boom made Bahrain's financial system increasingly attractive to banking business. As a result, the number of commercial banks reached fifteen by 1977. Moreover, two specialized banks were added to the Bahraini banking structure, namely the Housing Bank and the Bahrain Development Bank.

Because the government of Bahrain was conscious about its declining oil reserves, Bahrain was among the first GCC countries to undertake initiatives aimed at diversifying its economy away from oil (Bahrain Monetary Agency, 1994). Bahrain focused on developing itself as a centre for financial services in the Gulf region with the aim of attracting oil revenues from the neighbouring Gulf countries. In fact, Bahrain has successfully attracted offshore banking units (OBUs) and has developed the main offshore financial centre in the Gulf region. Offshore banks located in Bahrain are not required to pay income taxes. Moreover, they are exempted from foreign exchange controls and cash reserve requirements. On the other hand, OBUs must not accept deposits from citizens and residents of Bahrain, and must refrain from transactions involving Bahraini Dinars. In return, Bahrain benefits from employment opportunities for its national labour force and collects annual licence fees. The first OBUs to operate in Bahrain were Citibank and Algemene Bank Nederland (opened in 1975). One of the main factors that induced the fast growth of Bahrain's OBUs market was the shift of OBUs located in Lebanon to Bahrain. The number of OBUs in Bahrain reached a maximum of seventy-six in 1984. However, owing to the dramatic decline in oil prices in the mid-1980s, many OBUs contracted their business, resulting in non-renewal of various licences. Moreover, trends towards consolidation within and between banking groups increased. As a result, the number of OBUs in Bahrain declined and, by 2002, around forty-eight were active in the country. According to the Bahrain Monetary Agency (2001), around 32.9 per cent of the assets of OBUs are from Arab countries (mostly from other GCC countries). Western European banks account for 32 per cent, American banks 21.3 per cent, and Asian banks 11.3 per cent of total OBU banking sector assets.

In 1977, Bahrain also introduced a third category of banking licences, called Investment Banking licences (IBs), for banks intending to carry out investment business (Bahrain Monetary Agency, 1994). The first of these banks was Bahrain Investment Bank (in 1977). The number of these types of banks increased from a handful in the late 1970s to thirty-four by 2001.

Bahrain also aims to establish itself as a centre for Islamic banking and finance. Early on, Bahrain took the lead in introducing a comprehensive prudential set of regulations for Islamic banks, which follow guidelines from the Bahrain-based Accounting and Auditing Organization for Islamic Financial Institutions and the Basel Committee on Banking Supervision, as well as guidelines from the accounting firm Ernst & Young. These regulations aim mainly to cover regulatory issues concerning capital adequacy, asset quality, and liquidity management. These regulations may give Bahrain-based Islamic banks a competitive edge and may create interest among other countries to adopt Islamic banking regulations similar to those developed by Bahrain (Standard and Poor's *Creditweek*, October 16, 2002).[6]

In 2000, total banking sector assets amounted to around $106 billion, a GDP multiple of about fourteen, with OBUs' assets occupying the largest stake (87.4 per cent), followed by commercial bank assets (9.4 per cent) and investment banks (3.2 per cent).

Although the Bahraini commercial banking sector is the smallest in the GCC region, Bahrain commercial banks have achieved significant growth over the last decade or so. Commercial banking credit experienced a growth of 112 per cent from the year 1990 to 2000, increasing annually by an average of 9 per cent and totalling $3.7 billion by 2000.[7] Over the same period, deposits increased by 70 per cent, with an annual growth rate of 7 per cent. These deposits totalled $6.5 billion in 2000. In addition, capital and reserves of the banking sector amounted to $0.6 billion by 2000. The assets size of Bahrain commercial banks reached $7.9 billion by the year 2000.

Overall, Bahraini banking sector development reflects its special position as a major financial centre in the Gulf region. The country aims to provide an environment conducive to banking and financial activity, and has recently made various moves to establish itself as the major Islamic finance centre in the region. While there is increasing competitive pressure from Dubai, Bahrain remains one of the world's premier financial centres. Given its role as an offshore centre, the domestic banking sector remains relatively small, in fact the smallest in the GCC; nevertheless, the domestic banks continue to provide an important role in mobilizing domestic savings and financing economic development within the country.

Bahrain's financial markets

The government of Bahrain established an organized stock market in Manama in 1989 to regulate the listing and trading of securities and to control the members of the market. The objectives of the stock exchange market are to enhance the exchange in a way that serves economic and development policies. Foreign or non-Bahraini companies listed on the BSE must be either joint-stock companies or closed companies that have been incorporated at least three years prior to listing, and must have a paid-up capital of at least $US 10 million and have been making net profits from their principal activity three years before listing. Equities, bonds, mutual funds and currency warrants are currently the main listed securities on the exchange. Efforts are under way to strengthen the role of the stock exchange in the economy by increasing the number of listed companies, introducing new investment instruments, cross-listing shares at the regional level, and developing automated depository, clearing and settlement procedures. The exchange's operations became fully automated in 1999, a service that enhanced its regional links and other services. By the end of 1999, there were 41 listed companies, with a market capitalization amounting to around BD 2.7 billion (Bahrain Monetary Agency, Annual Report, 2001). The exchange is heavily dominated by commercial banks, investment firms, and insurance companies. Overall, the Bahraini financial system has been set up to be a financial centre in the Arab world that plays a major role in attracting oil money and reinvesting this in international markets (Azzam, 1998). The participants in the Bahraini market, especially the offshore banking units, are offered attractive packages in terms of regulatory and fiscal incentives. Recently, the Bahraini authorities have introduced various international prudential regulations in line with the Basel supervisory core-principles. In addition, Islamic banking activity developments are well-advanced and are supported by the Bahraini authorities.

Since the end of 1992 the BMA, which issues government bonds and treasury bills on behalf of the government, has only made new issues to cover maturing issues. The total outstanding bills remain a little below the government-imposed ceiling of BD 300 m ($800 m). Bills have a maturity of 91 days and the bonds range from five years to seven years. In late 1998, Alba issued $50 m in medium-term bonds and further issues were planned by other local companies. The Alba issue was well received and the fact that it was tradable on the Bahrain Stock Exchange (BSE) added to the issue's attraction. The BSE itself is taking steps to widen share ownership and trading. In the mid-1990s trading was still thin, but in time the BSE aims to become a more important part of the local financial scene (Al-Mannai, 2001).

There is a limited amount of corporate advisory work required by local industries which are contemplating expansion or privatization. New ventures, such as various proposed infrastructure projects, are likely to be financed on a build–operate–transfer basis. These also offer opportunities for advisory work. However, Azzam (1998) notes that only the bigger banks have the expertise to undertake this (just as only they have the expertise to structure bond issues) and they usually face competition from offshore banks, which can easily get permission to engage in this type of local business.

Banking sector development in Kuwait

According to Al-Sharrah (1999), the first attempt to establish a bank in Kuwait was in 1935 when both the Ottoman Bank and the British Bank of the Middle East competed to establish a branch for their banks. Neither succeeded because of the hesitant Kuwaiti rulers. In 1941, the British Bank of the Middle East was permitted to set up a branch in Kuwait. Many banks tried later to enter the Kuwaiti banking market, but the authorities prohibited foreign banks from conducting banking business in the country. When the British Bank's concession ended in 1971, this bank changed its name to the Kuwait Bank for the Middle East and Kuwaitis purchased 60 per cent of the bank's capital.

Foreign currencies – largely the Indian Rupee and then the Gulf Rupee – circulated in Kuwait between 1930 and 1961. However, in May 1961, Kuwait issued its own currency, called Dinar (Al-Sharrah, 1999). The Kuwaiti Dinar (KD) came into existence after the Kuwaiti economy was strengthened, primarily through increased revenues from oil, which led to the development of the financial and other economic sectors. Moreover, the need for its own currency came because Kuwait wanted a stronger and stable currency, hoping to avoid the fluctuations associated with the Gulf Rupee. Prior to the establishment of the Kuwait Central Bank, a Currency Board was in charge of issuing the Kuwaiti Dinar and administering money exchange. In 1959, the Central Bank of Kuwait was created and took over the functions of the Currency Board.

In 1952, a group of Kuwaiti families founded the first national bank in Kuwait, known as the National Bank of Kuwait, which is currently the largest commercial bank in the country. In fact, after Kuwait gained its independence in 1961, the establishment of several other banks, all under Kuwaiti ownership, followed. Moreover, some specialized financial institutions also emerged: the Credit and Savings Bank was established in 1965 by the government to channel funds into domestic projects, agriculture, and housing; the Industrial Bank of Kuwait, established in 1973, aimed to fill the gap in medium- and long-term industrial financing; and the private Real Estate Bank of Kuwait emerged in 1973 as a financier of property developments in the country. By 1978, the number of commercial banks operating in Kuwait amounted to seven, the same as today (2004).

The huge revenues generated from oil production that coincided with the rise in oil prices after 1973 resulted in a substantial increase in the wealth of Kuwait and its inhabitants. Some of the increased prosperity was channelled into speculative activities on the Kuwaiti stock market and this resulted in a small stock market crash in 1977.[8] As a response to these difficulties, the government provided compensation for certain investors and also introduced reforms and stricter regulations. The introduction of tougher capital market regulations unintentionally contributed to the creation of an illegal stock market, known as the Suq al-Manakh. The Suq al-Manakh emerged as an unofficial stock market operating alongside the official one and its stocks were mainly traded by wealthy families trading in large amounts. Because deals were undertaken using post-dated cheques, this created a huge demand for credit, and when stock prices fell in 1982, the Suq al-Manakh crashed creating a severe shake-out of the Kuwaiti financial sector and the entire economy. The officials revealed that total outstanding cheques amounted to $94 billion from about 6,000 investors. The debts from the crash left all but one bank in Kuwait technically insolvent. Only the National Bank of Kuwait, the largest commercial bank, survived the crisis. In response, the government devised a complicated set of policies, embodied in the Difficult Credit Facilities Resettlement Program, to bail out banks and investors.

During the Iraqi invasion of Kuwait in 1990, the largest commercial bank in Kuwait (National Bank of Kuwait) was the bank least affected thanks to its substantial international funds.[9] It controlled the exiled government's finances during the invasion. However, over the 1990–4 period in the aftermath of the Iraqi invasion, the annual decline in the Kuwaiti banks' assets reached 6.5 per cent, and the decline in these banks' foreign assets reached 13.4 per cent as the Kuwait government directed these banks to fulfil their international liabilities so as to maintain international confidence in the institutions (Al-Sharrah, 1999).

Since April 1993, the domestic interest rate structure has been linked to the KD discount rate and banks have been permitted to set their interest charges with a margin (not to exceed a certain level) set with reference to the Central Bank of Kuwait's rate. However, since January 1995, all ceiling rates on deposit's were lifted and are now determined according to the market mechanism.

In sum, the Kuwaiti banking sector has been restoring its pre-invasion position. If we look at banking credit over the last decade (see Figure 5.1), we notice that Kuwaiti banking credits were severely affected in the years after the Iraqi invasion. However, banking credit recovered and reached $17.1 billion by 2000, showing more confidence. Total deposits in the banking sector reached $25.8 billion by the end of the decade. Moreover, the level of financial capital and reserves of the banking system reached $5.7 billion, increasing by 50 per cent over the decade and suggesting a strengthened banking environment.

The banking sector in Kuwait has experienced difficult periods over the last twenty years or so resulting from the Suq al-Manakh crash and the Iraqi invasion. However the Kuwaiti banking system has illustrated its resilience in these difficult periods and has emerged as a solid banking system.

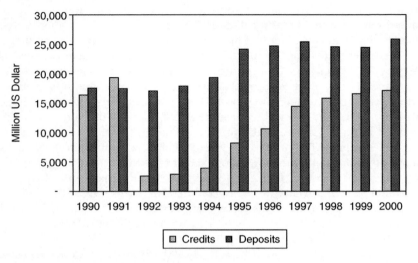

Figure 5.1   Credits and deposits of Kuwaiti commercial banks, 1990–2000
Source: GCC Secretariat General's Economic Bulletin, 2001.

Kuwaiti financial markets

In general, the heyday of Kuwaiti financial markets was in the years before the 1982 stock market crash, when local companies and banks played a leading role in channelling surplus oil revenues from the Gulf into Western capital markets (Presley, 1992). The year of the crash also marked the high point of Arab oil revenues, and by the mid-1980s lower oil prices and healthy economic growth in Western countries had diminished the importance of Arab money to the world financial system. Arab financial institutions in general, and Kuwaiti ones in particular, focused more on internal markets and on readjusting to increasingly strained economic circumstances. From 1982 until the early 1990s Kuwaiti financial markets were in limbo as they reeled from the effects of the crash and were then hit by the Iraqi invasion (Wilson and Presley, 1992). The only significant development of the market was the launching, in 1987, of Central Bank treasury bills and bonds. The general downturn in the Gulf economies at this time meant that banks were looking abroad for assets and that treasury instruments were a way of keeping the money in the country (Presley, 1992).

The commercial bond market started to revive in 1994–5. Kuwait Real Estate Bank issued KD15 m ($50 m) in five-year bonds at the end of 1995 to replace an issue which was maturing. It then issued a further KD20 m in May 1996 to provide additional funding. In October 1997 the Kuwait Investment Projects Company issued KD12 m in five-year bonds. The only other issue since the Iraqi invasion was for a local leasing company, Commercial Facilities Company. Demand for all the issues was healthy and it is expected that the bond market will continue its revival in the years ahead. Both of the Real Estate Bank issues were managed by National Bank of Kuwait while the Projects Company issue was managed by Kuwait Investment Company.

The Kuwait Stock Exchange (KSE) plays a major role in local financial markets and the government has committed itself to an extensive privatization programme which will involve the floating of large blocks of shares in local companies (Al-Attar, 2000). These sales were expected to be the main force reviving stock market activity during the late 1990s. In mid-1998 two stock market investment funds were launched with the aim of attracting new money into local stocks. For the first time, subscription was opened to resident expatriates. However, neither was well received by the market and government companies had to step in to cover the subscription (Al-Ganim, 2000). The KSE has languished since trading resumed after the Iraqi occupation, and at the time when the funds were launched the prospects for significant capital growth across the index as a whole were minimal. While the success of the Commercial Facilities Company issue was expected to lead to subsequent successful offers for existing companies, there was little expectation that the stock market would develop as a vehicle for raising new capital, as was starting to happen in other Gulf countries.

The Kuwaiti government periodically commissions consultants to propose long-term strategic plans for the economy. The best known of these was a lengthy study by the Massachusetts Institute of Technology, which was circulated around government ministries in 1998. These studies invariably propose a liberalization of financial markets and the development of Kuwait into a regional financial centre. Offshore banking is sometimes mentioned as an option. There is little evidence to suggest that the government wants to pursue this course. The development of a major offshore banking centre appears unlikely and developments of capital markets businesses will probably occur at a gradual pace.

Banking in Oman

Banking activities in the Sultanate of Oman commenced a few years following the end of World War II, when the British Bank of the Middle East was the only available bank in the Sultanate, starting its operations in 1948. Although banking activities were relatively limited until the exploration of oil in 1967, the situation changed just three years after the start of the commercial exporting of oil when the Omani banking structure expanded with the opening of three new banks (Central Bank of Oman, 1996; Al-Sharrah, 1999).

Prior to 1970, Oman did not have its own national currency. In 1970, Oman announced a decree establishing the Muscat Currency Authority to act as an official entity issuing Oman's currency (called the Riyal Omani, RO), managing Oman's foreign assets, and accepting deposits from banks in Oman. The British Bank of the Middle East (its Omani branch) was entrusted with administering this entity. In 1972, Oman established the Muscat Currency

Authority to issue the national currency, manage government accounts, and to execute banking transactions with commercial banks and international institutions. Moreover, all banks were asked to acquire licences from this entity in order to practise banking business (Al-Sharrah, 1999).

Together, the Muscat Currency Authority and the Oman Currency Board were the first steps taken towards the creation of the Oman Central Bank. In November 1974, a banking law established the Central Bank of Oman (CBO) that began operations in April 1975. The CBO is empowered to make advances to the government to cover temporary deficiencies in current revenues; to purchase government treasury notes and securities with a maximum maturity of ten years; to make advances to commercial banks; and to buy, sell, discount, and rediscount commercial paper.

The law establishing CBO also facilitated the entry of foreign-owned banks and permitted an increase in the number of local banks in the Sultanate. During the 1970s (the period that witnessed an oil price boom), the number of banks operating in Oman increased, reaching twenty by the end of the decade. In addition, three specialized development banks were established: the Oman Development Bank (1977), the Oman Housing Bank (1977), and the Oman Bank for Agriculture and Fisheries (1981). Although the increase in the number of banks facilitated an inflow of foreign capital and increased funds to the development process, during the early 1980s the CBO froze new bank licensing, fearing that the available number of banks might lead to excess capacity in the Omani banking system. Moreover, the steep fall in oil prices in the mid 1980s exposed the Omani banking system to pressures that led to a rationalization of various lending schemes and forced the authorities to encourage banks to strengthen their capital and to make adequate provisions and reserves.

Bank licensing was relaxed from the mid-1980s onwards and the number of banks increased to twenty-two by the end of 1980s, with nine national and thirteen foreign banks. In 1991, the CBO was given increased powers allowing the central bank to suspend or withdraw licences of banks violating regulatory rules. In fact, the CBO exercised its new power on the Bank of Credit and Commerce International (BCCI) because of the institution's engagement in illegal practices such as weapon finances.[10] The CBO liquidated the BCCI branch in Oman and offered it to a national bank (Bank Dhofar al-Omani al-Fransi), which agreed to take over the BCCI branch in 1992. After this event, Bank Dhofar al-Omani al-Fransi became the second largest bank in the Sultanate after the National Bank of Oman. The restructuring trend in the Omani banking system had already started in January 1989 when the Bank of Muscat purchased the assets and liabilities of the Oman Banking Corporation. Moreover, the first half of the 1990s witnessed a decrease in the number of Omani national banks, falling to only seven banks as a result of various mergers, while the number of foreign banks fell to eleven.

The Central Bank also offered incentives to merger in the form of a five-year tax break and cheap deposits which would be awarded according to the size of the new bank's capital. Oman is also the only Gulf country to have successfully implemented a policy of bank mergers (Azzam, 1998). Several local banks have non-Omani shareholders. The position at the end of 2000 can be summarized as follows:

- Bank Muscat Al-Ahli Al-Omani: Société Générale has a 10 per cent stake.
- Oman Arab Bank: Jordan's Arab Bank has a 49 per cent stake and the managing director is seconded from the Arab Bank.
- Bank Dhofar Al-Omani Al-Fransi: Banque Paribas has a 10 per cent stake and the general manager is seconded from Paribas.
- Bank of Oman, Bahrain and Kuwait: Bahrain-based Bank of Bahrain and Kuwait, itself 50 per cent owned by Kuwaiti financial institutions, has a 49 per cent stake.
- Commercial Bank of Oman: GIBCORP, the local joint venture between Bahrain-based Gulf International Bank and local interests, has a 42 per cent stake and a management contract.
- National Bank of Oman and Oman International Bank are wholly owned by local interests. Bank of Credit and Commerce International (BCCI) had a 40 per cent stake in National Bank and a management contract before it was closed in July 1991.

Three of the local banks are clearly bigger than the others: Bank Muscat Al-Ahli al-Omani, National Bank of Oman and Oman International Bank. All had assets of around $14,800 m and deposits of around $13,500 m at the end of 2000.

The Omani banking system is the smallest in the GCC. The banking system is regulated by the Central Bank of Oman. The Central Bank exercises considerable influence over local banks and there have been no recent examples of commercial banks in Oman defying their central bank's wishes. The Central Bank regularly reviews banking regulations. Changes to the rules are published in its twice-monthly English-language newsletter *Al Markazi* and in the annual report. The most important regulations affecting Omani banks, as listed in the Central Bank of Oman Report in 2001, are the following:

- Banks may not lend more than 15 per cent of their net worth to any one client.
- Total lending may not exceed 75 per cent of deposits and net worth. This ratio rises to 85 per cent when bills of exchange are included in the loan portfolio.
- Banks' open foreign exchange position may not exceed 40 per cent of their net worth.

- 5 per cent of customers' deposits must be kept with the Central Bank. Treasury bills may account for up to 60 per cent of this 5 per cent (that is, 3 per cent of customers' deposits). In this and other Central Bank calculations, borrowings from banks overseas are counted as customers' deposits, while borrowings from local banks are not.

During the 1990s, certain banking regulations were put in force in order to advance the soundness of the Omani banking system. In 1991, the CBO amended the ceiling on the amount banks could lend to their directors from a maximum of 20 per cent to 15 per cent of their capital. Moreover, although banks in Oman had been in full compliance with the Basel capital adequacy minimum requirement of 8 per cent since 1992, the CBO wanted to further enhance the capital cushion, and thus it asked banks in Oman to achieve a minimum ratio of 12 per cent by 1998 (Central Bank of Oman, 2000). This led all banks in Oman to achieve a ratio even higher than the 12 per cent target. Moreover, an expansion in personal lending in 1997 and 1998 induced the CBO to put a ceiling of 30 per cent on the proportion of personal loans in total private sector lending. However, this limit was relaxed in 2000 as the ceiling increased to 35 per cent (owing to the improved macroeconomic climate). The loan to deposit or lending ratio is currently set at 87.5 per cent. The minimum reserve requirement for banks is set at 5 per cent of total deposits. Until 1993, the authorities set ceilings on the interest rates commercial banks could charge on both deposits and loans. In a move toward deregulation, the authorities decided to gradually prepare the banking market for market-determined interest rates. Oman freed up the ceiling imposed on deposits of Riyal Omanis in the last quarter of 1993. In mid-1994, the authorities also deregulated interest rates on consumer loans of RO 9,000 or less. By January 1999, consumer loans were fully deregulated (Central Bank of Oman, 2000).

Over the period 1990–2000, Omani banking credit grew by 198 per cent, increasing annually by an average of 13 per cent over the period, and totalling $7.7 billion by 2000. Total deposits in the banking sector stood at $6.8 billion. In addition, capital and reserves of the banking sector reached $1.1 billion in 2000, reflecting an average annual growth of 15 per cent. Total commercial bank assets reached $15.2 billion in 2000. Overall, these indicators show that, as in other GCC markets, the Omani financial sector has expanded substantially over the last decade. Following a series of mergers during the 1990s, the number of commercial banks at the end of 2000 stood at fifteen; six are locally incorporated and nine are branches of foreign banks.

Omani financial markets

Omani financial markets are based on bank lending and trade finance for the major private sector companies (Azzam, 1998). In 1987 the Central Bank started issuing treasury bills and in 1991 began issues of bonds. The stock market opened in 1989 and has become an important feature of the local financial scene from the mid-1990s onwards. Treasury bills, which have 90-day maturities, are issued by the Central Bank every two weeks. The value of bills outstanding can vary considerably from year to year depending on the banks' liquidity position. In 1999–2000 bills outstanding were valued at about $300–400 m and accounted for about 1–1.5 per cent of banks' total assets. The introduction of Government Development Bonds (GDBs) was a significant addition to Omani capital markets. The bonds are used as a way of funding the government deficit and may be bought by Gulf citizens as well as Omanis. The bonds usually have maturities of 5–7 years although there are occasional issues with longer or shorter maturities.

During 1999 the Muscat Securities Market (MSM) increased its role in local financial markets. During the year $186 m in equity finance was raised by new companies and a further $63 m was raised by existing companies seeking additional capital. The government is committed to privatizing part of its holdings in local companies, and new investment opportunities will also arise from the government's policy of having new infrastructural projects, such as power stations and sewerage systems, constructed on a build–own–operate–transfer basis. The first such project, the Manah power station, was awarded in 1997 to an international consortium led by Belgium's Tractebel and including four local contractors. Authorities are keen to encourage overseas fund managers to invest in Oman and various regulations covering foreign direct investment have been upgraded and clarified during the 1990s. In theory, foreign direct investment is already possible, although in practice it shall remain subject to various restrictions.

Banking sector development in Qatar

Prior to commercial export of oil, Qatar did not have any practising banking activities (Qatar Monetary Agency, 1992). The first-ever bank in Qatar was established in 1950, when the Eastern Bank (known today as Standard Chartered Bank) established its Qatar branch after Qatar's oil exports commenced in December 1949. In 1954 and 1956, the British Bank of the Middle East (now operating as HSBC bank) and the Ottoman Bank (currently known as the Grindlays Bank) respectively opened their Qatar branches. Two Arab banks were also established later: the Arab Bank Limited in 1957 and the Intra Bank (known later as Al-Mashrek Bank) in 1960. Until the mid-1960s, foreign bank branches dominated banking activities, until Qatar established its first national bank (know as the Qatar National Bank) in 1965 with joint-venture capital shared equally between the government of Qatar and the public. The economic expansion in Qatar attracted more foreign banks; thus, in the second half of the 1960s, the government authorized four new foreign banks.

Because of the strong presence of the British administration in the Gulf region, the dominant currencies formerly in circulation were either the Pound Sterling or the currencies that were linked to it, such as the Indian Rupee and the Gulf Rupee (the Gulf Rupee was issued in India and used especially for the Gulf region's cash transactions) (see Qatar Monetary Agency, 1992; Bahrain Monetary Agency, 2002). While these currencies were considered to be the main media of exchange to obtain goods and services in the Gulf region, negotiations between Qatar, Bahrain, Dubai, and Abu Dhabi had been taking place in order to create a common Gulf currency that would replace the aforementioned currencies. However, these negotiations failed to achieve this goal, but they did, at least, lead to a successful agreement, reached in 1966 between Qatar and Dubai, to create one currency to circulate within these two Gulf emirates. The responsibility for issuing and managing this currency was vested in the Qatar – Dubai Currency Board. Prior to the circulation of this new currency (called the Qatar-Dubai Riyal), the Indian government devalued the Indian Rupee by 35 per cent, which was followed by a parallel depreciation of the Gulf Rupee. To ensure a successful debut of the Qatar-Dubai Riyal, the two governments asked existing banks to exchange the Gulf Rupee with this new currency at the pre-devaluation rate. However, for technical reasons, the two governments decided to circulate the Saudi Riyal and withdraw the Gulf Rupee. This was followed by the issuance of the Qatar-Dubai Riyal in the last quarter of 1966 with a value equal to the pre-devaluation Gulf Rupee. The Qatar-Dubai Riyal was also covered by the Pound Sterling; however, when the Pound Sterling was devalued in 1967, the two Emirates agreed to maintain the value of the new currency against gold.

According to the Qatar Monetary Agency (1992), the Qatar-Dubai currency circulated in Qatar until 1972, the year in which Dubai merged in the United Arab Emirates (UAE) and issued its own currency. After gaining independence in 1972, Qatar became a member of the International Monetary Fund (IMF) and in 1973 introduced its own currency (the Qatari Riyal), which was pegged to the IMF's special drawing rights, and then pegged to the US Dollar at a rate of QR 3.64 per $1, which is in effect till today.

Qatar established in 1973 the country's central bank known as the Qatar Monetary Agency (QMA, later called the Qatar Central Bank, QCB). The QMA regulates banking credit and finances, issues currency, and manages the foreign reserves necessary to support the Qatari Riyal. One of the first steps taken by the QMA was to restrict the licensing of new bank establishments or branch openings of foreign banks. The oil boom started in 1973, promoting economic growth, and this resulted in an expansion of the banking sector as three national banks were established during the latter part of the 1970s. Furthermore, another two national banks were added to the banking structure during the 1980s. However, one foreign bank, the Qatar branch of Al-Mashrek Bank – headquartered in Beirut – was closed and put into liquidation in 1989 (Qatar Monetary Agency, 1992).

As a result of the Iraqi invasion of Kuwait, banks in Qatar lost an estimated 15 to 30 per cent of deposits in late 1990, while QMA (with its ready reserves) left banks free to accept or reject the withdrawal of deposits before their maturity but in accordance with their liquidity status.[11] Moreover, QMA directed money exchangers to sell dollars at the official rate, with penalties to be set for any reported violation. These measures adopted during the Gulf crisis maintained confidence and soundness in the financial system that resulted throughout the 1990s.

According to *Gulf Business* (August 2002), one important banking problem occurred in 2000 when one of Qatar's national banks (Al-Ahli Bank of Qatar) was hit by a severe loan problem caused by one of its major corporate client's defaulting. Al-Ahli Bank's credit risk exposure to this corporate was discovered to approach 40 per cent of the total bank loan portfolio. To bail out the bank, QCB rescued the bank on an agreement providing a 10-year guarantee with an amount close to the amount of the bank's non-performing loan ($28 million). QCB has also changed the bank's management and required significant bank restructuring. It has been argued that confidence in Qatar's banking sector would have been harmed if the QCB let this bank fail. Moreover, one of the major weaknesses that appeared to have led to this problem was that the bank's management generally remained under the influence of key shareholders and political figures. This necessitated moves to enhance the management and monitoring systems in order to reduce the likelihood of conflicts of interest in the future.

The current regulations indicate that banks' credits are limited to 95 per cent of their total deposits. In addition, banks must maintain a ratio of no less than 6 per cent of their capital to total assets at all times. Moreover, capital adequacy must maintain a minimum of 8 per cent, in line with the Basel 1988 recommendations. Nevertheless, it should be noted that, starting from the mid-1990s, QCB has gradually lifted the restriction on deposit rates and, currently, all deposit rates are set according to market forces. Banks are also permitted to offer interest on demand deposit accounts with balances exceeding QR 2 million. QCB amended the reserve requirements from 19 per cent on demand deposits to 2.75 per cent effective on the total of all deposit accounts.

Within the period 1990–2000, the level of credit in the economy increased by 188 per cent, progressing by an average annual rate of 13 per cent and reaching $7.6 billion by 2000. Deposits increased by 136 per cent with an annual growth of 11 per cent totalling $9.9 billion by the end of the decade. Bank capital and reserves grew by 61 per cent, achieving an average annual growth of 6 per cent and reaching some $1.7 billion by 2000.[12] Moreover, the level of assets stood at $14.8 billion. The Qatari banking system currently includes fourteen commercial banks, seven national and seven foreign, as well as one specialized bank (Qatar Central Bank, 2000).[13]

Overall, the Qatari banking sector has substantially developed over the last decade or so. The authorities continue to strengthen supervision of the banking system in order to ensure improved soundness and to comply with various international standards. Moreover, the relaxation of various barriers, such as interest rate ceilings, should help facilitate greater competition in the banking system.

Qatari financial markets

Qatari financial markets are among the smallest in the Gulf and are unlikely to develop much during the next few years (Al-Mannai, 2001). The banks' overwhelming focus on the liabilities side is on attracting deposits (especially from the government). The Qatari market is highly liquid and Qatari banks remained net placers of interbank funds even after banking conditions started to tighten in the early 1990s. The government of Qatar raised its first Euroloan in 1989 – $400 m for the first phase of a major gas development project – and has since borrowed a number of times on international markets. Almost all the money raised in this way has come from international banks, with QNB the only local bank to have had any significant role in the syndications (it often takes the role of agent bank). Project finance for industrial expansion has also been dominated by foreign banks. The stock exchange opened in early 1999. Limited share trading is conducted through local banks but the market is currently not a significant factor in the domestic financial scene.

Recent performance of GCC banking systems

In this section we analyze a range of indicators reflecting the main financial features of GCC countries' banking systems. As noted in earlier chapters, one broad type of indicator that can be used to judge the development of the banking system relates to the ratio of bank deposits to the size of the economy. Typically, one can examine the relationship between various monetary aggregates, such as M1 and M2, to GDP (see Figure 5.2).[14, 15] Total GCC countries' money supply in its narrower definition (M1) varied around 20 per cent of GDP over the period 1995–2000. The ratio M2/GDP, which also measures financial deepening, is relatively high, averaging around 50 and 60 per cent over the period. These measures reflect how the GCC banking sector is able to attract deposits, and this degree of monetization reflects the high use of money (cash and banks accounts) in preference to other means of exchange. This also reflects increased confidence in the banking system and suggests a readiness to use technology to serve customer financial needs (Jbili, Galbis and Bisat, 1997).

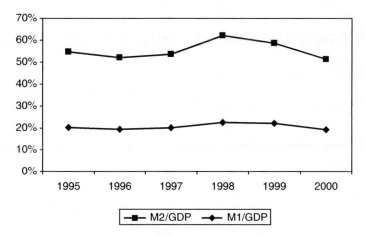

Figure 5.2 Degree of monetization in the GCC countries' banking systems, 1995–2000.
Source: GCC Secretariat General's Economic Bulletin, 2001.

Moreover, the contribution of the financial sector to GCC countries GDP increased from 4.5 per cent in 1990 to 6.6 per cent in 2000, reflecting an increase in importance of the sector. In 2000, the ratio of commercial bank assets to GDP in GCC countries suggested that the banking sector was relatively important since this ratio ranged from about 70 per cent in Saudi Arabia to 125 per cent in Bahrain (excluding offshore banking units assets) and these levels appear relatively high by international standards (see Figure 5.3).

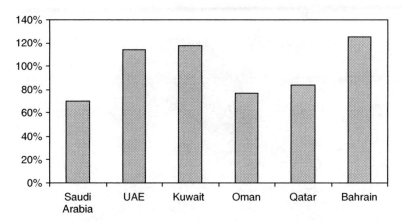

Figure 5.3 GCC commercial bank assets relative to GCC countries' GDPs, 2000
Sources: GCC Secretariat General's Economic Bulletin, 2001; Annual Reports of GCC central banks, 2000.

In terms of size, Table 5.2 shows that the Saudi commercial banking sector was the largest among those of the GCC countries. As of 2000, the figures express the size of the GCC banking market in terms of assets, loans, and deposits.

Bank lending was mainly concentrated in two economic sectors of trade and construction that jointly occupied a stake of 37.4 per cent of total loans in 2000 (see Figure 5.4 and Table 5.3). Over the period 1995–2000, the GCC banks witnessed a remarkable average annual growth of 18.2 per cent in loans to the personal sector, the second position after the trade sector, with 17.1 per cent of total bank loans. This suggests the growing importance of retail banking in the Gulf (Jbili, Galbis and Bisat, 1997).

Table 5.2 Size of commercial banking sector across GCC states, 2000 ($ billion)

	Assets	*Loans*	*Deposits*
Saudi Arabia	121.1	46.2	71.2
UAE	75.5	37.6	36.8
Kuwait	70.4	17.1	25.8
Oman	15.2	7.7	6.8
Qatar	14.8	7.6	9.9
Bahrain	7.9	3.7	6.5

Sources: GCC Secretariat General's Economic Bulletin, 2001; Annual Reports of GCC central banks, 2000.

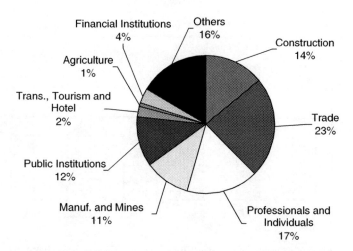

Figure 5.4   Share of commercial banks' credits to the economic sectors, 2000
Source: Authors' calculations based on GCC Secretariat General's Economic Bulletin, 2001.

Table 5.3 GCC commercial banks: credit structure (1995–2000)

Year	Construction	Trade	Professionals & individuals	Manuf. & mining	Public institutions	Trans., tourism & hotels	Agriculture	Financial institutions	Others
1995	13.2%	23.3%	8.4%	9.3%	18.3%	2.6%	0.9%	3.9%	20.1%
1996	12.7%	24.2%	9.1%	8.9%	16.8%	2.0%	0.9%	4.4%	20.9%
1997	13.7%	25.3%	10.6%	9.2%	14.8%	1.9%	0.6%	3.4%	20.5%
1998	13.5%	25.0%	9.7%	10.1%	11.8%	1.6%	0.6%	3.3%	24.5%
1999	14.2%	23.6%	16.7%	11.0%	13.4%	2.6%	0.8%	3.4%	14.2%
2000	13.8%	23.6%	17.1%	10.6%	11.6%	2.5%	0.8%	3.8%	16.3%
Average annual growth (1995–2000)	1.1%	0.3%	18.2%	2.8%	–8.1%	2.9%	–2.2%	0.1%	–1.0%

Source: Authors' calculations based on GCC Secretariat General's Economic Bulletin, 2001.

The main source of deposits generated by commercial banks is interest-bearing accounts (mainly consisting of savings, time deposits, and foreign currency deposits), which account for 65 per cent of total commercial bank deposits, followed by demand deposits (27 per cent) and government deposits (7 per cent) as of 2000.

GCC banking sectors are characterized by high levels of market concentration. In 2000, the three largest banks in Kuwait accounted for about 89 per cent of total commercial banking sector assets, whereas in the least concentrated market, the UAE, the top three held around a third share of banking sector assets. The Qatari banking sector was also highly concentrated, with a three-firm concentration ratio of 69 per cent. Saudi Arabia's three largest banks accounted for half of the domestic banking sector, and both Oman and Bahrain's three-largest banks constituted around 40 per cent of their respective banking sectors. Moreover, the largest bank in Qatar controls around 50 per cent of the banking sector. Similarly, the biggest bank in Kuwait has 44 per cent of the market. The high degree of concentration and the dominant market share of the top banks are also noticeable in Saudi Arabia and Oman (see Figure 5.5). Overall, the high degree of concentration in GCC banking markets (apart from the UAE) suggests that the strict licensing rules and restrictions on foreign bank entry have helped create these market structures. It can be seen that the UAE has the lowest level of concentration and this is almost a consequence of laxity in restrictions on the licensing of domestic and foreign banks that increased the number of such institutions, especially in the late 1970s and 1980s, as was mentioned earlier.

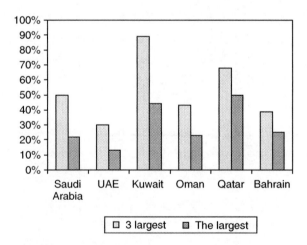

Figure 5.5 Three largest and the largest banks' assets relative to total banking sector assets, 2000

Sources: Authors' estimates calculated using Bankscope (January, 2002); and Annual Reports of foreign banks in Qatar and the UAE (2000).

The following indicators analyze the overall performance and soundness of GCC banks, including the foreign banks that operate in both Qatar and the UAE. Table 5.4 summarizes these indicators that reflect the growth, profitability, capital strength, and asset quality of GCC banks between 1995 and 2000.

As mentioned earlier, GCC countries' commercial banks experienced substantial growth during the 1990s. In general, whether one considers assets, loans, or deposits growth, annual growth rates range around the 10 per cent level. In addition, the equity of the banking systems has increased at an annual rate of around 6 per cent. The growth of the banking system overall is also mirrored by the increased importance of foreign banks in the UAE. For instance, foreign banks in the UAE occupied 26 per cent of the total commercial banking sector in 2000, a percentage that increased from the 22 per cent in 1995. In this country, foreign bank assets have grown faster than those of the national banks, experiencing an annual average growth rate of 9 per cent over the period (UAE national bank assets grew by 6.1 per cent annually over the same period).

In contrast, the share of foreign bank assets in Qatar's banking sector remained unchanged over the 1995–2000 period. While they accounted for 14 per cent of total commercial bank assets in 2000, their assets have grown at a slower rate compared with national banks. Foreign bank assets increased by 50 per cent between 1995 and 2000, while national bank assets grew by 54 per cent. Foreign bank deposits also increased by a lower percentage (51.2 per cent) and with lower average annual growth compared with national banks. However, loans made by foreign banks increased at a faster rate than those of domestic banks, presumably a reflection of the involvement of these banks in financing major gas-industry projects.

The widely used financial accounting profits indicators, return-on-equity (ROE) and return-on-assets (ROA), show that on average GCC banks performed very well in the second half of the 1990s. This was clearly reflected in the average ROEs of 27 per cent and ROAs of 4.0 per cent, which were high figures by international standards. Across GCC countries, banks in Qatar, the UAE, and Oman have generated the highest returns, although profitability elsewhere has been high. Moreover, ROE and ROA indicators show that foreign banks in both Qatar and the UAE generate higher profits than do their domestic peers probably reflecting the different market segments in which the former operate.

The capital ratios (capital-to-loan and capital-to-assets) for Qatari and Omani banks are slightly lower than those of other GCC countries, but they are still high relative to those of many banks in the developed world. Overall, the equity to loans and the equity to assets ratios for the GCC countries (19.3 and 14.8 per cent respectively) show a strong capital position

Table 5.4 Indicators of GCC countries' commercial banks' performance and soundness

The indicators	Qatar			UAE			Saudi	Kuwait	Bahrain	Oman	GCC
	Foreign	National	Overall	Foreign	National	Overall					
Growth indicators											
Total assets annual growth (1995–2000)	4.8%	5.6%	5.5%	9.0%	6.1%	6.7%	6.5%	3.5%	4.4%	16.9%	6.2%
Total deposits annual growth (1995–2000)	5.0%	5.7%	5.6%	8.5%	5.1%	8.2%	6.4%	3.2%	3.7%	14.9%	5.5%
Total loans annual growth (1995–2000)	5.6%	4.7%	4.8%	8.0%	5.7%	6.2%	6.1%	6.8%	4.4%	19.0%	6.9%
Equity annual growth (1995–2000)	5.7%	7.9%	7.6%	6.6%	7.7%	7.5%	5.7%	5.3%	5.0%	21.4%	6.7%
Profitability indicators											
ROE (average 1995–2000)	45.0%	34.0%	39.5%	38.0%	24.1%	31.1%	19.4%	18.4%	21.1%	32.3%	35.4%
ROA (average 1995–2000)	10.0%	3.1%	6.6%	6.6%	4.6%	5.6%	1.9%	2.8%	3.4%	3.7%	4.8%
Capital strength											
Equity to total loans (average 1995–2000)	16.2%	15.9%	16.1%	20.0%	23.0%	21.5%	18.6%	20.8%	22.0%	16.9%	19.3%
Equity to total assets (average 1995–2000)	10.6%	10.1%	10.3%	15.3%	18.1%	16.7%	10.1%	15.4%	17.8%	11.9%	14.8%
Liquid assets to total assets (average 1995–2000)	7.6%	6.7%	6.8%	9.4%	8.6%	8.7%	6.1%	6.8%	4.4%	19.0%	6.9%
Asset quality											
Loan Provisions annual growth (1995–2000)	38.6%	31.1%	34.9%	36.7%	5.3%	21.0%	42.9%	0.6%	37.3%	54.4%	31.8%
Loan to deposit ratio (average 1995–2000)	–	–	–	–	–	–	–	–	–	–	77%
Number of banks	8	6	14	24	19	43	9	10	11	6	93

Notes:
Annual growth (1995–2000) is the average of the rate of change from year to year taken for the whole period.
Average (1995–2000) is the average (or the mean) of the period.
'Overall' is the average for both national and foreign banks.
Sources: Authors' own calculations using Bankscope (January, 2002); and annual financial reports of foreign banks in Qatar and the UAE (1995–2000).

that maintains soundness in accordance with local and international guidelines.

In terms of banking sector liquidity, the ratio of liquid assets to total assets, which includes cash and amounts due from banks, measures the ability of banks to meet unplanned withdrawals. This ratio shows a very high level of liquidity in the Omani banking sector, as it averaged 19 per cent over the period 1995–2000. Liquidity ratios vary between 6 and 10 per cent in most other GCC banking systems, with Bahraini banks having the lowest level of liquidity at 4.4 per cent.

If one considers accounting indicators of credit risk, the average annual growth of loan loss provisions shows high levels for GCC banks; and the annual growth of loan provisions of foreign banks operating in Qatar and the UAE is even greater than that of their national peers. Generally, this indicates the presence of loan problems facing GCC banks during this period, probably a reflection of non-performing loans resulting from the substantial economic downturn and contraction of expenditure in 1998. Moreover, in Qatar, the default of a major corporate borrower of one of Qatar's banks in the late 1990s induced the central bank to take measures assuring the adequacy of provisions to meet possible future defaults in the banking sector.

Despite the high level of loan loss provisioning, the GCC banking sectors have expanded and shown positive performance during the second half of the 1990s. However, an ongoing regulatory process aimed at strengthening prudent regulation and improving loan assessment methods continues to take place in order to ensure that GCC banks comply with both domestic and international safety and soundness standards.

Prospects for financial sector development

The formation of the GCC by Arab Gulf countries aims to establish a foundation for cooperation between countries that will lead to greater economic convergence and a more unified and integrated market. From the date the GCC agreement was signed (1981), negotiations have commenced aimed at increasing the free flow of products and factors of production within GCC countries. The Council's negotiations yielded an agreement, signed in 1999, aimed at unifying trade customs charges. This agreement took effect from January 2003, and under it all products entering the GCC zone will face a unified customs rate. This is expected to increase non-price competition within the GCC zone by encouraging each country to improve their ports and alter trade facilities (by attracting higher volumes, cheaper warehousing services, and so on) so that the cost of imports may foster re-exporting business.

A major part of the GCC economic integration programme focuses on the creation of an economic and monetary union. In achieving this goal, the

GCC has agreed to introduce a unified currency by 2010. Certain steps have clearly been accomplished that will gradually help pave the way to establishing the unified currency. For example, GCC countries have completed a project linking all ATM networks throughout the region. In essence, residents within the GCC countries will be able to obtain money from their own bank accounts at the same cost they pay in their own countries and at the same official exchange rate of GCC countries' currencies. Moreover, the GCC countries agreed at the Omani summit (in 2000) to establish a timetable that enables them to adopt the Dollar as a currency to which all current GCC countries' currencies' will be pegged. (This was in place at the start of 2003 as Kuwait, the only GCC country adopting a basket of currency, pegged its Dinar currency to the US Dollar commencing January 2003.)

The committee of GCC central bank governors is also currently studying ways in which to develop GCC capital markets and especially bond markets, because of their expected positive effect on attracting investment and enhancing monetary policy tools. Moreover, with the aim of encouraging GCC banks to expand regionally, the GCC summit of 2000 issued a resolution urging central banks to allow banks from GCC countries to open branches throughout the region. This calls for GCC countries to change their local laws in order to permit greater bank entry. The impact of this resolution is already bearing fruit. For example, branches of a bank from the UAE have been opened in Saudi Arabia and Bahrain. Bahrain has also permitted the establishment of branches from Oman and the UAE. Qatar also has one branch of a UAE bank. In fact, the phased opening up of GCC banking markets should foster greater competitiveness and this may encourage increased mergers and alliances between banks within the region.

During the 1980s and 1990s, the number of banks operating in the region increased, improving the sophistication of financial activity. In addition, regulatory authorities started to place greater emphasis on financial sector soundness and prudential regulation. As the competitive environment has heightened, this has been accompanied by consolidation and gradual deregulation of various banking and financial systems, a process which will continue.

Conclusion

This chapter reviews the main features of GCC financial systems, namely those of Kuwait, Oman, Qatar, United Arab Emirates, Saudi Arabia and Bahrain. In general, these countries have experienced various financial reforms aimed at strengthening the positive role of their financial systems in the economic growth process. The reforms in the six countries have mainly included moves to deregulate as well as to improve prudential standards. Stock markets have been upgraded and they have begun to play a wider role in financing various economic sectors within their respective countries, although their importance remains limited. Commercial banks still dominate Gulf systems and these are highly concentrated. Gulf systems show favourable growth in terms of their asset quality, capital adequacy and profitability during the 1990s. Such indicators reflect an enhanced role for financial intermediaries in the process of economic growth and exhibit the positive impact of economic and financial reforms undertaken in these countries. Furthermore, financial systems have deepened in these countries and the proportion of credit allocated to the private sector as a percentage of GDP has increased in all six countries, suggesting that banks have become more efficient in allocating financial resources within the respective countries.

Overall it seems that the performance and efficiency of Gulf financial and banking systems have improved during the 1990s. Although it is difficult to say specifically whether this improvement is a result of various reforms or improvements in the general macroeconomic environment, perhaps one can at least suggest that the reform process has had some positive influence. There is also still an ongoing process of liberalization and the moves to create a single GCC economic and monetary union are likely to provide a further impetus to restructuring opportunities and capital market development across the region.

6
Islamic Banking

Introduction

The Arab world has been the cradle of Islamic banking and there are now around one hundred Islamic banks and financial institutions working in the private sector. Islamic financial principles are nowadays a fast-growing feature of all Arab economies. As such, the aim of this chapter is to highlight the history and features of Islamic banking business and analyze its development.

In every economy, there is a need to transfer funds from savers to entrepreneurs. This function is performed through the process of financial intermediation in the financial markets, where banks are the most important operators. Financial intermediation enhances the efficiency of the saving/investment process by eliminating the mismatches inherent in the requirements and availability of financial resources of savers and entrepreneurs in an economy. Savers are often small households who save relatively small amounts and entrepreneurs are firms who often need relatively large amounts of cash. Financial intermediaries remove this size mismatch by collecting the small savings and packaging them to suit the needs of entrepreneurs. In addition, entrepreneurs may require funds for periods relatively longer than would suit individual savers. Intermediaries resolve this mismatch of maturity and liquidity preferences again by pooling small funds.

Moreover, the risk preferences of savers and entrepreneurs are also different. It is often considered that small savers are risk averse and prefer safer placements whereas entrepreneurs deploy funds in risky projects. The role of the intermediary again becomes crucial. They can substantially reduce their own risks through different techniques of proper risk management. Furthermore, small savers cannot efficiently gather information about opportunities to place their funds. Financial intermediaries are in a much better position to collect such information, which is crucial for making a successful placement of funds.

The role and functions of banks outlined above are indeed highly useful and socially desirable, but interest, which is prohibited in Islam, plays a central role in each of these functions. Therefore, Islamic economies have to find alternative ways of performing various banking functions. This challenge provides the rationale of Islamic banking. Islamic scholars and practitioners have developed a number of alternative ways of performing necessary banking activities.

An Islamic bank, like other banks, is a company whose main business is to mobilize funds from savers and supply these funds to businessmen/entrepreneurs. It is organized as a joint stock company with the shareholders supplying the initial capital. It is managed by shareholders through their representatives on the Board of Directors. While a conventional bank uses the rate of interest for both obtaining funds from savers and supplying these funds to businessmen, an Islamic bank performs these functions using various financial modes compatible with the *Sharīʿ ah* (Islamic jurisprudence). A wide variety of such modes of financing are now available. Some of these are described in the Appendix to this chapter.

History of Islamic banking

When commercial banking emerged after the industrial revolution, a very large majority of Muslim scholars expressed their serious reservations with this model of financial intermediation due to its reliance on interest rate, and called for the development of alternative mechanisms to perform the financial intermediation function in Muslim societies. Muslim masses to a very significant extent refrained from dealing with commercial banks. However, growing needs of traders, industrialists and other entrepreneurs in rapidly monetizing economies were pressing. The Muslim economists and banks took up the challenge of developing alternative models of financial intermediation. Valuable theoretical work was done in the early nineteenth century. At that time most of the Muslim world was under colonial rule. When Muslim countries gained their independence after World War II, practical experiments in interest-free financing started on a modest scale and gradually expanded in scope.

While credit societies and cooperatives working on an interest-free basis existed in several Muslim countries even during the colonial period, the semblance of banking institutions started emerging in the early 1960s. A pioneering experiment of putting the Islamic principles governing financial dealings into practice was conducted in Mit-Ghamr, Egypt, from 1963 to 1967. Deriving inspiration from the idea of German saving banks, the Mit-Ghamr initiative mobilized small savings from the rural sector largely through savings accounts. No interest was paid to the account holders. However, as an incentive they were eligible for small short-term interest-free loans for productive purposes. They were allowed to withdraw their deposits on demand. In addition, investment accounts on the basis of profit sharing were also introduced. The funds so mobilized were invested on the basis of profit-sharing with entrepreneurs.

The first interest-free institution with 'bank' in its name, Nasser Social Bank, was also established in Egypt in 1971. This was the first time that a government in a Muslim country showed an interest in incorporating an interest-free institution. Even though the objectives of the Nasser Social Bank were mainly social – such as providing interest-free loans to the poor and needy; scholarships to students; and micro-credits to small projects on a profit-sharing basis – the involvement of a public authority in interest-free banking sent important signals to Muslim businessmen having surplus funds. A group of such businessmen took the initiative of establishing the Dubai Islamic Bank in 1975 in Dubai, United Arab Emirates (UAE). This was the first Islamic Bank established on private initiative. However, the official support was crucial, with the governments of UAE and Kuwait contributing respectively 20 per cent and 10 per cent of the capital.

The most important development in the history of Islamic banking took place with the establishment of the Islamic Development Bank (IDB) in 1975. The IDB was established as an international financial institution in pursuance of the declaration of intent issued by a conference of finance ministers of Islamic countries held in Jeddah, Saudi Arabia in December 1973. The declaration was signed by the representatives of twenty-three member countries of the Organization of the Islamic Conference (OIC). The second conference of finance ministers, held in Jeddah, in August 1974, adopted the Articles of Agreement establishing the Islamic Development Bank. The inaugural meeting of the Board of Governors of the IDB took place in Riyadh, Saudi Arabia, in July 1975 and the Bank started functioning on 20 October 1975.

The period between 1975 and 1990 was the most important period in the history of the development of the Islamic financial industry. During this period, it matured into a viable alternative model of financial intermediation. It won respect and credibility in terms of both theoretical developments and practical experiences. On the one hand, several financial products compatible with *Sharī'ah* were developed, and on the other, Islamic banks showed good results in practice while using these products. The period was not only marked by establishment of a large number of Islamic financial institutions in the private corporate sector under different socio-economic milieu, but also witnessed the expression of intent from three countries, namely, Pakistan, Iran and Sudan, to gradually eliminate interest from their entire economies and substituting it with a complete banking systems based on Islamic principles. Several practical steps were also taken in these countries towards achieving that objective. Even more important was the fact that several important multinational banks started offering Islamic financial products. These included Hong Kong and Shanghai Banking Corporation

(HSBC), Chase Manhattan, Grindlays and Citibank to name only a few. That was a clear recognition of the viability of the new model and its acceptance by international players. The International Monetary Fund and the World Bank also recognized Islamic financial products as genuine means of financial intermediation and produced papers to that effect. Throughout the 1980s, the Islamic banking industry grew at an annual average growth rate of about 15 per cent. In terms of the number of institutions, starting with two in 1975, the number passed 50 by 1990.

In the 1990s while the growth of the banking industry continued, though at a slower rate, attention was also given to non-bank financial institutions. Islamic financial institutions other than banks started coming on the scene in increasing numbers. These included insurance companies and investment funds. While the Islamic insurance sector has not registered sufficient growth, Islamic investment funds have witnessed significant progress.

Initiatives for the establishment of some of infrastructure institutions supporting the Islamic financial industry also started in 1990s. In the beginning, Islamic banking institutions had to work within the institutional framework that supports conventional banking. They were at a comparative disadvantage because that framework was not specifically geared to their needs. A beginning has been made towards constructing a network of supporting institutions for the Islamic financial industry. Some very important institutions have recently come on scene. These include:

- The Accounting and Auditing Organization for Islamic Financial Institutions (AAOIFI)

Shareholders, depositors, investors and regulators utilize information provided in financial statements. If all these statements are prepared on the basis of uniform standards, it facilitates objective comparison between different financial institutions and enables the market discipline to work more effectively. In this regard the Accounting and Auditing Organization for the Islamic Financial Institutions (AAOIFI) is adapting the international standards to suit Islamic financial institutions. The AAOIFI standards were introduced for the first time in 1993 for Islamic financial institutions. The Islamic financial institutions are adopting these standards in increasing numbers.

- International Islamic Financial Market (IIFM)

Islamic financial services industry faces greater liquidity risk due to the absence of a secondary market for Islamic financial instruments. The non-existence of an inter-bank Islamic money market makes liquidity management a challenging task. The Islamic banks are thus under a constraint to maintain liquidity that is higher than what conventional banks do. This adversely affects the Islamic banks' competitiveness. The establishment of an IIFM in

2002 in Bahrain is thus one of the most important building blocks for the Islamic financial services infrastructure.

- Liquidity Management Centre (LMC)

One of the most acute problems facing Islamic banking industry is lack of short-term liquidity instruments and a market for them. It is estimated that the total liquid funds available to the Islamic financial institutions for short-term investments are US$ 20–30 billion. The need of a money market for efficient managing of short-term liquidity is evident. To address this need, the LMC as an operating arm of the IIFM Board was incorporated in Bahrain in February 2002.

- The Islamic Financial Services Board (IFSB)

Proper regulation and supervision of banks and financial institutions is also important for financial efficiency and stability. Some of the risks faced by the Islamic financial industry are unique due to the *Sharīʿah* compliance requirements. Bank supervisors utilizing the traditional standards cannot assess such risks. The need for special guidelines for the regulation and supervision of Islamic banks has long been felt. Some regulatory authorities have already introduced guidelines for Islamic banking supervision in their respective jurisdictions. With an active involvement of the International Monetary Fund (IMF), the IDB and support of the Bahrain Monetary Agency (BMA), Bank Negara Malaysia (BNM) and other central banks, an Islamic Financial Services Board was established in Malaysia in November 2002. Its mandate is to develop prudential standards in accordance with the unique features of the Islamic financial institutions in coordination with the existing standard setting bodies. This will contribute towards the development of a robust and resilient Islamic financial system that can effectively preserve financial stability and contribute to balanced growth and development. This will also facilitate the integration of the Islamic financial system as a viable component of the global financial system.

- The International Islamic Rating Agency (IIRA)

Market discipline is important for an efficient and stable financial system. In this regard, external rating systems and accounting standards play a vital role in improving the availability of information to depositors, bankers and regulators. Existing conventional rating systems are primarily concerned with the financial strength of counterparties and ignore compliance with the *Sharīʿah* requirements. Since non-compliance of even a financially sound Islamic bank with the *Sharīʿah* requirements can be a serious cause of systemic instability, the need for an Islamic rating agency has always been felt. Keeping this need in view, an International Islamic Rating Agency (IIRA) was incorporated in Bahrain in 2002. The IIRA will also scrutinize *Sharīʿah* aspects of financial institutions and products, which will be of major importance to the Islamic financial industry having in mind the global character/appeal of the agency. As a specialized rating agency, the IIRA will be complementary to the existing agencies, adding value to the market. By assessing fiduciary relationship and credit risk inherent in any instrument or issuer, the IIRA will help create a higher degree of confidence and acceptability of products among the players in the industry.

Distinguishing features of Islamic banking

While Islamic banks perform mostly the same functions as the conventional banks, they do it in distinctly different ways. Some of the distinguishing features of Islamic banking are given below:

Risk-sharing

The most important feature of Islamic banking is that it promotes risk sharing between the provider of funds (investor) and the user of funds (entrepreneur). By contrast, under conventional banking, the investor is assured of a predetermined rate of interest. Since the nature of this world is uncertain, the results of any project are not known with certainty *ex-ante*. Therefore, there is always some risk involved. In conventional banking, all this risk is borne by the entrepreneur. Whether the project succeeds and produces a profit or fails and produces a loss, the owner of capital gets away with a predetermined return.[1] In Islam, this kind of unjust distribution is not allowed. In the Islamic banking both the investor and the entrepreneur share the results of the project in an equitable way. In the case of profit, both share it in pre-agreed proportion. In the case of loss, all financial loss is borne by the capitalist and the entrepreneur loses his labour.

Emphasis on productivity as compared to creditworthiness

Under conventional banking, almost all that matters to a bank is that its loan and the interest thereupon are paid to it on time. Therefore, in granting loans, the dominant consideration is the credit-worthiness of the borrower. Under Profit and Loss Sharing (PLS) banking, the bank will receive a return only if the project succeeds and produces a profit. Therefore, an Islamic bank will be more concerned with the soundness of the project and the business acumen and managerial competence of the entrepreneur. This feature has important implications for the distribution of credit as well as the stability of the system.

Moral dimension

The conventional banking is secular in its orientation. As against this, in the Islamic system all economic agents have to work within the moral value system of Islam. Islamic banks are no exception. As such, they cannot finance any project which conflicts with the moral value system of Islam. For example, they will not finance a wine factory, a casino, a night club or any other activity which is prohibited by Islam or is known to be harmful for the society. In this respect Islamic banks are somewhat similar to 'Ethical Funds' now becoming popular in the Western world.

Wider set of products

An important point to be noted in the way Islamic banking works is that it offers a wider choice of products. In addition to some fixed-return modes that can serve necessarily the same functions that interest serves in conventional banking, Islamic banks can use some profit-sharing modes also. The addition of profit-sharing modes to the available menu renders several advantages. Some of these are:

- The allocation of financial resources on the basis of profit-and-loss sharing gives maximum weight to the profitability of the investment, whereas an interest-based allocation gives it to creditworthiness. We can expect the allocation made on the basis of profitability to be more efficient than that made on the basis of interest.
- A system based on profit sharing would be more stable compared to one based on a fixed interest rate on capital. In the first, the bank is obliged to pay a fixed return on its obligations regardless of their fate, should the economic conditions deteriorate. In the latter, the return paid on the bank's obligations depends directly on the returns of its portfolio of assets. Consequently, the cost of capital would adjust itself automatically to suit changes in production and in other business conditions. Furthermore, any shock that might befall the obligations side of the balance sheet would be automatically absorbed. This flexibility not only prevents the failure of the enterprises seeking funds, but also ensures the existence of a necessary harmony between the firm's cash flow and its repayment obligations, that element which enables the financial system to work smoothly.
- Since depositors of Islamic banks, except demand deposit holders, share in the actual performance of the banks, they are expected to remain more vigilant about the performance of banks. That will also contribute to financial stability.
- Since bank assets are created in response to investment opportunities in the real sector of the economy, the real factors related to the production of goods and services (in contrast with the financial factors) become the prime movers of the rates of return to the financial sector.

The transformation of an interest-based system into one based on profit-sharing helps achieve economic growth as this results in increasing the supply of venture or risk capital and, consequently, encourages new project owners to enter the realm of production as a result of more participation in the risk-taking.

Closer link between monetary and real sectors

Another important feature of Islamic banking to be noted is that even in the case of fixed return modes that create debt, like interest-based financing does, there is a crucial difference. Debt creation in Islamic finance is generally not possible without the backing of goods and services and the resultant debt instruments are not tradable except against goods and services. Monetary flows through Islamic financial modes are tied directly to the flow of goods and services. Therefore, there is little room for a sudden and mass movement of such funds as compared to the flow of interest-based short-term funds. Hence destabilizing speculation is expected to be significantly curtailed.

Islamic banking in the Arab world

The Arab world has been the cradle of Islamic banking. As mentioned before, the pioneering experiment (Mit-Ghamr) as well as the first interest-free bank (Nasser Social Bank) started in Egypt. Thereafter also the Middle East remained dominant in the Islamic financial industry. Now there are around a hundred Islamic banks and financial institutions working in the private sector, excluding those in the three countries, namely, Pakistan, Iran and Sudan, which have declared their intention to convert their entire banking sector to Islamic banking.[2] These institutions are spread in a number of countries and continents. The geographical distribution of these Islamic banks is given in Table 6.1. These figures show that the largest number of Islamic banks is in the Gulf Cooperation Council (GCC) countries followed by other Middle Eastern countries. The share of the Arab world in the number of Islamic banks is 58 per cent.

Table 6.1   Islamic banks by regions (2002)

Region	Number of institutions	%
South and South East Asia	18	18.56
GCC	42	43.30
Other ME	14	14.43
Africa	9	9.28
Rest of the world	14	14.43
Total	97	100

Source: Islamic Banking Information System (IBIS), under construction at the Islamic Research and Training Institute, Jeddah.

But that is not the end of the story. While this gives us an idea about the 'spread' of Islamic banking, it does not reflect the relative 'strength' of Islamic banking in various regions because of the relative size of various institutions. In order to see the relative 'strength' of Islamic banking in various regions, the assets of a sample of 30 Islamic banks for which data are available for 2002 are shown Table 6.2.

It can be seen that Islamic banking activity is concentrated in the Middle East, especially GCC countries. This region accounts for 83 per cent of the total assets of Islamic banks. In addition, two major international holding companies, namely, the Dar al-Māl al-Islami and the Al-Baraka Group each of which control about a dozen Islamic banks and finance companies, some of which are operating outside Middle East, are both controlled by Middle Eastern owners. Thus, the real importance of the region in the Islamic banking industry is even higher.

Furthermore, as mentioned above, in Sudan an attempt is being made to convert the whole banking and financial system to the Islamic model. The process of the economy-wide Islamization of the banking system in Sudan started in 1984 when a presidential decree was issued directing all commercial banks to stop interest-based dealings with immediate effect and to negotiate the conversion of their then existing interest-bearing deposits and advances into Islamically acceptable forms. Foreign transactions were allowed to be continued on the basis of interest temporarily. It is reported that this sudden change forced the banks to adopt the nearest Islamic alternative available, that is, *murābaḥah*, which soon constituted 90 per cent of their financial operations. It is also reported that the banks applied Islamic financing techniques only formally in their ledger books and in the reports submitted to the central bank of the country. However, policy-makers in the central bank were also discontented with this procedure of transforming the banking system. They considered it as a mere political decision imposed by the government without being preceded by adequate detailed studies.[3] This

Table 6.2   Assets of Islamic banks by regions (2002)

Region	Assets (million $)	%
South and South East Asia	6765.00	13.05
GCC	38374.50	74.04
Other ME	4806.86	9.27
Africa	NA	NA
Rest of the world	1879.68	3.63
Total	51826.04	100

Source: Islamic Banking Information System (IBIS), under construction at the Islamic Research and Training Institute, Jeddah.

experiment with economy-wide Islamization of the banking system came to an end in 1985 with the change in government. The government revived the process in May 1990 by reactivating an existing Islamic banking law and issued a more comprehensive law in 1992 which envisions an economy-wide Islamization of the financial system including the government sector. The effort is much more earnest and much better organized this time. Now all banks operating in Sudan are using Islamic modes of finance, including branches of foreign banks. Altogether there are 25 banks that are offering Islamic financial products in Sudan.

An important development worth mentioning is the attempt being made to eliminate interest from the government sector also. Other countries have found this a hard nut to crack. The government of Sudan has launched two Funds based on the principle of *mushārakah* to mobilize resources for the public sector. The first is the Government Mushārakah Certificate (GMC). It is an instrument that enables the government to raise funds through issuance of securities that promise the investor a negotiable return linked to developments in government revenue in return for their investment in the provision of general government services. The other is the Central Bank Mushārakah Certificate (CMC). This is an equity-based instrument that is issued against the government (or central bank) ownership in commercial banks. Under CMC, the central bank becomes a partner with the investors in profits of the underlying assets. The distribution of profit between the central bank and the investors is negotiable and the Certificate can be sold on the secondary market to another bank or the central bank.

In Bahrain a different approach towards Islamic banking is being pursued. While the government is not committed to complete Islamization of its banking sector, it lends active support to the Islamic banking industry in a number of ways. Bahrain was amongst the first countries to recognize the importance of the concept of Islamic banking and finance and as a consequence has been both supportive of the development of the industry in general and welcoming to the new institutions in particular. Consequently, Bahrain has gathered a concentration of specialist Islamic institutions on its shores. Today Bahrain has the largest number of Islamic financial institutions not only in the Gulf but anywhere in the world. It is playing host to 25 Islamic banks and financial institutions, five industry-support organizations, six Islamic insurance companies and 34 Islamic mutual funds. A comprehensive prudential set of regulations for Islamic banks was introduced in early 2000 by the Bahrain Monetary Agency (BMA). This is referred to as the Prudential Information and Regulatory Framework (PIRI). The framework covers areas such as capital adequacy, asset quality, management of investment accounts, corporate governance and liquidity management. Within such an environment, the Islamic financial industry in Bahrain is expected to enjoy sustainable growth based upon strong investor and customer confidence, attractive product design and expanding markets. The Bahrain Monetary Agency's statutory responsibility as the sole regulator for the financial sector and the sector's adherence to the Prudential Information and Regulations for Islamic Banks (PIRI) framework ensures that Islamic institutions will continue to operate according to standards comparable to those of the conventional financial sector.

Saudi Arabia is the largest market for Islamic finance in terms of size. The largest Islamic bank in the world, Al Rajhi Banking and Investment Corporation, is based in Saudi Arabia. The bank had $15.8 billion in assets at the end of 2002. In addition, almost all other banks operating in Saudi Arabia are offering Islamic products besides their conventional operations. Saudi Arabia is also home to the largest concentration of Islamic funds. The most important Islamic banking institution, the Islamic Development Bank (IDB), is also headquartered in Saudi Arabia.

The Islamic Development Bank is a Multilateral Development Bank serving the Muslim countries. Its present membership stands at 55 countries. Its purpose is to foster economic development and social progress of member countries and Muslim communities, individually and collectively, in accordance with the principles of the *Sharīʿah*. In order to meet the growing and diverse needs of its member countries, the Bank has established a number of institutions and funds with distinct administrative arrangements and operational rules. These entities and funds, affiliated with the Bank, enable the IDB to mobilize supplementary financial resources in line with the *Sharīʿah* principles and to focus on those functions and activities, which cannot be covered under its normal financing arrangements. With these affiliated entities and funds, the Bank has evolved over time into a group called the IDB Group. During the span of about three decades of existence, the Bank has made significant strides. The Bank has not only successfully attained a respectable position among the multilateral development financing institutions, but also proved to be a model emulated by other Islamic banks. At the end of February 2003 (corresponding to the latest accounting year of the Bank), the authorized capital of the Bank stood at 15 billion Islamic Dinars[4] (ID) (US$ 20.55 billion). Its subscribed capital amounted to 8.1 billion Islamic Dinars (US$ 11.10 billion), whereas its paid-up capital amounted to Islamic Dinars 2.68 billion (US$ 3.67 billion). The ordinary resources of the Bank consist of members' subscriptions (paid-up capital, reserves and retained profits), which amounted to Islamic Dinars 3.90 billion (US$ 5.34 billion).

Several other countries in the Arab world have significant presence of Islamic finance. Kuwait is host to the second largest Islamic commercial bank, the Kuwait Finance House. In addition, there are ten Islamic investment banks and finance companies working in Kuwait. Qatar, Jordan and Yemen also have some Islamic banks and finance companies.

Islamic investment funds and insurance products

Investment funds are considered as one of the most efficient and cost-effective ways of participating in stock markets. Though this investment vehicle suits all categories of investors in the medium and long term, they have several special advantages for small investors. These include, economies of scale and lower transactions cost, lower risk through diversification over industries, countries and currencies, access to global markets and professional portfolio management by fund managers who are more qualified and better informed.

Another reason in favour of the establishment of investment funds is the need for long-term finance in all economies. In a conventional system, this is provided through long-term bonds and equities. Securities markets and specialized equity institutions perform this function. In addition to the general public, the most important sources of these long-term investments are investment banks, mutual funds, insurance companies and pension funds. Since in an Islamic economy use cannot be made of interest-bearing bonds, the need for equity-based institutions is much higher.

Therefore, the important question we need to ask is: can investment funds run on an Islamic basis? Since in most of the Muslim countries, which are the natural domain of Islamic finance, security markets are not well established, another question needs to be posed. Can Islamic investment funds invest in international stock markets, and if so, what *Sharīʿah* conditions need to be satisfied? We deal with these questions in turn.

The basic concept of investment funds, whereby funds are pooled from several investors and managed by others on their behalf, is acceptable under the principle of *wakālah*. The Fund promoter is the *wakīl* (agent) of the unit holders and charges a fixed fee for his services. He can in turn appoint a fund manager on a fixed salary or on a profit-sharing basis. Both of these arrangements are acceptable from an Islamic point of view and are well established. Therefore, investment funds satisfy fundamental principles of Islamic theory of contracts. It is worth noting that investment funds are different from *muḍārabah* accounts in the Islamic banks. The basic difference between the two is that in the latter case the bank is *muḍārib* (working partner) and hence shares in the risk of investment.[5] In the case of investment funds all risk is borne by the unit holders. For the same reason, the fund promoters have no share in profits, all of which after deducting fixed management fees of the promoters is passed on to the unit holders. At the operational level, the basic concept of unit trusts is that risks and rewards are shared by investors (unit holders) who benefit from the expertise of professionals.

Therefore, from a contractual point of view the case for investment funds is well established. However, since the fund promoter is only a '*wakīl*' of the unit holders, it is the unit holders' responsibility to ensure that the particular businesses in which the money of the fund is invested do not violate any *Sharīʿah* principles. These conditions must be specified in the agreement governing the participation in the fund. Once that is done, the Islamic responsibilities of a *wakīl* are well known. He is supposed to work according to the terms of the trust reposed in him. If he violates the terms of that trust, he is liable to penalties.

Once the funds are pooled, they can be used in any *ḥalāl* (Islamically permissible) business. Investment funds can take many forms. They can be 'income funds' targeting at regular incomes, or 'growth funds' targeting at capital gains. They can also be classified by type of business, e.g. Lease Funds, or by industry, e.g. Real Estate Funds, or by commodities, e.g. Commodity Funds or Petroleum Funds, etc. All of these are permissible.

One important type of investment funds needs further comment. These are 'Equity Funds', funds whose main activity is buying and selling of shares of other companies. In this case, it has to be ensured that the business activities of the companies whose shares are bought and sold, themselves are acceptable from the *Sharīʿah* point of view. This is so because shareholders are the owners of the company and as such are collectively as well as individually responsible for its deeds. Islamic scholars have opined that investment in equity funds is permissible if certain conditions are satisfied. They have prescribed three minimum requirements: (i) the fund must not deal in equities of companies whose basic business activity is banned by the Islamic *Sharīʿah* – e.g. breweries, casinos, conventional banks etc.; (ii) interest income earned by the fund must be negligible and separable so that the fund's income can be cleansed of it; (iii) since sale of debt is not permissible except at face value, the proportion of debts receivable in the portfolio of the company should not exceed an 'acceptable' proportion. How these conditions can be complied with in practice is discussed below.

To ensure that the companies selected for the investment are acceptable from the perspective of the *Sharīʿah*, a fund management group can screen the prospective companies to be included in the portfolio. As with other types of ethical investment selection, both positive and negative criteria can be used. Negative criteria involve excluding companies whose major purpose is the production or distribution of alcohol or pork products or the management of gambling facilities or investment in *ribā*-based financial institutions. Some investors may prefer to avoid investing in airlines, hotels or supermarket chains, which serve alcohol, even though this is a minor part of their business. This would however result in a much more restricted potential portfolio. Usually businesses are defined by their prime activity, which makes a hotel group or airline acceptable, but a brewery unacceptable. There are parallels with ethical investment funds, which avoid investing in tobacco companies, but may invest in retail groups selling cigarettes alongside other items.

Second, since according to *Shari'ah* principles both giving and taking interest is forbidden, ideally it would be desirable to avoid investing in companies which have any dealing with *ribā*-based banks, but practically, this would mean the exclusion of virtually all quoted companies, including those whose stocks are traded in the equity markets of Muslim countries. In practice, fund management groups seeking to comply with the *Shari'ah* adopt two criteria. First they examine the extent to which a company's income is derived from interest, any proportion in excess of 10 per cent being unacceptable.[6] The second criterion is to consider the extent of debt to equity finance, a proportion in excess of one-third being unacceptable.

The *Shari'ah* law itself does not specify ratios such as those suggested by some scholars, nor does it establish what factors should be used in any calculations, such as debt to market capitalization versus debt to book values. The latter is arguably more stable, as it is not subject to daily changes in market valuation, and there may be a case for using book values rather than market capitalization as the appropriate screening variable.

It is worth stressing that if all quoted companies that are leveraged are excluded there would be nothing left to include in any investment portfolio. There are also the issues of any interest that quoted companies obtain on their bank balances. Information on such receipts should be available in the annual reports of any quoted company and in the interim statements. One possible solution to this problem is for the fund manager to pay an amount equivalent to the proportion of any dividends derived from interest to charity in order to purify the income. Alternatively the income may be distributed, but the *Shari'ah* committee advising the fund manager may make a recommendation to the investor about the amount he or she should donate to an appropriate charitable cause. It is worth stressing that any manager of a fund designated as Islamic should be able to draw on the services of a *Shari'ah* advisor, or, even better, have the opinion of a *Shari'ah* committee charged with overseeing all operations of the fund to ensure compliance with Islamic law.

Third, according to the majority of Islamic scholars, sale of debt is not permissible except at face value. Now most companies have accounts receivable in their portfolios, i.e. debts. Can shares of these companies be bought and sold? Some *Shari'ah* scholars have argued that the ruling of permissibility depends on what is the dominant component. If the ratio of debts receivable is less than 50 per cent in a company's portfolio, then buying and selling of its shares would be permissible.

As to practice, some Islamic investment funds were established in the early 1970s. Many of them did not survive. The real growth in this sector took place in the 1990s. While definite information on the number of Islamic funds and their size is not available, one source[7] gives a list of known Islamic funds that includes 85 equity funds. This list is, of course, not exhaustive. If we also add other investment funds, e.g. commodity funds, lease funds, trade funds, etc., the number of Islamic investment funds would be in excess of 150. Both Dow Jones and FTSE have launched several Islamic indices which track more than two thousand companies worldwide. They use various screens to produce these indices meeting Islamic criteria for holding equity in these companies. This has led to the involvement of several well-known Western fund managers in the Islamic fund management.

Another segment of the Islamic financial industry relates to insurance. Unfortunately, due to juridical issues which have not been satisfactorily resolved, this segment has not shown enough growth. Due to the element of 'chance' in all insurance contracts, some Islamic scholars likened the insurance business to gambling which is prohibited in Islam. Other scholars have pointed out that the element of 'chance' emerges from the nature of risk. They further point out that all risks that one faces in life are not of the same kind. They make a distinction between three types of risks.

First, there is the risk that can be termed 'entrepreneurial risk'. This risk is part of the normal course of business. Every economic activity involves uncertainty that generates risks. Some agents, called entrepreneurs take those risks. An enterprising person makes profit, as well as, on occasion, incurring losses. However, the fact that society always has such enterprising people is testimony to the fact that, by and large, profit outweighs loss. Willingness to take such risks does not imply any moral evil. Rather, it is a need that no society can do away with.

The second type of risk which is also part of life arises from the possibility of occurrence of natural disasters and calamities. People throughout history have sought ways and means to protect themselves from the occurrence of personal losses due to such calamities. This is the essence of insurance.

The third type of risk arises from uncertainties that are not part of every-day life. They arise from various types of 'games' that people create for themselves. These risks are unnecessary. They are unnecessary for the individual in the sense that if someone chooses not to participate in these 'games', he will face no such risk. They are also unnecessary for the society in the sense that they do not add any economic value to the wealth of the society.

It is the third type of risk that is the essence of gambling which is prohibited by Islam. As to the other two types of risks, both are a natural part of everyday life and must be reckoned and dealt with. Once this is accepted, the concept of insurance becomes acceptable in principle. However, it must be noted that there is an important difference between the first and the second type of risk mentioned above. While the basic motivation for taking the entrepreneurial risk is 'profit', the basic motivation to seek protection against the second type of risk is 'fear'. The loss resulting from such calamities is often huge and may in many cases be beyond the capacity of individuals on which these calamities fall. By paying a small price, called a premium, one can buy 'protection' against such happenings.

Many Islamic scholars have pointed out that there is nothing wrong in seeking protection against sufferings if one can manage to do so, but that nobody should make a profitable business out of the sufferings that naturally befall humanity. This led to the development of Islamic insurance which is based on the concept of *takāful*, which means taking care of one another. Thus, an Islamic insurance company, usually called *Takāful*, has the following features:

- The company is not the one who assumes risks nor the one taking any profit. Rather, it is the participants, the policy-holders, who cover each other.
- All contributions (premiums) are accumulated into a fund. This fund is invested using Islamic modes of investment, and the net profit resulting from these investments is credited back to the fund.
- All claims are paid from this fund. The policy-holders, as a group, are the owners of any net profit that remains after paying all the claims. They are also collectively responsible if the claims exceed the balance in the fund.
- The company acts as a trustee on behalf of the participants to manage the operations of the *Takāful* business. The relationship between the company and the policy-holders is governed by the terms of *muḍārabah* contract. Therefore, should there be a surplus from the operations the company (*muḍārib*) will share the surplus with the participants (*rabb al-māl*) according to a pre-agreed profit-sharing ratio.

In practice, there are about 40 Islamic insurance companies operating in the world outside Iran and Sudan, which as mentioned before, are attempting to Islamize their entire economies.

Regulating Islamic banks

There are three main reasons why regulation and supervision of the banking industry is important: to increase the information available to investors (transparency), to ensure the soundness of the financial system, and to improve control of monetary policy. In the case of Islamic banks, there is an additional dimension of supervision which relates to *Sharī'ah* supervision of their activities. Therefore, regulation and supervision of Islamic banks is as important as, if not more so, than that of conventional banks.

To protect the public and the economy from financial panics, most governments have created elaborate regulatory bodies. As a result, the banking industry has become one of the most heavily regulated industries in the world. In most countries Islamic banks are put under the supervision of the central bank of the country and are given the same treatment as given to conventional commercial banks. Some countries issue special Islamic banking acts to govern the operations of specific Islamic banks and their relationship with the central bank.[8] Some others issue laws that set general rules for the operations of Islamic banks side by side with conventional banks.[9] The regulatory and supervisory framework prevailing at present for Islamic banks in a cross-section of countries in the Arab world is summarized in Table 6.3.

It may be noticed that, by and large, regulatory authorities subject Islamic banks to the same controls, conditions and regulations that they apply to the interest based banks. However, there are certain factors that require that Islamic banks should be treated on a different footing. Some of these factors are now examined

Table 6.3 Salient features of regulation and supervision for Islamic banks in some Arab countries

Country	Salient features of Islamic banking supervisory systems
Bahrain	Regulated by the Bahrain Monetary Agency (BMA). ♦ BMA regulates both commercial banks and investment banks (securities firms); insurance companies are under separate regulatory authority. ♦ Dual banking (Islamic and conventional) banking system; Basel capital requirements and core principles adopted for both groups. ♦ Four Islamic banking groups: (a) Islamic commercial banks, (b) Islamic investment banks, (c) Islamic offshore banks, and (d) Islamic banking windows in conventional banks. ♦ Consolidated supervision. ♦ International Accounting Standards adopted. ♦ Each Islamic bank must have a *Sharī'ah* board. ♦ Compliance with AAOIFI standards under active consideration. ♦ Investment deposits, current accounts and capital allocation for assets must be declared. ♦ Mandatory liquidity management by adopting the standardized maturity buckets of assets. ♦ Islamic and conventional mixed system.
Jordan	Regulated by the Central Bank of Jordan (CBJ). ♦ Separate regulatory bodies for banks and securities firms. ♦ Islamic banking law exists. ♦ Dual system. ♦ Separate *Sharī'ah* board required. ♦ Consolidated supervision. ♦ Basel capital requirements and core principles adopted. ♦ International Accounting Standards adopted.
Kuwait	Supervised by the Central Bank of Kuwait (CBK). ♦ CBK regulates both commercial banks and investment banks (securities firms); insurance companies are under separate regulatory authority. ♦ Dual banking system. ♦ Two Islamic banking groups: (a) Islamic commercial banks, and (b) Islamic investment banks. Conventional banks not allowed to have Islamic banking windows. ♦ Consolidated supervision. ♦ Basel capital requirements and supervisory standards adopted. ♦ International Accounting Standards adopted. ♦ Separate Islamic banking law under active consideration. ♦ Separate *Sharī'ah* board for each bank necessary.
Qatar	Regulated by the Central Bank of Qatar (CBQ). ♦ Dual banking and separate regulatory system. ♦ No separate Islamic banking law exists. ♦ Islamic banks supervised by special directives of CBQ. ♦ Separate *Sharī'ah* boards for banks required. ♦ Standardized transparency requirements for Islamic banks exist.

Sudan	Regulated by the Central Bank of Sudan (CBS). ♦ Single (Islamic) system. ♦ Islamic banking law in place. ♦ Separate *Sharī'ah* boards for banks required, also the Central Bank has a *Sharī'ah* Supervisory Board. ♦ Substantial public sector control; supervision and regulation is effected by other government policies. ♦ Evolution of financial instruments under way. ♦ Compliance with the capital adequacy and supervisory oversight standards of the Basel Committee not clear. ♦ Major bank merger is planned to strengthen bank capital.
UAE	Regulated by the Central Bank of UAE. ♦ Islamic banking law exists. ♦ Dual system. ♦ Islamic banking windows allowed. ♦ Separate *Sharī'ah* boards required. ♦ Basel Committee capital adequacy requirements and supervisory standards in place. ♦ International Accounting Standards in place.
Yemen	Regulated by the Central Bank of Yemen (CBY). ♦ Islamic banking law exists. ♦ Dual system. ♦ Islamic banking windows allowed. ♦ Separate *Sharī'ah* board required. ♦ Major policies and standards set by the CBY are equally applicable to all banks. ♦ Separate supervisory office for Islamic banks inside the CBY under active consideration. ♦ Compliance with the Basel standards not clear.

Source: Adopted from Exhibit 1 in Chapra and Khan, 2000.

Islamic banks, like all other commercial banks, are required to keep some of their deposits with central banks. Central banks usually pay interest on those deposits which Islamic banks cannot accept. An alternative is needed to ensure that Islamic banks get a fair return on their deposits with the central banks.

Central banks function as lenders of last resort to commercial banks, providing loans at times of liquidity crunch. Although most Islamic banks function under the supervision of a central bank, they cannot legitimately benefit from such a facility because such funds are usually provided on the basis of interest. It is understandable that such assistance cannot be free of cost. However, there is a need to devise and implement an interest-free framework for such assistance. The Pakistan Council of Islamic Ideology suggested a profit-sharing mechanism whereby profit can be calculated on a 'daily-product' basis.[10] Another suggestion is to build a 'common pool' by Islamic banks under the supervision of central banks to provide relief to one another in case of liquidity problems on a cooperative basis.[11]

Legal reserves imposed on deposits with conventional banks are meant to meet possible withdrawals, whose rates vary between demand, saving and time deposits. This may apply to the same extent only in the case of Islamic banks' demand deposits. However, the *muḍārabah* deposits are like bank equity. Therefore, Islamic banks should not be required to maintain reserves against them just as equity capital is not subject to those reserves.[12]

In countries where the central bank conducts open market operations, Islamic banks are not able to participate in these operations because of the interest-based nature of the securities bought and sold. Thus, Islamic banks are constrained by the fact that financial assets that could be liquidated quickly are not available to them. This introduces some rigidity in the asset structure of Islamic banks.

Lack of understanding of the correct nature of Islamic financing techniques may also be partially responsible for rather inappropriate policies of the central banks towards Islamic banks. This is particularly true of *mushārakah* and *muḍārabah*. In debt financing, granting a loan by a bank is a one-time activity, no matter what the size of the loan. But *mushārakah* and *muḍārabah* are on-going activities and participation of an Islamic bank in these activities continues as long as the project financed is in operation. This may have important implications for reporting as well as control and regulation of Islamic banks by the central banks.

Central bank regulators are sometimes unclear about the exact role of the *Sharīʿah* Boards. It is sometimes felt that these Boards may interfere in the banks' decisions with regard to monetary policy tools such as reserve requirements, open market operations, etc. It would be desirable to determine the exact role of the *Sharīʿah* Boards and take the central bankers into their confidence.

Prospects for Islamic banking

There is a definite desire amongst Muslim savers to invest their savings in ways that do not involve interest. Prohibition of interest by Islam does not mean zero rate of return for savers and investors. They must be provided with returns on savings and investments through permissible means and modes that are competitive in the market. While Islamic banking fulfils the religious requirements for Muslims, it also broadens the choice-set available to others by offering sales-finance, low-risk products (i.e. buying and selling) and products based on sharing risks and returns.

The development of the Islamic financial industry was greatly helped by the oil boom of the 1970s. Flush with money, Muslim businessmen in the Middle East, who were hitherto reluctant to deal with commercial banks working on the basis of interest, poured billions of dollars into newly established Islamic banks. There is still plenty of scope for expansion in the Islamic financial industry but to exploit that scope the industry has to respond to the challenges from both within and outside. The future of the industry depends on how it faces those challenges. In the rest of this section we discuss what we see as the most important of those challenges.

Until recently, Islamic banks had a fairly large degree of 'monopoly' over the financial resources of Islamically motivated clients. This situation is changing fast. From a specialized niche market, Islamic finance has grown into an attractive global industry. The competition from conventional banks is expected to increase in the near future due to globalization. Electronic banking and widespread use of computers in banking has transformed the way banking is done. The communication revolution through faxes, telexes and emails has reduced the cost of international communication. Now, the saving of one country can be invested in other countries by the click of a mouse. Customers in many countries can now 'navigate' on the internet between competing banks, unit trusts, mutual funds and even business firms. Due to liberalization, the world markets are rapidly converging into a single market place.

This poses opportunities as well as challenges for Islamic banks. On the one hand, it will allow more portfolio diversification and hence reduce the risk in profit sharing modes. This will open up opportunities for Islamic banks to increase the use of such modes. It is also expected that Islamic banks may be allowed to open more and more branches in non-Muslim countries. The possibilities of further deposit mobilization by Islamic banks are the greatest in this area, especially in the Muslim communities of these countries. On the other hand, to benefit from the opportunities offered by globalization, the Islamic banks need to improve the quality of their services and develop suitable new financial products.

At present, Islamic banks are too small to benefit from, or even participate effectively in the process of globalization. In the wake of technological change and globalization, Islamic banks must prepare themselves to handle a much larger size of operations and to deal with internationally minded and financially sophisticated customers. The required infrastructure and the larger and geographically wider scope of operations call for a larger bank size. There is a worldwide trend of mergers. Since the year 2000 alone, dozens of banks and financial companies, which were already very big, have merged to form mega-banks. As against this, the available data show that Islamic banks and financial institutions are much below the optimum size. Considering that Islamic banks and financial institutions are generally very small in size, serious consideration should be given to mergers, syndicated finance, and the creation and management of joint financial services companies. Islamic banks also need to form strategic alliances with Western banks to cope with the implications of globalization in the field of finance. Financial markets can no longer be restricted to national boundaries. Furthermore, there are large Muslim communities in several Western countries. Cooperation with Western banks is also needed to provide financial services to these communities in accordance with their faith.

So far, Islamic banking has largely concentrated on providing short-term finance. This made sense as a beginning because Islamic banking emerged as an alternative for commercial banking which has a strong bias towards short-term finance. However, in all businesses there is need for long-term finance. In the conventional system, this is provided through long-term bonds and equities. This function is performed by securities markets and specialized equity institutions. In addition to the general public, the most important sources of these investments are mutual funds, insurance companies and pension funds. Islamic banks do not deal with interest-bearing bonds. Therefore, the need for equity markets is much higher in an Islamic framework. It may be mentioned here that even in conventional finance there is an increasing trend towards the use of equities as a source of business finance. Islamic financial institutions need to be involved in equity markets. Giving more importance to 'fund management' and building more stock companies, mutual funds, and offering equity-based instruments are some of the actions required. This trend is already gaining ground. We believe this is the area having the most potential for growth in the coming years.

In the aftermath of the Asian financial crisis, the regulation and supervision of financial firms has assumed greater importance. New regulatory standards are being actively discussed. It is important at this stage that Islamic financial institutions are also integrated into the international financial system. It is pertinent to note in this regard that Islamic banking products are unique, and their operational modes are distinct. The regulatory and supervisory standards applied to conventional banking would therefore be insufficient to provide the necessary safeguards for Islamic banking. Ignoring such a fact would leave the whole banking sector exposed, simply because a part of it is not supervised properly. Countries that host Islamic banking and financial institutions have real interests in closing this hole. This can only be done through a coordinating body that produces and enforces sound regulatory and supervisory standards, which would be tailored for the needs of Islamic banking and finance. In this regard, establishment of the Islamic Financial Services Board is expected to fill an important gap. The regulatory framework in the Islamic financial industry needs to address the unique characteristics and attributes associated with Islamic banking operations and Islamic financial instruments. The complexities of the respective risks in the Islamic financial instruments need to be fully explored and quantified to provide for their effective assessment and management. With the advent of Basel II that advocates a higher degree of risk-focused regulatory approach, the Islamic financial institutions would be required to identify and 'unbundle' the risks inherent in Islamic financial instruments. The players in the Islamic financial industry must therefore have in place robust risk management practices and systems.

Most Islamic banks exist as single stand-alone entities. The strength of commercial banking is derived not from individual institutions but by taking all banks together. Inter-bank transactions among Islamic banks are minimal because in most countries the number of Islamic banks is very small. The evolution of short-term financial assets that Islamic banks may hold and transact among them would go a long way towards making an Islamic money market a reality. The establishment of an International Islamic Financial Market is a welcome step, but to make it effective there is an urgent need for developing suitable money market instruments that are compatible with *Sharīʿah*.

Islamic financial transactions are of two kinds. One is based on fixed charge on capital and the other is based on profit sharing. At present, the modes of financing being used by most Islamic banks are dominated by fixed-return modes such as *murābaḥah* and leasing. Even though such modes are clearly distinguishable from interest-based modes since transactions with these modes are always done through real commodities, they do not yield the full benefits expected of an Islamic financial system. Islamic economics specialists had built up their hopes on Islamic banks to provide a significant amount of profit-sharing finance. This would have economic effects similar to direct investment and produce a strong economic development impact. However, due to some practical difficulties, profit-sharing finance has remained negligible in the operations of Islamic banks.

Financing modes like *murābaḥah* are serving a useful purpose: that of providing investors high liquidity with low risk. However, an overwhelming use of these modes has led to some undesirable results, including the problems of default, illiquidity of assets and short-term asset structure.[13] Unfortunately, until a proper institutional set-up is built, and necessary products, including those for managing risk, are developed, it may not be possible for Islamic banks to drastically increase the use of risky modes. However, Islamic banks can be encouraged to provide more profit-sharing finance, if arrangements are made to reduce the costs involved by appropriate institutional arrangements as well as financial engineering consistent with the preferences of fund users. The benefits of direct investment in terms of economic development may not always be fully reflected in the rate of return. They occur to the society as a whole. It may therefore pay to support the involvement of Islamic banks into profit-sharing finance. Until such arrangements are made, banks will not increase their risk exposure to any large extent. In the short run, therefore, the emphasis should move to a greater reliance by businesses on equity and smaller reliance on credit. For this purpose attempts should be made to increase the number of equity institutions such as mutual funds, unit trusts, and so on.

Conclusion

Islamic banking, like any other banking system, must be viewed as an evolving system. Serious research work of the past fifty years has established that Islamic banking is a viable and efficient way of financial intermediation. Islamic scholars and practical bankers have developed a number of financial instruments which can be used by Islamic banks in performing various banking functions in a modern economy. Islamic banking practice which started in the early 1970s on a modest scale has shown tremendous progress during the last thirty years. A number of Islamic banks and other Islamic financial institutions have been established under heterogeneous, social and economic milieu. Recently, many conventional banks, including some major multinational Western banks, have also started using Islamic banking techniques. Various components of the Islamic financial system are now available in different parts of the world in varying depth and quality. A detailed and integrated system of Islamic banking and finance is gradually evolving. To design various parameters of such a system and establish supporting institutions are the biggest challenges facing the scholars and practitioners of Islamic finance in the new millennium.

While Islamic banking fulfils the religious requirements for Muslims, it also broadens the choice-set available to others by offering sales-finance, and low-risk products (i.e. buying and selling), as well as products based on sharing risks and returns. In addition to providing more choices to clients, this mix of fixed and variable return modes has a number of healthy effects for the efficiency and stability of the system. Islamic banking should not be seen as a religious movement. It is simply another way of performing the financial intermediation function, and experience has shown it to be an attractive one.

Appendix: main Islamic banking and finance contracts

An Islamic bank, like other banks, is a company whose main business is to mobilize funds from savers and supply these funds to businessmen/ entrepreneurs. The functions of Islamic banks and other financial intermediaries are similar to their conventional counterparts. Muslim economists have shown that there are alternative Islamic modes and models through which these functions can be performed. While a conventional bank uses the rate of interest for both obtaining funds from savers and supplying these funds to businessmen, an Islamic bank performs these functions using various financial modes compatible with the *Sharīʿah*. The major Islamic modes being used at present are briefly described below.

1. *Muḍārabah* (passive partnership)

This is a contract between two parties: a capital owner (*rabb al-māl*) and an investment manager (*muḍārib*). Profit is distributed between the two parties in accordance with the ratio that they agree upon at the time of the contract. Financial loss is borne by the capital owner; the loss to the manager being the opportunity cost of his own labour, which failed to generate any income for him. Except in the case of a violation of the agreement or default, the investment manager does not guarantee either the capital extended to him or any profit generation. Some other important features of the *muḍārabah* contract include:

- While the provider of capital can impose certain mutually agreed conditions on the manager he has no right to interfere in the day-to-day work of the manager.

- *Muḍārabah* is one of the fiduciary contracts (*'uqūd al-amānah*). *Muḍārib* is expected to act with utmost honesty, otherwise he is considered to have committed a grave sin (in addition to worldly penalties). This has important implications for the moral hazard problem.
- The liability of the *rabb al-māl* is limited to the extent of his contribution to the capital and no more.
- The *muḍārib* is not allowed to commit the *muḍārabah* business for any sum greater than the capital contributed by the *rabb al-māl*.
- All normal expenses related to *muḍārabah* business, but not the personal expenses of the *muḍārib*, can be charged to the *muḍārabah* account.
- No profit distribution can take place (except as an ad hoc arrangement, and subject to final settlement) unless all liabilities have been settled and the equity of the *rabb al-māl* restored.

As a mode of finance applied by Islamic banks, on the liabilities side, the depositors serve as *rabb-al-māl* and the bank as the *muḍārib*. *Muḍārabah* deposits can be either general, which enter into a common pool, or restricted to a certain project or line of business. On the assets side, the bank serves as the *rabb-al-māl* and the businessman as the *muḍārib* (manager). However the manager is often allowed to mix the *muḍārabah* capital with his own funds. In this case profit may be distributed in accordance with any ratio agreed upon between the two parties, but the loss must be borne in proportion to the capital provided by each of them.

2. Mushārakah (active partnership)

A *mushārakah* contract is similar to *muḍārabah*, with the difference that in the case of *mushārakah* both partners participate in the management and provision of capital and also share in the profit and loss. Profits are distributed between partners in accordance with agreed ratios, but the loss must be distributed in proportion to the share of each in the total capital.

3. Diminishing partnership

This is a contract between a financier (the bank) and a beneficiary in which the two agree to enter into a partnership to own an asset, as described above, but on the condition that the financier will gradually sell his share to the beneficiary at an agreed price and in accordance with an agreed schedule.

4. Bay' murābaḥah (sales contract at a profit mark-up)

In the classical *fiqh* literature, there is a sales contract called *bay' mu'ajjal* which refers to sale of goods or property against deferred payment (either in lump sum or instalments). *Bay' mu'ajjal* need not have any reference to the profit margin that the supplier may earn. Its essential element that distinguishes it from cash sale is that the payment is deferred. Strictly speaking, the deferred payment can be higher than, equal to or lower than the cash price. In practice, however, this sale takes the form of *bayʿ al-murābaḥah*, which stands for the supply of goods or property by the seller to the buyer at cost plus a specified profit margin agreed between them.

Islamic banks now use this contract as a mode of finance in the following manner. The client orders an Islamic bank to purchase for him a certain commodity at a specific cash price, promising to purchase such commodity from the bank once it has been bought, but at a deferred price, which includes an agreed-upon profit margin called mark-up in favour of the bank.

Thus, the transaction involves an order accompanied by a promise to purchase and two sales contracts. The first contract is concluded between the Islamic bank and the supplier of the commodity. The second is concluded between the bank and the client who placed the order, after the bank has possessed the commodity, but at a deferred price, which includes a mark-up. The deferred price may be paid as a lump sum or in instalments. In the contract between the Islamic bank and the supplier, the bank often appoints the person placing the order (the ultimate purchaser) as its agent to receive the goods purchased by the bank.

5. *Ijārah* (leasing)

In the simple lease contract the usufruct generated over time by an asset, such as machinery, airplanes, ships or trains, is sold to the lessee at a predetermined price. This is called an operating lease, as against a finance lease. The operating lease has a number of features that distinguish it from other forms of leasing. Firstly, the lessor is himself the real owner of the leased asset and therefore bears all the risks and responsibilities of ownership. All defects, which prevent the use of the equipment by the lessee, are his responsibility, even though it is possible to make the lessee responsible for the day-to-day maintenance and normal repairs of the leased asset. Secondly, the lease is not for the entire useful life of the leased asset but rather for a specified short-term period (for a month, a quarter, or a year) unless renewed by consent of both the parties.

6. A lease ending in the purchase of the leased asset

Since the entire risk is borne by the lessor in the operating lease, there is a danger of misuse of the leased asset by the lessee. The financial lease helps take care of this problem by making the lease period long enough (usually the entire useful life of the leased asset) to enable the lessor to amortize the cost of the asset with profit. At the end of the lease period the lessee has the option to purchase the asset from the lessor at its market value at that time. The lease is not cancellable before the expiry of the lease period without the consent of both the parties. There is therefore little danger of misuse of the asset.

A financial lease has other advantages too. The leased asset serves as security and, in case of default on the part of the lessee, the lessor can take possession of the equipment without court order. It also helps reduce the lessor's tax liability due to the high depreciation allowances generally allowed by tax laws in many countries. The lessor can also sell the equipment during the lease period such that the lease payments accrue to the new buyer.[14] This enables the lessor to get cash when he needs liquidity. This is not possible in the case of a debt because, while the *Sharīʿah* allows the sale of physical assets, it does not allow the sale of monetary debts except at their nominal value.

Some of the jurists have expressed doubts about the permissibility of financial leases. The rationale they give is that the long-term and non-cancellable nature of the lease contract shifts the entire risk to the lessee, particularly if the 'residual' value of the asset is also fixed in advance. The end result for the lessee may turn out to be worse than the outright purchase of the asset through an interest-bearing loan. A financial lease has thus the potential of becoming more exploitative than outright purchase. Suppose the lease contract is for five years. The lessee would have to continue making lease payments even if he does not need the asset, say, after two years. In the case of a purchase through an interest-bearing loan, the purchaser can sell the asset in the market and repay the loan, thus reducing his loss. This he cannot do in a financial lease. If he is unable to make lease payments, he may lose his stake in the asset even though he has paid a part of the asset price beyond the rental charge he would normally pay in an operating lease.

However, there are jurists who consider financial leases to be permissible if certain conditions are satisfied. Firstly, the lessor must bear the risks of leasing by being the real owner of the leased asset. He cannot leases what he does not own and possess, and should be responsible for all the risks and responsibilities related to ownership. Therefore, a leasing contract where the lessor acts only as an intermediary between the supplier and the lessee and plays the role of only a financier, with ownership of the asset being nothing more than a legal device to provide security for repayment of the loan and legal protection in case of default, is not allowed. In this case the lessor leases an asset before buying it and taking possession of it, and gets a reward without bearing any risk. Secondly, lease payments cannot start until the lessee has actually received possession of the leased asset and can continue only as long as it remains usable by him. Thirdly, all manufacturing defects and later damages which are beyond the control of the lessee, should be the lessor's responsibility.[15] The lessee can, however, be made responsible for the proper upkeep and maintenance of the leased asset.

As a form of financing used by Islamic banks in practice, the contract takes the form of an order by a client to the bank, requesting the bank to purchase a piece of equipment, promising, at the same time, to lease it from the bank after it has been purchased. Rent instalments are calculated in such a manner as to include, in reality, recovery of the cost of the asset plus the desired profit margin. Thus, this mode of financing includes a purchase order, a promise to lease, and a leasing contract with a provision to transfer ownership of the leased asset to the lessee at the end of the lease agreement. This transfer of ownership is made through a new contract, in which the leased asset is either given to the lessee as a gift or is sold to him at a nominal price at the end of the lease agreement. According to a decision of the OIC Fiqh Academy, this second transfer-of-ownership contract should be signed only after termination of the lease term, on the basis of an advance promise to effect such a transfer of ownership to the lessee.

7. *Al-Istiṣnāʿ* (contract of manufacture) and *Al- Istiṣnāʿ Al-Tamwīlī* (financing by way of *Istiṣnāʿ*)

Al-Istiṣnāʿ is a contract in which a party orders another to manufacture and provide a commodity, the description of which, delivery date, price and payment date are all set in the contract. According to a decision of the OIC Fiqh Academy, this type of contract is of a binding nature, and the payment of price could be deferred.

Al- Istiṣnāʿ Al-Tamwīlī, which is used by Islamic banks, consists of two separate *istiṣnāʿ* contracts. The first is concluded between the beneficiary and the bank, in which the price is payable by the purchaser in future, in agreed instalments, and the bank undertakes to deliver the requested manufactured commodity at an agreed time. The second *istiṣnāʿ* contract is a subcontract concluded between the bank and a contractor to manufacture the product according to prescribed specifications. The bank would normally pay the price in advance or during the manufacturing process in instalments. The latter undertakes to deliver the product to the bank on the date prescribed in the contract, which is the same date as that stated in the first *istiṣnāʿ* contract. The original purchaser (i.e. the bank's client) may be authorized to receive the manufactured commodity directly from the manufacturer.

8. *Salam*

Salam is a sales contract in which the price is paid in advance at the time of contracting, against delivery of the purchased goods/services at a specified future date. Not every commodity is suitable for a *salam* contract. It is usually applied only to fungible commodities.

Islamic banks can provide financing by way of a *salam* contract by entering into two separate *salam* contracts, or one *salam* contract and an instalments sale contract. For example, the bank could buy a commodity by making an advance payment to the supplier and fixing the date of delivery as the date desired by its client. It can then sell the commodity to a third party either on *a salam* or instalments sale basis. If the two were *salam* contracts, the second contract would be for delivery of the same quantity, description, etc. as that constituting the subject-matter of the first *salam* contract. This second contract is often concluded after the first contract, as its price has to be paid immediately upon conclusion of the contract. To be valid from the

Sharī'ah point of view, the second contract must be independent, i.e. not linked to the delivery in the first contract. Should the second contract consist of an instalments sale, its date should be subsequent to the date on which the bank would receive the commodity.

9. *Wakālah* (agentship)

Wakālah is a contract whereby somebody (principal) hires someone else to act on his behalf, i.e. as his agent for a specific task. The agent is entitled to receive a predetermined fee irrespective of whether he is able to accomplish the assigned task to the satisfaction of the principal or not, as long as he acts in a trustworthy manner. He would be liable to penalties only if it can be proved that he violated the terms of the trust or acted dishonestly.

In the case of a financial *wakālah* contract, clients give funds to the bank/company that serves as their investment manager. The bank/company charges a predetermined fee for its managerial services. Entire profit or loss is passed back to the fund providers after deducting such a fee.

7
Financial System Efficiency

Introduction

We have already noted various features of Arab banking and financial systems and also identified that a major objective of the various financial liberalization programmes undertaken aim to promote more competitive, stable and better-performing operating environments. Inextricably linked to these objectives is the improvement in the efficiency of banks and the financial system overall. This chapter examines the main issues concerning the study of financial system efficiency. Among many functions the financial system performs, there are two that are essential for any economy: one is the administration of the payments mechanism, and the other is intermediation between ultimate savers and borrowers. However, undertaking these functions may not be sufficient for the financial system to maintain its wellbeing and performance. The experience of many financial systems that have experienced financial crises suggests an essential element in the functioning of the financial system is the extent of its efficient operation. This is crucially linked to the soundness and safety of the financial system overall.

The first part of the chapter outlines why an efficient banking and financial system is desirable from a policy standpoint and then goes on to look at different efficiency aspects. The second part of the chapter examines how one can measure banking system efficiency and the main results from the empirical literature. The next chapter will discuss recent empirical evidence on Arab banking sector efficiency.

Why should we be concerned about the efficiency of the financial system?

As the core function of the financial system is to mobilize internal financial resources to finance productive investment, the efficiency of the financial system is an important determinant of its soundness. Over the last two decades, many financial systems have experienced severe currency and banking crises. Such crises occurred in the US banking sector in 1985–92, Mexico in 1994–5, and Asia in 1997–8 (see Krugman, 1998; Mishkin, 2001). One of the major features of these crises was the lack of efficiency in these systems, as well as the lack of adequate regulations to enhance efficiency. For example, Krugman (1998) points out that among the reasons for the Asian crisis was the severity of the moral hazard problem. Banks had been provided with implicit guarantees, which distorted incentives towards making risky loans.[1] These types of loans, which in the case of East Asia were typically loans made to the real estate sector, created a boom in asset prices. When the asset market crashed, many banks faced insolvency problems because borrowers were unable to repay their loans.

In general, international investors seeking more internationally diversified portfolios and better returns on investments may have learned from these crises that questions about how strong (and how efficient) a financial system is really matter.[2] However, it might be hard for an investor to tell which financial system is more efficient than another, especially when it comes to developing countries. The difficulty in choosing an efficient financial system might be due to the lack of any well-known indicators that could be useful to guide international investors to answer the question of how efficient a financial system is. Chen and Khan (1997) argue that foreign incentives to invest internationally depend on the return on foreign investment, which in turn depends on the level of financial development and the country's economic growth. Moreover, empirical studies by Demirgüc-Kunt and Levine (1996) and Levine (1996) on financial development and economic growth provide a set of indicators to measure the level of development of a financial system and how it relates to economic development. From these studies, one may conclude that more developed financial systems may indicate more efficient financial systems. However, the level of development of a financial system does not mean that all efficiency aspects are mature. East Asian financial systems have witnessed relatively high levels of development, but they were inefficient in the sense that they had market imperfections that resulted in an inefficient allocation of financial resources prior to the financial crises.

The study of the efficiency of financial systems before and after crises can provide valuable information for policy-makers (see Berger and Humphrey, 1997). Therefore, it is important that there should be studies evaluating financial systems from an efficiency perspective to judge the health of the financial system and its suitability to encourage capital flow. Studies that measure bank efficiency and performance, stock market efficiency and volatility, regulation and supervisory effectiveness, can help in determining the efficiency features of a financial system.

Defining financial system efficiency

In economics, the word 'efficiency' is always linked to the allocation of resources. Its narrow definition usually refers to resources being employed in a way that gives the maximum production of goods and services. When this is achieved, then allocation is said to be optimal. Generally, the concept of economic efficiency means that the economy produces goods and services that fully reflect the preferences of consumers, given that the production of these goods and services is made with minimum cost. In addition to this, economists may also include environmental and social aspects in the calculus of economic efficiency.

The concept of economic efficiency dates back to the classical school of economics (see Nicholson, 1995, pp. 561–2). Adam Smith's 'invisible hand' and laissez-faire arguments stress that when there is no government involvement in economic activities, the market mechanism will be capable of maximizing individual welfare and allocating resources efficiently. This is because the market mechanism can independently coordinate between buyer and seller interests and reach equilibrium; thus, whenever imbalances in the supply and demand of goods and services occur, the market will automatically readjust itself to achieve equilibrium.

The classical economic view of the predominance of the invisible hand, however, became increasingly questioned in the light of various developments in the early twentieth century. In particular, the Great Depression created a paradigm shift that resulted in Keynes's *General Theory of Employment, Interest and Money* (1936) (see Mankiw, 1994, p. 275). The persistence of depressions has shown that the pure market economy (of the invisible hand and laissez-faire) fails to reach equilibrium and full employment of resources. Keynes stressed the significance of government involvement to revive and stimulate the economy and to help the market to increase efficient allocation of resources. The idea of Keynes has been extended to show other reasons in which market failure (failure to achieve optimal allocation) provides welfare grounds for government involvement in economic activity. For example, the government may intervene to set anti-trust laws that protect market competition.

The aim of both classical and Keynesian schools, when explaining their approaches to methods of achieving an efficient allocation of resources, is to enable the economy to obtain economic stability (i.e. avoid severe fluctuations and crisis) in order to foster productivity. While the aforementioned schools of thought focused mainly on the efficiency of the real sector, the concepts are (obviously) applicable to the financial industry. Based on this link, we can view financial system efficiency as the various elements that should be available to minimize market imperfections and waste in a way that enhances stability and fosters economic productivity. In other words, when financial resources are used efficiently, then stability in the system is enhanced as market imperfections (such as price distortions) are eliminated, and the economy will reflect fundamentals.

Aspects of efficiency as applied to the financial system

The following section presents a wide range of efficiency concepts that have been discussed in the financial literature. Based on the vast literature, the related issues of efficiency, applicable to the financial system can be viewed from several perspectives. Tobin (1984) identifies four major aspects of financial system efficiency. These are: information arbitrage efficiency, fundamental valuation efficiency, full insurance efficiency (or hedging), and functional efficiency. We argue that Tobin's efficiency aspects can be reintroduced in a framework that covers broader aspects of financial system efficiency. As shown in Figure 7.1, there are four main efficiency aspects of the financial system: structural efficiency, informational efficiency (in which Tobin's fundamental valuations efficiency and informational arbitrage efficiency concepts are discussed), operational efficiency (in which Tobin's risk pooling and full insurance efficiency concepts are discussed), and regulatory efficiency. Within this classification, the following also covers, in addition to Tobin's efficiency concepts, various other related issues that impact on financial firm performance.

Informational efficiency

Informational efficiency refers to the extent to which a financial system is able to provide information that helps allocate financial resources to their most productive uses. Indeed, information is one of the most important factors affecting the process of funds allocation. This is because the acquisition of information by both lenders and borrowers may be the main determinant for financing activities.[3] In addition, the more information available on the quality of borrowers (i.e. their success in loans repayment and their projects' feasibility) the more funds the lenders are willing to provide for borrowers.

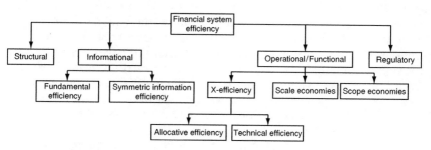

Figure 7.1 Aspects of financial system efficiency

If the lenders lack information, the risk of non-payment of the debt will increase, and risk-averse lenders will be less willing to finance borrowers. In this case, informational inefficiency leads to more market imperfections, which reduces the supply of funds available for economic growth.

Informational efficiency in the financial literature has two related aspects. The first could be viewed as how parties deal with asymmetric information problems. The second is about the ability of the financial markets to reflect the financial asset prices according to market fundamentals.

Symmetric information efficiency

Symmetric information efficiency deals with how the financial system is able to provide all relevant information for parties engaged in financial deals. When the distribution of information between these parties is uneven, then this is known as an asymmetric information problem. That is, when the less informed party deals in a transaction with the more informed party, it is difficult for the less informed party to make accurate decisions.

Asymmetric information in the financial system can appear before and/or after the transaction. Pre-transaction asymmetric information problems relate to adverse selection; while moral hazard comes after the transaction (Mishkin, 1998, pp. 35–6). Adverse selection occurs when the lack of information makes it difficult for the financier to make successful selections. In the case of banking, adverse selection exists when a bank is not able to distinguish between borrowers with low or high default probabilities. In this case, the quality of borrowers would be indistinguishable to the bank. By applying Akerlof's (1970) lemons model, the credit market will suffer from market imperfections in which the lack of information will induce lenders to raise the interest rate. Lenders will tend to do this since a higher interest rate will compensate for unexpected defaults. However, this will bring more low-quality borrowers with high risk and drive out good-quality borrowers with lower risk.

In the case of financial markets, the problem of adverse selection may appear before purchasing a firm's stock. If the securities market fails to reflect the fundamentals in the stock price of the underlying firm, then information about the firm's quality will be difficult to evaluate. For example, when the firm's stock price is overvalued and does not match the firm's profitability, then investors will be reluctant to buy the stock because it is difficult for them to determine the quality of the firm. In this case, the firm might fail to raise the funds it needs. On the other hand, when the overvalued firm succeeds in raising the funds it needs, then it can be said that, due to market imperfections, the stock market has failed to allocate funds to their most productive uses.

The second sort of asymmetric information is called moral hazard. It appears after the parties agree to make a transaction. The hazard in the transaction exists when one of the parties engages in behaviour that is undesirable to the other party. In banking, moral hazard arises when the borrower uses funds in activities that increase the probability of default. In financial markets, since a firm has no obligation to repay the nominal value of the stock, the incentive of firms' managers to undertake risky investments is more likely.[4]

When funds allocation to risky uses becomes a norm for getting high returns, instability in the economy will become more likely. If borrowers fail to repay their loans and firm failure increases, it would be difficult for banks to meet savers withdrawals, and this could make banks insolvent. Moreover, as the likelihood of firms' failures increases, stockholders will still rush to sell shares of these firms, and the stock market might crash.

Therefore, in the absence of an efficient market, asymmetric information problems will increase market imperfections that may destabilize the financial system and the economy. In order to overcome asymmetric information problems, these informational efficiencies (obviously) have to be improved. The literature explains several methods that the financier might use to increase information about the quality of the funds' applicants. Among theses are screening, credit rationing, monitoring and commitment (Stiglitz, 1989; Mishkin, 1998). The first two, screening and credit rationing, are used to alleviate the adverse selection problem. The others, monitoring and commitment, are used to reduce moral hazard.

Screening is a method used by the lender and intermediaries to screen good from bad loans. The lenders collect information on the borrower's historical credit record and evaluate the current status of their creditworthiness as well as how successful the borrowers' future ability to repay the loan. In financial markets, the collection of information about the performance of firms is the tool used by investors to screen firms' quality. Therefore, in order for an investor to accurately judge the stock price of a firm, information available on the firm's performance plays a major role in assessing its stock price. This point will be elaborated below when we talk about fundamental efficiency.

Credit rationing is used by banks in order to reduce the effects of adverse selection. Stiglitz and Weiss (1981) show that as uncertainty and the distribution of information widens, the lack of information on borrowers and their projects may induce the bank to increase interest rates. However, an increase in interest rates will bring another problem to the bank. It will face riskier borrowers instead of safer borrowers since, as in Williamson (1975), high risk increases the adverse selection problem. This is because high interest rates induce the current borrowers to shift to riskier investments as the rate of return increases with the level of risk.

Instead of increasing the rate of interest, banks may ration credit so as to limit the amount of loans according to the expected risk attached to a borrower. Some authors (such as Stiglitz, 1998) have voiced concern about the effect of this method since it causes the level of investment to fall. However, the existence of other sources of funds, such as the securities market, will help mitigate the negative impact of credit rationing on economic growth. Nevertheless, the success of a firm to raise funds from other sources when it fails to do so from banks depends on other elements specific to the firm, such as its reputation and rating records. Also, the level of development of the capital market and the overall financial system are important factors in financing financial deficit agents to find better alternatives to raise funds. In this case, the level of investment will be much less affected (Thakor, 1996).

Monitoring is the method used by the party offering the finance in order to alleviate the problem of moral hazard. The lender oversees the behaviour of the borrower in order to ensure that borrower activities are in line with the contract. In banking, the commercial borrower, for instance, will be asked to provide the bank with audited accounts and other information. In financial markets, firms are enforced to publicize their audited accounts and to have investors informed of the firms' activities. This will make it easier for investors to judge on how well a firm is performing.

Commitment deals with the ways to tackle the incentive distortions that lead to moral hazard. It aims to increase the credibility of the borrowers to maintain the interest of the lenders. Many methods can be used to enhance commitments. For example, banks may design restrictive contracts that confine the loans to be made to only particular projects and activities. Moreover, banks may enforce borrowers to present periodical reports to monitor how the loan is spent on the project. Banks may also ask borrowers to provide collateral in order to get loans. The collateral can effectively influence the incentive of borrowers since it induces them not to use the loans in activities that increase the probability of default; otherwise, they might lose their collateral.

The importance of informational efficiency aspects in alleviating asymmetric information problems is that they contribute to real economy efficiency by deriving social benefits. For example, Boyd and Prescott (1986) show how the screening process allows the financial system to achieve socially beneficial projects by reducing or eliminating inferior projects and diverting resources to more productive projects. Moreover, the collection of information about investors' creditworthiness creates a valuable database for intermediaries and a network of information that facilitates information transmission (Greenwood and Jovanovic, 1990). For example, the existence of private firms (such as Moody's and Standard and Poor's in the US and London-based Fitch IBCA credit rating agencies) specializing in collecting information and evaluating the performance of firms will guide financiers who purchase such information to determine which firms are worthy of receiving funds. These agencies typically rate relatively large companies. However, banks may use consumer credit rating firms (like Experian in the

UK) to credit score retail customers as well as using their own extensive internal databases.

Fundamental efficiency – efficient stock markets

'Fundamental valuations efficiency' is the term used by Tobin (1984) to express how current market prices of assets reflect fundamentals.[5] More precisely, the market is called fundamentally efficient when it is able to set a price of a financial asset equal to the present value of the asset's future income stream. When the market is fundamentally efficient, no one will have an incentive to pay more than what the asset's future income is worth today.

Stock market efficiency may be viewed as the market's ability to reflect fundamental firm value. Since market participants' interaction (ask and bid mechanisms) determine the price of financial assets, it is important that they have accurate information so as to be able to predict (with some degree of certainty) what the future income stream of the stock will be. If they make their decisions according to all information available in the market, then the price of the stock would be the present value of its future income stream. The more information available, the better will be the expectation of the future income placed on it by investors and the more accurate the price set by the stock market. In this sense, the stock market is called efficient when it fully and correctly reveals information on the stock prices of the listed firms.

Efficiency of the stock market may be reduced when there are imbalances in the distribution of information. When there are differences in the level of information obtained, investors with more information would be able to make gains from the trade. From this perspective, Tobin's informational arbitrage efficiency term can be applied here. Tobin views this as when information is equally distributed across all market participants, the investor cannot make any profit from engaging in trade (of a financial asset). This notion can also be applied to explain the role of information in affecting stock market activity. That is, when information is equally distributed across all stock market investors, they cannot make abnormal profits; investors can only make such profits when they have access to some information that is not known to others.

Fama (1970) has utilized the idea of fundamental efficiency to develop hypotheses (weak, semi-strong, and strong form) that assess market efficiency in terms of pricing accuracy. Moreover, Fama's efficient market hypotheses incorporate rational expectations theory to evaluate how information may be used to make abnormal profits. Accordingly, the stock market is efficient when investors cannot make use of historical information (weak form), publicly available information (semi-strong form), and private information (strong form) to make abnormal profits. Therefore, Fama's famous hypotheses assess how far the stock market reveals information so that the stock prices reflect the fundamentals.

It is important that stock markets provide correct price signals for listed firms as stock prices can affect firms' sources of finance. For example, a firm's stock price is the cost at which funds are raised for the expansion of the firm. The higher the price, the cheaper the funds; and the lower the price, the more expensive it is for the firm to attract finance from the primary market. Another reason is that inefficient price signals may affect the net worth (the firm's capital) of the listed firm. If the firm's value is under-priced, it means that the value of the firm's net worth will decline. This might affect the lenders/financiers' attitude towards financing a firm that is not backed by strong capital. In addition, the undervalued firm may further suffer from the contraction of its financial sources, especially when the firm's internal sources of finance are not sufficient.

As noted earlier, incorrect pricing of a firm's stock will also increase the severity of asymmetric information (Greenwald, Stiglitz and Weiss, 1984). Lenders will find it difficult to distinguish good firms from bad firms. That is, they may lend to a firm with high stock prices when in fact the firm's stocks are overvalued; conversely, they may become more reluctant to lend to a good firm when its stock price is undervalued. When the financier feels that the stock market makes the screening of the quality of the firm more difficult, the amount of the funds raised by the firm will be less than needed and therefore stock markets will channel funds inefficiently.[6] Moreover, under-priced firms will face moral hazard problems since managers will have incentives to make riskier investments (in order to generate greater profits) with the aim of appreciating the share value of the company.

Thus, fundamental efficiency stresses the role of stock market efficiency in setting the correct stock prices according to information available. An efficient stock market will reduce price distortions caused by asymmetric information, improve market perfections, minimize moral hazard and should provide greater stability in share prices.

Operational efficiency

Operational efficiency in the financial system relates to the system's ability to organise the channelling of funds with minimum cost. As we will show below, when the cost of intermediation is at a minimum, this means that fewer resources are utilized to channel a greater volume of funds. Operational efficiency has mostly been studied in the context of financial institutions, such as banks (although it can also relate to the operational characteristics of capital market organizations and exchanges).

Before talking about the operational efficiency elements of financial inter-mediaries, it is essential that we explain the bank production process.

Namely, we need to define what a bank or financial firm produces before we can say whether it is relatively efficient or not. The measurement of what a bank produces (its outputs) is a controversial issue in financial studies since the production of financial institutions is characterized by its non-physical (service) nature. In banking studies, there are however two views of measuring outputs: the production and the intermediation approaches. In the production approach, banks are viewed as firms that use labour and capital to produce loans, deposits and other earning assets. In addition, this approach measures outputs as the number of loans and deposits accounts. The intermediation approach views banks as firms that use labour, capital and deposits to produce loans and other earning assets. The intermediation approach measures outputs in terms of their values, but not number of accounts. Therefore, the difference between both approaches lies mainly in whether deposits should be considered among inputs or outputs; and whether banks' inputs and outputs are measured according to the number or value of accounts. Most of the banking efficiency studies adopt the intermediation approach because it is easier in terms of data availability, and because it is at the heart of measuring the cost of intermediating deposits to the receivers of loans (Berger and Mester, 1997).

Returning to operational efficiency, most of the work undertaken in the financial area focuses on modelling the efficiency of banks. In particular, substantial emphasis in recent years has been made attempting to measure X-inefficiency (a term initially coined by Leibenstein, 1966).

X-efficiency exists when banks' cost (or profit) does not deviate from the best-practice cost (profit) frontier. In fact, X-efficiency is the most important part of operational efficiency. As Berger *et al.* (1993b) state, '[t]he one result upon which there is virtual consensus is that X-efficiency differences across banks are relatively large and dominate scale and scope efficiencies'. (This is also noted in Berger and Humphrey, 1991, and Evanoff and Israilevich, 1991.)

X-efficiency is usually decomposed into technical and allocative efficiency. In welfare economics, allocative efficiency is used to show the situation in which the prices of goods and services produced in the economy reflect the minimum cost of supplying them. Thus in perfect competition, consumers pay prices that reflect the minimum cost of production at which producers receive normal profits that are adequate to make their businesses continue supplying the products. In a market with a sole producer, the price is set above the minimum cost, where the price consumers pay deviates from being allocatively efficient. In financial studies, specifically banking, allocative efficiency denotes the ability of a bank to use inputs in optimal proportions with respect to their prices (Farrell, 1957). In banking studies, most authors, including Berger *et al.* (1993a), find that banks' inefficiencies are technical in nature rather than allocative. Therefore, many authors, such as Mester (1993) and Altunbas *et al.* (2000) do not decompose the X-efficiency measurements.

In general, the empirical banking literature provides more attention to technical rather than allocative efficiency.

Technical efficiency relates to the avoidance of excessive use of inputs, i.e. more than that which is optimal for the given level of output (Berger *et al.*, 1993). In banking, the measurement of the optimal use of inputs, once technical efficiency is achieved, involves analysis of the cost or price of inputs. From society's point of view, society is better off if a cost-inefficient bank improved its operational efficiency towards reducing the inefficient and unproductive usage of its inputs. There are many reasons why technical inefficiency might exist. A managerial element might have an influence on a firm's operations through mistakes in choosing the optimal size of inputs. Banks may mistakenly agree to pay high rates for deposits in order to increase their deposits base that would enable them to make larger, more profitable loans. However, if sub-optimal levels of deposits are obtained using this strategy then the bank may not be able to fulfil its output obligations, resulting in a misuse of inputs.

Moreover, the level of competition in the banking system may influence X-efficiency. When competition increases, bank managers may be more inclined to reduce prices to fight against potential erosion of their market share. Also, banks may have incentives to incur high costs in order to provide services that are more attractive to their customers. Banks may even channel the amounts of deposits by making risky loans or by making loans to too many low-return investments. This will lead banks to face delays and probably defaults of their loans, which induce higher monitoring costs accompanied by a reduction in the amount of interest received from loans. In this case, banks will face higher-cost X-inefficiency. The higher-cost X-inefficiency may lead the bank not only to be forced to increase their margins but also to set higher fees on the bank's services to its customers. This may reduce the bank's competitiveness and again expose it to potential solvency problems.

Scale economies exist when a bank operates on its decreasing long-run total average cost curve. There are many empirical studies that investigate the existence of scale and scope economies. Most of them have been undertaken on the US banking system. Generally, one might expect that large or merged banks realize greater scale economies, making them more efficient. However, empirical research has suggested that this is not the case. As an example, the survey article on US banks by Humphrey (1991) has deduced that, on average, banks operate on the constant portion of their average cost curve; where medium-sized banks, rather than large and small banks, tend to be more scale efficient. In a later study, Humphrey (1993) uses different output measures on a sample of US banks and finds that small banks realize scale economies, but medium and large size banks operate at constant and decreasing scale economies respectively. In general, the empirical evidence finds that long-run average cost curves for banks are relatively flat; however, recent studies that look more at large banks tend to find greater evidence of scale and scope economies (this is discussed in more detail later in this chapter).

Scope economies exist when it costs the same or less if one or more outputs are added (to the available output set) than if different firms produce each output separately. Scope economies may be realized when mergers or acquisitions take place between firms producing different outputs. Individual banks producing a variety of services may also be enjoying scope economies. As an example, one bank may provide loans and another bank may engage in portfolio investments. If these two banks join together and produce both loans and investments, scope economies may be achieved when joint production of these two outputs are less costly than the total cost of these outputs being produced separately by individual banks. The majority of empirical studies on scope economies in banking have been undertaken on the US banking industry. Evidence to support the hypothesis that multi-product banks have lower costs than specialists has been put forward in studies such as by Gilligan and Smirlock (1984) and Lawrence and Shay (1986). However, others, including Hunter, Timme and Yang (1990) and Mester (1987) find no strong support for the existence of scope economies in banking.

Other aspects of operational efficiency

Risk-pooling comes from the role of diversification and spread of assets being invested in the financial system (Tobin, 1984). Banks can spread risk across large numbers of borrowers with different risk types, different projects and different sectors of an economy. Also, financial markets allow investors to make their portfolios more efficient by choosing well-diversified assets. The general idea behind risk spreading is to avoid non-systematic risk; that is, the fall in the return of an investment will be recovered by the rise of return of another.[7]

Uncertainty reduction has been explained by Tobin as an aspect of efficiency, which he calls 'full insurance efficiency'. Insurance efficiency implies that the financial system enables its participants to have their financial assets delivered and obtained with insurance against all future contingencies. In other words, this is called 'hedging' against uncertainty. Since the volatility of stocks, interest rates, and exchange rates impede the trade of financial assets, financial derivatives (such as forward contracts, financial futures, options, swaps, and so on) are tools that allow individuals and companies to engage in contracts that contain the delivery of a specified amount and quantity of assets on a certain date. Therefore, future financial instruments are, in general, important for financial system efficiency because they reduce the risk associated with the volatility of asset prices and provide confidence and stability in the transactions within the financial system.

Funds-pooling refers to the law of aggregation as an important efficiency feature of the financial system, which helps maximize the level of funds intermediated in the economy. Banks are the main financial system institutions able to aggregate and pool small savings in order to make large loans. Financial markets can also aggregate small funds from the new issues of reasonably priced stocks and bonds. The law of aggregation can help all society's wealth classes to participate with their funds in a way that matches their wealth capacities.

Structural efficiency

Efficiency is also studied from the view of market structure. Market structure usually refers to the way in which the market is organized in order to provide products for end users (Rutherford, 2000, p. 288). In the financial sector, market structure embraces market competition, the nature of products produced, and the regulatory environment. The study of market structure may also go further to include the question of whether a bank-based or a market-based financial system is more efficient in the allocation of financial resources (see Levine, 2002). For example, the US and the UK financial systems are characterized by market-based finance since the financial markets play a major role in raising funds. In contrast, Japan and most European countries are bank-based financial systems. For developing countries, where financial systems are not so advanced, it may be more preferable that their financial systems be bank-based since banks are better suited in resolving market imperfections created by information asymmetry problems, which may be more severe in developing countries.

If one considers market structure, the level of competition is probably the most important aspect. In the banking industry, one might consider a more competitive market as better in allocating financial resources, increasing consumer welfare and achieving market stability. Although high levels of competition can contribute to the welfare of end users, it may also destabilize the banking system. Stiglitz (1994) has pointed out that increased competition erodes profits and increases the insolvency threat of poorly functioning banks.

When there is a contraction in banks' profitability because of high competition, banks face two main choices: one is to be more cost efficient; the other is to make riskier loans. The problem is that the second choice may tend to be dominant during periods of intense competition. Therefore, when risky loans end up defaulting, the banking system may correct itself by restructuring through takeovers and mergers by banks that are more efficient. However, this usually happens after a crash that may be harmful to the banking system and the economy. As mentioned earlier, in the mid-1980s to 1992, the US savings and loan industry experienced a crisis resulting from severe competition. Moreover, among the causes of the Great Depression's financial crises was the high competition in the banking industry. There-fore, one of the procedures used to restore stability to the banking industry is to limit competition and restrict entry barriers (Dziobek, 1998).

Today, many banking markets around the world appear to have an oligopolistic structure. It has been argued that having a smaller number of banks is preferable, for the following reasons (see Cetorelli and Peretto, 2000). (i) In terms of stability provision, an oligopolistic structure means that banks will face less threat to their profitability, which helps maintain stronger solvency. Policy-makers should not be concerned about consumer welfare issues as long as domestic rates and fees charged by banks are reasonable when compared to other international banking sectors. (ii) A large number of banks means that there might be banks that are poorly capitalized. These banks can be the source of inefficiency and instability to the banking system because insufficient capital may induce them to undertake risky activities (Wachtel, 2000). (iii) Having a small number of banks makes it much easier for the central bank to supervise these banks.

Regulatory efficiency

Financial regulations include a set of rules that organize the operation of the financial sector. Regulatory efficiency relates to how appropriate these rules are in that their benefits should easily outweigh their costs and they should be effective in providing the appropriate level of prudential safeguards. Regulations are said to be prudent when they offer safety and soundness to the financial system in order to protect systems from financial crises. The efficiency of financial regulation derives also from effective supervision. Moreover, regulatory efficiency can also relate to how these regulations enhance efficiency aspects in order to further reduce market imperfections. However, it is known that policy-makers, who set regulations, are also subject to information asymmetries. While regulatory efficiency is difficult to measure, a close watch on the performance of the financial system and its regulatory effectiveness should provide policy-makers with some feedback as to how efficient and effective the regulatory framework is in achieving its goals.

Appropriate surveillance, the collection of information, and the effective implementation of regulations and good supervision are important elements for enhancing the efficiency of the financial system. For example, in cases where financial systems are liberalized, when there are inadequate regulations to restrict the banking and financial sector from taking on excessive risks that expose the system to financial distress, it is then said that regulations are inadequate and inefficient. This is because inadequate financial supervi-sion and regulation is one source of financial instability and crisis (Stiglitz, 1998).

Government regulations aim to improve various sorts of efficiency in the financial system. The government, through either the central bank or other regulatory body, supervises banks' activities to reduce risks, maintain solvency, and enhance/maintain the soundness of individual banks and the system overall. Central banks typically impose reserve requirements as a safety line for banks to provide enough liquidity to meet banks' daily requirement. Banks may also be asked to periodically report their financial transactions to the central bank to check that they abide by these requirements.

One important feature that aims to reinforce the stability of the financial system is that various regulations are set in order to provide guarantees to protect depositors. The deposits guarantee idea originates from the US as a way to rehabilitate and restore confidence in the financial system (e.g. after the Great Depression).[8] Although deposit guarantees can be a way of enhancing the efficiency of the financial system, guarantees may also erode efficiency, as they encourage moral hazard. That is, depositors may care less about imposing discipline on banks' behaviour. Banks know that when they are in trouble their depositors will not withdraw their money because deposits are protected. Moreover, guarantees may further distort banks' incentives since they will be more inclined towards taking risky activities (Mishkin, 1998).

Stock markets, which in most countries are overseen by government agencies, set regulations in such a way as to enhance stock market efficiency. Regulations require listed firms to maintain high reporting and other standards. For transparency purposes, which alleviate the adverse selection problem, firms are required to make their financial reports available to the public. These types of requirements improve stock market efficiency since market participants will make their decisions according to the information being available for all market participants. Moreover, obligations on the minimum accounting standards and contract enforcements limit managerial cheating and correct incentives, which can alleviate the moral hazard problem. Therefore, market prices that are backed by effective regulation are likely to be set on the basis of firms' performance. If this is the case, managers will always try to direct their firms towards productive activities that boost the value of their firms in the stock market.

On the other hand, some government regulations, backed by interventionist policies, have induced substantial inefficiencies. For example, many financial systems, especially in developing economies, have suffered from heavy financial restraints (interest ceilings, high reserve requirements, and exchange rate controls) in order to finance priority sectors (such as the import substitutions industries), as well as to finance government financial requirements (such as budget deficits). These heavy financial restraints created distortions in the prices of resources being allocated in the economy. They also impeded the growth of the size of the financial system since depressed interest rates did not encourage the taking of deposits and thereby investments.

The view that financial repression in developing countries creates an impediment to economic growth and financial sector development has already been covered earlier in this text. For a brief re-cap, McKinnon (1973) and Shaw (1973) note that in order to remove market distortions and promote economic growth, all forms of financial repression should be removed. However, the experience of developing countries that shifted to greater liberalization of their financial sectors (such as in Mexico and East Asia) has provided evidence of the failure of some financial liberalization policies (Stiglitz, 1998). This may be because the context in which financial liberalization was implemented lacked to some extent a variety of regulatory efficiency and other efficiency aspects. For example, in terms of regulatory efficiency, many studies, including Fry (1995), indicate that an adequate level of supervision and regulation must be accompanied by financial liberalization policies. Adequate supervision and regulation must therefore enhance efficiency, resulting in stability and financial (banking) productivity.

Others, such as Stiglitz (1998), reacted to the recent Asian financial crises by advocating mild financial repression that will result in various efficiency gains. Stiglitz argues that, previously, financial restraints were a policy used by various governments to earn 'rents' that enabled them to finance growth projects.[9] In mild financial repression, governments administer interest rates but let the rent be contained within the market. That is, investors and household borrowers will privately allocate the generated rents. The reason why mild financial restraints can lead to more efficiency is that it encourages higher investment since the administered interest rate is meant to be slightly lower than the rate of return on investments. Though savings will be affected, individuals will have more incentive to seek better returns on their financial assets than deposits, given that the elasticity of savings in response to the changes in the interest rate is at least low if not close to zero. The other efficiency benefit of mild financial repression is that low interest rates will induce safer investors to show up (compared to the situation where high interest rates attract risk-seeking investors). Thus the likelihood of defaults will decline, leading to safer and prudent financial systems (see Caprio and Summers, 1993). Therefore, according to these arguments, mild financial repression can improve the efficiency of the financial system.

Measuring banking sector efficiency – theory and empirical evidence

There are many studies that tackle various aspects of the efficiency features of the financial system. These studies have many objectives; although, generally speaking, it is rare to find a single study that examines all the efficiency features of a financial system. In the remainder of this chapter we aim to narrow the focus and examine the theory and empirical evidence on banking sector efficiency.

Importance of bank efficiency studies

Studies on bank efficiency (that examine scale economies, scope economies, and X-efficiency) have gained more attention from financial system policy-makers and regulators, researchers, managers, and owners of financial institutions in recent years.

Policy-makers and regulators can benefit from a further understanding of the efficiency of banks as the performance of the banking sector can impact on certain policies implemented in the financial system. For example, bank efficiency studies are helpful in judging the extent to which changes in the regulatory environment impact on efficiency. For instance, the removal of restrictions (e.g. interest rate restrictions and entry barriers) should stimulate industry performance and create social benefits by reducing waste in resources. Deregulation should foster competition and reduce the market prices of financial services (Berger and Humphrey, 1997). The study of banking sector efficiency can therefore help identify whether policy actions are effective.

Regulators can also use efficiency studies to investigate market structure and performance issues, especially in examining whether bank profitability is driven by market power factors or efficient operations (see Berger, 1995; Molyneux, Altunbas and Gardener, 1996, Ch. 4). Concentrated banking sectors may make banks operating in the same industries earn high profits through setting prices of financial products and services at levels unfavourable to customers. This situation is known as the market-power hypothesis. An alternative view, known as the efficient-structure hypothesis, suggests that more efficient banks are able to generate higher market shares and earn high profits that are mostly induced by competitive prices enabled by efficient operations rather than market power practices. Hence, testing whether the efficient-structure or market-power hypothesis prevails can provide regulators with information about the appropriate conduct of the banking industry.

Studies on efficiency can also provide signals as to the health of the financial sector. They can help to identify efficiency sources that could either strengthen or harm the performance of the banking industry. For example, many studies have found that strong capital levels are connected to efficient bank performance, because banks that perform well are able to generate higher profits that strengthen their solvency base. On the other hand, the level of problem loans is found to be negatively related to bank efficiency (Berger and Humphrey, 1992; Hermalin and Wallace, 1994; Mester, 1996). Studies that link bank efficiency to financial soundness help to provide regulators with information about the source of inefficiency and how this may be related to banking sector risk.

Efficiency studies are important for managers, since, from the point of view of business strategy, managers need to take the steps or find the reasons and the determinants for why and how they can improve their efficient performance from both the input side (by improving cost efficiency using better information technology, managerial practices, and enhancing capital) and the output side (by improving profit efficiency through their marketing and pricing strategies). Efficiency studies can also help managers benchmark the performance of their banks with their main competitors (they can also be used to compare the efficiency of their own branch networks).

Studies on bank efficiency may also be important from a shareholders' perspective because they appoint managers and expect them to run their financial firms efficiently. Having a wider range of best-practice benchmark indicators may help shareholders monitor their managers more effectively. It is clearly in shareholders' interest that managers maintain efficient performance that ensures stable profits and soundness for the bank or banks in question.

Overall, bank efficiency studies can provide results that are of interest to financial policy-makers, financial institution managers and owners. The study of banking sector efficiency can provide useful added information as to the extent of resource deployment in the banking sector, financial institutions' profitability, market power, and the overall safety and soundness of the financial system.

What do banks produce? Defining the bank production process

Before we can measure the efficiency of banks we need to define the production process. In the context of the traditional theory of the firm, banks could be viewed as financial firms that employ certain input resources and transform them into certain outputs. However, the treatment of banks in the context of the theory of the firm is relatively complex, mainly because there is no consensus as to what a bank actually produces. If one considers the production process, it is important to 'appropriately classify outputs and inputs of the financial firm by considering the criteria on which the financial firm makes economic decisions' (Sealey and Lindley, 1977, p.1251). Problems arise, as it is by no means certain as to what constitutes the input or output side of bank production. For example, there is no consensus as to whether deposits should be treated as services that banks produce because deposits are items used as inputs transformed into loans.

Another difficulty associated with banks' production is related to the nature of the bank as a financial firm since its production is characterized by non-physical items, which could lead to measurement difficulty. For example, there is no consensus as to whether it is better to measure banks' output in terms of the number of accounts or the value of these accounts. A bank may appear to have a large number of accounts, but when it is compared to another bank in the same sample, the value of its accounts might be less than the value of accounts of another bank with a lower number of accounts (Heffernan, 1996). In extension, this difficulty in defining bank output may lead to problems in the measurement of bank productivity. For example, is it best to use loans, deposits, or assets to measure the productivity of employees and/or branches? Moreover, even if one defines bank output, problems still remain in identifying the quality of the output.

Since balance sheet accounts are designed to give information on a bank's resources (e.g. financial capital and other liabilities) and the uses of these resources (e.g. the assets side), these accounts may also provide information on a bank's inputs (from the liabilities side) and outputs (on the assets side). As Berger and Humphrey (1990, p. 247) have stressed, '[v]irtually all observers would agree that banks' liabilities have some characteristics of inputs, because they provide the raw material of investable funds, and that bank assets have some characteristics of outputs as they are ultimate users of funds that generate the bulk of the direct revenue that banks earn'. Therefore, although the bank balance sheet may give a potential insight of a bank's inputs and outputs, there is however no consensus as to whether the balance sheet classification of liabilities and assets should be used in explaining the production process of a bank.

The pivotal issue in defining bank inputs and outputs lies on one of the main items of the balance sheet – deposits – an item that has created controversy as to whether this should be considered under the inputs or the outputs classification of a bank production technology. Some studies adopt a dual approach in order to resolve how deposits should be treated. For example, Hughes and Mester (1993) and Bauer *et al.* (1993) have used demand deposits as outputs and time deposits as inputs, considering interest paid as a price of inputs as well as the treatment of interest paid as a part of total cost. However, other researchers have attempted to test empirically whether deposits should be classified as inputs or outputs (see, for example, Hughes and Mester, 1993; Favero and Papi, 1995). The test is generally based on the idea that when the use of some inputs increases, expenditure on other inputs should decrease. The findings of these studies tend to show that deposits are negatively related to other inputs for given outputs, suggesting that deposits are better considered as inputs rather than outputs.

In the banking literature, anyhow, it appears that there are two main lines in defining inputs and outputs of banking institutions: these are the intermediation and the production approaches (see Humphrey, 1985; Berger and Humphrey, 1990). In both approaches, the treatment of deposits is clearly identified.

Basically, both the intermediation and the production approaches agree on the view that labour and physical capital items are inputs used in the banking production process. The main differences between the two approaches lies in how to view deposits and how banks' inputs and outputs should be measured. The intermediation approach treats deposits as a category of inputs since a banking firm's decision-making process relies on deposits to produce earning assets such as loans (Sealey and Lindley, 1977). In contrast, the production approach sees deposits as a part of a bank's outputs, on the grounds that deposits are attracted using bank resources (such as labour and capital) so as to offer customers value-added outputs in the form of clearing, record-keeping, and security services (Bauer *et al.*, 1993; Resti, 1997).

For the measurement of inputs and outputs, the intermediation approach uses the currency value of accounts and considers both operating and interest costs. In contrast, the production approach measures banks' outputs by physical quantities (such as the number of deposit accounts, loans accounts, current accounts, and so on) and considers only operating costs.

Along with the intermediation and the production classification, various other approaches to defining banks' inputs and outputs have been applied in various banking studies. Among these are: the user-cost approach and the value-added approach (see Berger and Humphrey, 1990).

The user-cost approach emphasizes how a category in the bank balance sheet adds to the net contribution of total revenue. Under this approach, a category in the bank's assets is considered an output if its returns exceed the opportunity cost of funds. If not, then this category is considered an input. Likewise, a category of the bank's liability is considered an output if its costs are less than the opportunity cost of the funds; otherwise it is an input.

The value-added approach claims that a category, whether it is in the liabilities or assets sides of the balance sheet, should be considered as a bank's output if the category generates an important value added to a bank. On the other hand, a bank's activities from which the bank creates low added value are treated as unimportant outputs, intermediate outputs, or inputs. For example, balance sheet items such as loans and deposits are expected to be treated as a bank's output since they add a significant amount to the majority of banks' value-added; however, purchased funds are considered as inputs, and government securities are classified as banks' 'unimportant' outputs because of their low value added.

In practice, the intermediation approach is the most widely used in the bank efficiency literature. Many studies adopt this approach for various reasons.[10] Firstly, it conforms with the microeconomic theory of intermediation since this approach emphasizes that funds deposited are intermediated to lenders with minimum costs (Berger *et al.*, 1987; Ferrier and Lovell, 1990). Secondly, Kaparakis *et al.* (1994) adds that it is better to use the intermediation approach when large banks are to be included in the sample; this is because they fund a large share of their assets from non-deposit sources. Thirdly, data on the number of accounts is difficult to obtain, as this information is usually proprietary in nature. Typically, the production approach has been used to study the efficiencies of branches of financial institutions because branches deals with customer documents and process them for the financial institution as a whole, and the managers of these branches have little influence over banks' funding and investment decisions.

Economies of scale in banking

A firm enjoys economies of scale when the production of one more unit of an output leads to a decline in unit production costs. Put simply, scale economies exist when the average cost of production falls as output becomes larger (all other things being equal). If average costs remain the same as output increases we have constant returns to scale, and if they increase, diseconomies of scale are realized.

There are several reasons why bank business may be characterized by scale economies. Forestieri (1993) identifies a number of possible factors that may bring about scale economies in banking:

- Administrative procedures associated with monitoring and screening of borrowers are likely to fall when a firm applies such techniques to a larger number of customers, and this should lead to a declining average cost for loan granting (Arrow *et al*, 1961; Williamson, 1975; Berger *et al.*, 1987; Shaffer, 1991; Humphrey, 1991).
- Larger banks may exploit their size by employing specialized labour (technical and managerial labour) that adopts more efficient organizational forms (Clark, 1988).
- As bank size increases, the use of IT (information technology) helps better utilization of resources because of imperfect divisibility of investments and the facilitation of more flexible production processes (Landi, 1990).
- Some inputs may have excess capacity so that an increase in output only accounts for the exploitation of this capacity, given that the increase in output does not require an increase in all inputs over the entire production period (Bell and Murphy, 1968).[11]

Estimates of the degree of scale economies have important implications for firm expansions as well as for policy implications (Binger and Hoffman, 1988). For banks, it is important to discover the relationship between scale and cost so that the bank, with the scale and output information, knows whether such an expansion leads to an increase or decrease in costs. From a policy perspective, a firm's return to scale has important implications for market structure and entry policies. For example, it is generally expected that when an industry exhibits substantial increasing returns to scale then the industry could become monopolistic in structure. Moreover, a market with a certain group of firms that enjoy increasing returns to scale could be viewed as a concentrated market. This is because economies of scale allow firms to offer more competitive prices and thus capture a larger share of the market. This has implications for merger and competition policy if one knows that economies of scale are important over time. For instance, it helps policy-makers to identify at what levels of concentration further merger and acquisition (M&A) activity may be prohibited. It also informs policy concerning how new entry can be encouraged in the sector. For instance, if optimal size is very large this may limit entry of new firms.

Overall, the studies undertaken prior to 1965 on US banks (for instance, Alhadeff 1954; Schweiger and McGee, 1961; and Gramley, 1962) tend to show that scale economies exist in US banking. Moreover, these studies find that small US banks benefit from scale economies, although there is less agreement on evidence of scale economies for large and medium-sized banks. From the mid-1960s onwards, Benston (1965) and Bell and Murphy (1968) use more sophisticated cost function approaches and tend to find that scale economies are evident for large and medium-sized banks, while large bank exhibit diseconomies of scale. Moreover, these studies generally also tend to show that branch banks operate at higher average cost than unit banks.

Other issues motivated later studies on scale economies. Most importantly, in realization of the shortcomings of the limitations of using the Cobb–Douglas cost function approach, later studies tended to use the more flexible translog cost function approach to model bank costs. For instance, Benston *et al.* (1982) and Berger *et al.* (1987) use the translog approach to distinguish between scale economies at the level of the bank branch office and at the level of the banking firm. They note that holding the number of branches fixed in the cost or production equation does not provide the possibility that both the number and size of branches may expand as production increases. They generally find that scale economies occur at the branch level and scale diseconomies at the banking firm level.[12]

Kolari and Zardkoohi (1987) used US Federal Reserve Functional Cost Analysis (FCA) data for the period 1979–83. The authors estimate three different models representing various aspects of bank production. The first defines bank output as the Dollar value of demand and time deposits, the second uses an output as the Dollar value of loans and securities, and the third model specifies output as the Dollar value of loans and total deposits. Generally, the main findings suggest that cost curves for all US banks are U-shaped. These findings also indicate that unit banks have relatively flat cost curves (constant returns to scale), while branch banks exhibit U-shaped cost curves but these tend to be more upward-sloping – suggesting scale economies at relatively low levels of output.

Humphrey (1987) examined scale economies by investigating cost dispersion among similar banks sizes. He pointed out that the source of cost difference across banks' size could be explained by scale economies across different bank sizes and cost variations across similar-sized banks. In a sample of 13,959 US banks observed over 1980, 1982, and 1984, Humphrey divides bank data into 13 size classes and looks at the average cost of these banks. The author finds that the variation in average costs between banks that have the highest cost in comparison with those having the lowest cost is two to four times larger than the observed differences in the average cost across bank size classes. Moreover, the result on cost economies does not show strong evidence of competitive advantage for large banks over small banks.

Studies that use the translog functional form to model US bank costs, and mostly undertaken in the 1980s, suggest that the estimated cost function is characterized by a U-shaped average cost curve. Although these studies do not consistently show the optimal size for a US banking firm, they suggest that scale economies exist at relatively low bank size levels, somewhere between $25 and $200 million in deposits. As with the earlier Cobb–Douglas studies, while scale economies are found at low levels of bank output they seem to disappear when banks become larger.

Most of the studies on bank cost functions during the 1980s and 1990s focus on identifying the bank size where economies of scale are realized. For example, Humphrey's (1990) survey suggests that very large banks do not tend to exhibit economies of scale. Berger *et al.* (1993b) refer to various other studies (including Berger *et al.*, 1987; Ferrier and Lovell, 1990; Berger and Humphrey, 1991; Bauer *et al.*, 1993) that focus on estimating the minimum level of the U-shaped average cost curve. Taken together, these studies tend to show that banks with assets between $75 million and $300 million tend to have the minimum average cost. Berger *et al.* (1993b), summarizing the findings of Hunter and Timme (1986, 1991), Noulas *et al.* (1990), and Hunter *et al.* (1990), note that for larger banks, having assets over $1 billion, the minimum efficient scale is achieved at assets of $2–10 billion.

While differences in methodological approaches may be one reason for the differences in results, the above evidence indicates little evidence of substantial economies for large banks. Other evidence from the US banking sector that uses alternative nonparametric approaches to model bank costs finds that increasing returns to scale are evident for banks at least up to $500 million in assets size, and constant returns to scale thereafter (McAllister and McManus, 1993; Mitchell and Onvural, 1996).

Similar to the earlier studies, most of the European cost economies studies prior to the mid-1980s used the Cobb–Douglas and CES functional forms to model bank costs. From the mid-1980s the literature uses more flexible functional forms, such as the translog to model banks' production process. Overall, while there is greater evidence of scale economies in European banking compared to the US, there remains little evidence to support the view that scale economies are prevalent for large banks.

Fanjul and Maravall (1985), for instance, study 83 commercial banks and 54 savings banks and use the Cobb–Douglas functional form to estimate scale economies in the Spanish banking market in 1979. Rodriguez, Alvarez and Gomez (1993) also examine scale economies for 64 Spanish savings banks in 1990. Using a hybrid translog function, the results revealed scale economies for medium-sized saving banks, but scale diseconomies were reported for larger institutions.

Vennet (1993) uses the translog functional form and studies 2,600 credit institutions operating in the EU banking industry for the year 1991. The author found scale economies were realized for bank assets sizes in the range between \$3 and \$10 billion. In the cross-country studies on scale economies undertaken by Altunbas and Molyneux (1996) on four European countries (France, Germany, Italy, and Spain), the authors find that scale economies were evident across a wide range of bank sizes. Their findings also indicate strong evidence of economies of scale across all output sizes for French, German, and Spanish banking systems, but not for the Italian banks, which tended to exhibit constant returns to scale. Cavello and Rossi (2001) examine the cost features of 442 European banks over the period 1992–7, and find evidence that scale economies existed in the main banking systems although they were more pronounced for small-sized banks. On studying 15 European countries over the period 1989–97, Altunbas, Gardener, Molyneux and Moore (2001) find that economies of scale were extensive across the smallest banks and banks that range between ECU 1 billion and ECU 5 billion size.

In general, the findings from the European studies reveal greater evidence of economies of scale in banking than the US; however, there is no consensus as to the level of output at which these economies are exhausted (for a more detailed review, see Goddard *et al.*, 2001)

Scope economies

Economies of scope exist when a firm achieves cost savings by increasing the variety of products and services it produces. Unlike economies of scale, which are related to declining average costs for additional unit output produced, economies of scope are related to a decline in the total cost when outputs are produced together in a single firm relative to producing them separately in different firms; or it is cheaper for a firm to produce varieties of outputs by one branch rather than producing them by different branches (see Baumol *et al.*, 1988; Binger and Hoffman, 1988; Sinkey, 1992).

This can be shown in a formal way as follows. Suppose that there are two branches of a single financial firm, A and B, where branch A produces product X and branch B produces product Y; the cost functions for these products in each branch is given by $TC^A (Q_x, 0)$ and $TC^B (0, Q_y)$ respectively. If the financial firm finds that both products X and Y should be produced by only one branch, say A, then the total cost of producing both products by branch A becomes $TC^A (Q_x, Q_y)$, and economies of scope could then be achieved when:

$$TC^A(Q_x, Q_y) < [TC^A(Q_x, 0) + TC^B(0, Q_y)]$$

This mathematical expression says that the total cost of the joint production of both products X and Y, TC (Q_x, Q_y), produced by a single branch, branch A, is less than the sum of total cost of each product produced separately in both branches A and B. The extent to which scope economies can exist for a firm (or a branch) can be measured by:

$$S = \frac{[TC^A(Q_x, 0) + TC^B(0, Q_y)] - TC^A(Q_x, Q_y)}{[TC^A(Q_x, 0) + TC^B(0, Q_y)]}$$

A negative value for S would mean diseconomies of scope because it is more expensive to combine the production of X and Y in one branch, A. It is only when S is positive that economies of scope exist, and the closer the value of S to one the more important it is to limit the production of the two outputs to a single branch A.

Several reasons can be put forward to explain why joint production may be less costly than producing the same products separately by different entities. Berger *et al.* (1987) point out several reasons, such as: fixed costs can be spread over a wider range of outputs and levels, information economies exist that can lead to a reuse of the same information on the other types of output that share similar characteristics, and risk reductions obtained through more diversified outputs. Mester (1994) notes that the most important source of economies of scope relates to the share of a large range of inputs in the production of several outputs. As fixed inputs are heavily used in the production of both outputs, the firm witnesses a decline in average costs as fixed costs can be spread across multiple outputs. From this perception, one can find a connection between economies of scale and scope, where the spreading of fixed costs over a wider range of output volumes leads to greater cost savings per unit of outputs.

Scope economies are often cited as the reason why a bank may diversify into different product areas – such as selling insurance and mutual funds; the argument being that there is cost savings associated with the cross-selling of financial products. As such, the scope economy argument is used to justify the rationale for universal banking and bancassurance business.

The results of cost economies studies on the US banking industry generally suggest a weak presence of scope economies. Gilligan and Smirlock (1984) use a sample of 2,700 US banks with balance sheet data covering the period 1973–8 to examine scope economies. They use two outputs defined in terms of either liabilities (demand and time deposits), or assets (securities and loans outstanding). Their results indicate that the costs of producing one output depend on the level of other outputs, implying the existence of economies of scope. Mester (1987) reviews a number of studies that investigate economies of scale and scope in US banks between the period 1983 and 1986. Mester infers that the surveyed studies tend to find no evidence of the existence of economies of scope in US banking. Lawrence and Shay (1986) examine economies of scope in US banking over the period 1978–82. Using a generalized functional form and three outputs (deposits, investments, and loans), the authors find that cost complementarities are present in the joint production of these outputs, thus suggesting the presence of the economies of scope. On the other hand, Hunter, Timme and Yang (1990) examine economies of scope in a sample of 311 large US banks at the end of 1986. The results indicate non-presence of a sub-additive cost function which also indicates the absence of cost complementarities. Their conclusion stresses that there is no evidence found for the presence of economies of scope in large US banks.[13]

As in the case of the US literature, little evidence is available on scope economies in European banking. Altunbas and Molyneux (1996) tested for the presence of economies of scope on the basis that joint production of loans and securities is less costly than their production in separate banks. The study covers a number of European countries, and the results they find are mixed. In France, the authors found that medium-sized banks show economies of scope. In Spain, banks with less than $1 billion in assets are found to enjoy substantial economies of scope, while German banks of the same assets size experience scope diseconomies. In Vennet's (1993) study on cost economies of credit institutions operating in the EU, large banks were found to enjoy economies of scope. Moreover, Lang and Welzel (1996) examined cost economies for German cooperative banks. Using the standard translog cost function, the authors found that economies of scope were prevalent for the largest banks.

Overall, there is rather limited evidence on scope economies in banking. This relates to the difficulty in estimating scope economies, as estimates tend to be sensitive to different output and input specifications. In addition, scale economies seem to be more prevalent than scope economies, given evidence from the empirical literature. The next section examines efficiencies unrelated to size (scale) and product mix (scope) and these are known as X-efficiency.

X-efficiency in banking

In the previous sections we show that scale economies are realized by producing outputs at levels where a bank operates on the decreasing average cost. Scope economies are achieved when a bank jointly produces outputs that result in cost savings compared to the cost of separate production of these outputs. In fact, until the late 1980s, the focus of the literature was extensively directed towards the study of scale and scope economies. These studies are mostly concerned with the issue of inefficiency due to non-exploitation in the utilized output mix or scale of production.[14] In this sense, Fukuyama (1993) and Drake and Simper (1999) assert that, in these studies, it is implicitly or sometimes explicitly assumed that banks are efficient, that is, their input mix is at the cost frontier, or their output mix is on the production frontier.

X-(in)efficiency is part of operational efficiency and is a term introduced by Leibenstein (1966). Leibenstein's view on X-inefficiency is based on the description of a firm that produces at less than the optimum level. In general, the banking literature considers X-inefficiency as having two components: allocative inefficiency and technical inefficiency. Allocative inefficiency reflects the failure to choose an optimal input mix in reaction to relative input prices. Technical inefficiency exists when employing an excessive level of inputs for certain output production.

The banking efficiency literature considers that the term X-inefficiency incorporates both allocative and technical inefficiency. Failure to achieve both technical and allocative efficiencies leads to X-inefficiency, which is defined as the deviation of banks' cost (or profit) function from the best-practice cost (or profit) function. This best-practice cost function is the frontier towards which the firm cost function should move in order to become more X-efficient.

The efficient frontier, or the benchmark, is estimated depending on the objective that a financial firm wishes to pursue. One can estimate cost or profit X-efficiency depending on whether one wishes to estimate X-efficiency on the input side (cost X-efficiency) or input and output side (profit X-efficiency).

If cost minimization is the banks' objective, then cost efficiency shows how close the estimated cost function of a financial firm is to the estimated best-practice cost function. If profit maximization is the main objective, profit X-efficiency estimates how close a bank's profit function is to the maximum or the best performing bank's profit function in the industry. Berger and Mester (1997) suggest two concepts of profit efficiency: standard profit and alternative profit efficiency. The two profit efficiency concepts measure how close a bank is to achieving the maximum possible profit given particular levels of input and output prices.

Measures of profit X-efficiency are believed to be superior to cost X-efficiency, as profit X-efficiency measures allow us to take into account inefficiency from both input and output sides. In this sense, banks can be cost efficient from the view of their input side, but they might be inefficient with respect to outputs. For instance, a bank may minimize costs (thus making it cost efficient) but if it does not maximize revenues it will not be profit efficient. Alternatively, banks can be cost inefficient yet profit efficient if they have high costs that result in greater revenues.

Studies on efficiency measurement date back to the late 1950s, specifically to the work of Farrell (1957). He measured inefficiency by calculating the deviation of the actual behaviour from the optimum. By following Farrell, nearly all approaches to efficiency measurement concentrate on his idea where there must be a frontier representing an optimum capacity, and the deviation from the frontier is considered as inefficiency. However, the estimation approach of the optimum benchmark or the frontier, and the measurement of the distance the estimated observations are placed away from this theoretical estimated frontier, is the area where many empirical studies have differed. There are two main statistical approaches used to measure the efficient frontier: non-parametric and parametric approaches.

Non-parametric approaches

Non-parametric (or linear-programming) approaches (see Aigner and Chu, 1968; Afriat, 1972; Richmond, 1974; Berger and Humphrey, 1997) specify no functional form to estimate the best-practice frontier. It assigns the best-practice banks on the frontier and other banks are considered less efficient relative to the ones defining the frontier. In fact, most non-parametric approaches do not allow for any random disturbances, so no stochastic term is included in the model.[15] Deviations of the data from the frontier are the inefficiency residuals that are strictly one-sided and negative for the production frontier model and positive for the cost frontier. This is because the data cannot lie above the estimated maximum production function or fall below the minimum cost function. The major disadvantage of the deterministic frontier approach is that because it does not take into account random noise, the inefficiency term may be overestimated since the latter may include random noise.

Non-parametric studies mainly use Data Envelopment Analysis (DEA), which is a linear programming technique utilized to construct the frontier and measure efficiency. This technique as constructed by Farrell (1957) has been subject to many extensions (Charnes *et al.*, 1978; Banker *et al.*, 1984). DEA approximates the efficient frontier through the envelope of hyper-planes in the input space. It uses a linear programming algorithm method to measure how far a given observed input vector is from the frontier; the inefficiency of the firm is computed as the ratio of the firm's input costs relative to the least input cost of the best-practice firm which lies on the efficient frontier (Evanoff and Israilevich, 1991).

Some researches such as Elyasiani and Mehdian (1990) envisage DEA, and therefore the deterministic frontier, as having the advantage of no standard specification of what functional form must be used. In essence, however, there are a number of drawbacks concerning this approach. First, since DEA is a non-parametric approach in which the frontier estimates are deterministic, it does not allow for errors or any stochastic variables to enter the model; therefore, any deviation from the estimated frontier is considered inefficiency. The problem here is that the calculated efficiency might contain information of data shocks or measurement errors which may result in mis-estimation of inefficiency. Second, DEA does not estimate the model parameters, and there is no test that makes the researcher sure of how accurate the estimation is, and because DEA does not produce standard errors, inferences are not available (Greene, 1993). Third, inefficiency represents only an upper bound of the DEA estimates, a matter that makes comparison between banks unreliable (Schmidt, 1986).

The Free Disposal Hull (FDH) approach as introduced by Deprins *et al.* (1984) develops the DEA technique. This approach has been gaining increased acceptance, as it is seen as an alternative non-parametric approach competing with the DEA technique to measure inefficiency (DeBorger, Ferrier and Kerstens, 1995). FDH differs from DEA in that it does not take into consideration the convexity assumption, which is a property related to the production possibility set. In referring to Tulkens (1993), Berger and Humphrey (1997, p. 177) state that 'the points on lines connecting the DEA vertices are not included in the frontier. Instead, the FDH production possibilities set is composed only of the DEA vertices and the free disposal hull points interior to these vertices. Because the FDH frontier is either congruent with or interior to the DEA frontier, FDH will typically generate larger estimates of average efficiency than DEA.' Similar to DEA, however, the principal shortcoming of the FDH is that it ignores random error. However, FDH considers the variation of efficiency over time and makes no assumption as to the type of distribution of the inefficiency component, and thus the measured distance between the estimated observation and the frontier is wholly considered as inefficiency.

Parametric approaches

The parametric approach assumes an explicit functional form to estimate the frontier of either cost or profit functions. The parametric method is stochastic, in that it allows random disturbance along with inefficiency residuals to be accounted for when estimating the efficient frontier. There are various parametric techniques that have been used to estimate bank efficiency, the most common of which is known as the stochastic frontier approach.

The stochastic frontier model was developed by Aigner *et al.* (1977) and, later, by Jondrow *et al.* (1982). Realizing the disadvantages of the deterministic frontier approach, especially the non-consideration of random noise, this induced a significant development in the efficiency measurement literature; that is, the estimation of a frontier comprising both inefficiency and stochastic (or random noise) terms (Aigner *et al.*, 1977; Meeusen and van den Broeck, 1977). The reason why one includes a stochastic term is to account for random noise that can either increase or decrease the frontier due to luck or other measurement error factors (Berger and Humphrey, 1991). In the case of the stochastic frontier one assumes that the frontier shifts from one observation to another. Here, the inefficiency term implies that, in the case of cost studies, inefficiency raises costs above the minimum estimated cost function (the cost frontier). Inefficiency also decreases profit below the profit frontier if one is studying profit efficiency.

In the stochastic frontier approach, strong distributional assumptions are necessarily needed to decompose the residual into inefficiency and noise components. The distributional assumption for the stochastic term component is typically characterized by a two-sided normal distribution; while the inefficiency term is always assumed to be a one-sided distribution representing the shortfall of output from the production frontier or the increase of the cost beyond the cost frontier. Aigner, Lovell and Schmidt (1977) provide two ways of estimating the inefficiency, assuming the distribution of the inefficiency term takes a half-normal distribution in one estimation and an exponential distribution in another. Meeusen and van den Broeck (1977) consider inefficiency to take only the exponential distribution. Cebenoyan *et al.* (1993) and Berger and DeYoung (1997) use the truncated normal distribution, while the gamma distribution is considered by Richmond (1974), Stevenson (1980) and Greene (1990). One difficulty related to the stochastic frontier approach is that there is no consensus as to the type of distribution one should choose to arrive at the inefficiency measure, although Greene (1990) suggests that the distributional assumptions do not have much impact on the efficiency estimates.

Other econometric approaches to deriving X-efficiency are known as the distribution-free (DFA) and the thick-frontier approaches (TFA). The DFA assumes that the inefficiency term is stable and does not change over time; whereas other coefficients and variables are allowed to vary, leaving the random error component to average out over time (see Berger *et al.*, 1993a; Berger and Humphrey, 1992). Therefore, unlike the stochastic frontier approach, the DFA places no specific type of distribution on the inefficiency term. This approach usually requires a panel data set so that the cancellation of the error term finds enough time to retain a zero value. Berger and Humphrey (1991) propose the thick-frontier approach. The thick-frontier approach estimates the cost function of banks in the lowest average cost quartile, which is the thick-frontier, and compares it with the cost function of banks in the highest average cost quartile. It then decomposes the deviations into random noise and an inefficiency residual. In order to distinguish between both error terms, the thick-frontier approach assumes that the random noise is embodied within the lowest and the highest average cost quartile, which appears as the deviations from the predicted costs of each quartile. Differences between the lowest and the highest average cost quartiles are measured as the inefficiency component. This approach avoids making any assumptions on how the error components are distributed.

The bulk of banking studies that use the econometric approach (stochastic frontier, thick frontier, and distribution-free approaches) – although they use different assumptions regarding the error term components – typically find similar X-inefficiency results. That is, for different studies using various data sets, mean levels of banking sector inefficiency lie within the range of 5 to 30 per cent. In contrast, DEA studies report a wider divergence of banking X-inefficiency, averaging from less than 5 per cent to more than 50 per cent (Berger *et al.*, 1993a).

In their review of the financial sector X-efficiency literature, Berger and Humphrey (1997) surveyed some 130 studies. This survey examines various studies covering different financial institutions (such as banks, bank branches, saving and loans, and other financial service firms), using different approaches to measuring efficiency (parametric and non-parametric approaches), and also covering different countries and regions. In their survey, Berger and Humphrey find that the mean inefficiency across all studies included in the survey was 27 per cent, with standard deviation of 13 per cent. This means that, on average, financial firms could produce 27 per cent more outputs, given current inputs, if they operated as efficiently as the most efficient firms. In a comparison between the parametric and non-parametric approaches, the mean inefficiency measures of these approaches are relatively close to one another, 29 per cent and 19 per cent, for the non-parametric and parametric studies respectively. However, the standard deviation of the non-parametric studies, at 17 per cent, is higher than that of the parametric approach, at 6 per cent. This indicates that the mean efficiency measures found by parametric studies are more likely to be closer to each other compared to those found in non-parametric studies.

With regard to the rankings of inefficiency estimates, there are only a few studies that calculate the range between the efficiency estimates for both parametric and non-parametric approaches. In Berger and Humphrey's (1997) survey, only two studies report a Spearman rank correlation coefficient (R) between the DEA and SFA estimates: the study by Ferrier and Lovell (1990) found $R = 0.02$, and the study by Eisenbeis *et al.* (1996) found R ranging between 0.44 and 0.59. These findings suggest a weak ordinal association between the two approaches.

Berger *et al.* (1993a) stress that there is no rule or standard guide to researchers in choosing the most reliable approach that fully describes the nature of the banking data. However, because the interpretation of bank efficiency levels has important implications for owners, managers, regulatory and policy decision makers, Bauer *et al.* (1998) propose a set of consistency tests. These tests are stated as follows:

1. Efficiency scores obtained using different approaches should yield comparable statistical means, standard deviations, and distributional properties.

2. Different approaches should approximately rank the efficiency of the financial institutions in the same order.
3. Relating to point 2, different approaches should generate similar estimates on best and worst practice financial institutions so that it eases the identification of successful and unsuccessful financial firms.
4. In order to identify the effect of the implementation of regulatory policies, different approaches should generate consistent results of efficiency over time.
5. Efficiency scores should be consistent with market competitive condition since banks of old establishment and matured ones are expected to be more competitive than newer banks.
6. Efficiency results should match the financial ratios that are used to evaluate the profitability and the performance of these firms.

Bauer *et al.* (1998) suggest that consistency conditions 1 to 3 should be used to check how the efficiency scores from different approaches could arrive at a degree where they are mutually consistent and could provide useful insights for policy questions. Moreover, consistency conditions 4 to 6 can evaluate the extent to which efficiency scores from different approaches yield credible and reasonable measures. Overall, these consistency conditions tests, if passed, should increase the confidence in efficiency scores using different approaches and advance judgment on the efficiency features of the financial industry under study.

Estimating efficient frontiers and the choice of functional forms

Parametric approaches have been widely used in the bank efficiency literature and they all rely on the choice of an appropriate cost or (more recently) profit function. As we noted previously, early studies extensively used the Cobb–Douglas functional form,[16] although since the mid-1970s until the late 1980s more studies have adopted the translog functional form to model bank costs.[17] More recently the Fourier Flexible functional form has been the preferred choice for estimating cost and profit efficiencies in banking.

For most studies published in the late 1960s until the late 1970s, the use of the Cobb–Douglas functional form was the main approach and these studies estimated the relevant cost functions in order to obtain economies of scale estimates (for example, Bell and Murphy, 1968; Schweitzer, 1972; Murphy, 1972; Kalish and Gilbert, 1973; Mullineaux, 1975 and 1978). In later studies, Benston, Hanweck and Humphrey (1982) claimed that the Cobb–Douglas functional form suffered from certain shortcomings: namely, the function was not the most appropriate model to estimate a cost function that exhibited a U-shaped average cost curve, since the Cobb–Douglas specification only allowed for one aspect of the estimation of increasing, decreasing, or constant average cost for all banks. Benston, Hanweck and Humphrey (1982) suggested a more flexible cost function, the translog functional form, to estimate bank costs. The authors claimed that the translog function overcomes the shortcomings of the Cobb–Douglas functional form in the sense that the translog form is more able to account for U-shaped average costs, and to estimate the cost function across firms of different sizes in an industry. Moreover, the translog model allows homogeneity of the degree one by simply imposing restrictions on the translog model parameters (McAllister and McManus, 1993). In practice, a great deal of research in the banking efficiency literature has used the translog functional form to estimate the cost characteristics of banking firms (see, for example, Kwan and Eisenbeis,1995; Altunbas *et al.*, 2001; Berger *et al.*, 2000).

However, some studies have cast doubt on the result of efficiency, scale, and scope economies obtained using the translog model. In showing the shortcomings of the translog function, McAllister and McManus (1993) tested four model specifications: translog, kernel, spline, and Fourier functional form.[18] As shown in Figure 7.2, these authors find that (within the global approximation) all specifications behaved well, except for the translog

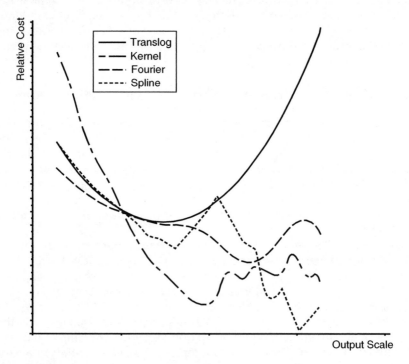

Figure 7.2 Translog, kernel, spline, and Fourier cost function estimates
Source: Adapted from McAllister and McManus, 1993, p. 396.

model where its cost function started to suffer from bias caused by large outputs, resulting in incorrect estimates of average costs for large-sized banks.

In addition, non-parametric approaches such as Kernel regression as well as the Fourier Flexible form (which are to be considered semi-parametric approaches) overcome this shortcoming of the translog function because they allow more flexibility and freedom for the shaping of the cost function given different bank sizes.

The principal technique that has been used in the recent banking efficiency studies to overcome the disadvantages of the translog function is the Fourier Flexible form. In contrast to the translog model the Fourier Flexible form can provide more accurate approximations to the true function over the whole range of data (Gallant, 1982). As the Fourier Flexible form adds trigonometric terms (which are mutually orthogonal over the $[0,2\pi]$ interval) to the translog specification, '[the] linear combination of sine and cosine functions called a Fourier series can represent exactly any well-behaved multivariate function' (Mitchell and Onvural, 1996, p. 140).[19] Thus, the use of trigonometric terms will narrow the edge between the approximated function and the true path of data (Gallant, 1982; Mitchell and Onvural, 1996; Berger and Mester, 1997).[20] However, it should be noted that although it has been argued that the translog has deficiencies regarding the estimation of global approximations, a study by Altunbas and Chakravarty (2001) indicates that, in general, while the Fourier Flexible form is better in terms of goodness of fit, its forecasting ability is worse. This may imply that the use of translog form could be justified by its predictive abilities.

Overall, the development of various functional forms to estimate cost and profit efficiency in banking is still ongoing. The greater use of the Fourier Flexible functional form complemented with translog estimates provides another consistency test for efficiency measure.

Empirical evidence on X-efficiency in banking

In this section we present the findings of some recent empirical studies undertaken to examine X-efficiency in banking systems. We start with the empirical evidence on US and European banking studies, and then discuss recent work that examines banking sector efficiency in some other systems.

Kaparakis, Miller and Noulas (1994) use data covering 5,548 US banks with assets over $50 million in the year 1986. By employing the stochastic cost frontier and using the translog function, the authors find overall mean inefficiencies of 10 per cent. Their findings also suggest that banks generally become less efficient with increasing size. Moreover, by moving to a more competitive environment, the authors find that banking may become costly and more inefficient. The study by Mester (1993) investigates efficiency in mutual and stock Saving and Loan's (S & L) using 1991 data. By employing the stochastic cost frontier approach, the results suggest that deregulation of interest rates and increased competition may, to some extent, contribute to a shifting of a large number of costly and inefficient S & L institutions from mutual to stock ownership. Moreover, the author finds that capital–assets ratios are positively correlated – but uninsured deposits are negatively correlated – with efficiency.

Berger, Hancock and Humphrey (1993) study US commercial banks with data including three panels of 384 to 599 banks each covering the period 1984–9. Their results, which are obtained using the distribution-free approach (DFA), show that the mean profit X-efficiency ranged from 52 to 66 per cent, suggesting that larger banks are found to be more X-efficient than smaller banks. Moreover, the authors find that technical inefficiencies dominate allocative inefficiency, suggesting that banks are not particularly poor in choosing input and output plans, but they are poor in running and carrying out these plans. Moreover, the findings suggest that most of the profit inefficiencies stem from revenue deficiencies, rather than excessive costs.

Elyasiani and Mehdian (1995) aim at identifying how cost efficiency in US small and large banks differs in order to explore the relationship between size and productive efficiency and to examine how changes in regulations affected banking sector efficiency during the 1980s. The sample contains 150 US banks studied over the period between 1979 and 1986. Using the non-parametric DEA approach, their findings show that the mean efficiency estimated ranged between 95 and 97 per cent. They also show that in the pre-deregulation era, small banks were more efficient than large banks, and post-deregulation both small and large banks were almost equally efficient.

Kwan and Eisenbeis (1995) studied 254 US bank holding companies observed on a semi-annual basis over the years 1986 to 1991. Using the stochastic frontier approach (SFA), the authors find that mean inefficiency declined over the study period. Their results suggested also that small-sized banks were less efficient (81 per cent) than their larger counterparts (92 per cent).

Mester (1997) studied 214 banks in the Third Federal Reserve District over the years 1991–2. Using the SFA and accounting for risk and quality factors in banking outputs, the author finds that although the studied banks are operating at cost-efficient output levels and product mixes, there appears to be a significant level of X-inefficiency at the banks considered.

Berger and Mester (1997) examined 6,000 US banks over a six-year period 1990–5. They employed three efficiency concepts – cost, standard profit, and alternative profit efficiency measures. Using the distribution-free approach (DFA) to estimate these efficiency types, and using the preferred model including risk and quality variables, the efficiency scores are found to be 86 per cent, 54 per cent, and 46 per cent, respectively. Moreover, the authors find that profit inefficiencies are not positively correlated with accounting profits.

Rogers (1998) used the parametric approach to estimate the efficiency of 10,000 US commercial banks over the period 1991–5. The author estimates stochastic translog cost, revenue, and profit frontiers where each included net non-interest income as a measure of non-traditional output. Under all three frontier specifications, the restricted model which omitted these activities is rejected in favour of the unrestricted model. Overall, mean cost efficiency is found to range between 71 and 76 per cent for the unrestricted model, compared to 65 and 66 per cent for the restricted one. The mean revenue efficiency ranged between 41 and 44 per cent and 50 and 51 per cent for the restricted and unrestricted models respectively. The mean profit efficiency ranged between 60 and 71 per cent and 65 and 68 per cent for the restricted and unrestricted models respectively.

The recent US bank studies therefore suggest the existence of inefficiency on both input and output sides, with mixed results on whether small or large banks are more efficient.

Generally, profit and revenue inefficiencies are found to be substantially larger than cost inefficiency. In addition, controlling for asset quality and risk can also influence efficiency results. Taking this (and other evidence) into consideration it seems that US bank cost inefficiencies are generally found to be between 15 per cent and 25 per cent whereas profit inefficiencies are in the region of 30 per cent to 55 per cent.

In addition to the US literature there is also a growing interest in European banking sector efficiency. The following just covers the findings from some of the main studies.

Berg *et al.* (1993) use the DEA approach to study banking sector efficiency in Finland, Norway and Sweden in the year 1990. The authors find that the largest banks in Sweden are among the most efficient units in the whole sample, whereas only one large Finnish bank and no large Norwegian banks score efficiency above 90 per cent. In a later study, Berg *et al.* (1995) examine the efficiency of banks in Denmark, Finland, Sweden, and Norway. The authors also find that large banks in Sweden as well as in Denmark are the most efficient units in the pooled sample.

Altunbas *et al.* (1994) study the efficiency of German banks with a data set containing 196 banks covering the year 1988. Using the stochastic frontier approach, the authors find that the mean cost inefficiency in German banking is around 24 per cent. Pastor *et al.* (1995) estimate efficiency of banking sectors in eight European countries using a non-parametric approach. Their findings show that the most efficient banks in the sample are those of France (95 per cent), Spain (82 per cent), and Belgium (80 per cent); while the least efficient banks come from Germany (65 per cent), Austria (60 per cent), and UK (53 per cent). In addition, a European Commission (1997) study covering 10 European Union countries over 1987 to 1994 used the stochastic frontier approach and found that the average banking system efficiency ranged between 71 per cent and 77 per cent over the five years and these decreased over the last four years of the study period. Altunbas *et al.* (2001) use the Fourier Flexible functional form to estimate the characteristics of banking costs in European countries over the period 1988–95. The authors find the mean cost X-inefficiency at the level of 25 per cent. The authors also examine whether large banks are more X-efficient than small banks. They do not find any evidence supporting this claim for their sample of European banks. Dietsch and Weill (1998) also studied the efficiency of 11 European Union countries using data on 661 commercial banks, mutual, and saving banks covering the period 1992–6. Generally, their estimates on the efficiency and productivity over the study period suggest an increase in cost and profit inefficiency levels. Casu and Girardone (1998) investigated 32 Italian banking groups and 78 bank parent companies and subsidiaries in 1995. Using both parametric (SFA) and non-parametric (DEA) approaches, the authors find that the mean efficiency using the parametric approach was 92 per cent for banking groups, and 94 per cent for banks' parents and companies; for the DEA estimates, the mean efficiency is found to be 88 per cent for banking groups and 90 per cent for bank parent and companies.

Turati (2001) estimates the cost efficiency in European banking markets from 1992 to 1999. The author specifies three different translog cost functions. All the three models consider 3 inputs (labour, physical capital, and deposits) and 2 outputs (loans and other earning assets). Correlation between scores obtained with different specifications of the cost function is very high. The author also finds no major differences in mean efficiency among European countries. Mean efficiency across countries shows a decline from 1992 to 1998 and an increase from 1998 to 1999. Turati suggests that the low correlations between cost efficiency scores and profitability may indicate the presence of market power in the banking industry.

Maudos *et al.* (2002) advance their earlier work by examining both cost and profit efficiencies using a sample of banks for ten countries of the European Union, using IBCA bank accounting data for the period 1993–6. Using panel data frontier approaches, the authors find high levels of cost efficiency but lower levels of profit efficiency. This result points to the importance of inefficiencies on the revenue side of banking activity. Also, their results show low but positive correlation between the rankings of cost and profit efficiency. In their analysis, the authors use four groups of variables: size, specialization, other characteristics specific to each bank, and characteristics of the markets in which they operate. The results show that medium-sized banks enjoy the highest levels of efficiency in both costs and profits; the type of banking specialization is not significant in explaining differences of efficiency between banks; and the banks with a higher loans/assets ratio are more efficient. Overall, the authors conclude that there is a notably wide range of variation in efficiency levels in the banking systems of the European Union, with variation in terms of profit efficiency being greater than in terms of cost efficiency.

Overall, the European bank efficiency studies (like their US counterparts) tend to find that cost inefficiency levels are around 25 per cent or lower, and in the majority of cases this tends to be decreasing over time, probably due to greater competitiveness within the European integrated market. The more limited evidence on profit inefficiency suggests that this is typically higher, around 40–50 per cent. However, the literature provides little consensus as to the size of banks that appear to be the most efficient.

Bank X-efficiency in emerging and developing countries

The banking literature also now includes a growing number of efficiency studies on emerging and developing countries. Table 7.1 provides a summary of these studies.

Bhattacharya, Lovell and Sahay (1997) use data on 70 Indian commercial banks over the period 1986–91. Using the DEA approach, the authors find efficiency to be at the level of 80 per cent for the sample. Publicly owned banks report higher efficiency levels (87 per cent) than privately owned banks (75 per cent) and foreign-owned counterparts. Taylor, Thompson, Thrall and Dharmapala (1997) study 13 Mexican commercial banks over the period 1989–91. Using the DEA approach, the study finds the mean efficiency to range between 69 per cent and 75 per cent, with a decreasing trend over the three years under study. Kraft and Tirtiroglu (1998) obtain data from the audited final accounts on 43 Croatian commercial banks in 1994 and 1995. The authors estimate X-efficiency and scale-efficiencies for both old and new state and private banks. Cost X-efficiencies are found to range from 55 per cent to 88 per cent. Amongst the 43 banks, 27 banks have efficiency levels above 80 per cent. New banks are shown to be more X-inefficient and more scale-inefficient than either old privatized banks or old state banks. However, new private banks are highly profitable. Srivastava (1999) estimates the efficiency of 85 Indian commercial and public banks over the period 1994–5. The findings suggest that the mean cost efficiencies of private and public banks are similar at 98 per cent. Moreover, the mean efficiency of recent entrants (mostly foreign banks as well as some private banks) shows a higher level than current banks. In terms of bank size, the highest cost efficiency is, generally, reported for middle-sized banks, followed by small and large-sized banks.

Intarachote (2000) uses a sample on 15 Thai banks, 14 foreign banks, and other finance and specialized institutions. The study, which uses the nonparametric DEA approach, finds that inefficiency ranges from 26 per cent to 48 per cent for national banks, 33 per cent to 50 per cent for foreign banks, and 6 per cent to 14 per cent for the finance and specialized institutions.

Isik and Hassan (2002) estimate cost and profit efficiencies for Turkish banks over the 1988 to 1996 period. Over these years, they find that the overall cost and profit efficiencies for the Turkish banks are 72 per cent and 83 per cent, respectively. The results also indicate that the production efficiencies of the industry consistently have declined over time. Moreover,

Table 7.1 Bank efficiency in emerging and developing countries

Study and year	Country	Data and period of study	Methodology	Main findings
Oral and Yolalan (1990)	Turkey	Data on Turkish bank branches.	DEA	Inefficiency estimates are within the range 13–47%.
Zaim (1995)	Turkey	95 banks for the two years of 1981 and 1990.	DEA	Average inefficiency estimates are found 17% in 1991 and 6% in 1990.
Bhattacharya, Lovell and Sahay (1997)	India	Data on 70 commercial banks over the deregulation period 1986–91.	DEA	Inefficiency scores are found to be within the range 17.19–80.44% over the period of analysis. Government-owned banks are more efficient (87%) than privately and foreign-owned banks (75%).
Taylor, Thompson, Thrall and Dharmapala (1997)	Mexico	Data on 13 commercial banks for the years 1989, 1990 and 1991.	DEA	Average inefficiency scores are found to be 25% in 1989, 28% in 1990, and 31% in 1991.
Isik and Hassan (2002)	Turkey	Data on a sample of commercial banks over the years 1988, 1992 and 1996.	DEA	Average cost efficiency of the sample consistently fell over time, from 78% in 1988, to 71% in 1992 and 68% in 1996.
Leightner and Lovell (1998)	Thailand	Data on 31 banks for the period 1989–91.	SFA	Average annual efficiency estimates are found to be 58%, 49%, 45%, 42%, 34% and 31% for the years under investigation, respectively.
Okuda and Mieno (1999)	Thailand	Data on a sample of Thai domestic banks over the period 1985–94.	SFA Translog	Average inefficiency score is found to be just over 25%. Large banks are found to be the most cost efficient.
Hao, Hunter and Yang (1999)	Korea	Data on 19 private banks over the period 1985–95.	SFA	Inefficiency estimates are found to be within the range 9–15%. The financial deregulation of 1991 was found to have had little or no significant effects on the level of sample bank efficiency.

Study	Country	Data	Method	Findings
Intarachote (2000)	Thailand	Data on an unbalanced sample of 15 Thai banks and 15 foreign-owned banks and a number of finance and specialized institutions.	DEA	Overall cost inefficiency scores are found to be within the range 52–47% for Thai banks, 50–67% for foreign-owned banks, and 86–95% for other financial institutions.
Jackson and Fethi (2000)	Turkey	Data on sample of 48 commercial banks for the year 1998.	DEA	Average inefficiency estimates are found to be 23%.
Hasan and Marton (2000)	Hungary	Data on all Hungarian banks that reported during the 1993–7 period, 154 bank observations.	SFA Fourier-Flexible	Average cost and alternative profit efficiency estimates are found to be 21.62% and 29.08%, respectively. The higher the foreign involvement in bank ownership, the lower is the inefficiency.
Saha and Ravishankar (2000)	India	Data on 25 public sector banks for the year 1995.	DEA	Efficiency estimates are found to be within the range 58–74% with an average efficiency of 69%.
Mertens and Urga (2001)	Ukraine	Data on sample of 79 commercial banks for the year 1998.	SFA and TFA	Average cost efficiency was found to be 67.2% using the SFA and 80.5% using the TFA. Average profit efficiency was found to be 71.99% using the SFA and 65.77% using the TFA. Small banks are found to operate more efficiently in cost terms but less efficiently in profit terms.
Cook, Hababou and Roberts (2001)	Tunisia	Data on 10 Tunisian banks (5 public and 5 private) for the period 1992–7.	DEA	Average inefficiency is found to be 45% using the intermediary approach. Publicly-owned banks (55%) are found to be more inefficient than private-owned banks (36%).

Table 7.1 (Continued)

Study and year	Country	Data and period of study	Methodology	Main findings
Sathye (2001)	India	Data on 94 commercial banks for the period 1997–8 (27 publicly-owned banks, 33 private-owned banks and 34 foreign-owned banks).	DEA	Average efficiency score is found to be 83% as per Model A, and 62% as per Model B. Foreign-owned banks are found to be in the highest efficiency quartiles in both models.
Kwan (2002)	Hong Kong	Quarterly data on a number of multi-branch banks for the period 1992–9.	SFA	Average efficiency estimates are found to be within the range 16–30%.
Darrat, Topuz and Yousef (2002)	Kuwait	Data on 8 banks for the period 1994–7.	DEA	Average cost inefficiency is found to be 32%.
Rao (2002)	GAE	Data on 35 banks for the period 1998–2000.	SFA Translog and Flexible-Fourier	Average inefficiency estimates increased from 14% in 1988 to 25.21% in 2000 using the Fourier-Flexible, but decreased from 30.48% in 1998 to 25.53% in 2000, using the translog. Small banks are found to be more efficient than large and medium-sized banks.
Williams and Intarachote (2002)	Thailand	Data on 29 banks for the period 1990–7.	SFA	Average alternative profit inefficiency is found to be 15.14% for domestic-owned banks, and 14.74% for foreign-owned banks. Small banks are found to be more efficient than large and medium-sized banks. Efficiency decreased at an increasing rate over time.

Study	Country	Data	Method	Findings
Weill (2003)	Czech Republic and Poland	Data on a sample of 31 Polish banks (of which 12 foreign-owned) and 16 Czech banks (of which 8 are foreign-owned) for the year 1997.	SFA Translog	Foreign-owned banks are found to be more efficient than other banks, suggesting better management.
Bonin, Hasan and Wachtel (2003)	11 Eastern European countries	Data on unbalanced sample of 220 banks and 830 observations for the period 1996–2000.	SFA Translog	Government-owned banks are less efficient than private and foreign-owned banks. Foreign-owned banks are more profit efficient than cost efficient.
Fuentes and Vergara (2003)	Chile	Data on all Chilean banks 1990 to 2000.	SFA Translog	Cost inefficiency 9% and profit inefficiency around 25%. Subsidiaries more efficient than branches of foreign banks.
Burki and Khan Niazi (2003)	Pakistan	23 commercial banks for the year 1991, 36 banks for the period 1992–4, 39 banks for 1995, 40 banks for 1996–8, 39 banks for 1999, and 37 banks for 2000.	DEA	Mean cost efficiency found to be 74.5%. Allocative inefficiency (83.6%) contributes more than technical inefficiency (88.2%). The highest levels of efficiency were achieved by foreign banks (79.7%), followed by private banks (75.1%) while state-owned banks achieved least cost efficiency (60.5%).

their analysis suggests that the relationship between bank size and efficiency is strongly negative. In general, they also find that foreign banks operating in Turkey seem to be significantly more efficient than their domestic peers. In addition, private banks are found to be more efficient than public banks in terms of all types of efficiency.

An interesting study of UAE banking is undertaken by Rao (2002) who uses a sample of 35 banks between 1998 and 2000 to investigate the efficiency features of different sized banks. Overall, Rao finds conflicting results in efficiency trends. Using the Fourier flexible functional form he finds average inefficiency increases from 14 per cent in 1988 to 25 per cent in 2000. However, the translog estimates reveal the opposite, with inefficiency falling from 30 per cent to around 25 per cent. Overall, however, small banks are found to be more efficient than large and medium-sized banks.

In general, the results of bank efficiency studies in the above countries tend to be similar to that of the US and European literature. Cost inefficiencies are smaller than profit inefficiencies and there are differences between foreign and domestic banks (and also sometimes between state and private banks). While this section by no means provides an exhaustive survey it at least gives a flavour of the recent features of the bank efficiency literature. The increasing number of studies on banking sector efficiency in systems other than the US and Europe also suggests the growing interest in examining such issues, especially in the light of greater banking sector deregulation.

Conclusion

This chapter outlines the main features associated with banking and financial sector efficiency. The first part of the chapter discusses why an efficient banking and financial system is desirable from a policy perspective and shows how financial sector deregulation is inextricably linked to various efficiency concepts. The remainder of the chapter examines how one can measure banking system efficiency and the main results from the empirical literature. The following chapter presents some recent evidence on banking sector efficiency from the Arab world.

8
Efficiency in Arab Banking

Introduction

This chapter investigates the efficiency features of a variety of Arab banking systems. In particular we report recent evidence on banking sector efficiency in Egypt, Jordan, the Gulf and various Maghreb countries. The empirical evidence on bank efficiency in these countries can be used to provide insights into the impact of economic and financial reforms. The first part of the chapter examines in detail the recent study by Al-Jarrah (2002) and Al-Jarrah and Molyneux (2003) who examine the cost and profit performance of a sample of banks operating in Jordan, Egypt, Saudi Arabia and Bahrain between 1992 and 2002. The second part of the chapter examines the efficiency of Gulf banks, summarizing the results from Al-Shammari (2003) and Mohamed (2003). The final part of the chapter discusses recent evidence from Bakhouche (2004) who analyzes the cost and profit efficiency of Algerian, Moroccan and Tunisian banks up to 2002. Despite the extensive literature that has examined productive efficiency, especially in the US banking system and other European markets, empirical research on financial sectors in developing countries, including Arabian countries, is limited. The chapter therefore aims to bring together studies on Arab banking systems in order to examine the impact of economic and financial reforms which have taken place in these countries over the past two decades.

Why study Arab bank efficiency?

There are various reasons for examining efficiency levels in Arabian banking systems. First, little empirical work has been undertaken to investigate efficiency levels in Arabian banking and an empirical investigation may yield interesting insights that could be of use to policy-makers operating in these countries and to the financial institutions themselves. Second, such a study should help in assessing the impact of the economic and financial reforms that have taken place in the countries under study. In addition, assessing the impact of financial reforms on banking sector efficiency levels should provide useful policy information. Furthermore, this chapter aims to provide empirical evidence about efficiency differences across various Arabian banking industries (and across various types of financial institutions operating in these countries such as commercial, investment and Islamic banks). We also seek to assess, for instance, whether there is a link between bank size, and cost and profit efficiency levels. If we find a positive size and efficiency relationship, there will be a tendency for continued consolidation and concentration in the industry. Furthermore, the recent literature also aims to investigate the determinants of Arab banks' efficiency and as such investigates how factors such as asset quality, capital levels and other environmental variables (such as bank size, market characteristics, geographic position and liquidity ratios) influence banks' efficiency levels. This chapter therefore presents contemporary evidence on the efficiency features of Arab banking systems which we hope also adds to the broader debate on developing financial systems.

Measuring the efficiency of Arab banks

In their study of bank efficiency in Egypt, Jordan, Saudi Arabia and Bahrain, Al-Jarrah (2002) and Al-Jarrah and Molyneux (2003) chose the stochastic frontier, with the Fourier-flexible functional form, as the main methodology to be employed to derive efficiency measures in the countries under study. While the translog functional form has been probably the most widely utilized to derive efficiency estimates, the Fourier-Flexible (FF) has received more focus in the recent efficiency literature. The Fourier-flexible functional form is preferred over the translog because it better approximates the underlying cost function across a broad range of outputs as suggested by Spong *et al.* (1995), Mitchell and Onvural (1996). Besides, Berger and Mester (1997) note that the local approximations of the translog may distort scale economy measurements since it imposes a symmetric U-shaped average cost curve. This aspect of the translog might not fit very well with data that are far from the mean in terms of output size or mix. The FF alleviates this problem since it can approximate any continuous function and any of its derivatives (up to a fixed order). Any inferences that are drawn from estimates of the FF are unaffected by specification errors (Ivaldi *et al.*, 1996). Carbo *et al.* (2000) indicate that since the FF is a combination of polynomial and trigonometric expansions, the order of approximation can increase with the size of the sample. Finally, the FF has several appealing properties in terms of modelling bank cost or profit structures, as pointed out by Williams and Gardener (2000). Unlike other commonly used functional forms such as the translog, the FF form is unaffected by specification errors. Furthermore, it has been widely accepted that the global property is important in banking where scale, product mix and other inefficiencies are often heterogeneous.

Therefore, local approximations (such as those generated by the translog function) may be relatively poor approximation to the underlying true cost (or profit) function. Specifically, the Fourier-flexible functional form augments the translog by including Fourier trigonometric terms.

To arrive at the Fourier-flexible functional form we start with a standard stochastic cost model for a sample of N firms that can be written as:

$$\ln TC_i = \ln TC(y_i, w_i, z_i; B) + u_i + v_i, \ i = 1, \ldots, N$$

where TC_i is observed cost of bank i, y_i is the vector of output levels and w_i is the vector of input prices for bank i. z_i represents a vector of control variables which in the case of our estimates includes the quality of bank's output (q_i), the level of its financial capital (k_i) and the time trend (T_i). B is a vector of parameters, v_i is a two-sided error term representing the statistical noise (assumed to be independently and identically distributed and have a normal distribution with mean 0 and variance σ_V^2).

u_i are non-negative random variables that account for technical inefficiency. In order to estimate cost and profit efficiencies Al-Jarrah and Molyneux (2003) adopt the two approaches suggested by Battese and Coelli (1992 and 1995). In the case of Battese and Coelli's (1995) model, u_i are assumed to be independently distributed as truncations at zero of the $N(m_i, \sigma_u^2)$ distribution; where $m_i = \delta_i d$, where δ_i is a set of environmental variables (defined in the previous section) which are employed to control for firms' specific factors that may help to explain the differences in the efficiency estimates, and d is a vector of parameters to be estimated. For the Battese and Coelli (1992) model, u_i are assumed to be *iid* as truncations at zero of the $N(\mu, \sigma_u^2)$ distribution.

The following outlines the model specification for estimating the cost functions.[1] The translog functional form for the cost frontier is specified as:

$$
\ln(C/w_3) = \alpha + \sum_{i=1}^{2} B_i \ln(w_i/w_3) + \sum_{k=1}^{3} \gamma_k \ln y_k + \sum_{r=1}^{3} \psi_r \ln z_r
$$

$$
+ \frac{1}{2} \left[\sum_{i=1}^{2} \sum_{j=1}^{2} B_{ij} \ln(w_i/w_3) \ln(w_j/w_3) \right] + \frac{1}{2} \left[\sum_{k=1}^{3} \sum_{m=1}^{3} \gamma_{km} \ln y_k \ln y_m \right]
$$

$$
+ \frac{1}{2} \left[\sum_{r=1}^{3} \sum_{s=1}^{3} \psi_{rs} \ln z_r \ln z_s \right] + \sum_{i=1}^{2} \sum_{k=1}^{3} \eta_{ik} \ln(w_i/w_3) \ln(y_k)
$$

$$
+ \sum_{i=1}^{2} \sum_{r=1}^{3} \rho_{ir} \ln(w_i/w_3) \ln(z_r) + \sum_{k=1}^{3} \sum_{r=1}^{3} \tau_{kr} \ln y_k \ln z_r + u_{it} + v_{it}
$$

By augmenting the previous translog form by Fourier trigonometric terms, we get the Fourier-flexible functional form written as:

$$\ln(C/w_3) = \alpha + \sum_{i=1}^{2} B_i \ln(w_i/w_3) + \sum_{k=1}^{3} \gamma_k \ln y_k + \sum_{r=1}^{3} \psi_r \ln z_r$$

$$+ \frac{1}{2}\left[\sum_{i=1}^{2}\sum_{j=1}^{2} B_{ij} \ln(w_i/w_3) \ln(w_j/w_3)\right] + \frac{1}{2}\left[\sum_{k=1}^{3}\sum_{m=1}^{3} \gamma_{km} \ln y_k \ln y_m\right]$$

$$+ \frac{1}{2}\left[\sum_{r=1}^{3}\sum_{s=1}^{3} \psi_{rs} \ln z_r \ln z_s\right] + \sum_{i=1}^{2}\sum_{k=1}^{3} \eta_{ik} \ln(w_i/w_3) \ln(y_k)$$

$$+ \sum_{i=1}^{2}\sum_{r=1}^{3} \rho_{ir} \ln(w_i/w_3) \ln(z_r) + \sum_{k=1}^{3}\sum_{r=1}^{3} \tau_{kr} \ln y_k \ln z_r$$

$$+ \sum_{n=1}^{8} [\phi_n \cos(x_n) + w_n \sin(x_n)] +$$

$$\sum_{n=1}^{8}\sum_{q=n}^{8} [\phi_{nq} \cos(x_n + x_q) + w_{nq} \sin(x_n + x_q)]$$

$$\sum_{n=1}^{8} [\phi_{nnn} \cos(x_n + x_n + x_n) + w_{nnn} \sin(x_n + x_n + x_n)] + u_{it} + v_{it}$$

where *lnC* is the natural logarithm of total costs (operating and financial); *ln* y_i is the natural logarithm of bank outputs (i.e. loans, securities, off-balance sheet items); *ln* w_i is the natural logarithm of *i*th input prices (i.e. wage rate, interest rate and physical capital price); the x_n terms, $n = 1, \ldots, 8$ are rescaled values of the $\ln(w_i / w_3)$, $i = 1,2$, $\ln(y_k)$, $k = 1,2,3$, and $\ln(z_r)$, $r = 1,2,3$, such that each of the x_n span the interval $[0, 2\pi]$, and π refers to the number of radians here (not profits), and α, β, γ, ψ, ρ, τ, η, d, ω, ϕ and t are coefficients to be estimated.

Since the duality theorem requires that the cost function be linearly homogeneous in input prices and continuity requires that the second order parameters are symmetric, the following restrictions apply to the parameters of the cost function in the equation above:

$$\sum_{i=1}^{3} \beta_j = 1 \; ; \quad \sum_{i=1}^{3} B_{ij} = 0 \; ; \quad \sum_{i=1}^{3} \eta_{ij} = 0 \; ; \quad \sum_{i=1}^{n} \rho_{ij} = 0$$

Moreover, the second order parameters of the cost function must be symmetric, that is, $B_{ij} = B_{ji}$ and $\eta_{ik} = \eta_{ki}$, for all i, k. The scaled log-output quantities x_i are calculated as in Berger and Mester (1997) by cutting 10 per cent off each end of the $[0, 2\pi]$ interval so that the z_i span $[0.1 \times 2\pi, .9 \times 2\pi]$ to reduce approximation problems near endpoints. The formula for z_i is $[0.2\pi - \mu x\,a + \mu x\,\text{variable}]$, where $[a, b]$ is the range of the variable being transformed, and $\mu \equiv (0.9 \times 2\pi - 0.1 \times 2\pi/(9b-a))$. Fourier terms are only applied to the outputs, leaving the input price effects to be defined entirely by the translog terms, following Berger and Mester (1997). The primary aim is to maintain the limited number of Fourier terms for describing the scale and inefficiency measures associated with differences in bank size. Moreover, the usual input price homogeneity restrictions can be imposed on logarithmic price terms, whereas they cannot be easily imposed on the trigonometric terms.

The maximum-likelihood estimates for the parameters in the Fourier-flexible stochastic frontier for Cost, Standard and Alternative profit efficiency functions – that includes efficiency correlates – are estimated using the computer program FRONTIER Version 4.0 (see Coelli, 1996). This program uses three steps to obtain the maximum-likelihood estimates. The first step involves obtaining ordinary least squares (OLS) estimates of the equation. These estimates are unbiased because of the non-zero expectation of u_{it}. The second step involves evaluating the log-likelihood function for a number of values of γ between zero and one. During this procedure, d_i are set to zero and the values of B_0 and σ^2 are adjusted according to the corrected ordinary least squares formulae for the half-normal model. The estimates corresponding to the largest log-likelihood value in this second step are used as starting values in the iterative maximization procedure in the third and final part of the estimation procedure.

In addition to estimating cost efficiencies, Al-Jarrah and Molyneux (2003) also estimate alternative profit efficiency and standard profit efficiency using the same methodology. For the case of the standard profit function, they specify variable profits in place of variable costs and take variable output prices as given but allow output quantities to vary. On the other hand, the alternative profit function employs the same dependent variable as the standard profit function and the same exogenous variables as the cost function but it measures how close a bank comes to earning maximum profits given its output levels rather than its output prices. Studies by Al-Shammari (2003) and Mohamed (2003) use similar approaches as outlined above to estimate Gulf banking efficiency.

The Al-Jarrah and Molyneux (2003) study uses a sample of 82 banks operating in Jordan, Egypt, Saudi Arabia and Bahrain over the 1992–2000 period. This sample represents around 78 per cent, 88 per cent, 63 per cent and 55 per cent of the banking system assets of these countries (excluding the assets of foreign branches and central banks). Table 8.1 shows the details.

The sample represents the major financial institutions that have consistently published their financial statements over the last ten years in the countries under study. The relative size of Bahrain's banks in the sample looks small, and the reason is that the financial system in this country has been dominated by offshore banking units which are excluded from the sample as these belong to large international financial institutions and their data are unavailable. In Saudi Arabia, the specialized government institutions, while important, do not publish detailed financial statements and so these are not included in the sample.

Table 8.1 Size of the study sample relative to the banking sectors of Jordan, Egypt, Saudi Arabia and Bahrain over 1992–2000 (US$ million)

Year	Bahrain			Egypt			Jordan			Saudi Arabia		
	Sample assets	Total banking assets	%	Sample assets	Total banking assets	%	Sample assets	Total banking assets	%	Sample assets	Total banking assets	%
1992	34,200	77,500	44	52,200	62,500	84	6,900	9,100	75	77,600	129,600	60
1993	34,300	68,400	50	54,300	60,900	89	7,100	9,600	74	82,700	142,800	58
1994	37,000	73,700	50	57,200	62,300	92	8,000	10,700	75	85,400	146,300	58
1995	40,000	73,700	54	63,900	69,800	92	9,100	11,900	77	89,600	150,100	60
1996	42,500	76,600	55	67,600	77,100	88	9,800	12,500	79	93,900	156,400	60
1997	44,900	83,500	54	77,200	89,100	87	11,100	13,700	81	105,000	163,900	64
1998	48,700	99,400	49	82,600	97,300	85	12,000	14,800	81	111,500	171,400	65
1999	55,200	102,100	54	88,700	103,300	86	13,000	16,300	80	121,700	172,200	71
2000	57,400	106,400	54	93,800	103,600	90	14,500	18,900	77	131,900	181,300	73
Average	43,800	84,600	52	70,800	80,600	88	10,200	13,100	78	99,900	157,100	63

Sources: The total assets were extracted from the annual financial reports of the monetary agencies in the countries under study (the consolidated financial statements of the banks) while the sample was drawn from the London Bankscope database (January, 2000 and 2002).

Table 8.2 shows the specialization of the banks included in the sample. The number of commercial banks comprises around 66 per cent of the total sample. The percentage of commercial banks operating in each country varies, ranging from 42 per cent in Bahrain to 77 per cent in Saudi Arabia.

Table 8.3 shows that the size of total assets of all the banks included in the present study increased from about US$ 180 billion in 1992 to about US$ 310 billion in 2000 and averaged about US$ 235 billion over the whole period. Dividing these financial institutions into nine size categories, the share of the largest banks (with assets size greater than US$ 5 billion) constituted around 70 per cent of the total assets of all the banks over the period 1992–2000.

Al-Jarrah and Molyneux (2003) employ the intermediation approach, as indicated earlier, for defining bank inputs and outputs. Following Aly *et al.* (1990), the inputs used in the calculation of the various efficiency measures are deposits (w_1), labour (w_2) and physical capital (w_3). The deposits include time and savings deposits, notes and debentures, and other borrowed funds. The price of loanable funds was derived by taking the sum of interest expenses of the time deposits[2] and other loanable funds divided by loanable funds. Labour is measured by personnel expenses as a percent of total assets. Bank physical capital is measured by the book value of premises and fixed assets (including capitalized leases). The price of capital was derived by taking total expenditures on premises and fixed assets divided by total assets. The three outputs used in the study includes total customer loans (y_1), all other earning assets (y_2), and off-balance sheet items (y_3), measured in millions of US dollars.

The off-balance sheet items (measured in nominal terms) were included as a third output. Although the latter are technically not earning assets, these constitute an increasing source of income for banks and therefore should be included when modelling the banks' cost characteristics; otherwise, total banks' output would tend to be understated (Jagtiani and Khanthavit, 1996). Furthermore, these items are included in the model because they are often effective substitutes for directly issued loans, requiring similar

Table 8.2 Specialization of banks under study, 1992–2000 (per cent of total)

	Bahrain	Egypt	Jordan	Saudi Arabia	All
Commercial	44	76	57	77	66
Investment	28	8	29	8	16
Islamic	17	5	7	0	7
Other	11	11	7	15	11
Total number	18	37	14	13	82

Source: Calculated from Bankscope (Jan. 2000 and 2002).

Table 8.3 Distribution of banks' assets in Jordan, Egypt, Saudi Arabia and Bahrain, 1992–2000

Bank asset size ($ m)	1992	1993	1994	1995	1996	1997	1998	1999	2000	Avg.
	%	%	%	%	%	%	%	%	%	US$, mil.
1–99.9	0.11	0.08	0.14	0.16	0.14	0.10	0.06	0.02	0.02	202
100–199.9	1.16	1.05	0.78	0.35	0.31	0.18	0.21	0.29	0.27	1,073
200–299.9	1.76	1.35	1.10	1.78	1.04	0.80	0.67	0.36	0.32	2,173
300–499.9	3.78	4.08	3.47	2.79	2.92	2.75	2.49	2.04	1.58	6,422
500–999.9	2.56	2.73	4.64	4.57	4.51	3.53	3.67	3.47	3.29	8,569
1,000–2,499.9	11.87	11.50	9.89	13.09	10.02	11.31	11.84	10.51	10.15	25,911
2,500–4,999.9	8.29	8.56	4.68	4.94	7.12	6.65	6.50	7.66	8.26	16,470
5,000–9,999	18.22	19.28	24.51	26.23	24.40	26.82	14.88	19.13	9.28	46,196
10,000+	52.26	51.37	50.78	54.22	49.54	47.85	59.67	56.53	66.83	129,190
T. assets (US$, billion, nominal values)	179	187	197	213	225	250	268	293	313	

Source: Calculated from Bankscope (Jan. 2000 and 2002).

information-gathering costs of origination and ongoing monitoring and control of the counterparts, and presumably similar revenues as these items are competitive substitutes for direct loans.

The definitions, means, and standards of deviation of the input and output variables used in the stochastic frontier estimations are reported in Table 8.4. The table shows that the average bank had US$ 1.26 billion in loans,

Table 8.4 Descriptive statistics of the banks' inputs and outputs for Jordan, Egypt, Saudi Arabia and Bahrain over 1992–2000

Variables	Description	Mean	St. dev	Min.	Max.
TC	Total cost (includes Interest expense, Personnel expense, Commission expense, Fee expense, Trading expense, other operating expense) (US$ millions).	170	300	0	1,720
W1	Price of funds (%) (total interest expense/total customer deposits (demand, saving and time deposits)).	0.07	0.09	0.00	1.98
W2	Price of labour (%) (total personnel expense/total assets).	0.02	0.01	0.00	0.21
W3	Price of physical capital (non-interest expense/average assets).	0.01	0.01	0.00	0.21
Y1	The US $ value of total aggregate loans(all types of loans) (US$ millions).	1,260	2,280	1	15,060
Y2	The US $ value of total aggregate other earning assets (short-term investment, equity and other investment and public sector securities (US$ millions)).	1,390	2,470	1	13,600
Y3	The US $ value of the off-balance sheet activities (nominal values, US$ millions).	1,320	3,510	1	26,740
p1	Price of loans (%) (total earned interest/total loans).	0.15	0.07	0.01	0.87
p2	Price of other earning assets (%) (trading income and other operating income excluding commission and fees income/other earning assets).	0.05	0.04	0.01	0.33
P3	Price of off-balance sheet items (%) (commission and fees income/off-balance sheet items).	0.01	0.02	0.00	0.20

Source: Calculated from Bankscope (Jan. 2000 and 2002).

US$ 1.39 billion other earning assets and US$ 1.32 billion of balance sheet items over 1992–2000. The cost of input variables averaged about 7.0 per cent for purchased funds, 2.0 per cent for labour and 1.0 per cent for physical capital over the period 1992–2000. On the other hand, the prices of banks' output averaged about 15.0 per cent for loans; 5.0 per cent for other earning assets and 1.0 per cent for off-balance sheet items over the same period.

In addition to the above input and output variables, the study also employs a variety of control and environmental variables[3] to rule out the effect of other factors that might explain differences among efficiency estimates for the banks under study. The three control variables included in our model include the size of loan loss reserves as a percent of banks' credit portfolio, the capital adequacy ratio, and a time trend (see Table 8.5 below for details). The loan loss reserves as a proportion of gross loans ranged between 0.01 and 19.68 per cent; the latter figure suggests that some banks faced substantial credit quality problems. The total banks' capital as a percentage of total assets averaged around 14.0 per cent with a standard deviation of 12.0 per cent; this reflects sizeable differences in the capital adequacy of the banks under study.

The size of loan loss reserves as a proportion of gross loans is added to the model to control for the banks' risk structure. It is also used as a measure of banks' asset quality and as a measure of the banks' management efficiency in monitoring the credit portfolio. A lack of diversity in a bank's asset portfolio may be associated with increases in problem loans without sufficient provisioning, exposing a bank's capital to risk and potential bankruptcy that might be closely related to the quality of bank management. Banks facing financial distress have been found to carry large proportions of nonperforming loans (Whalen, 1991). Furthermore, studies on bank failures suggest a positive relationship between operating inefficiency and failure rates (see, for example, Cebenoyan, Cooperman and Register, 1993; Hermalin and Wallace, 1994; Wheelock and Wilson, 1995). Barr, Seiford and Siems (1994) found that this positive relationship between inefficiency and failure is evident a number of years ahead of eventual failure. Kwan and Eisenbeis (1995) report that problem loans are negatively related to efficiency even in non-failing banks. Berger and DeYoung (1997) found a link between management quality and problem loans by reporting that an increase in management quality reduces banks' problem loans.

Hughes *et al.* (1996a, b) and Mester (1996) included the volume of nonperforming loans as a control for loan quality in studies of US banks, and Berg *et al.* (1993) included loan losses as an indicator of loan quality evaluations in a DEA study of Norwegian bank productivity. Whether it is appropriate to include nonperforming loans and loan losses in banks' cost, standard and alternative profit functions depends on the extent to which these variables are exogenous. Such variables would be exogenous if caused by negative economic shocks ('bad luck'), but they could be endogenous, either because management is inefficient in managing its portfolio ('bad management') or because it has made a conscious decision to reduce short-run expenses by cutting back on loan origination and monitoring resources ('skimping'). Berger and DeYoung (1997) tested the bad-luck, bad-management, and skimping hypotheses and found mixed evidence on the exogeneity of nonperforming loans.

Another important aspect of efficiency measurement is the treatment of financial capital. A bank's insolvency risk depends on the financial capital available to absorb portfolio losses, as well as on the portfolio risks themselves. Even apart from risk, a bank's capital level directly affects costs by providing an alternative to deposits as a funding source for loans. On the other hand, raising equity typically involves higher costs than raising deposits. If the first effect dominates, measured costs will be higher for banks using a higher proportion of debt financing; if the second effect dominates, measured costs will be lower for these banks. Large banks depend more on debt financing to finance their portfolios than small banks do, so failure to control for equity could yield a scale bias. The specification of capital in the cost and profit functions also goes part of the way toward accounting for different risk preferences on the part of banks. Therefore, if some banks are more risk averse than others, they may hold a higher level of financial capital than maximizing profits or minimizing costs. If financial capital is ignored, the efficiency of these banks would be mismeasured, even though they behave optimally given their risk preferences. Hughes *et al.* (1996a, b, and 1997) and Hughes *et al.* (1995) tested and rejected the assumption of risk neutrality for banks. Clark (1996) included capital in a model of economic cost and found that it eliminated measured scale diseconomies in production costs alone. The cost studies of Hughes, *et al.* (1995) and the Hughes *et al.* (1996a, 1997) profit studies incorporated financial capital and found increasing returns to scale at large-asset-size banks. A possible reason is that large size confers diversification benefits that allow large banks to have lower capital ratios than smaller banks. Akhavein *et al.* (1997) controlled for equity capital and found that profit efficiency increases as a result of mergers of large banks. Banks' capital is also included in the model of Berger and Mester (1997) who find that well-capitalized firms are more efficient. This positive relationship between capital and efficiency may indicate that inefficient banks with lower capital have less to lose in taking more risky projects than an efficient bank. This is consistent with moral hazard and agency conflict between managers and shareholders where less monitored managers with lower equity have incentives to expense preference (to divert profits to senior executives' pay at a cost to shareholders).

The environmental variables (or efficiency correlates) were also added to the model to investigate the reason for the differences in efficiency scores across banks under study. These include variables that control for market structure and organizational characteristics, geographical segmentation and bank liquidity. Al-Jarrah and Molyneux (2003) identify variables to account for bank specialization, bank size and concentration in the respective banking industries. Financial institutions in each country are divided into four categories: commercial, investment, Islamic and other financial institutions (that perform various bank functions). Furthermore, they employ the 3-firm asset concentration ratio that is widely used to test for monopoly characteristics. They also include a dummy variable to control for bank geographical (country) location.

The total assets variable is used to control for bank size where bank size may be associated with efficiency, as size may be required to utilize scale and (maybe) scope economies (if large banks are more diversified). Furthermore, larger banks may have more professional management teams and/or might be more cost conscious due to greater pressure from owners concerning the bottom-line profits (Evanoff and Israilevich, 1991). Berger *et al.* (1993a) found that most of the efficiency differences among large banks was on the output side, as larger banks might be better able to reach their optimal mix and scale of outputs. On the other hand, Hermalin and Wallace (1994), Kaparakis *et al.* (1994), and DeYoung and Nolle (1996) found significant negative relationships. Other studies, however, report no significant relationship between bank size and efficiency, such as Berger and Mester (1997) and Chang *et al.* (1998).

The 3-firm concentration ratio and market share variables were included to control for oligopoly behaviour along the lines of the traditional structure–conduct–performance paradigm (see Molyneux *et al.*, 1996) and as an indicator of the characteristics of the respective banking industry structures. The Cournot model of oligopolistic behaviour suggests that there is a positive relationship between concentration and profitability. Consistent with this model, some studies have found a positive relationship between market concentration and profitability (Berger and Hannan, 1995; Berger and Mester, 1997). The market power that prevails in less competitive markets enables some banks to charge higher prices for their services and make supernormal profits. Banks may exert their own market power through size, as noted by Berger (1995), and so we include a market share variable to control for what Berger refers to as 'relative market power'.

Dummy variables for bank specialization are also included in the model so as to control for the product diversity, as efficiency may be associated with a firm's strength in carefully targeting its market niches. The cost of producing various products may be lower when specialized banks produce them rather than when a single bank produces all the products, due to diseconomies of scope. There are a number of studies that have examined the impact of product diversity on efficiency. Aly *et al.* (1990) found a negative relationship between product diversity and cost efficiency. Ferrier, Grosskopf, Hayes and Yaisawarng (1993) found that banks with greater product diversity tend to have lower cost efficiency. Chaffai and

Dietsch (1995) compared the efficiency of universal versus non-universal (more specialized) banks in Europe and found the former to be less cost efficient.

Finally, the liquidity ratio is included to account for banks' liquidity risk. Banks that hold more liquidity may be expected to have lower liquidity risk but may be less profit efficient as liquid assets tend to yield lower returns. In contrast, as liquid assets are controlled in outputs, one would expect banks with higher liquid assets (all other things being equal) to be more cost efficient.

Bank efficiency in Egypt, Jordan, Saudi Arabia and Bahrain

Using the methodology and data sources outlined above, Al-Jarrah and Molyneux (2003) find that cost efficiency estimates for banks in the countries under study averaged 95 per cent and these estimates have slightly varied over time from 95 per cent in 1992 to 94 per cent in 2000. This suggests that the same level of output could be produced with approximately 95 per cent of current inputs if banks under study were operating on the most efficient frontier. This level of technical inefficiency is somewhat less than the range of 10–15 per cent for the 130 studies surveyed by Berger and Humphrey (1997) and Berger and DeYoung (1997). These results are also less than the level of inefficiency found in European studies, including Carbo *et al.*'s (2000) whose findings for a sample of banks, from twelve countries, show mean cost inefficiency of around 22 per cent for the period 1989 to 1996.

Referring to Table 8.5, the average cost efficiency based on bank specialization ranged from 93 per cent for investment banks to 98 per cent for Islamic banks. The efficiency scores, based on geographical location, ranged from 89 per cent in Jordan to 99 per cent in Bahrain. Finally, based on asset size, the differences among technical efficiency scores are not significant where optimal bank size is US$ 2.5–5.0 billion and the largest banks seem to be somewhat more efficient.

As indicated earlier, the bank efficiency literature considers the estimation of both cost and profit efficiencies to reveal more accurate information about firm-level performance (see Berger and Mester, 1999). Referring to Tables 8.6 and 8.7, the standard and alternative profit functions results show average technical efficiency estimates are around 66 per cent and 58 per cent respectively over the period 1992–2000. It should be noted that this level of efficiency is somewhat similar to the typical range of profit efficiency found in US studies, which is about half of the industry's potential profits, according to Berger and Humphrey (1997). Profit inefficiencies in Arab banking are less than those found in European banking. For instance, Williams and Gardener (2000) estimate profit efficiency to be 79.7 per cent in European banking during the 1990s. The mean profit efficiency given the

Table 8.5   Cost efficiency in Jordan, Egypt, Saudi Arabia and Bahrain banking over 1992–2000

	1992	1993	1994	1995	1996	1997	1998	1999	2000	All
Bahrain	100	100	100	100	100	99	99	99	99	99
Egypt	94	94	94	94	94	93	93	93	93	94
Jordan	90	89	89	89	89	89	89	88	88	89
Saudi Arabia	97	97	97	97	97	97	97	97	96	97
Commercial	95	95	95	95	94	94	94	94	94	94
Investment	93	93	93	93	93	93	93	93	93	93
Islamic	98	98	98	98	99	99	98	98	98	98
Other	97	96	96	96	96	96	96	96	96	96
All	95	95	95	95	95	94	94	94	94	95

Asset size (US$ million)

	1–199	200–299	300–499	500–999	1,000–2,499	2,500–4,999	5,000–9,900	10000+	All
Bahrain	100	99	100	99	99	99	99	99	99
Egypt	95	94	94	94	94	93	92	90	94
Jordan	88	87	88	91	90			91	89
Saudi Arabia				98	98	98	98	95	97
All	95	93	94	95	95	96	96	94	95

Asset size (US$ million)

	1992	1993	1994	1995	1996	1997	1998	1999	2000	All
1–199.9	94	94	95	95	96	96	95	96	95	95
200–299	93	94	92	93	92	92	95	95	95	93
300–499	95	95	95	95	94	94	92	92	91	94
500–999	96	94	94	94	94	95	96	95	96	95
1,000–2,499	96	96	95	96	96	94	94	94	94	95
2,500–4,999	95	96	99	96	96	96	96	96	96	96
5,000–9,999	98	98	97	96	96	96	95	96	95	96
10000+	95	95	94	94	94	93	94	93	94	94
All	95	95	95	95	95	94	94	94	94	95

Source: Al-Jarrah and Molyneux, 2003.

standard profit function, suggests that banks under study lose around 34 per cent of profits that could be earned by a best-practice institution. The profit efficiency, given both the standard profit and alternative profit function, witnessed volatility over the period 1992–2000. While over the period 1993–9 the efficiency estimates derived from both profit function specifications fluctuate slightly around their average, the year 2000 exhibits a fall in profit efficiency across banks under study. This might reflect the response of economic and financial activities to the instability in the oil prices and the

Table 8.6 Standard profit efficiency in Jordan, Egypt, Saudi Arabia and Bahrain banking over 1992–2000

	1992	1993	1994	1995	1996	1997	1998	1999	2000	All
Bahrain	69	78	67	71	66	72	67	68	57	68
Egypt	66	64	66	70	66	64	65	73	63	66
Jordan	84	60	61	61	63	56	56	59	50	61
Saudi Arabia	67	68	66	69	69	65	59	63	63	65
Commercial	70	67	68	72	69	65	62	68	62	67
Investment	65	69	55	55	48	51	57	60	43	56
Islamic	83	73	78	79	75	80	67	67	76	75
Other	64	58	57	61	64	73	74	78	55	65
All	70	67	65	68	66	65	63	68	59	66

Asset size (US$ million)

	1–199	200–299	300–499	500–999	1,000–2,499	2,500–4,999	5,000–9,900	10000+	All
Bahrain	75	67	71	62	66	66	78	56	68
Egypt	74	59	60	70	69	70	58	72	66
Jordan	53	66	56	73	53			68	61
Saudi Arabia				43	62	65	68	68	65
All	70	63	62	68	65	67	67	67	66

Asset size (US$ million)

	1992	1993	1994	1995	1996	1997	1998	1999	2000	All
1–199.9	72	68	75	70	65	70	76	70	56	70
200–299	65	75	60	65	62	60	57	63	44	63
300–499	71	65	60	60	58	63	59	64	55	62
500–999	61	66	62	76	71	64	63	75	66	68
1,000–2,499	78	62	64	66	65	67	66	67	56	65
2,500–4,999	59	49	79	79	78	63	64	77	62	67
5,000–9,999	65	73	71	72	64	60	61	70	64	67
10000+	70	73	64	73	76	71	60	61	63	67
All	70	67	65	68	66	65	63	68	59	66

Source: Al-Jarrah and Molyneux, 2003.

political instability aroused from recent conflict aggravation in Palestine and the Gulf.

Given the standard profit function, profit efficiency ranged from around 61 per cent in Jordan to 68 per cent in Bahrain. Based on specialization, the results show that the efficiency scores ranged from 56 per cent for investment banks to 75 per cent for the Islamic banks (see Table 8.6 for details). This result might explain the increase in Islamic banking activities, especially in Bahrain, over the past few years, as the cost of funds for Islamic banks is relatively lower than the cost of funds for other financial institutions.

Table 8.7 Alternative profit efficiency in Jordan, Egypt, Saudi Arabia and Bahrain banking over 1992–2000

	1992	1993	1994	1995	1996	1997	1998	1999	2000	All
Bahrain	58	72	60	66	58	64	51	61	58	61
Egypt	65	58	60	62	59	60	56	68	55	60
Jordan	59	51	54	53	49	39	42	52	46	49
Saudi Arabia	56	56	54	51	61	59	51	61	61	57
Commercial	60	59	61	63	63	58	53	62	56	60
Investment	55	61	52	50	43	46	46	62	44	51
Islamic	76	57	60	64	54	63	51	55	78	62
Other	69	62	47	53	48	63	56	67	47	57
All	61	60	58	60	58	57	52	62	55	58

Asset size (US$ million)

	1–199	200–299	300–499	500–999	1,000–2,499	2,500–4,999	5,000–9,900	10000+	All
Bahrain	63	66	59	54	55	59	86	68	61
Egypt	59	55	54	63	64	61	64	78	60
Jordan	42	46	46	59	43			74	49
Saudi Arabia				23	50	65	56	63	57
All	56	55	54	59	57	62	61	69	58

Asset size (US$ million)

	1992	1993	1994	1995	1996	1997	1998	1999	2000	All
1–199.9	61	47	57	68	49	62	63	55	48	56
200–299	56	72	47	58	57	45	46	59	46	55
300–499	58	64	56	52	50	57	44	53	44	54
500–999	62	53	55	61	63	55	51	70	56	59
1,000–2,499	70	57	63	54	49	57	50	64	53	57
2,500–4,999	58	50	66	66	64	52	55	73	66	62
5,000–9,999	58	55	67	64	64	58	63	65	56	61
10000+	62	80	62	74	84	77	60	62	68	69
All	61	60	58	60	58	57	52	62	55	58

Source: Al-Jarrah and Molyneux, 2003.

Islamic banks, as noted in Chapter 6, do not pay interest but rather a mark-up which is a profit margin based on the way in which the funds are utilized. Given the geographical location, Jordan is a much poorer country compared to Saudi Arabia and Bahrain (oil-producing countries) and banks may be able to sell higher profit generating products in these markets. This might explain why the Jordanian banks are relatively less profit efficient than the banks in other countries under study.

Based on the size of assets, apart from the smallest banks which are the most profit efficient, larger banks seem to be more profit efficient, in general. This result supports the theory that large banks enjoy several advantages compared to small banks. These advantages include the ability of large banks to utilize more efficient technology with less cost, the ability of these banks to prepare more specialized staff for the most profitable activities and their ability to provide higher-quality output resulting in higher prices.

Similar results are obtained from the alternative profit function estimates where profit efficiency ranges from 49 per cent in Jordan to 61 per cent in Bahrain. Based on specialization, Islamic banking is again the most profit efficient while investment banking is the least efficient. Based on asset size, the largest banks also seem to be the most efficient. Overall, the results of both the standard and alternative profit function, while varying in absolute efficiency levels, are identical in terms of profit efficiency ranking in terms of country, specialization and bank asset size.

To summarize, the main findings of the Al-Jarrah and Molyneux (2003) study are that cost efficiency levels averaged around 95 per cent over the period 1992–2000, without noticeable change over the 1992–9 period but experiencing a fall in 2000. On the other hand, both standard (and alternative) profit efficiency averaged around 66 per cent (and 56 per cent) over the sample period. Standard profit and alternative profit efficiency of Arabic banking systems did not witness significant changes over the 1993–9 period but also experienced a fall in 2000. That is, profit efficiency has recently fallen.

Profit efficiency estimates for the Arabic banks under study are not noticeably different from those observed from previous studies on the US and European banking industries. Islamic banks are found to be the most cost and profit efficient while investment banks are the least efficient. This result may partially explain the motives behind the increase in Islamic banking activities over the past few years, as the cost of funds for Islamic banks is lower than the cost of funds for other financial institutions. On the other hand, intense competition between investment and commercial banks might explain the competitive disadvantages of the investment banks in terms of their market share and expose the motives for increased mergers and consolidation activity between such banks.

Based on assets size, large banks seems to be relatively more cost and profit efficient, in general. This result suggests that large banks enjoy several advantages compared to small banks. These include the ability of large banks to utilize more efficient technology with less cost, the ability of these banks to set up more specialized staff for the most profitable activities and the ability of these banks to provide better-quality output and therefore charge higher prices. Geographically, Bahrain is the most cost and profit efficient banking systems while Jordan is the least cost and profit efficient.

Finally, while the countries under study have implemented many economic and financial reforms over the last twenty years or so, as indicated earlier, these reforms do not appear to have had much impact on banking sector efficiency. Given our findings, it seems that more reform may be needed to improve (especially) their profit efficiency. Perhaps the move to create a single GCC market may help to facilitate these developments as the creation of a similar European single market appears to have had a positive impact on European bank efficiency (see European Commission, 1997).

Efficiency in GCC banking systems

This section reports evidence on bank efficiency on a wider range of GCC banking systems over the period 1995–2000. Using various model specifications, Mohamed (2003) examines the efficiency features of GCC banks and Figure 8.1 shows the mean cost and profit inefficiencies for each country. In general, cost inefficiency estimates across GCC countries are more or less similar to each other. This is true for different model estimations. Nevertheless, because the use of the distribution-free approach provides closer inefficiency estimates to the half-normal model, Mohamed (2003) tends to accept the half-normal estimates as those that are more likely to reflect the 'actual' level of inefficiency in GCC banking markets.

Figure 8.1 indicates that Omani banks appear to be the least cost inefficient (i.e. the most efficient), scoring a level of 7.1 per cent cost inefficiency. The next least cost inefficient banks are Saudi banks, with cost inefficiency levels of 7.9 per cent. Bahraini and Kuwaiti banks occupy the middle ground of GCC cost inefficiency with levels of 7.5 per cent. Qatari and UAE banks have been the most cost inefficient with cost inefficiency levels of 8.3 and 8.8 per cent respectively. The findings on cost efficiency are similar to those by Al-Jarrah and Molyneux (2003) who find Bahraini and Saudia Arabian banks to be the most cost efficient. However, it should be noted that Al-Jarrah and Molyneux (2003) compared the efficiency of Bahrain and Saudi banks with those in Jordan and Egypt, whereas Mohamed's study focuses solely on GGC banking systems. As such, one would expect to arrive at different results given that the peer group of best-practice banks will come from different banking systems. On the profit side, standard and alternative profit inefficiencies across GCC countries tend to vary. In general, Figure 8.1 shows that banks from Saudi Arabia and Bahrain are the most profit inefficient, with a profit inefficiency difference of at least 7 per cent points higher than for other GCC countries' banks.

Omani banks remain the least profit inefficient, while the rest of the GCC countries' banks fall in the middle positions.

Figures 8.2 and 8.3 compare the inefficiency across bank ownership and asset size, respectively. Figure 8.2 shows that foreign banks are more cost inefficient than national banks; in contrast, foreign banks are more profit efficient than national banks. Figure 8.3 presents efficiency scores according to the size of bank; generally, large banks are less cost inefficient than

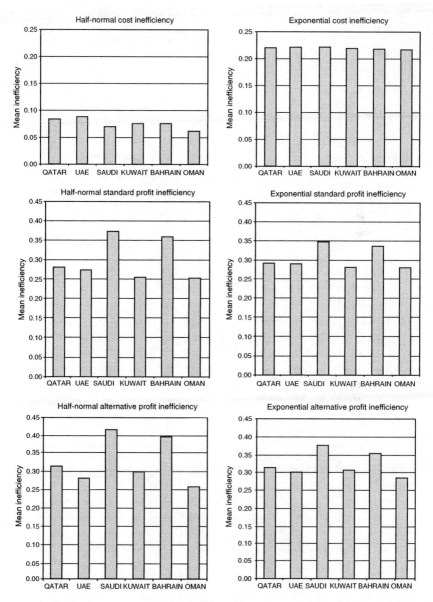

Figure 8.1 Cost and profit inefficiencies across GCC banking systems, 1995–2000 (average)

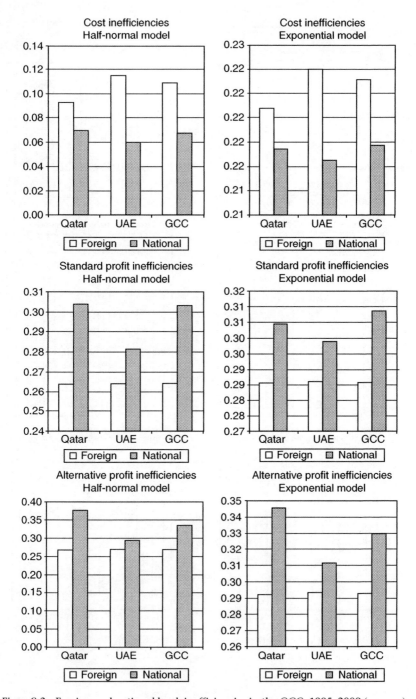

Figure 8.2 Foreign and national bank inefficiencies in the GCC, 1995–2000 (average)

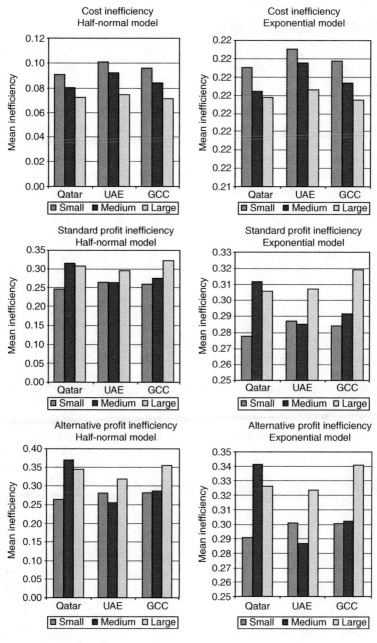

Small banks are under $300 million in assets; Medium: $300 million to $1 billion in assets; Large: Over $1 billion in assets.

Figure 8.3 Cost and profit inefficiencies across bank size in the GCC, 1995–2000 (average)

medium-sized and small banks. On the other hand, small banks are less profit inefficient than medium and large banks.

Mohamed (2003) shows that when the size class ranges, the conclusions drawn regarding banks' cost and profit inefficiencies according to the size of banks remain almost unchanged. That is, large banks are less cost inefficient but more profit inefficient than small banks.

It may not be surprising that Omani banks are the least cost inefficient in the GCC banking industry, although the differences in inefficiency scores are relatively small between these countries. In addition, although the number of the Omani banks included in the sample is relatively small (6 banks), the Omani banking system witnessed the most active M & A (Merger and Acquisition) activity taking place in the GCC region over the study period, enabling Omani banks to show the highest cost and profit efficiency scores. These mergers have materialized due to authorities' encouragements.

One may expect that banks with higher cost inefficiency will have higher profit inefficiency since cost inefficiency is included in profit inefficiency. However, the results tend to indicate that this is not the case, at least for GCC banking. For example, UAE banks, which are more cost inefficient than Kuwaiti banks, have lower profit inefficiency.

Bearing in mind that across the whole GCC banking system there is a common frontier for profit and cost functions, the results may imply that the best-practice bank in terms of cost is not necessarily the same as that in terms of profit, since the cost-efficient bank may do better at choosing the appropriate input mix but may do worse in terms of output mix.

The question as to why one country's banks are more cost or profit efficient than another may be related to the size of banks in a country. For instance, with reference to Figures 8.2 and 8.3, countries that have relatively small banks, such as the UAE and Qatar, tend to show higher cost inefficiency but lower profit inefficiency. On the other hand, banking industries that are dominated by larger banks, such as those in Saudi Arabia, Bahrain, and Kuwait, tend to show lower cost inefficiency but higher profit inefficiency. In fact, large banks may have lower cost inefficiencies because their per unit cost decreases as the scale increases. However, scale effects may induce profit inefficiency because large banks may face more difficulty in generating revenues efficiently. Berger and Mester (1997, p. 936) state that '[t]he cost and profit efficiency results together seem to imply that as banks grow larger, they are equally able to control costs, but it becomes harder to create revenues efficiently'. Moreover, this finding is consistent with the conventional fact that small banks typically have higher profitability ratios than larger banks. Having said this, however, the scale effects that induce profit inefficiency are unlikely to be large.

This scale effect could also explain differences in the inefficiency of foreign and national banks. For instance, the majority of foreign banks operating in the GCC countries are classified in terms of size as small to medium-sized banks. Therefore, as is shown in Figure 8.3, foreign banks are found to be less cost efficient but more profit efficient than national banks.

Scale economies in Gulf banking

Scale economies measure how a unit change in output affects total costs.[4] The economies of scale results from Mohamed (2003) are shown in Table 8.8. With reference to the cross-country scale economies comparisons, the results in Table 8.8 show that both (the half-normal and exponential) estimates assign Saudi and Kuwaiti banks as realizing scale economies over the period under study. Bahraini banks experience constant returns to scale. However, UAE, Omani, and Qatari banks exhibit scale diseconomies.

Overall, Mohamed (2003) finds that the GCC banking industry has been exhibiting scale diseconomies driven mostly by banks from the UAE, Oman, and Qatar.

It is also found that large GCC banks are much closer to unity than those of small and medium banks. Moreover, small banks show more scale diseconomies than medium-size banks. Scale economies have also been calculated for the foreign banks operating in the GCC banking system (specifically, foreign banks operating in the UAE and Qatar). In comparison to the GCC national banks, foreign banks have on average been operating with higher scale diseconomies than national banks over the six-year period.

Scale inefficiency in Gulf banking

The reason for computing scale inefficiency is that we cannot compare between the estimates of both scale economy and X-inefficiency since they measure different aspects of a bank's cost characteristics. That is, scale economies is a measure of scale elasticity that expresses a percentage change in the total cost with respect to a percentage change in output, and X-inefficiency

Table 8.8 Scale economies in the GCC banking industry, by country

	Scale economies(Half-normal inefficiency distribution)	Scale economies (Exponential inefficiency distribution model)
GCC	1.108	1.177
Qatar	1.222	1.281
UAE	1.166	1.229
Saudi Arabia	0.903	0.995
Kuwait	0.886	0.970
Bahrain	1.027	1.097
Oman	1.256	1.329

Source: Mohamed, 2003, various pages.

expresses the percentage of the cost function that bank i needs to alter so that it can reach the cost function of the industry's best-practice bank.

In order to find a common ground for comparing the estimates of these two concepts, scale economies must be transformed into scale inefficiency, which expresses the percentage the cost function ought to change if a bank needs to move to the minimum efficient scale. Using the approach suggested by Evanoff and Israilevich (1995),[5] scale inefficiencies for Gulf banks are calculated by Mohamed (2003) and his results are shown in Figure 8.4. This shows comparisons between X-inefficiency and scale inefficiency estimates and illustrates that X-inefficiencies are consistently larger than scale inefficiencies.

Many other studies find that cost X-inefficiency dominates both scale and scope efficiencies. For example, Berger and Humphrey (1991) find that X-inefficiencies dominate scale and scope inefficiencies in commercial banking.[6] In contrast, Altunbas *et al.* (2000) find that scale inefficiencies dominate X-inefficiencies in Japanese banking. On a country-wide basis, Mohamed (2003) finds that Saudi banks are the most scale-efficient banks within the GCC. The Kuwaiti and Bahraini banks are together the second most scale-efficient banks. Larger banks are also found to be more scale efficient than smaller competitors.

Mohamed's (2003) overall results that large banks (mostly national banks) realize greater scale economies and are more scale efficient than small banks

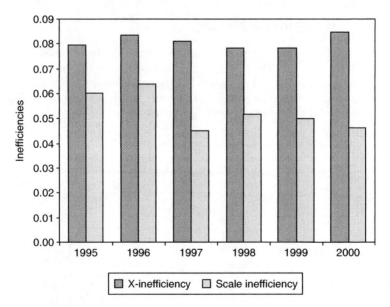

Figure 8.4   Comparisons between scale and X-inefficiency in GCC banking
Source: Mohamed, 2003.

in the GCC banking industries could be explained in a number of ways. One explanation is related to the issue of the bank's age. Older banks have increased their size over time and become more scale exploitive. This explanation applies also to foreign banks since long-established foreign banks have increased their size over time in response to economic development and this has led to a better exploitation of resources and per unit cost reduction. For example, foreign banks that were established in the 1950s, 1960s, and 1970s were probably better placed to profit from financing the early stages of the GCC growth period during the 1970s.[7] However, while a share of large foreign banks' domestic financing has, to a certain extent, been crowded out by national banks established mainly in the 1970s and 1980s, large foreign banks still have a sizable share of the foreign banks' sector (about 70 per cent of total foreign bank assets, which represent nearly 24 per cent of the total GCC commercial banking market).

Large banks are also seen to have greater geographical coverage in the GCC than small and medium-size banks. Large foreign banks have opened branches, particularly in Qatar and the UAE. They may, perhaps, have been able to realize economies from this type of expansion.

Another issue relating to the exploitation of economies and scale efficiencies is that if a country is over-banked with commercial banks, scale economies and scale efficiencies might be affected. This being so, banks that operate in relatively small GCC countries that appear over-banked, such as Qatar and the UAE, may have less opportunity to exploit scale and other cost efficiencies. Countries that restrict new bank licensing like Saudi Arabia and Kuwait potentially provide greater scale and cost efficiency advantages for locally operating banks.

Large banks may realize greater scale economies and scale efficiencies because they have greater access to better information technology. This relates to such things as more sophisticated ATM networks, better credit scoring systems, and improved internal and external monitoring and screening systems. Taken together, big banks in the GCC may have technology, managerial, and other advantages over smaller banks, resulting ultimately in improved cost performance.

Since most of the large banks operating in the GCC banking sector are national banks, it is important to note that many of these have been established and promoted by government regulation and ownership. For example, Saudi Arabia and Kuwait have strict regulations governing the establishment of any new commercial banks. Similarly, in Qatar and the UAE, there are limits associated with foreign bank branches. This limitation has created an opportunity for existing banks, especially national banks, to expand their services to absorb increases in the demand for credit and other banking services.

Apart from the regulations that inhibit foreign bank presence or/ and expansion in these markets, foreign banks may also suffer from other limitations. For instance, GCC governments mainly favour national banks to fulfil the majority, if not all, of their government financing needs. This can have the adverse effect of distorting the price mechanism since the choice of the government may not be based on market disciplines. Government practice, in this case, could also affect foreign interests in investing in the country, discourage potential foreign banking, and distort national bank competitiveness.

Foreign banking business is also characterized mainly by relatively narrow banking activities such as money transfer and the facilitation of moderate commercial trade between the host country and the country of origin, while larger foreign banks undertake a broad range of commercial and corporate banking activities. Many of the smaller foreign banks have located in the GCC to remit transfers mainly for expatriate workers. However, because deposits of expatriate workers (in most cases) tend to be relatively small, and because there are restrictions on foreign banks' operations, many foreign banks have remained small in size. This may explain these banks' inability to grow in order to realize greater scale economies and scale efficiency.

Nonetheless, small banks (mostly foreign banks) can find ways to continue their business alongside large banks. '[S]mall banks are better at relationship banking than large banks due to superior information and greater discretion in applying information' (Chen, Mason and Higgins, 2001). Moreover, loan officers at large banks tend to be more strict in following bank rules and criteria than their counterparts in small banks (Nakamura, 1994). This also suggests why smaller banks (or foreign banks) are able to survive under restrictions and less efficient performance.

Determinants of Gulf bank efficiency

The final part of Mohamed's (2003) study examines the determinants of banking sector inefficiency in GCC banking systems over 1995–2000. For this purpose, he uses the logistic regression model, in which he regresses inefficiency variables (cost and profit inefficiency measures) on a variety of bank and market-specific variables that are believed to be most likely to influence inefficiency levels. The results are shown in Tables 8.9 and 8.10. Starting with the relationship between inefficiency and financial capital, in both cost and profit inefficiency determinants, the coefficient is negative and is significantly different from zero. This indicates that banks with low inefficiency levels tend to hold higher levels of capital. Generally, in this analysis, the results suggest that more efficient GCC banks generate higher earnings, which are translated into higher levels of capital.

The results also show that accounting profits (return-on-assets) is negative and is significantly different from zero as well. The return-on-assets coefficient

Table 8.9 Determinants of GCC bank cost inefficiency (logistic regression)

Independent variables	Dependent variable Cost inefficiency		
	Coefficient	std. error	T-value
Constant	8.13E-02	7.71E-03	10.548
Equity	−4.12E-08	1.33E-08	−3.108
Return on assets	−0.2483704	4.46E-02	−5.575
Loan-loss provisions	8.23E-02	4.27E-02	1.928
Foreign bank (dummy variable)	2.59E-02	4.18E-03	6.203
Loans-to-total assets	−5.05E-02	8.63E-03	−5.857
Fixed assets to total assets	2.42E-08	2.57E-08	0.943
Total assets	2.14E-09	1.35E-09	1.59
Banking sector assets/GDP	−3.45E-04	8.38E-04	−0.412
CN[−1]*	0.4309832	3.61E-02	11.942
Durbin-Watson statistic =	1.91243	Rho =	0.04379
Adjusted R-squared =	0.46058		
Observations =	558		

* The lagged dependent variable is used to remove auto-correlation.
Source: Mohamed, 2003.

in both cost and profit inefficiency regressions confirms that more efficient banks may be expected to achieve, on average, better accounting profits performance than less efficient banks. Therefore, this may underline the perception that more efficient banks can consolidate their capital through better profit performance, enabling them to accumulate higher capital, in turn making them less risky firms.

With respect to loan quality, both the cost and profit inefficiency dependent variables are positively correlated with the level of provisions; the variable is significant at the 10 per cent level in the cost inefficiency regression but insignificant in the profit inefficiency regression. This positive correlation suggests that inefficient banks are forced by regulation to increase the level of provisions when their loans are facing default problems. In other words, a high level of provisions indicates loan quality deterioration and, as a result, inefficiency generally increases in response to the higher level of problem loans. This may also suggests that efficient banks with lower levels of loan provisions are better at evaluating credit risk.

Turning to the issue of ownership, the dummy variable for foreign banks shows a positive and statistically significant relationship with cost inefficiency but a statistically insignificant relationship with profit inefficiency. Taking at least the relationship between cost inefficiency and the variable for foreign banks, it is inferred that the existence of foreign banks has contributed to the inefficiency level in the GCC banking industry during the study period.

Table 8.10　Determinants of GCC bank profit inefficiency (logistic regression)

Variable	Dependent variable Standard profit inefficiency		
	Coefficient std.	error	T-value
Constant	0.2588479	3.13E-02	8.274
Equity	−2.66E-07	5.65E-08	−4.705
Return on assets	−1.006451	0.18616	−5.406
Loan-loss Provisions	1.11E-02	0.18015	0.062
Foreign bank (dummy variable)	8.52E-03	1.62E-02	0.527
Loans-to-total assets	−7.09E-02	3.53E-02	−2.005
Fixed assets to total assets	−9.05E-08	1.08E-07	−0.838
Total assets	2.33E-08	5.74E-09	4.069
Banking sector assets/GDP	1.99E-03	3.53E-03	0.564
SN[−1]*	0.5102705	3.46E-02	14.757
Durbin-Watson statistic =	1.95567	Rho =	0.02217
Adjusted R-squared =	0.38476		
Observations =	558		

* The lagged dependent variable is used to remove auto-correlation.
Source: Mohamed, 2003.

This result is consistent with the finding that foreign banks operating in GCC countries tend to be less cost efficient than their national peers. In fact, regulatory restrictions on foreign bank business, such as restrictions on bank size, taxes, and bank branching, could also be the main factors inducing foreign banks to contribute to inefficiency in the GCC banking industry.

As for the rest of the control variables, the negative correlation between the loan to assets ratio and the inefficiency levels indicate that banks with higher proportions of lending business in their balance sheets are more efficient. This finding may indicate that the GCC countries' larger banks emphasized lending business during the second half of the 1990s in order to respond to market demand. Moreover, bank total assets which approximate the size of a bank, shows a clearer relationship between bank profit inefficiency and bank size (than bank cost inefficiency and bank size). As we previously noted, large banks usually experience higher profit inefficiency than small banks. The statistically significant and positive relationship between total assets and profit inefficiency indicates that as banks increase in size, their profit inefficiency increases. Nevertheless, this relationship is not evident in case of cost inefficiency since the total assets coefficient is not significant, although its sign is positive.

Taken together, the main results from Mohamed's (2003) logistic regression are that the strengthening of financial capital is a central element explaining bank efficiency in the GCC region. On the other hand, the erosion in loan quality reduces banking sector efficiency. Overall, the policy implication is that regulations in the region need to focus on building a safe and sound banking system with adequate prudential rules. This should ultimately feed into improved banking sector efficiency levels.

Banking sector efficiency in Algeria, Morocco and Tunisia

A recent study by Bakhouche (2004) provides the first detailed study of banking sector efficiency in the three main Maghreb countries – Algeria, Morocco and Tunisia. Using a sample of banks from 1994 to 2001 he estimates both cost and profit efficiency for different types of financial firms. Banks are classified into five main types: commercial banks, specialized governmental banks, multi-lateral governmental banks, merchant banks (or investment houses) and finally, other non-banking financial institutions include leasing and factoring firms. These are shown in Table 8.11.

Bakhouche (2004) uses two model specifications according to Battese and Coelli (1992) and Battese and Coelli (1995) to arrive at a preferred model specification.[8] Tables 8.12 and 8.13 display the technical efficiency estimates of banks in Algeria, Morocco and Tunisia for the cost and alternative profit efficiency derived from the preferred models over the period of study 1994–2001.

Table 8.12 shows that cost inefficiency averages around 28 per cent for the whole sample (cost efficiency is 72.21 per cent overall). This suggests that the same level of output could be produced with approximately three-quarters of current inputs if the banking institutions under study operated on the most cost efficient frontier. For comparison, the average level of cost inefficiency found in Maghreb banking is higher than inefficiency levels indicated by Berger and Humphrey's (1997) survey of 130 previous bank efficiency studies and Carbo *et al.* (2000) who compared cost inefficiency in a number of EU countries, who found an inefficiency range between 10 and 15 per cent, and around 22 per cent, respectively. However, these results are found to be within the range of similar studies on developing countries, such as Rao (2002) on the UAE banking system (25–31 per cent), but higher than the results obtained on other studies such as Mertens and Urga (2000) on the Ukrainian banking system (23 per cent) and Hasan and Marton (2000) for Hungarian banks (21 per cent).

In the case of profit efficiency, average inefficiency levels are found to be slightly higher than cost inefficiency at about 30 per cent. This suggests that the level of profit can be increased by approximately a third, keeping the same level of outputs if the banking institutions under study were operating on the most profit efficient frontier. For comparison, the level of alternative profit inefficiency of Maghreb banking is higher than that suggested by Williams and Intarachote (2002), who estimate the alternative profit inefficiency of 29 banks operating in Thailand and found inefficiency levels

Table 8.11 Maghreb banking sample

Algeria		Morocco		
Commercial banks	*Specialized governmental banks*	*Commercial banks*	*Specialized governmental banks*	*Other banks*
• Al-Ryan Bank-Algeria	• Banque Algérienne de Développement	• Banque Centrale Populaire	• Banque Nationale de Développement Economique	• Société d'Équipement Domestique et Menager
• Al-Baraka Bank		• Banque Commercial du Maroc	• Caisse Nationale de Crédit Agrocole	
• Arab Banking Corporation-Algeria		• Banque Marocaine du Commerce Extérieure		
• Banque de Développement Local		• Banque Marocaine pour le Commerce et l'Industrie		
• Banque Algériénne de Développement Local		• CitiBank (offshore branch)		
• Banque extérieure de l'Algérie		• Crédit du Maroc		
• Banque Nationale d'Algérie		• Crédit Immobilier et Hôtelier		
• Compagnie Algérienne de Banques		• Société Générale Marocaine de Banques		
• Crédit Populaire d'Algérie		• Wafabank		

Table 8.11 (Continued)

Tunisia

Commercial banks	Specialized governmental banks	Multi-lateral governmental banks	Merchant banks	Other banks
• Amen Bank	• Banque de Développement Économique en Tunisie	• Banque Arabe Tuniso-Libyenne de Développement et du Commerce Extérieur	• Beit Ettamouil Saoudi Tounsi	• Amen Lease
• Arab Banking Corporation-Tunisia	• Banque Nationale de Développement Touristique	• Banque de Tunisie et des Émirats d'Investissement		• Arab Tunisian Lease
• Arab Tunisian Bank		• Tunisian Kuwaiti Development Bank		• Compagnie Internationale de Leasing
• Banque de l'Habitat		• Banque Tuniso-Qatari d'Investissements		• General Leasing
• Banque de Tunisie				• Tunisie Factoring
• Banque du Sud				
• Banque Franco-Tunisienne				
• Banque Internationale Arabe de Tunisie				
• Banque Nationale Agricole				
• Banque Tunisienne de Solidarité				
• North Africa International Bank				

Table 8.11 (Continued)

Tunisia

Commercial banks	Specialized governmental banks	Multi-lateral governmental banks	Merchant banks	Other banks

- Société Tunisienne de Banques
- Tunis International Bank
- Union Bancaire pour le Commerce et l'Industrie
- Union Internationale de Banques

Banks[1]	Algeria	Morocco	Tunisia	All
Commercial banks	80%	96%	85%	86%
Specialized governmental banks	20%	3%	6%	12%
Multi-lateral governmental banks	0%	0%	3%	0.8%
Investment/security houses	0%	0%	3%	0.6%
Non-banking financial institutions (leasing and factoring)	0%	1%	3%	0.6%

[1] Assets percentage as a proportion of sample total.
Source: Bankscope (Dec. 2002).

Table 8.12 Cost efficiency in Algeria, Morocco, and Tunisia banking over 1994–2001

	1994	1995	1996	1997	1998	1999	2000	2001	All
Algeria	87.05	78.96	79.37	79.30	84.44	75.80	67.57	60.68	69.73
Morocco	76.29	76.02	80.11	77.91	80.58	80.02	82.37	75.20	75.49
Tunisia	67.45	67.19	70.33	72.45	70.17	66.29	67.73	64.01	66.59
Commercial	78.12	72.60	77.24	78.86	80.66	76.10	75.04	70.07	72.69
Non-commercial	69.97	65.89	64.74	68.84	66.86	65.53	67.72	54.35	64.53
Investment	*	57.90	70.40	66.89	67.32	64.23	68.42	53.63	65.21
Specialized banks	74.81	74.66	72.18	70.63	72.22	72.60	74.92	56.54	71.00
Non banking ins.	*	*	45.41	44.35	46.75	43.85	45.37	57.62	48.27
Multi-lateral bank	65.13	65.12	70.95	93.48	81.15	81.42	82.17	49.62	73.63
All	75.81	71.86	73.99	74.66	74.23	70.61	70.95	65.54	72.21

Asset size (US$ million)

	1994	1995	1996	1997	1998	1999	2000	2001	All
1–99	58.30	38.18	53.25	44.35	51.82	46.11	45.20	37.12	46.79
100–249	65.98	58.47	66.99	69.57	72.30	61.70	58.58	60.40	64.25
250–499	75.71	77.57	88.02	91.05	58.78	52.51	50.51	41.71	66.98
500–999	64.45	66.58	73.29	72.55	76.64	75.68	76.87	78.16	73.03
1,000–1,999	75.86	76.10	71.60	78.02	86.46	83.07	85.16	76.13	79.05
2,000–2,999	75.12	76.36	80.84	80.23	82.34	87.11	86.45	93.23	82.71
3,000–3,999	92.89	78.29	88.62	91.84	92.77	95.38	90.22	96.03	90.76
4,000–4,999	*	91.66	*	91.37	88.53	86.89	92.11	93.90	90.74
5,000+	90.03	92.19	91.60	91.11	95.01	95.40	95.21	93.35	92.99
All	74.79	72.82	76.78	78.90	78.30	75.98	75.59	74.45	75.95

Table 8.12 (Continued)

Assets in million US dollars	1–99	100–249	250–499	500–999	1,000–1,999	2,000–2,999	3,000–3,999	4,000–4,999	5,000+
Algeria	30.32	43.31	28.50	*	70.73	72.60	86.46	89.94	92.68
Morocco	*	*	56.59	66.37	80.02	78.84	92.56	93.90	*
Tunisia	49.21	65.95	69.44	74.07	82.90	91.67	*	*	*
Commercial	48.01	57.77	37.48	74.69	81.49	85.03	91.33	90.71	92.57
Non-commercial	52.02	62.83	64.94	69.84	70.73	72.60	86.64	91.66	94.57
Investment	60.31	68.92	54.93	*	*	*	*	*	*
Specialized banks	*	*	61.57	69.84	70.73	72.60	86.64	91.66	94.57
Non banking ins.	43.72	44.83	56.59	*	*	*	*	*	*
Multi-lateral bank	*	74.73	86.68	*	*	*	*	*	*

Source: Adapted from Bakhouche, 2004.

Table 8.13 Alternative profit efficiency in Algeria, Morocco, and Tunisia banking over 1994–2001

	1994	1995	1996	1997	1998	1999	2000	2001	All
Algeria	73.18	71.15	76.11	79.12	74.49	82.05	78.08	44.77	66.87
Morocco	68.11	67.14	64.28	59.63	58.01	46.03	53.09	90.68	63.81
Tunisia	71.14	72.70	73.49	73.66	73.82	74.44	73.76	69.64	72.69
Commercial	70.40	70.73	71.22	71.02	72.20	69.76	68.75	74.33	69.65
Non-commercial	72.52	74.43	74.81	74.77	71.08	72.66	73.98	60.45	71.19
Investment	*	80.88	77.54	76.31	74.42	74.46	75.12	65.53	75.28
Specialized banks	70.52	71.71	74.08	70.62	67.81	75.49	79.99	47.82	69.62
Non-banking ins.	*	*	75.41	74.43	67.30	74.76	73.93	46.13	66.72
Multi-lateral bank	74.52	70.72	72.22	77.70	74.81	65.95	66.86	82.32	73.14
All	70.85	71.18	72.21	71.84	71.09	70.57	70.03	68.90	70.83

Asset size (US$ million)

	1994	1995	1996	1997	1998	1999	2000	2001	All
1–99	72.43	72.53	77.03	74.43	73.32	71.49	71.36	58.14	71.34
100–249	75.00	72.79	75.05	76.04	74.29	71.85	73.41	55.74	71.77
250–499	69.00	68.52	75.36	74.96	61.58	64.51	62.72	66.92	67.95
500–999	62.57	73.94	71.97	69.96	72.68	70.17	73.01	71.19	70.69
1,000–1,999	71.18	74.38	72.69	72.84	69.19	71.30	72.58	69.88	71.75
2,000–2,999	66.63	59.59	67.12	68.25	68.87	72.89	72.73	78.94	69.38
3,000–3,999	64.27	60.11	60.53	53.36	53.13	49.78	55.93	78.39	59.44
4,000–4,999	*	77.55	*	84.20	76.99	64.72	60.25	70.38	72.35
5,000+	74.73	70.10	78.84	75.47	77.25	73.17	80.09	71.84	75.19
All	69.48	69.95	72.32	72.17	69.70	67.76	69.12	69.05	69.94

Table 8.13 (Continued)

Assets in million US dollars	1–99	100–249	250–499	500–999	1,000–1,999	2,000–2,999	3,000–3,999	4,000–4,999	5,000+
Algeria	68.26	72.57	72.40	*	72.76	75.39	64.98	69.81	75.27
Morocco	*	*	51.52	61.46	70.03	64.50	55.88	70.38	*
Tunisia	71.71	70.11	70.99	72.66	72.96	74.11	*	*	*
Commercial	68.18	71.89	73.11	73.85	71.53	68.74	57.04	68.99	75.00
Non-commercial	72.16	64.63	65.06	65.76	72.76	75.39	74.82	77.55	79.82
Investment	80.69	72.06	61.44	*	*	*	*	*	*
Specialized banks	*	*	68.50	65.76	72.76	75.39	74.82	77.55	79.82
Non-banking ins.	72.16	60.93	51.52	*	*	*	*	*	*
Multi-lateral bank	*	68.33	75.16	*	*	*	*	*	*

Source: Adapted from Bakhouche, 2004.

averaged 15 per cent, but approximately similar to that found by Mertens and Urga (2000) and Hasan and Marton (2000), 28 per cent and 29 per cent, respectively. The level of alternative profit inefficiency can be explained by factors linked to profit-related activities. Banks in the three countries are strongly influenced by political pressure and other non-market forces that may force them to allocate resources to activities or firms that have experienced low levels of profits. This factor is particularly observed in Algeria, where, for decades, banking institutions have made significant amounts of lending to the non-performing government-owned sectors. The paltry selection of credits as well as government influence, importance of public sector, and relative weakness of private sector might have led the banking sector to subsequently absorb non-performing loans, and as a result record high levels of profit inefficiency. Thus, the hypotheses of 'bad luck' and 'bad management' suggested by Berger and De Young (1997) may explain the relatively low level of (cost and) profit efficiency in Algeria, Morocco and Tunisia banking.

The results can also be viewed in terms of bank type, geographic location and size. First, in terms of bank type, it seem that commercial banks are more cost efficient but slightly less profit efficient than other types of banks. Second, in terms of geographic location, Moroccan banks are more cost efficient than Algerian and Tunisian banks, whereas Tunisian banks are more profit efficient than Algerian and Moroccan banks. Third, in terms of size, large and medium-sized banks tend to be more cost efficient than smaller banks, but small and larger banks tend to be more profit efficient than their medium-sized counterparts. The results may imply that macro-economic conditions and regulatory measures in Morocco and Tunisia are relatively more favourable for obtaining lower cost inefficiencies than in Algeria. Country-specific characteristics can be important in influencing bank efficiency levels, including macroeconomic conditions and the degree and speed of financial, economic and regulatory reforms. Within this context, Tunisia and Morocco commenced implementing financial liberalization and economic reforms in favour of private and foreign capital earlier and faster than Algeria – nearly more than half of banks' capital in Tunisia and Morocco is owned by foreign investors. Privatization programmes in Morocco and Tunisia have strengthened the role of both domestic private and foreign-owned sectors in the economy compared to Algeria. The link between the size of the private sector and banking efficiency may indicate that the privatization of state-owned enterprises to boost competition is significant in improving commercial bank efficiency. Besides, in the case of Tunisia, the country is characterized by higher rates of GDP per capita, and this may suggest that its banks are more successful in attracting deposits and generating stronger cash flows than banks in Morocco and Algeria. Higher GDP per capita tends to generate more savings, and hence more deposits and consequently more bank lending.

Overall it is found that cost and alternative profit inefficiency averaged about 30 per cent over the period 1994–2001. It is also found that commercial banks are more cost efficient and less profit efficient than other types of banks. In addition, large and medium-sized banks tend to be more cost efficient but less profit efficient than small-sized banks. Overall, in the three countries, it seems that cost inefficiency and alternative profit inefficiency experienced an increase over the period from 1994 to 2001, although it is higher in Algeria than in Morocco and Tunisia. This would suggest financial and economic reforms have not made an influential impact on the cost and profit efficiency performance of the banking sectors in the three countries under study. Anecdotal evidence also suggests that the financial sectors in the three countries still seem to be suffering from limited competition and market pressures.

Bakhouche (2004) also finds that scale economies are present in Algeria, Morocco and Tunisia banking and they lie in the range of 1 per cent and 10 per cent. Economies of scale rise with bank size. For instance, constant returns to scale are recorded for banks with less than $250 million in total assets (a value of 0.995 is recorded). Banks with total assets of more than $500 million broadly display increasing returns to scale. Maghreb banking systems are characterized as systems where scale economies get larger as banks become bigger, which is a clear incentive for consolidation within the respective banking systems. Thus, positive economies of scale are found for the overall Maghreb banking industry. Specifically, commercial banks and medium and large-sized banks in Morocco and Tunisia tend to realize the largest scale economies.

Conclusion

In this chapter we have discussed the results of the main rationale for investigating the efficiency features of Arab banking systems and outlined the main findings from the recent empirical literature. Overall, profit inefficiencies appear to be greater than cost inefficiencies in most systems, a finding similar to that found for US and European banking systems. This means that there is greater variation in bank profit performance compared with cost differences across systems. Banks therefore need to focus more on revenue generation coupled with appropriate risk management practices if they are to boost performance and emulate best practice. X-inefficiencies also typically exceed scale economies, although with regard to bank size the largest institutions appear to realize substantial economies, perhaps creating further incentive for merger activity. The findings for Gulf banks also reveal that foreign banks are less cost efficient, but more profit efficient than national banks. This suggests that foreign banks focus more on revenue generating than do their domestic counterparts. As foreign banks tend to have a different business mix (high-end retail clients, large corporate banking services, and so on), it is perhaps not surprising that they are found to be less cost efficient but more profit efficient. The literature also finds that Islamic banks appear, on average, to be more efficient than their traditional banking competitors. This may be another reason why this type of banking business is gaining popularity in the region. It also seems to have better potential for growth in the future.

While substantial variations in the cost and profit features of Arab banks exist, the main findings generally concur with the results on banking sector efficiency in the US and Europe. What is surprising is that there is little evidence to suggest that the major financial reforms had a noticeable impact in improving banking sector efficiency during the 1990s. This may be because the efficiency gains associated with liberalization programmes are counterbalanced by changes in the economic environment and/or other operating conditions faced by Arab banks. The high degree of concentration and role of the government in Arab banking systems may also mitigate financial liberalization effects. Nevertheless, there does appear to be consensus that Arab banking markets are becoming more competitive, and this is highlighted in the following chapter where we discuss contemporary developments and expected future trends in Arab banking systems.

9
Current Developments and Prospects for Arab Banks

Introduction

Since the late 1990s banks throughout the Arab world have been generating strong returns to their shareholders. This performance has resulted mainly from banks' emphasis on improving their cost and revenue performance and also managing their risk exposures more effectively. Shareholder (or stakeholder) value has become a critical driver of bank strategy. Much greater attention is nowadays placed on the efficient allocation of capital throughout the banking firm. Risk and return features of banks' operations are managed more effectively and this has also encouraged the trend to more performance-enhancing balance sheet and risk management practices, such as the growing use of sophisticated securitization and credit risk management techniques. Arab banks now place much more emphasis on boosting their non-margin income from off-balance sheet activities such as from trading, underwriting, private banking and asset management business. The banking industry has also been transformed by consolidation and profits strengthened by buoyant domestic economies. Banking markets have become more concentrated and at the same time more competitive as new financial and non-financial entrants make the banking business more contestable. In addition, universal banking continues to be the dominant form of bank operational model.

Similar to their counterparts in the West, Arab banks aim to maintain their performance by developing long-term customer relationships and capturing an increased range of clients' (both retail and corporate) financial activity. Given this strategic focus, many banks are focusing on developing their non-traditional business in areas like insurance, private banking, asset management, pensions and other investment services. The focus on developing a wider array of retail financial services is driven by the rapidly changing demographics and client demand in the region. Corporate and investment banking business is increasingly overlapping with traditional lending business being supplemented with a growing array of more specialized and capital market based services.

The operating environment for Arab banks is also being influenced by various international regulatory developments. Bank for International Settlements' initiatives aimed at enhancing bank supervision and corporate governance have generally been taken on-board, as have the OECD's Financial Action Task Force's (FATF) recommendations on anti-money-laundering and terrorist financing. The introduction of the new Basel 2 capital adequacy rules and the formation of the single GCC banking market will also impact on the strategies of many banks. These issues are discussed in the present chapter.

Trends in the structural features of Arab banking

Financial sectors in the Arab world have traditionally been characterized by relatively high levels of government controls where regulatory authorities maintained a protected banking environment that inhibited competition. However, market conditions have undergone extensive changes over recent years. On the demand side, customer preferences have changed substantially, becoming more sophisticated and price conscious. On the supply side, the globalization of financial markets has been accompanied by governmental deregulation, financial innovation and automation. Both factors imply an increase in the number of competitors and a tougher operating environment. In addition, progress in technology, especially phone-based and internet banking, has enabled financial firms to extend their activities beyond narrow local or national boundaries and to increase their market share by providing competitive products to wider markets at a lower price. As in the West, new suppliers of retail financial services, such as retailers, automobile manufactures, and so on, have entered the market. As such, banks are now faced with strong competition from both banks and non-bank institutions, and this also accentuates competition within the banking and financial services sector overall.

To assist banks in confronting the new challenges, financial authorities throughout the Arab world have become more aware of the importance of financial deregulation to promote competition in the market, the aim being to concurrently increase both the efficiency and soundness of banking systems. In this respect Arab countries have passed a substantial body of legislation aimed at liberalizing their financial systems. The liberalization process has been accompanied by financial deregulation through the reduction of direct government control. At the same time it is associated with upgrades of prudential regulations.

The process of deregulation has some important implications for banks. First, deregulation removes or reduces collusive and/or restrictive practices, promoting competition between banks, thereby increasing the banks' risk.

Second, changes arise from the ability of banks to seek new business in much wider fields of activity such as loan purchases and off-balance sheet transactions. Moves into new business areas and an increased competitive environment change the nature of banks' risks and perhaps substantially increase the cost of funds to established players, thus reducing their competitive advantage. This induces banks to pay greater attention to the areas of pricing and upgrading the quality of their products. Therefore, banks become more concerned about analyzing and controlling their costs and revenues, as well as dealing with risks taken to produce acceptable returns. In this context, maximizing shareholders' wealth and promoting improvements in productive efficiency have become much more important strategic targets for banks.

While increases in competition are apparent throughout Arab banking markets, structural developments appear to have encouraged a trend towards greater market concentration. This parallels developments in Europe and the US. According to a report by the Bank for International Settlements (2000) the preference for national consolidation is that it offers clearer opportunities for reducing costs and fewer complications in terms of handling the merger due to a normally more homogeneous corporate culture. Besides, firms try first to gain a stronger national presence so that they could be large enough to compete in a likely later cross-country consolidation phase.

Developments in retail banking

As in other banking markets, the retail financial services industry has become an increasingly important segment of Arab banking business. Traditionally, banks focused on the corporate sector, which left a large proportion of population un-banked. This has all changed. The offer of a wide array of retail products and services is now the norm for banks operating throughout the Arab world and all banks provide the usual deposits, consumer loans and credit-card services. Some Gulf banks now rival their Western counterparts in the implementation of automated teller machines (ATM) and electronic funds transfer at the point of sale (EFTPOS) networks. Others provide advanced phone and internet based banking services. Some of the larger banks offer sophisticated private banking and asset management services to their wealthier clients. Retail insurance products are among the fastest growing product segments in Saudi Arabia and other Gulf countries. Islamic retail financial services are also widespread. Even in countries such as Egypt where it is recognized that retail banking is relatively underdeveloped, the four large state banks (National Bank of Egypt, Banque Misr, Banque du Caire and Bank of Alexandria) have gradually transformed their retail banking strategies to fight off competition from foreign interlopers (Citibank and Société Générale).

The continued success of Arab banks' retail business will depend strongly on how the banks adapt to provide products and services that meet the demands of a rapidly growing and relatively young population. It will also be influenced by the way in which banks adapt to new technology. Advances in technology will continue to influence the ways in which financial service firms do their business. Typically, technological advances contribute to reducing costs associated with the management of information (collection, storage, processing and transmission), mainly by substituting automation for paper-based and labour-intensive activity. They also change the ways in which customers have access to banks' services and products, mainly through 'new' distribution channels such as the internet, phone-based and other remote channels. According to Morgan Stanley Dean Witter[1] there is 'strong evidence that a clicks-and-mortar approach maximises the ability of financial institutions to capture a greater proportion of a customer's overall financial assets'. This is based on the view that having a substantial physical presence strengthens brand image and provides customers with greater product confidence compared with internet-only offerings. In addition, extra service, advice and sales elements that come with the integrated approach encourage customers to place more of their financial services with one provider. There is also evidence that various products, such as consumer loans, mortgage products and life insurance, lend themselves more readily to different distribution channels, so by offering a multi-channel platform customers can be given a more tailored and cost efficient service, dependent on their needs.

Many Arab banks are developing their fledgling internet activities. However, a wave of new technologies based on broadband telecommunications networks is set to transform the industry. In general, broadband networks allow for much more data to be transmitted at greater speeds. Put simply, it means that internet access will become much quicker, allowing users to take advantage of new types of content ranging from sophisticated web pages to real-time interactivity. Three types of device – the interactive television, the PC and the mobile handset – are able to receive broadband services that could revolutionize distribution channels. Broadband interactive TV in particular could provide Arab banks with access to a much bigger customer base, since far more customers or potential customers in the Arab world own a television than a PC. Interactive television could make it attractive for banks to cater to mass segments that have proved difficult to serve profitably in the past.

In addition to interactive TV, mobile financial services, provided via cellular phones, will also become commonplace with the evolution of broadband technology. Such services are already popular in Hong Kong and Japan where mobile balance checking, funds transfers and share trading are widely available. McKinsey (2001)[2] has noted that throughout Europe there is significant interest of financial firms establishing a mobile financial service presence. Some banks in the Gulf already provide banking and investment services via the cell phone. For Arab banks the attractions of putting services on mobiles relates to the addition of an alternative distribution channel, and they may also be able to earn fees from share-trading and various banking transactions. These gains however need to be compared with the costs of developing such services.

As with the internet revolution banks are reappraising their technology strategies given developments expected as a result of the introduction of broadband technology. The forces unleashed by the internet and attendant technologies are likely to be further magnified by the broadband revolution providing great benefits to customers and major challenges to the providers of financial services. In addition to customer-facing technology, banks are also considering opportunities that allow them to reorganize their back-offices.

Private banking

One area gaining significant attention by commercial banks globally is private banking – offering banking and investment services to high net worth individuals. The global onshore private banking business is worth around $20 trillion and the offshore market is estimated to be around $7 trillion. Offshore assets under management have grown around 6 per cent annually since the mid-1990s and it is likely to continue at this level to 2010. Demand for private banking services is very much driven by growing prosperity, as illustrated by higher GDP per capita and income levels. For oil-exporting Arab countries the demand for such services is likely to be strongly linked to oil revenues. More generally, demand for such services goes hand-in-hand with general economic development. While private banking services in various forms have long been present in the more prosperous Gulf banking markets there are good prospects in other Arab markets for such services. See Figures 9.1 and 9.2 that highlight estimates of the Gulf and global private banking business.

Over the last few years, American and European banks have rushed to develop their private banking and wealth management operations, particularly targeting the so-called mass affluent market. Typically, mass affluent clients are defined as individuals with $50,000 to $500,000 of funds to invest, whereas traditional private clients are those with more than $500,000 to invest. The very wealthy in the Arab world already deal with private bankers offshore in Switzerland, London and New York and this market is well established. However, banks are viewing private clients below the super-rich level as a group to target.

Commercial banks are particularly attracted to private banking business due to the growth prospects and low regulatory capital requirements (low risk) related to managing third-party assets. The market is considered to be relatively large and profitable and the industry fragmented. The hallmarks of a successful private banking operation are discretion, security and confidentiality. Clients demand decent relative returns from their investments and they tend to be financially sophisticated. To meet this demand, banks have to provide a

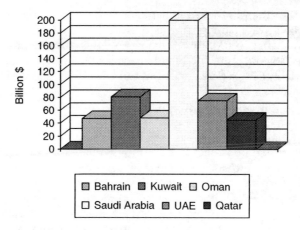

Figure 9.1   GCC private banking market size 2005 forecast
Source: Author's estimates.

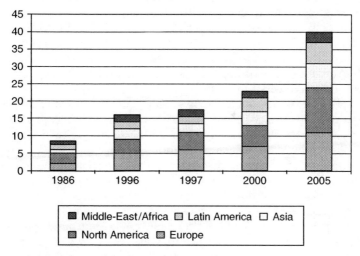

Figure 9.2   Global private banking market size (US$ trillion)
Source: Author's estimates.

multi-product capability offering a range of traditional banking services as well as a range of securities & funds services, cash management products, derivatives, mortgages & credit products, and alternative investments, to name but a few. While banks in the Arab world are relatively small compared with the largest Western banks, they can provide such services either in-house or obtain best-practice products by forming strategic alliances with partners.

In general, Gulf and other Arab banking markets offer substantial opportunities in the private banking area and incumbent banks are well placed to benefit from changes in the wealth management environment. Maintaining a strong domestic franchise and brand image coupled with good performance and appropriate client segmentation strategy are critical success ingredients.

Corporate and investment banking

The demand for corporate banking services has traditionally been the mainstay of Arab banking business and is strongly related to the business cycle. Typically, all banks provide payments, deposits and credit facilities and the larger banks provide a wider array of services for the larger corporate customers. As is the case with Western corporate banking practice, payment services are first and foremost provided by means of a business current account which gives firms access to a variety of specific money transmission facilities (e.g. cash and cheque deposit facilities, cheque writing facilities, access to automated payment services that facilitate the payment of direct debits and standing orders). The main deposit facilities include standard current account and term deposit services. With larger amounts being deposited then firms may seek more sophisticated cash management and treasury services from their banks (these are core products for medium-sized and larger companies). On the credit side, companies (and especially) smaller firms typically rely on overdraft and/or term loan facilities, although overdrafts are less common in certain systems.

During the 1990s firms increasingly sought to diversify their credit services, making more use of a wider array of asset finance products like factoring and leasing.[3] Such services (otherwise known as asset finance business) grew rapidly during the 1990s. This is for various reasons, including preferential accounting and tax treatment associated with lease finance, easier access to such products compared with overdraft finance, and the attraction associated with more certain credit flows.

As companies become larger the demand for corporate banking services becomes broader and more complex. Medium-sized companies require money transmission, deposit and credit facilities like their smaller counterparts. However, they also typically require a greater range of services relating to information about their business, risk management services, trade finance products and asset and investment management services (e.g. if they have to manage employees' pension fund assets or their own assets). Over the last decade or so, the range of banking products available to mid-size Arab corporations has grown substantially. This is because many banks have targeted this segment with products that previously were the sole preserve of just the largest companies. In Europe, it is now estimated that large commercial banks provide around 200 products to this segment, a breakdown of which is shown in Figure 9.3.

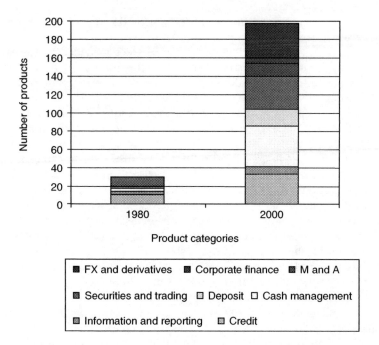

Figure 9.3 Number of middle-market business banking products offered by commercial banks

Note: FX = foreign exchange services; M & A = merger and acquisition finance and advisory
Source: Adapted from Goldman Sachs and McKinsey, 2001.

Commercial banks in the Arab world (like their counterparts in Europe) are increasingly looking to developments in the US corporate market to learn lessons as to how to adapt to the expected changes that are likely to impact on their business over the next decade or so. The reason is because the US is the most developed in providing capital market products to its medium-sized corporate clients – and this is a business expected to grow rapidly. Large multinational companies increasingly bypass the banking sector for their funding – by raising finance through equity and debt instrument (bond) issues. They can also raise funds in the international markets cheaper than many banks as their credit ratings tend to be higher. As such, lending to very large companies is a low margin (profit) business as banks have to compete at the finest terms and with capital markets. Commercial banks therefore are continuing to focus a significant part of their corporate banking focus on the middle-market segment, given that this is one of the most profitable parts of the corporate lending business. It should be noted, however, that there is less competition in the Arab world from capital markets. Domestic banks face greater competition from foreign banks in providing corporate banking services to the top corporations in the region.

At the top end of the ladder the main services provided to the largest firms are similar to those offered to mid-market firms although they usually have a greater international dimension. The type of products demanded by multinational Arab firms is shown in Table 9.1.

The largest Arab companies have the opportunity to tap international capital markets to raise finance and as such this provides some competition to the banking sector. However, it should be noted that in many countries the largest firms and financial institutions have strong relationships founded on long-established family and/or government relationships. Typically, the biggest firms and banks grew hand-in-hand in the recent development process and therefore can be viewed as having somewhat of a symbiotic relationship. This, of course, we would argue is a good thing as it has helped promote the development process in an ordered and constructive fashion. (Banking relationships tend to be stronger in the Arab world as the systems are primarily bank-based, as in Germany, compared with the market-based systems of the UK and US, although, as in the case of all bank-based systems they are slowly moving to a greater market orientation.)

A point that corporate bankers are aware of is the growing relevance of the disintermediation trend. Larger firms now have a wider range of capital market financing options than ever before and these compete with traditional bank lending products and services. It is a force that is encouraging many large investment banks increasingly to offer services to mid-sized firms – a market segment that was traditionally the sole preserve of commercial banks. Investment banks such as Goldman Sachs, Morgan Stanley, and Merrill Lynch that have a global expertise in capital markets, M & A and corporate advisory services are now actively competing with commercial banks to provide debt, equity and risk management services to the largest mid-market firms. (Mainly because this is viewed as a more profitable segment than the multinational corporation market segment that they have traditionally focused on.)

Table 9.1   Corporate banking products for multinational Arab corporations

Cash management (domestic & global)	M & A finance and advisory services	Investment loans
Foreign exchange (spot & forward transactions)	Institutional asset management	Custody
Deposits & term money	Corporate trust services	Credit lines
Trade finance	Project finance	Risk management services
Futures/options/swaps	Investor services	Payment facilities
Fixed income (bond issues)	Leasing	
Equities	Factoring	

Advances in technology, competition and other forces are also changing the way in which banks undertake corporate banking. The corporate credit market has changed, and demarcation lines between the services offered to different sized firms are eroding. In this changing environment it is not clear as to what types of corporate banking operation will be successful in the future.

Given the increasing segmentation of the business it seems likely that many banks will seek to adopt some form of specialist strategy targeting a narrower market, product or/and client base. This does not mean that corporate banking will become a mono-line business with individual banks offering one-product services. Rather it means that banks will specialize in a variety of areas of corporate banking business but will not (as has traditionally been the case) try to offer a universal corporate banking service to every type and size of firm. Commercial banks will seek to identify product or client areas they can be expert in and develop their business along such lines. McKinsey & Co. and Goldman Sachs[4] suggest a variety of potentially successful business models that may inform corporate banking developments in the Arab world. These are shown in Table 9.2.

Table 9.2 suggests a variety of business models for a successful corporate banking strategy. The study notes that revenue potential is greatest for the segments targeting investment banking services to mid-sized firms and multinational corporations, followed by the specialized finance provider and small-to-medium-sized enterprise banker. The largest banks are in a position to adopt a combination of all business model types apart from the independent adviser role – this is because their independence may be questioned given their strong proprietary product range. Large regional banks could undertake all business models apart from those that require comprehensive product ranges and massive financial strength such as in dealing with only top-end firms and credit trading. Other smaller banks will act as specialists in wholesale or/and local markets. It will be interesting to see whether this sort of market segmentation occurs in Arab banking systems over the following decade or so.

Technological developments impacting on Arab banks

Technological innovations have transformed most industrial sectors, especially due to the evolution of information-based technologies. In the case of the banking industry, due to the role of banks as information-based firms and their role in gathering and analyzing information, these changes have been even sharper. Information technologies offer savings in the cost and time of providing financial services, and increased revenues through the development of an array of new financial products often only limited by the level of potential demand, which can be created. Indeed, the rapid progress in information technology is transforming the way in which the banking

Table 9.2   Eight distinct winning formulas emerging in corporate banking

Strategic focus	Winning business models
Segment focus	1. *Growth specialist* – focuses on the distinct financial needs of approximately 50,000 fast growing companies including venture finance, IPO related business, M & A services.
	2. *SME (direct relationship) banker* – focuses on the standard needs of the majority of European midcorps offering standard packages, self diagnostic and advisory tools. Heavy reliance on direct channels to reduce costs on commodity products.
	3. *Midcorp (investment) banker* – targets the broader later stage financing needs of the established midcorp segment. Offering a comprehensive product mix with a strong investment banking element.
	4. *MNC bulge bracket* – is a formula that only a few banks can use as this requires the necessary skills to serve the 250 European MNCs and eventually the remaining 2,000 large corporates. Citigroup, Deutsche Bank and the top Swiss banks, United Bank of Switzerland and Crédit Suisse, the 'major aspirants'.
Product focus	5. *Specialized finance provider* – some commercial banks to build up a very strong position by focusing on selected commercial credit products. Areas of specialization presenting opportunities include: businesses with expert financial structuring skills in areas like cross-border leasing; international tax-related structures; large-scale factoring; long-term investment loans; and project finance. These types of business appeal to different clients ranging from utilities to computer manufacturers.
	6. *Credit trader* – takes a bet on the expected boom in credit trading. Majority of participants in this business are likely to outsource credit trading to a handful of 'powerhouses'. No examples of active debt traders in Europe although some US traders are trying to expand their product offering in Europe.
Functional focus	7. *Corporate financial services adviser* – corporate bank to act as an independent financial adviser to provide crafted individual financial solutions.
	8. *Factory provider* – offers services further down the value chain at the production level. Offers advisory tools, scoring models, products such as asset management or asset finance, either branded or white-labelled (products are processed by a third party firm on behalf of another company, e.g. Royal Bank of Scotland administers Tesco supermarket credit cards, but holders are probably unaware of this). Other services may include corporate ratings or credit/securities processing services.

Source: Adapted from Goldman Sachs and McKinsey, 2001, pp. 18–20.

industry works, through a dematerialization of informational sources, a substantial increase of information available, and the possibility of diversification into new business areas compatible with the banks' core activities.

Two main factors can be highlighted as consequences of technological innovation. First, the production function in banking has become more capital-intensive, given that the share of non-staff operating costs has increased in most of the European systems, at the expense of staff costs. Consequently, it has contributed to a reduction in the costs associated with the management of information (collection, storage, processing and transmission) by replacing paper-based and labour-intensive methods with automated processes. Secondly, diffusion of information technology is radically transforming banking delivery channels. In this respect, the competitive advantage which geographical proximity once provided by means of a large number of branches have been achieved through the installation of ATMs or alternative delivery systems and more recently through the introduction of internet banking.

Overall, progress in information technology has allowed the set-up of new delivery channels and products. It has also accelerated competition, making it easier to compare prices, lowering switching costs and diminishing barriers to entry into markets. Although these factors have intensified competition, they should increase efficiency as well, and other things being equal, reduce the amount of capital optimally held by banks. On the other hand, they may also contribute to the existence of over-capacity in terms of staffing levels in traditional or 'physical' delivery channels.

These forces are universal and Arab banks are well placed to take advantage of technological advances. However, given their size, most banks in the region are not well placed to develop their own innovative technology. This is a good thing. They can choose to implement best-practice systems when they have been tried and tested by their larger Western counterparts that have deeper pockets for investing in research and development and new innovative technologies. In fact, this is one of the reasons why relatively small banks tend to be more innovative than larger firms because they do not have to incur the larger development costs, can purchase bespoke best-practice systems and implement them with less disruption.

Regulatory trends

Arab banks, like those in other systems, have to comply with a barrage of rules and regulations from both national and international bodies. The main aim is to ensure safe, sound and efficient banking systems. Various recent recommendations have also been put in place to combat international money laundering business. This section focuses on the relatively recent international regulatory developments that impact on Arab banking.

BIS core principles on effective banking supervision

A landmark set of banking sector regulatory guidelines were issued by the Bank for International Settlements (1997) aimed at establishing minimum standards for bank supervision across all banking jurisdictions. These include principles relating to:

- Preconditions for effective supervision by advocating independence to bank supervisory authorities, effective legal frameworks under which these agencies operate, compliance and enforcement powers, rules relating to the sharing of information between supervisory authorities and other rules relating to confidentiality and immunity from prosecution for the regulatory agencies;
- Licensing and the role of the licensing authority;
- Transfers of significant ownership and controlling interests in banks;
- Major acquisitions;
- Capital adequacy requirements;
- Credit granting and monitoring standards;
- Assessment of asset quality and adequacy of loan-loss provisions and reserves;
- Concentration of risks and large exposures;
- Connected lending;
- Risk management and other internal controls;
- Rules relating to on-site and off-site inspection;
- Rules on consolidation supervision, validation of supervisory information and information requirements of banking organizations;
- Formal powers of supervision;
- Obligations of home country supervisors;
- Liaison and information exchange with overseas supervisors and;
- Obligations of host country supervisors.

The Basel Core Principles (BCP) comprises 25 basic proposals to make bank supervision more effective. These cover the main areas of concern to supervision, including the preconditions for effective banking supervision (Principle 1) and methods of ongoing banking supervision (Principles 16 to 20). These principles are seen by Basel as minimum requirements. They have also been designed to be verifiable by supervisors, regional supervisory groups and the market at large.

An important feature of the BCP regime is the perceived need for bank supervisors to have sufficient political autonomy to take necessary measures.[5] This needed autonomy has several operational dimensions. Compliance with these rules is clearly a major policy issue in Arab banking systems. But such regulatory compliance is not a 'black and white' matter. For one thing, considerable institutional differences exist between many jurisdictions, and these differences can be important in shaping both the specific implementation and impact of a new bank regulation. It must be said, on the other hand, that a more convergent pattern in regulatory practices has developed internationally. Nevertheless, these institutional differences remain and they can be very important in the degree and type of practical compliance pursued by a regulatory agency.

From available evidence it appears that the Arab banking systems are mainly compliant, although some fall short on providing information to overseas supervisors. Some Arab banking systems find it difficult to comply with all the principles because they have limited resources for supervising their banking systems. There are also questions concerning principles relating to ownership, connected lending, acquisitions, monitoring of risk positions, and so on. The main implications of these developments mean that Arab supervisors are constantly reviewing their licensing and other supervisory arrangements.

Impact of Basel 2 on Arab banks

Another major regulatory development relates to the implementation of the new Basel 2 capital adequacy regulations. On June 3, 1999, the Basel Committee on Banking Supervision formally launched proposals for a new capital adequacy framework (Basel 2). The original 1988 Accord established an international standard around a capital ratio of 8 per cent. The new Accord's main aim is to introduce a more comprehensive and risk-sensitive treatment of banking risks to ensure that regulatory capital bears a closer relationship to credit risk. In particular, the setting of minimum capital requirements will be based on an update of the current risk-weighting approach including the use of banks' internal risk ratings and external credit risk assessments. The New Basel Capital Accord has undergone an extensive review and the Basel Committee envisions implementation by 2006.

Basel 2 is built on three main pillars. Pillar 1 deals with the quantification of new capital charges and relies heavily on banks' internal risk-weighting models and on external rating agencies. Pillar 2 defines the supervisory review process and Pillar 3 focuses on market discipline, imposing greater disclosure standards on banks in order to increase transparency:

• *Pillar 1*, seeks to amend the old rules by introducing risk weightings that are more closely linked to borrowers' credit standing. The existing risk-weighting classification requires credit institutions (banks) and investment firms to hold at least 8 per cent of their assets as capital. Assets are adjusted using a risk-weighting formula, allowing loans judged to be less risky to be backed by less capital. However, this method has been criticized on grounds that the original Accord's risk-weighting categories are too crude, so that they bear little relationship to the actual likelihood of default. For instance, unsecured loans to large companies and sole traders are counted as bearing the same 100 per cent risk. This means banks have to hold the same amount of capital for regulatory purposes for these types of loans even if the former are viewed as being substantially less risky than the latter. In consequence, banks have tended to migrate towards riskier loans, which command higher interest rates while requiring the same level of capital backing.

The new Basel proposals refine the old methodology, to reflect with greater precision the varying underlying risks against which banks are required to hold capital. The new Accord does not propose changes to the current definition of capital or the minimum requirement of 8 per cent capital to risk-weighted assets. The proposal mainly affects how banking risks (credit risk, operational risk and market risk) are going to be measured. Methods for measuring credit risk are more complex than in the current Accord, a measure for operational risk has been explicitly proposed, while the measure of market risk remains unchanged.

The biggest changes relate to the calculation of capital backing for credit risk. Under Basel 2, banks will be able to choose between what is known as the 'standardized approach' and the Internal Ratings Based (IRB) approach. In the standardized approach the new Accord defines risk weights within broad categories of sovereigns, banks and companies, by reference to an external credit assessment firm (credit rating agency) subject to strict standards. Under IRB, banks are allowed to use their internal credit risk assessments subject to strict methodological and disclosure requirements.

Together with changes to the risk-weighting scheme (pillar 1), the proposed Accord rests on two other 'pillars', namely improved supervision and enhanced market discipline. These are intended to act as a lever to strengthen the safety and soundness of the banking system.

- *Pillar 2*, the supervisory review process, aims to ensure that a bank's capital adequacy position is consistent with its overall risk profile. To this end, bank regulators must be able to make qualitative judgements on the ability of each bank to measure and manage its own risks. The US Federal Reserve has recently supported the idea that bank examiners should evaluate capital management processes on a continuous basis, but also contends that supervisors should establish explicit capital adequacy goals after assessing the potential risks to the institution concerned. Supervisors should also have the ability to require banks to hold capital in excess of minimum regulatory requirements. The Basel Committee's discussions with regulators from outside the G10 area emphasized the need for higher capital requirements for weaker or riskier institutions. This is already the practice in some countries; for instance, some financial sector regulators in the G10 require various banks to hold capital equivalent to more than 20 per cent of their assets. However, such a practice is not common in most of Europe. Such a review process is likely to require a substantial increase in supervisory resources in many countries, where the regulatory systems are currently geared only towards adhering to standard quantitative guidelines.
- *Pillar 3*, seeks to enhance effective market discipline facilitated by introducing high disclosure standards with regard to bank capital. This requires banks to provide more reliable and timely information enabling market participants to make better risk assessments.

Taken together, Pillar 1 provides the rules for quantifying risk sensitivity and the minimum capital charges associated with these risks. This is balanced by the supervisory judgements available under Pillar 2 and market disclosure rules of Pillar 3. Ultimately, the new Accord seeks to create a more comprehensive and flexible regulatory framework, without sacrificing the safety and soundness achieved by the current Accord.

It is difficult to be definitive about the likely strategic impact of Basel 2. A great deal will also depend on its final form and the shape of banking markets when Basel 2 is finally implemented. Nevertheless, a number of surveys and views appear to exhibit some initial consensus on the proposals.

Peterson (2001, p. 52) reports a surprising feature of the release of the Basel proposals: that there was little movement in spreads linked to the proposals. Nevertheless, he argues that some of the biggest winners and losers under the Basel 2 proposals are comparatively easy to identify; we summarize these in Table 9.3 and discuss them below. During and since 2001, of course, there have been some developments that have modified parts of Basel 2 that bear on Table 9.3 and we will address these later.

Big, prudent banks should see a reduction in their regulatory capital as it converges towards economic capital. This will result from the ability of those banks to use and exploit the IRB approach. In the short term, however, they will have to meet the costs of upgrading their internal systems and technology. Compliance (and related disclosure) costs are also likely to be significant. As we saw in the previous section, the bigger and more sophisticated banks are likely to benefit, whilst the smaller and less sophisticated banks will lose.

Some of the biggest winners from the abolition of the old (Basel 1) risk-weighting bands are relatively creditworthy countries that are not members of the OECD. Risk weightings under the standardized approach will fall from 100 per cent to either 20 per cent or 0 per cent. Banks based in these countries will also be better off. Similarly, highly-rated corporates (all risk-weighted at 100 per cent under Basel 1) will also benefit from a much lower

Table 9.3 Potential winners and losers under Basel 2?

Winners	Losers
Big, prudent banks	Weak OECD credits
OECD outsiders	High-yield loan market
Highly-rated corporates	Retail banks
Asset-backed market	Credit derivatives
Multilateral development banks	Repos markets
High-yield bond market	Asset management
Unrated companies	

Source: Peterson, 2001, p. 52; *Risk*, 2001a and b.

risk weighting. As a result, banks will have an increased incentive to lend to these corporates.

All asset-backed securities (ABSs) were risk-weighted at 100 per cent under Basel 1. Under the Basel 2 standardized approach, asset-backed bonds will be risk-weighted according to their credit rating. This should make senior tranches more attractive for banks to hold and this may increase the respective demand.

Top-rated multilateral development banks have their asset weightings cut from 20 per cent to 0 per cent under the standardized approach. For high-yield bonds, banks will have to hold more capital under Basel 2 (but banks are not big investors anyway in high-yield bonds). But since bank lending to less creditworthy borrowers will be more heavily penalized under Basel 2, these companies may be pushed into the junk bond market, thereby increasing the supply of funds and depth of bond markets generally.

Under Basel 2, the weakest corporate and bank credits attract a weighting of 150 per cent (under the standardized approach), but unrated entities only attract a 100 per cent (albeit minimum) weight. This apparent preferential treatment of unrated companies seems likely to have some impact (Peterson, 2001, p. 52). For example, some companies might choose to remain unrated.

Initial views were that retail banks may be among the losers. Nevertheless, their capital treatment and the continuing calibration of retail banking credit risks seems to have reduced this potential. Problems also include the new operational risk charge and the increased costs of compliance.

Initial concerns were raised that the additional legal capital floor (w) for credit derivatives may adversely affect liquidity in the market for credit default swaps (*Risk*, 2001a, p. 26) and it has also been argued that there will be damaging consequences for repo market participants. Finally, concerns have also been expressed about the possible impact on asset management. In particular, the new operational risk capital charge will apply to the asset management operations of banks.

So what does this all mean for banks operating in the Arab world? Well, in reality there still appears to be considerable confusion about Basel 2. This is partly because of uncertainty about definitions, like operational risk. Consequently, there is uncertainty about measurement criteria and respective data needs. One of the biggest operational problems for Arab banks in meeting Basel 2 is getting the needed data and putting IT resources in place to do this. The Basel 2 risk methodology adopted by banks is likely to depend both on their size and the availability of needed (especially historic) data. For many Arab banks the extra investment and resources in moving to more sophisticated risk techniques are not cost-effective. Therefore, most banks will, perhaps, be adopting the standardized approach to calculating capital requirements.

Arab banks with large exposures to top-quality corporate names will be obvious winners, whereas in retail banking the higher probability of default may mean higher risk weightings (an exception being residential mortgage business). Morgan Stanley Dean Witter's (2001, p. 3) initial analysis suggests that Basel 2 could raise the risk weightings on retail products (excluding mortgages) as much as it lowers them on high-quality banking/capital market exposures. They believe that mid-market business and commercial lending will not be materially affected.

Basel 2 is likely to lead to some important portfolio changes in Arab banking. Investment banking/capital market activities should see an improvement. Retail activities, on the other hand, may experience reduced returns with greater regulatory capital. Mortgages and exposures to large rated corporates are two asset classes that should gain from Basel 2. These products will both require less regulatory capital. But banks will not be able to enjoy these advantages indefinitely since competitors will be attracted into these segments. Nevertheless, Basel 2 is likely to create a 'window of opportunity' for those Arab banks with mortgages and investment banking/capital market exposures to enjoy higher economic profit for a sustained period.

Having said all this, however, one must caution that banks in the Arab world are very much likely to rely on the standardized approach to capital calculations and this will place them at a competitive disadvantage to large Western banks. They are therefore unlikely to benefit from the IRB approach. This could be an important policy issue if large international banks compete with domestic Arab banks for large corporate and other business, as the former will have a substantial financing advantage.

FATF's anti-money-laundering and anti-terrorist-financing recommendations

The OECD Financial Action Task Force (FATF) was established at the G7 Summit of the Arch in 1989 and its main aim is to develop measures to help combat money-laundering activity. At the time of establishment, money laundering was only recognized as a specific criminal offence in seven of the Task Force member countries. Now it has 33 members including the Gulf Cooperation Council.

In 1990 the FATF established a range of recommendations that set the framework for anti-money-laundering efforts for the global financial system. These recommendations have been revised in 1996 and then more recently in 2003.[6] A summary of the main recommendations are shown in Table 9.4. No Arab financial system fails to cooperate on the FATF recommendations. As of March 2004, only seven jurisdictions had been listed as non-cooperative countries or territories (these were the Cook Islands; Guatemala; Indonesia; Myanmar; Nauru; Nigeria; and the Philippines).

Since the attacks in the United States on 11 September 2001, FATF has widened its mission beyond money-laundering in order to concentrate its expertise on the effort to combat global terrorist-financing. FATF has recently issued recommendation to combat terrorist-financing, encouraging all countries

Table 9.4 Summary of the principal recommendations of the Financial Actions Task Force on anti-money-laundering

---

A. LEGAL SYSTEMS

Scope of the criminal offence of money-laundering

- Countries should criminalize money-laundering on the basis of the United Nations Convention against Illicit Traffic in Narcotic Drugs and Psychotropic Substances, 1988 (the Vienna Convention), and the United Nations Convention against Transnational Organized Crime, 2000 (the Palermo Convention).
- Countries should ensure that the intent and knowledge required to prove the offence of money-laundering is consistent with the standards set forth in the Vienna and Palermo Conventions.

Provisional measures and confiscation

- Countries should adopt measures similar to those set forth in the Vienna and Palermo Conventions.

B. MEASURES TO BE TAKEN BY FINANCIAL INSTITUTIONS AND NONFINANCIAL BUSINESSES AND PROFESSIONS TO PREVENT MONEY-LAUNDERING AND TERRORIST-FINANCING

- Countries should ensure that financial institution secrecy laws do not inhibit implementation of the FATF Recommendations.

Customer due diligence and record-keeping

- Financial institutions should not keep anonymous accounts or accounts in obviously fictitious names and should undertake customer due diligence measures.
- Financial institutions should have appropriate risk management systems to determine whether the customer is a politically exposed person; obtain senior management approval for establishing business relationships with such customers.
- Financial institutions should, in relation to cross-border correspondent banking and other similar relationships, in addition to performing normal due diligence measures gather sufficient information about a respondent institution to understand fully the nature of the respondent's business and take other measures to ensure the identity of the customer.
- Financial institutions should pay special attention to any money-laundering threats that may arise from new or developing technologies.
- Financial institutions should maintain, for at least five years, all necessary records on transactions, both domestic or international, to enable them to comply swiftly with information requests from the competent authorities.
- Financial institutions should pay special attention to all complex, unusual, large transactions.
- The customer due diligence and record-keeping requirements set out in Recommendations are to apply to apply to Casinos; Real estate agents; Dealers in precious metals and stones; Lawyers, notaries, other independent legal professionals and accountants; Trust and company service providers.

Reporting of suspicious transactions and compliance

- If a financial institution suspects or has reasonable grounds to suspect that funds are the proceeds of a criminal activity, or are related to terrorist financing, it should be required, directly by law or regulation, to report promptly its suspicions to the financial intelligence unit.
- Financial institutions, their directors, officers and employees should be: protected by legal provisions from criminal and civil liability for breach of any restriction on disclosure of information; not prohibited by law from disclosing the fact that a suspicious transaction is being reported.
- Financial institutions should develop programmes against money-laundering and terrorist-financing.
- The requirements set out above also apply to the aforementioned non-financial businesses and professions, subject to various qualifications.

Other measures to deter money-laundering and terrorist-financing

- Countries should ensure that effective, proportionate and dissuasive sanctions, whether criminal, civil or administrative, are available to deal with natural or legal persons that fail to comply with anti-money-laundering or terrorist-financing requirements.
- Countries should not approve the establishment or accept the continued operation of shell companies.
- Countries should consider implementing feasible measures to detect or monitor the physical cross-border transportation of currency and bearer negotiable instruments, subject to strict safeguards.

Measures to be taken with respect to countries that do not or insufficiently comply with the FATF

- Financial institutions should give special attention to business relationships and transactions with persons, including companies and financial institutions, from countries which do not or insufficiently apply the FATF Recommendations.
- Financial institutions should ensure that the principles applicable to financial institutions are also applied to branches and majority owned subsidiaries located abroad.

Regulation and supervision

- Countries should ensure that financial institutions are subject to adequate regulation and supervision and are effectively implementing the FATF Recommendations.
- The competent authorities should establish guidelines, and provide feedback which will assist financial institutions and designated non-financial businesses and professions in applying national measures to combat money-laundering and terrorist-financing, and in particular, in detecting and reporting suspicious transactions.

276

Table 9.4 (Continued)

C. INSTITUTIONAL AND OTHER MEASURES NECESSARY IN SYSTEMS FOR COMBATING MONEY-LAUNDERING AND TERRORIST-FINANCING

Competent authorities, their powers and resources
- Countries should establish a Financial Investigation Unit (FIU) that serves as a national centre for the receiving (and, as permitted, requesting), analysis and dissemination of a Suspicious Transaction Report (STR) and other information regarding potential money-laundering or terrorist-financing.
- Countries should ensure that designated law enforcement authorities have responsibility for money-laundering and terrorist-financing investigations.
- When conducting investigations of money-laundering and underlying predicate offences, competent authorities should be able to obtain documents and information for use in those investigations, and in prosecutions and related actions.
- Supervisors should have adequate powers to monitor and ensure compliance by financial institutions with requirements to combat money-laundering and terrorist-financing, including the authority to conduct inspections.
- Countries should provide their competent authorities involved in combating money-laundering and terrorist-financing with adequate financial, human and technical resources.
- Countries should ensure that policy-makers, the FIU, law enforcement and supervisors have effective mechanisms in place which enable them to cooperate, and where appropriate coordinate domestically.
- Countries should ensure that their competent authorities can review the effectiveness of their systems to combat money-laundering and terrorist-financing systems by maintaining comprehensive statistics on matters relevant to the effectiveness and efficiency of such systems.

Transparency of legal persons and arrangements
- Countries should take measures to prevent the unlawful use of legal persons by money-launderers.
- Countries should take measures to prevent the unlawful use of legal arrangements by money-launderers.

D. INTERNATIONAL COOPERATION

- Countries should take immediate steps to become party to and implement fully the Vienna Convention, the Palermo Convention, and the 1999 United Nations International Convention for the Suppression of the Financing of Terrorism. Countries are also encouraged to ratify and implement other relevant international conventions, such as the 1990 Council of Europe Convention on Laundering, Search, Seizure and Confiscation of the Proceeds from Crime and the 2002 Inter-American Convention against Terrorism.

Mutual legal assistance and extradition
- Countries should rapidly, constructively and effectively provide the widest possible range of mutual legal assistance in relation to money-laundering and terrorist-financing investigations, prosecutions, and related proceedings.
- Countries should, to the greatest extent possible, render mutual legal assistance notwithstanding the absence of dual criminality.
- There should be authority to take expeditious action in response to requests by foreign countries to identify, freeze, seize and confiscate property laundered, proceeds from money-laundering or predicate offences, instrumentalities used in or intended for use in the commission of these offences, or property of corresponding value. There should also be arrangements for coordinating seizure and confiscation proceedings, which may include the sharing of confiscated assets.
- Countries should recognise money-laundering as an extraditable offence.

Other forms of cooperation
- Countries should ensure that their competent authorities provide the widest possible range of international cooperation to their foreign counterparts.

to adopt and implement these measures. The objective of these new rules is to deny terrorists and their supporters access to the international financial system. A summary of the FATF recommendations on terrorist-financing are listed in Table 9.5 and these are currently being put in place throughout the Arab world.

GCC single market and other Arab trading blocs

Another development that will have an effect on the operations and strategies of banks in the Gulf relates to the plans to create a GCC single market. As in the case of the European Union and the establishment of a single currency, the GCC's plan for further integration and the introduction of a Gulf single currency by 2008 places considerable emphasis on establishing a single financial services market. The single market for financial services is expected to benefit the GCC member states' economies as a whole. The full liberalization and integration of GCC member states' capital markets are expected to work towards the elimination of those distortions and negative effects that stem from misallocation of capital resources. Capital will move freely across national borders seeking the highest returns possible. Capital will have access to a wider range of markets and investments and therefore better allocation will result in attaining greater economic efficiency for the whole of the market. Furthermore, full integration of capital, money and banking markets will bring forward more converging real interest rates across the GCC member states with the positive consequences that are associated with such an outcome.

Table 9.5   Summary of the FATF special recommendations on terrorist-financing

- Each country should take immediate steps to ratify and to implement fully the 1999 United Nations International Convention for the Suppression of the Financing of Terrorism.
- Each country should criminalize the financing of terrorism, terrorist acts and terrorist organizations.
- Each country should implement measures to freeze without delay funds or other assets of terrorists, those who finance terrorism and terrorist organizations in accordance with the United Nations resolutions relating to the prevention and suppression of the financing of terrorist acts.
- If financial institutions, or other businesses or entities subject to anti-money-laundering obligations, suspect or have reasonable grounds to suspect that funds are linked or related to, or are to be used for terrorism, terrorist acts or by terrorist organizations,they should be required to report promptly their suspicions to the competent authorities.
- Each country should afford another country, on the basis of a treaty, arrangement or other mechanism for mutual legal assistance or information exchange, the greatest possible measure of assistance in connection with criminal, civil enforcement, and administrative investigations, inquiries and proceedings relating to the financing of terrorism, terrorist acts and terrorist organizations.
- Each country should take measures to ensure that persons or legal entities, including agents, that provide a service for the transmission of money or value, including transmission through an informal money or value transfer system or network, should be licensed or registered and subject to all the FATF Recommendations that apply to banks and non-bank financial institutions.
- Countries should take measures to require financial institutions, including money remitters, to include accurate and meaningful originator information (name, address and account number) on funds transfers and related messages that are sent, and the information should remain with the transfer or related message through the payment chain.
- Countries should review the adequacy of laws and regulations that relate to entities that can be abused for the financing of terrorism. Non-profit organizations are particularly vulnerable, and countries should ensure that they cannot be misused.

The Gulf Cooperation Council is now a very active body. It is framing the Gulf economy along similar lines to those of the European Union. Trade has already multiplied between member states as the industrialization process has continued. Trade barriers have been reduced, and an increasing number of Gulf institutions formed in order to accelerate economic cooperation. One item on the large agenda is monetary integration and, if the European experience is indicative, this will embrace the harmonization of banking regulations, monetary controls and fiscal instruments on the process towards one Gulf central bank and a common currency.

Conclusion

Major changes are impacting on the global financial systems. The Arab systems are not immune from these developments. Banking markets are becoming more concentrated, systems are liberalizing and the general environment is becoming more competitive overall. In such an environment, banks continually seek to improve their performance by focusing on bettering their efficiency and generating greater revenues. Linked to this is the need to manage capital and risks more effectively so that shareholders and stakeholders obtain good returns on their investments. Opportunities exist for Arab banks to develop their retail and corporate banking businesses in non-traditional areas such as in private banking and retail insurance. The desire to boost non-interest income relative to margin based revenue will undoubtedly continue. Technological advances continue to help reshape the economics of the financial services industry and many Arab banks are well placed to adopt state-of-the-art technology to broaden their delivery channels and streamline their back-office functions. Many are emulating their counterparts in Western banking systems.

In addition to these developments, changes in the international regulatory environment are also having an ever-increasing influence on Arab banking. Supervisory rules and regulations are being implemented to meet BIS recommendations. Recent initiatives aimed at countering money-laundering activity and terrorist-financing are also being introduced. None of the Arab countries is seen as non-compliant. All this is bringing Arab banking systems in-line with best practice internationally, which is a remarkable achievement given that most of the financial systems have only existed for around four decades or so.

Notes

2 An Overview of Arabian Economies

1. There were no official reports showing external indebtedness of Saudi Arabia and Bahrain, especially over the last part of the 1990s (reports by the Arab Monetary Fund, 2002, and World Bank, 2000, do not provide data on the indebtedness of these countries).

3 Economic Performance of Arabian Countries during the 1990s

1. See Fry (1988, p. 131).
2. GCC Secretariat General (http://www.gcc-sg.org/Foundations.html).
3. GCC Secretariat General's Economic Bulletin, 2001, pp. 12–13.
4. *Source*: Qatar Central Bank, Annual reports, 1998 and 1999.
5. Annual 2001 Reports GCC central banks.
6. *The World Factbook*, 2002 (http://www.cia.gov/cia/publications/factbook).
7. This percentage is calculated from the GCC Secretariat General/s Economic Bulletin, 2001, p. 28.
8. GCC Secretariat General's Economic Bulletin, 2001, p. 20.
9. All GCC countries are members of the Word Trade Organization except Saudi Arabia (which is in the process of joining).
10. This includes wholesale, retail, hotels, restaurants, transport, finance, insurance, real estate, government services, and other services (GCC Secretariat General's Economic Bulletin, 2001, p. 11).

4 Banking and Financial Systems in Non-Gulf Arab Countries

1. The solidarity of Maghreb countries was well seen during the independence war in Algeria. Algerian fighters used Tunisia and (intensively) Morocco to transport logistic aid.
2. Post-independence era starts from the day of independence from France until present. Algeria obtained its independence from France in 1962, while Morocco and Tunisia obtained their independence in 1956.
3. The CAD was transferred into a real development bank under the name of Banque Algérienne de Développement (BAD) according to Ordinance No. 72–66 of 7 June 1972.
4. Naas (2003, pp. 45–50) mentions that deposits at BNA, CPA and BEA represented approximately 70%, 10% and 20% of total commercial bank deposits, respectively, by the end of the 1960s.
5. Every government-owned enterprise had access to two accounts: the exploitation account and development account. The exploitation account was used to receive revenues, payment and short-term loans in order to finance working capital needs. The development account dealt with medium and long-term loans.
6. Banque du Maroc was established by the Dahir no. 1–59–233 of 30 June 1959 to replace the Banque d'État du Maroc and to ensure the functions of a Central Bank. It was created as a state-owned institution with legal personality and financial autonomy, entrusted with the privilege of issuing banknotes and coins, and the

mission of safeguarding the stability of the currency as well as preserving the soundness of the banking system. In March 1987, Banque du Maroc was replaced by Bank Al-Maghrib.

7. Banks were required to hold 6% of deposits as bonds issued by the Crédit Immobilier et Hôtelier (CIH), 5.5% of deposits as bonds issued by Banque Nationale pour le Développement Économique (BNDE), and 3.5% of deposits as bonds issued by Caisse Nationale de Crédit Agricole (CNCA).

8. Dahir enacting Law No. 1-93-147 of 6 July 1993.

9. For instance, the Property Savings Bank of Algeria and Tunisia, based in Algiers, now Amen Bank, remained subject to French jurisdiction until 1966. By this year, most of banks working in Algeria were nationalized.

10. Banks were required to obtain the approval of the central bank for credits exceeding TD100,000.

11. Bank Al-Maghrib Circular of 15 February 1996 related to interest rates.

12. Special saving deposits accounted before 40% of total deposits of the public in the banking sector at the end of 1998.

13. These banks are Banque Nationale pour le Développement Économique (BNDE), Crédit Immobilier et Agricole (CIA), and Caisse Nationale du Crédit Agricole (CNCA).

14. The Algerian government has now started privatizing its banks. The government plans to offer 50% capital of CPA to foreign and private investors in 2005.

15. The first joint-venture bank, which was licensed in 1991, is Al-Baraka Bank. This bank is owned equally between the Saudi-based private bank, Al-Baraka Group, and the Algerian government-owned bank BADR. The investment bank, Union Bank, was the first bank fully owned by Algerian private investors.

16. BADR and BNA increased their lending and loan concentration in the food and pharmaceutical importing agencies. These agencies suffered large losses originating from the 1994 devaluation of the Dinar. Iradian *et al.* (2000) report that between 1991 and 1997, public banks receive an equivalent of 11% of GDP to compensate them for foreign exchange losses incurred on past external borrowing contracted on behalf of the government. CNEP bank accumulated large amounts of non-performing loans to the housing and construction sector.

17. These are: Banque Centrale Populaire (BCP), Crédit Immobilier et Hôtelier (CIH), and Banque Nationale pour le Développement Économique (BNDE).

18. For instance, CNEP in Algeria was a saving bank, but was converted into a commercial bank in 1997. Similarly, the Crédit Immobilier and Hôtelier (CIH) was a specialized bank before 1993, but converted to a commercial bank. Also, in Tunisia, two commercial banks absorbed a number of non-commercial banks in 1999. First, the Union International de Banques (UIB) absorbed Tuniso-Emirates Investment Bank. Second, Société Tunisiénne de Banques (STB) took over Banque Économique pour le Développement en Tunisie (BEDT) and the Banque Nationale pour le Développement Touristique (BNDT).

19. The BCM has a market share of 17% in deposits and loans, and 25% of international transactions.

20. The BMCE and Wafabank are the second and third largest quoted banks with 22% and 15% of total banking market capitalization, and 6.4% and 4.4% of total market capitalization, respectively.

21. The Banque du Sud (BS) and Amen Bank (AM) are the second and third largest banks in terms of market capitalization. Each of them account for about 16% of total banking capitalization and about 3.6% of total market capitalization.

22. These banks are are Banque de Développement Local (BDL), Banque Extérieure d'Algérie (BEA), Banque Nationale d'Algérie (BNA), Crédit Populaire d'Algérie (CPA), Banque Algérienne du Développement Rural (BADR), and Caisse Nationale d'Epargne et de Prévoyance (CNEP). CNEP bank was converted into a commercial bank in 1997, after previously acting as the main public saving and housing loan institution.
23. Including Citibank, Société Générale, and Barclays.
24. These banks are Banque Nationale pour le Développement Economique (BNDE), Crédit Immobilier et Hôtelier (CIH), Caisse Nationale de Crédit Agricole (CNCA), and Banque Centrale Populaire (BCP). Vermeren (2002) mentions that in 1999 there was the 'CIH gate', the biggest financial scandal Morocco ever had since independence, involving nearly 11 billions of dirham (1.5 times the country's bill of hydrocarbon imports).
25. For instance, Banque Nationale de Paris (BNP) owned 56% of capital of Banque Morocaine du Commerce et de l'Industrie (BMCI), Crédit Lyonnais owns 51% of capital of Crédit du Maroc (CM), Société Générale owns 51% of capital of Société Générale Marocaine des Banques (SGMB). Foreign shareholders own 25.2%, 14.5% and 16.6% of capital of Banque Commerciale du Maroc (BCM), Banque Marocaine du Commerce Extérieur (BMCE), and Wafabank, respectively.
26. The latter is known in Morocco as the bank of the royal family.
27. This information is by James Drummond 'Northern lights: with a French-speaking population of 70 million, it is little wonder that Algeria, Morocco and Tunisia are attractive to French banks. (Middle East & Africa: Maghreb) ', published in the *Banker's Magazine* in Sept. 2002.
28. www.menareport.com (2 December 2003).
29. Private shareholders own nearly 6% of total capital of development banks. What remains is equally shared between the Tunisian government and a number of oil-exporting Gulf and Libyan governments.
30. In Algeria, the chief executives of government-owned banks are still nominated by political authorities.
31. Only 20% of these shares are floated on the Algiers Stock Exchange. These companies are Eriad-Setif (agro-industrial), Saidal (pharmaceuticals), and the Al-Aurassi Hotel.

5   Banking and Financial Systems in Gulf Cooperation Council (GCC) Countries

1. For example the Saudi British Bank and the Saudi American Bank.
2. Authors' own calculation based on the GCC Secretariat General's Economic Bulletin, 2001.
3. Economist Intelligence Unit, 1991.
4. Author's own calculation based on the GCC Secretariat General's Economic Bulletin, 2001.
5. Discussion on currency development is based on Bahrain Monetary Agency, 2002.
6. Bahrain hosted a first Islamic bank in 1975 and currently there are two commercial Islamic banks as well as a number of Islamic banks operating on the basis of OBUs and investment banks. According to the BMA (2001), the consolidated assets of Islamic banks stood at $6,051 million.
7. Author's own calculation based on the GCC Secretariat General's Economic Bulletin, 2001.
8. Economist Intelligence Unit, 1992.

9. Economist Intelligence Unit, 1992; Central Bank of Kuwait, 2002.
10. See Central Bank of Oman (1996).
11. Qatar Monetary Agency, 1992.
12. Author's own calculation based on the GCC Secretariat General's Economic Bulletin, 2001.
13. Among the national banks, two are Islamic. One of the foreign banks, the Grindlays Bank Ltd., changed into a national bank by 1 August 2000. The specialized bank is Qatar Industrial Development Bank, initiated in 1997 to provide loans to small and medium-sized manufacturing firms.
14. M1 consists of currency in circulation and demand deposits in local currency. M2 consists of M1 plus time deposits and deposits in foreign currencies.
15. Each M1, M2, and GDP are summed across GCC countries.

6 Islamic Banking

1. Except in the extreme case of bankruptcy.
2. This number does not include Islamic windows in conventional banks.
3. Osman Ahmed, in Wilson (1990, p. 77).
4. The Islamic Dinar is considered as the IDB accounting unit; it is equivalent in value to one Special Drawing Right (SDR) of the International Monetary Fund (IMF).
5. In a *mudarabah* contract both parties share in the risk. The *mudarib* risks his labour and the *rabb al-mal* (financier) risks his capital.
6. In practice most funds apply more stringent condition than this.
7. Failaka.com.
8. This was done in the cases of establishment of Islamic banks in Jordan and Egypt.
9. As in Malaysia, Turkey and the UAE.
10. Council of Islamic Ideology Pakistan (1980).
11. Chapra (1985).
12. For further arguments in favour of this proposal, see Chapra (1985, p. 161).
13. For a detailed discussion of these problems, see Iqbal *et al.* (1998).
14. The new buyer has to agree to continue the lease on the conditions previously agreed unless the lessee willingly agrees to new conditions.
15. Some of these can be insured against, but this has to be done by the lessor at his own cost.

7 Financial System Efficiency

1. Providers of funds to Asian financial institutions (especially in Thailand) believed that their funds would be protected from risk. In addition, the owners of financial institutions concluded, through their strong political connections, that the provision of such government guarantees would be available (see Krugman, 1998).
2. As we will analyze later, financial system efficiency includes both stock market efficiency and bank efficiency.
3. 'Lenders' can be financial institutions like banks, or individuals who buy bonds. The use of the word 'financier' may refer to those mentioned as lenders as well as buyers of stocks.
4. In terms of the informational aspect, Stiglitz (1989) gives more details on advantages and disadvantages of bonds, stocks and short-term finance.
5. Fundamentals refers to the analysis of evaluating the price of a stock on the basis of information on the micro-performance of the firm, such as earnings, dividends and financial statements, and on the macro-performance of the economy, such as interest rates, GNP, inflation and unemployment. The information is used to forecast the future price of the stock.

6. Greenwald, Stiglitz and Weiss (1984) refer to the situation in which adverse selection leads to lower funds raised as 'stock rationing'.

7. William Sharpe (1964) developed the capital asset pricing model that examines the systematic and non-systematic risks of holding a portfolio. Systematic risks are risks that cannot be avoided even by holding well-diversified portfolios. Non-systematic risks are risks that can be eliminated within well-diversified portfolios.

8. Such as that offered by the US Federal Deposit Insurance Corporation (FDIC), which provides insurance to deposits up to $100,000.

9. Rent denotes the difference between the administered interest rate and the rate that should be set by the market mechanism.

10. For example, see Berger and Mester (1997); Altunbas *et al.* (2001); Allen and Rai (1996).

11. On the other hand, there are several factors that may lead to scale diseconomies. Most of these could be related to size of the firm. Large firms may pay more for labour than small firms. Moreover, large firms may find it more difficult to monitor and evaluate employees' activities and there could be capacity constraints.

12. Using deterministic translog cost function to measure scale economies, expansion-path scale economies and expansion path sub-additivity, Berger *et al.* (1987) found that scale economies are shown slightly at the branch level, but large-scale diseconomies at the banking firm level.

13. Pulley and Humphrey (1993) showed that cost complementarities are less evident for both deposit and loan products, while the spread of the fixed costs over both these products is shared in the order of 4 to 5 per cent.

14. See Humphrey (1990) and McAllister and McManus (1993).

15. It also assumes that the frontier is fixed for all observations in the sample.

16. The other functional forms used are Constant Elasticity of Substitution or CES (Arrow *et al.*, 1961), and Leontief (Diewert, 1973), Box-Cox transformations of the translog model (Clark, 1984), hybrid translog function (Molyneux *et al.*, 1996), and the Fuss normalized quadratic variable profit function (Berger, Hancock and Humphrey, 1993).

17. Although there exist some studies that used the translog specification (for example, Turati, 2001; Maudos *et al.*, 2002), the majority of researchers nowadays tend to adopt the Fourier flexible form.

18. As defined by McAllister and McManus (1993, p. 395), 'The kernel regression technique [Hardle (1990) in a recent survey] builds a global estimate of the cost function by forming weighted averages over localized regions. Although this technique comes closest to the goal of "letting the data speak for themselves", it has the disadvantage of requiring very large samples to obtain accurate results, especially in applications in which there are more than a few explanatory variables.' 'The linear spline estimation technique [Porier (1976)] approximates the unknown cost function by a piecewise linear function. The grid of knot points becomes finer as the sample size increases, enabling the spline to approximate any continuous function. Experimentation suggested that a very simple spline-augmented translog function was an adequate approximation to the unknown cost function for purposes of the present comparison, with three knot points for each of the output variables.'

19. This is possible because the sine and cosine functions are mutually orthogonal and functions space-spanning; hence, representing an arbitrary function by a Fourier series is analogous to representing n-vectors.

20. Berger and Mester (1997) assure that Fourier-flexible has improved the fit of the data in every application they undertook.

8   Efficiency in Arab Banking

1. For the case of the standard profit function, Al-Jarrah and Molyneux (2003) specify variable profits in place of variable costs and take variable output prices as given but allow output quantities to vary. On the other hand, the alternative profit function employs the same dependent variable as the standard profit function and the same exogenous variables as the cost function but it measures how close a bank comes to earning maximum profits given its output levels rather than its output prices.
2. In the case of Islamic banks 'Depositors' share of profit' is used instead.
3. The control variables enter into the stochastic frontier model in the same way as the input variables (as betas) and these variables are fully interactive with other parameters of the model. On the other hand, the environmental variables are not interactive with other model parameters and are added to the model as delta (as will be shown later).
4. Scale economies are calculated using the following equation:

$$Scale\ economies = \sum_{i=1}^{2} \frac{\partial \ln TC}{\partial \ln Q_i} = \sum_{i=1}^{2} \alpha_i + \sum_{i=1}^{2}\sum_{j=1}^{2} \delta_{ij} \ln Q_j + \sum_{i=1}^{2}\sum_{j=1}^{2} p_{ij} \ln P_i$$

$$+ \mu_i \sum_{i=1}^{2} [-a_i \sin(Z_i) + b_i \cos(Z_i)]$$

$$+ 2\mu_i \sum_{i=1}^{2}\sum_{j=1}^{2} [-a_{ij}\sin(Z_i + Z_j) + b_{ij}\cos(Z_i + Z_j)].$$

If *scale economies* >1, <1, or = 1, then there are diseconomies, economies of scale, or constant returns to scale respectively.
5. Scale inefficiencies are calculated as *Scale inefficiency* $= e^{(.5/c)(1-\varepsilon)^2} - 1$, where ε is the first derivate of the cost function, that is the scale elasticity with respect to output; and c is the second derivative of the cost function with respect to output. After taking the first and second derivates of the cost function in terms of output quantities, the trigonometric terms are omitted in the calculations of scale inefficiency to avoid negative scale inefficiency values.
6. Berger *et al.* (1993a), Berger and Humphrey (1991), and Evanoff and Israilevich (1991) reach the same conclusions.
7. The start of sizable influxes of oil revenue in the 1970s enabled the establishment of national banks with both public and private, or purely private, ownership.
8. While the Battese and Coelli (1992) specification includes firm-specific variables to examine the firm-specific-related effects on efficiency, the Battese and Coelli (1995) specification extends the first specification to include a number of control and environmental variables. The model is estimated using FRONTIER 4.1, a package specifically designed for the estimation of stochastic production frontiers.

9   Current Developments and Prospects for Arab Banks

1. See Morgan Stanley Dean Witter, *The Internet & Financial Services*, 31 July 2000.
2. McKinsey & Co (2001), *Beyond Online*, Spring.

3. Factoring is simply a lending product that enables a firm to collect money on credit sales. The factor purchases a firm's invoice debts for cash at a discount, and then seeks repayment from the original purchaser of the company's goods or services. Leasing relates to an agreement where the owner of a product or service gives the customer the right to use equipment, such as a car, in return for a number of specified payments over an agreed time schedule. The equipment or vehicle leased is usually the only collateral security for the transaction. Hire purchase is similar to leasing although the difference is that the firm or individual making repayments also covers the initial cost of the asset and becomes the owner at the end of the payment period.
4. *The Future of Corporate Banking in Europe*, Goldman Sachs & McKinsey & Co, January 2001.
5. See, for example, Basel (1997, p. 8) and IMF (1998, p. 41).
6. See http://www1.oecd.org/fatf/ for full details of the FATF recommendations.

References

Abed, G.T. and M. Fischer (2003) 'Algeria: A Staff Report for the 2002 Article IV Consultation', *International Monetary Fund Country Report* No. 03/68, March 2003.

Achy, A. (2000) *Financial Markets and Growth in Morocco*, Institut National de Statistique et d'Économie Appliquée (INSEA) (National Institute of Statistics and Applied Economics, Rabat, Morocco).

Afriat, S. (1972) 'Efficiency Estimation of Production Functions', *International Economic Review*, 13, 568–98.

Aigner, D. and S. Chu (1968) 'On Estimating the Industry Production Function', *American Economic Review*, 58, 826–39.

Aigner, D., C. Lovell and P. Schmidt (1977) 'Formulation and Estimation of Stochastic Frontier Production Function Models', *Journal of Econometrics*, 6 (May), 21–37.

Akerlof, G. (1970) 'The Market for "Lemons": Qualitative Uncertainty and the Market Mechanism', *Quarterly Journal of Economics*, 84(3), 488–500.

Akhavein, J., A. Berger, and D. Humphrey (1997) 'The Effects of Megamergers on Efficiency and Prices: Evidence from a Bank Profit Function', *Review of Industrial Organization*, 12(1), February, pp. 95–139.

Al-Amri, A.M. (2000) *National Bank of Abu Dhabi, The Quarterly Economic and Financial Reports*, October.

Al-Attar, S. R. (2000) 'Recent Banking Developments in GCC Countries', *Kuwait Institute of Banking Studies Working Paper* (WP/3/00).

Al-Awad, B.K (2001) *Central Bank of United Arab Emirates Quarterly Economic Bulletin*, April.

Al-Ganim, A.G. (2000) 'An Overview of Kuwaiti Financial System Performance through the 1990's', *Kuwait Institute of Banking Studies Quarterly Economic Bulletin*, October.

Al-Jarhi, Mabid Ali and Munawar Iqbal (2001) *Islamic Banking: Answers to Some Frequently Asked Questions*, Occasional Paper No.4, Islamic Research and Training Institute, Islamic Development Bank, Jeddah.

Al-Jarrah, I. M. (2002) 'Efficiency in Arabian Banking', PhD, University of Wales, Bangor.

Al-Jarrah, I. M and P. Molyneux (2003) 'Efficiency in Arabian Banking', University of Wales, Bangor, *IEF Working Paper*.

Al-Mannai, A.A.(2001) 'The GCC Banking Industry and the Future Challenges', *Institute of Economic Studies and Banking Research Bahrain Working Paper*, (WP/10/2001).

Al-Owain, M.T. (2001) 'International Bank of Emirates', *The Quarterly Economic Review*, July.

Al-Sahlawi, K. (1997) 'The Role of Industrial Development Banks in Financing and Promoting Technological Change: The Case of the Saudi Industrial Development Fund', PhD, University of Wales, Bangor.

Al-Shammari, S. (2003) 'Structure–Conduct–Performance and the Efficiency of the GCC Banking Markets', PhD, University of Wales, Bangor.

Al-Sharrah, R. (1999) *The Specialised Banks in the Arab Gulf Countries*, Al-Falah Publishing, Kuwait (in Arabic).

Al-Suhaimi, J. (2001) 'Consolidation, Competition, Foreign Presence and Systemic Stability in the Saudi Banking Industry', *Bank for International Settlements Papers*, 4 August.

Alawode, A. and S. Ikhide (1997) 'Why Should Financial Liberalisation Induce Financial Crisis?', *Giordano Dell Amore Foundation: Centre for Assistance to Financial and Credit Institutions of Transitional Countries Quarterly Review*, no. 3.

Alhadeff, D.A. (1954) *Monopoly and Competition in Banking*, University of California Press, Berkeley, Calif.

Allen, F. and A. Santomero (1998) 'The Theory of Financial Intermediation', *Journal of Banking and Finance*, 21, 1461–85.

Allen, L. and A. Rai (1996) 'Operational Efficiency in Banking: An International Comparison', *Journal of Banking and Finance*, 20, 655–72.

Alonso-Gamo, P., A. Fedlino and S. Horvitz (1997a) 'Globalisation and Growth Prospects in Arab Countries', *International Monetary Fund Working Paper* (WP 125/97).

Alonso-Gamo, P., S. Fennell and K. Sakr (1997b) 'Adjusting to New Realities: MENA, The Uruguay Round, and the EU–Mediterranean Initiative', *International Monetary Fund Working Paper* (WP 5/97).

Altunbas, Y. and S. Chakravarty (2001) 'Frontier Cost Functions and Bank Efficiency', *Economics Letters*, 72, 233–40.

Altunbas, Y., L. Evans and P. Molyneux (1994) 'Universal Banks, Ownership and Efficiency: A Stochastic Frontier Analysis of the German Banking Market', University of Durham Economics Department, unpublished working paper.

Altunbas, Y., L. Evans and P. Molyneux (2001) 'Bank Ownership and Efficiency', *Journal of Money, Credit and Banking*, 33(4), 926–54.

Altunbas, Y., E. Gardener and P. Molyneux (1996) 'Cost Economies and Efficiency in EU Banking Systems', *Journal of Economics and Business*, 48, 217–30.

Altunbas Y., E. Gardener, P. Molyneux and B. Moore (2001) 'Efficiency in European Banking', *European Economic Review*, 45(10), 1931–55.

Altunbas, Y., M. Liu, P. Molyneux and R. Seth (2000) 'Efficiency and Risk in Japanese Banking', *Journal of Banking & Finance*, 24, 1605–28.

Altunbas, Y. and P. Molyneux (1996) 'Economies of Scale and Scope in European Banking', *Applied Financial Economics*, 6, 367–75.

Aly, H., R. Grabowski, C. Pasurka and N. Rangan (1990) 'Technical, Scale, and Allocative Efficiencies in U.S. Banking: An Empirical Investigation', *The Review of Economics and Statistics*, 72, 211–18.

Arab Chamber of Commerce (2001) 'Bahrain: Country Analysis Briefs', 'www.eia.doe.gov/cabs/bahrain.html'.

Arab Monetary Fund (2002) 'Statistics', 'www.amf.org.ae/vEnglish/default.asp'.

Arrow, K., H. Chenery, B. Minhas and R. Solow (1961) 'Capital Labor Substitution and Economic Efficiency', *The Review of Economics and Statistics*, 43 (3), August 1961, 225–50.

Azzam, H.T. (1998) *The Emerging Arab Capital Markets*, Kegan Paul International, London

Bagehot, W. [1873] (1991) *Lombard Street: A Description of the Money Market*, Orion Editions, Philadelphia.

Bahrain Monetary Agency (1994) *Bahrain, An International Financial Centre*, Bahrain.

Bahrain Monetary Agency (2001) *Annual Report*, Kingdom Bahrain.

Bahrain Monetary Agency (2002) *Bahrain Dinar Digest*, vol. 1 (January), Bahrain.

Bakhouche, R. (2004) 'Bank Efficiency in Maghreb Countries', PhD, University of Wales, Bangor.

Bank for International Settlements (2000) *Capital Requirements and Bank Behaviour – The Impact of the Basel Accord*, Basel Committee on Banking Supervision Working Paper 1.

Bank for International Settlements (2001) 'Development and Restructuring of the Saudi Banking System', *BIS Policy Papers*, Sept. 1999.

Banker, R., A. Charnes and W. Cooper (1984) 'Some Models for Estimating Technical and Scale Inefficiencies in Data Envelopment Analysis', *Management Science*, 30(9), 1078–92.

Barr, R., L. Seiford, and T. Siems (1994) 'Forecasting Bank Failure: A Non-Parametric Approach', *Recherches Economiques de Louvain*, 60, 411–29.

Basel Committee on Banking Supervision (1997) *Core Principles for Effective Banking Supervision*, September, Basel Committee on Banking Supervision, Basel.

Battese, G. and T. Coelli (1992) 'Frontier Production Functions, Technical Efficiency and Panel Data: With Application to Paddy Farmers in India', *Journal of Productivity Analysis*, 3, 153–69.

Battese, G. and T. Coelli (1993) 'A Stochastic Frontier Production Function Incorporating a Model for Technical Inefficiency Effects', Centre for Efficiency and Productivity Analysis (CEP A), Department of Econometrics, University of New England, Arrnidale, Australia, (WP 69/93).

Battese, G. and T. Coelli (1995) 'A Model for Technical Inefficiency Effects in a Stochastic Frontier Production Function for Panel Data', *Empirical Economics*, 20, 325–32.

Bauer, P., A. Berger, G. Ferrier and D. Humphrey (1998) 'Consistency Conditions for Regulatory Analysis of Financial Institutions: A Comparison of Frontier Efficiency Methods', *Journal of Economics and Business*, 50(2), 85–114.

Bauer, P.W., A.N. Berger and D.B. Humphrey (1993) 'Efficiency and Productivity Growth in U.S. Banking', in H.O. Fried, C.A.K. Lovell and S.S. Schmidt (eds), *The Measurement of Productive Efficiency: Techniques and Applications*, Oxford University Press, UK.

Baumol, W., J. Panzar and R. Willig (1988) *Contestable Markets and the Theory of Industry Structure*, Harcourt Brace Jovanovich, New York (revised edition).

Bayomi, K. (1995) 'Nahda Visions and Political Realities', http://www.hf.uib.noinstitutter/ smi/paj/Bayomi.html'.

Bell, F. and N. Murphy (1968) 'Economies of Scale and Division of Labour in Commercial Banking', *Southern Economic Journal*, October, 131–9.

BenBitour, A. (1998) *L'Algerie au Troisième Millenaire: Défis et Potentialités*, 1st edition, Edition Marinoor, Algiers.

BenHalima, A. (1987) *Le Système Bancaire Algérien: Textes et Réalités*, Edition Dahlab, Algiers.

Benston, G.J. (1965) 'Economies of Scale and Marginal Costs in Banking Operations', *National Banking Review*, 2(4), June, 507–49.

Benston, G., G. Hanweck and D. Humphrey (1982) 'Scale Economies in Banking: A Restructuring and Reassessment', *Journal of Money, Credit and Banking*, 14, 435–56.

Berg, S., F. Forsund and N. Bukh (1995) 'Banking Efficiency in the Nordic Countries: A Few-Country Malmquist Index Analysis', mimeo.

Berg, S., F. Forsund, L. Hjalmarsson and M. Suominen (1993) 'Banking Efficiency in the Nordic Countries', *Journal of Banking and Finance*, 17 (2–3), April, 371–88.

Berger, A. (1995) 'The Profit-Structure Relationship in Banking – Tests of Market Power and Efficient Structure Hypotheses', *Journal of Money, Credit and Banking*, 27, 404–31.

Berger, A. and R. DeYoung (1997) *Problem Loans and Cost Efficiency in Commercial Banks*, Federal Reserve Board, Washington, D.C. (WP 8/1997).

Berger, A., R. DeYoung and G. Udell (2000) 'Efficiency Barriers to the Consolidation of the European Financial Services Industry', *European Financial Management*, 6.

Berger, A. and T. Hannan (1998) 'The Efficiency Cost of Market Power in the Banking Industry: A Test of the Quiet Life and Related Hypotheses', *The Review of Economics and Statistics*, vol 3, August, pp. 454–65.

Berger, A., D. Hancock and D. Humphrey (1993b) 'Bank Efficiency Derived from the Profit Function', *Journal of Banking & Finance*, 17, 317–47.

Berger, A.N., G.A. Hanweck and D.B. Humphrey (1987) 'Competitive Viability in Banking. Scale, Scope and Product Mix Economies', *Journal of Monetary Economics*, 20, 501–20.

Berger, A. and D. Humphrey (1990) 'Measurement and Efficiency Issues in Commercial Banking', *Finance and Economics Discussion Series*, 151, Federal Reserve Board, USA.

Berger, A. and D. Humphrey (1991) 'The Dominance of Inefficiencies Over Scale and Product Mix Economies in Banking', *Journal of Monetary Economics*, 28(1), 117–48.

Berger, A. and D. Humphrey (1992) 'Measurement and Efficiency Issues in Commercial Banking', in Zvi Griliches (ed.), *Output Measurement in the Service Sectors*, National Bureau of Economic Research Studies in Income and Wealth, 56, University of Chicago Press, Chicago.

Berger, A. and D. Humphrey (1997) 'Efficiency of Financial Institutions: International Survey and Directions for Future Research', *European Journal of Operational Research*, 98, 175–212.

Berger, A., W. Hunter and S. Timme (1993a) 'The Efficiency of Financial Institutions: A Review and Preview of Research Past, Present, and Future', *Journal of Banking & Finance*, 17, 221–49.

Berger, A. and L. Mester (1997) 'Inside the Black Box: What Explains Differences in the Efficiencies of Financial Institutions?', *Journal of Banking & Finance*, 21, 895–947.

Berger, A. and L. Mester (1999) *What Explains the Dramatic Changes in Cost and Profit Performance of the U.S. Banking Industry*, Federal Reserve Board, Washington, D.C. (13/1999).

Besson, J.L. (1993) *Monnaie et Finances*, Office des Publications Universitaires, Algiers.

Bhattacharya, A., C. Lovell and P. Sahay (1997) 'The Impact of Liberalisation on the Productive Efficiency of Indian Banks', *European Journal of Operational Research*, 98, 332–45.

Binger, B. and E. Hoffman (1988) *Microeconomics with Calculus*, Harper Collins Publishers, New York.

Bisat, A., M. El-Erian and T. Helbing (1997) 'Growth, Investment, and Savings in the Arab Economies', *International Monetary Fund Working Paper* (WP 85/97).

Bonin, J. P., I. Hasan and P. Wachtel (2003) 'Bank Performance, Efficiency and Ownership in Transition Countries', Paper presented at the Ninth Dubrovnik Economic Conference, sponsored by the Bank of Croatia, June 26–28.

Boughrara, A. (2001) 'The Monetary Policy of the Central Bank of Tunisia: An Assessment', University of the Centre, Sousse. This paper presented at the 9th annual conference of the Economic Research Forum (ERF), held in Al-Sharja, UAE, October 26–28, 2002.

Boyd, J. and E. Prescott (1986) 'Financial Intermediation-Coalitions', *Journal of Economic Theory*, 38(2), 211–32.

Brownbridge, M. and S. Gayi (1999) 'Progress, Constraints and Limitations of Financial Sector Reforms in the Least Developed Countries', Institute for Development Policy and Management, University of Manchester, Finance and Development Research Programme, Paper No.7.

Bureau of Economic and Business Affairs (1998) 'US State Department Country Reports on Economic and Policy Trade Practices for Jordan, Egypt, Saudi Arabia and Bahrain', http://www.state.gov/www/issues/economic.

Burki, A. and G.S.K. Niazi (2003) 'The Effects of Privatization, Competition and Regulation on Banking Efficiency in Pakistan, 1991–2000', Paper presented at

CRC Conference on Regulatory Impact Assessment: Strengthening Regulation Policy and Practice, University of Manchester, Manchester, UK, 26–27 November, 2003.

Caprio, G. and L. Summers, (1993) *Finance and Its Reform: Beyond Laissez-Faire*, World Bank.

Carbo, S., E. Gardener and J. Williams (2000), 'Efficiency in Banking: Empirical Evidence from the Savings Banks Sector, Institute of European Finance, University of Wales, Bangor, unpublished.

Casu, B. and C. Girardone (1998) 'A Comparative Study of the Cost Efficiency of Italian Bank Conglomerates', Institute of European Finance, University of Wales, Bangor, unpublished (WP 3/98).

Cavello, L. and S. Rossi (2001) 'Scale and Scope Economies in the European Banking Systems', *Journal of Multinational Financial Management*, 11, 515–31.

Cebenoyan, A., E. Cooperman and C. Register (1993) 'Firm Inefficiency and the Regulatory Closure of S&Ls: An Empirical Investigation', *Review of Economics and Statistics*, 75, 540–45.

Cebenoyan, A.S., Elizabeth Cooperman, Charles A. Register and Sylvia Hudgins (1993) 'The Relative Efficiency of Stock versus Mutual S&Ls: A Stochastic Cost Frontier Approach', *Journal of Financial Services and Research*, 7, 151–70.

Central Bank of Jordan (1997) *Annual Report*, Jordan.

Central Bank of Jordan (2001) *Annual Report*, Jordan.

Central Bank of Kuwait (2002) *Annual Report*, Kuwait.

Central Bank of Oman (1996) and (2001) *Annual Report*, Oman.

Central Bank of Qatar (2001) *Annual Report*, Qatar.

Cetorelli, N. and M. Gambera (1999) 'Banking Market Structure, Financial Dependence and Growth: International Evidence from Industry Data', Wharton School Center for Financial Institutions, University of Pennsylvania, 1999/10, http://fic.wharton. upenn.edu/fic/papers/00/0019.pdf

Cetorelli, N. and P. Peretto (2000) 'Oligopoly Banking and Capital Accumulation', Federal Reserve Bank of Chicago, Working Paper 00–14.

Chabrier, P. and S. Ingves (2002) *Tunisia: Financial System Stability Assessment*, Monetary and Exchange Affairs and Middle Eastern Departments, IMF Country Report No. 02/119.

Chabrier, P. and I. Kabur (2000) *Algeria: Staff Report for the 2000 Consultation with Algeria*, IMF Country Report No. 00/93, July 2000.

Chaffai, M. and M. Dietsch (1995) 'Should Banks be "universal"? The Relationship between Economies of Scope and Efficiency in the French Banking Industry', *University of Robert Schuman of Strasbourg Working Paper*, France.

Chang, C., I. Hasan and W. Hunter (1998) 'Efficiency of Multinational Banks: An Empirical Investigation', *Applied Financial Economics*, 8, pp. 1–8.

Chapra, M. Umar (1985) *Towards a Just Monetary System*, The Islamic Foundation U.K., Leicester.

Chapra, M. Umar and Tariqullah Khan (2000) *Regulation and Supervision of Islamic Banks*, Occasional Paper No.3, Islamic Research and Training Institute, Islamic Development Bank, Jeddah.

Chaput, D., C. Delvoie, W. Grais and J.L. Sarbib (2000) *Kingdom of Morocco Financial Sector Strategy Note*, Private and Financial Sector Development, MENA Region, World Bank, Report No. 20885-MOR.

Charnes, A., W. Cooper and E. Rhodes (1978) 'Measuring the Efficiency of Decision Making Units', *European Journal of Operational Research*, 2, 429–44.

Chen, Z. and M. Khan (1997) 'Patterns of Capital Flows to Emerging Markets: A Theoretical Perspective', INF, WP/97/13, http://www.imf.org/external/pubs/ft/wp/wp9713.pdf.

Chen, Y., J. Mason and E. Higgins (2001) 'Economies of Scale in the Banking Industry: The Effects of Loan Specialization', Department of Business Administration and Education, Emporia State University, Emporia, Kansas State.

Clark, J. (1984) 'Estimation of Economies of Scale in Banking Using a Generalised Functional Form', *Journal of Money, Credit, and Banking*, 16(1), 53–68.

Clark, J. (1988) 'Economies of Scale and Scope At Depository Financial Institutions: A Review of the Literature', Federal Reserve Bank of Kansas City, *Economic Review*, 73, 16–33.

Clark, J. (1996) 'Economic Cost, Scale Efficiency, and Competitive Viability in Banking', *Journal of Money, Credit and Banking*, 28 (3), 342–64

Coelli, T.J. (1996) 'A Guide to Frontier Version 4.1: A Computer Program for Frontier Production Function Estimation', *Centre for Efficiency and Productivity Analysis Working Papers*, University of New England, Australia, No. 98/07.

Cook, W. D., M. Hababou and G.S. Roberts (2001) 'The Effects of Financial Liberalization on the Tunisian Banking Industry: A Non-Parametric Approach', *Schulich School of Business York University Working Paper.*

Council of Islamic Ideology Pakistan (1980) *Report of the Council of Islamic Ideology on the Elimination of Interest from the Economy*, Islamabad, Pakistan.

Cunningham, A. (1995) *Banking in the Middle East*, FT Financial Publishing, London.

Darrat, A.F. and A. Pennnathur (2002) 'Are the Maghreb Countries Really Integrable: Some Evidence from the Theory of Co-Integrated Systems', *Review of Financial Economics*, No. 11, 79–90.

Darrat, A.F., C. Topuz and T. Yousef (2002) 'Assessing Cost and Technical Efficiency of Banks in Kuwait', Paper presented at the Economic Research Forum for the Arab Countries, Iran and Turkey (ERF's) 8th Annual Conference in Cairo, January 2002.

DeBorger, B., G. Ferrier and K. Kerstens (1995) 'The Choice of a Technical Efficiency Measure on the Free Disposal Hull Reference Technology: A Comparison Using Banking Data', *Working Paper*, University of Arkansas, USA.

Demirgüç-Kunt, A. and R. Levine (1996) 'Stock Market Development and Financial Intermediaries: Stylised Facts', *World Bank Economic Review*, 10(2), 291–321.

Deprins, D., L. Simar and H. Tulkens (1984) 'Measuring Labour-Efficiency in Post Offices', in M. Marchand, P. Pestieau and H. Tulkens (eds), *The Performance of Public Enterprises: Concepts and Measurements*, North-Holland, Amsterdam.

DeYoung, R. and D. Nolle (1996) 'Foreign-Owned Banks in the US: Earning Market Share or Buying It?', *Journal of Money, Credit and Banking*, 28(4), 622–36.

Dietsch, M. and L. Weill (1998) 'Banking Efficiency and European Integration: Productivity, Cost and Profit Approaches', Paper presented at the 21st Colloquium of the SUERF, Frankfurt, 15–17, November.

Diewert, W. (1973) 'Functional Forms for Profit and Transformation Functions', *Journal of Economic Theory*, 7, 284–316.

Drake, L. and R. Simper (1999) 'X-efficiency and Scale Economies in Policing: A Comparative Study Using the Distribution Free Approach and DEA', Loughborough University, Economic Paper (7/97).

Dziobek, C. (1998) 'Market-Based Policy Instruments for Systemic Bank Restructuring', *IMF Working Paper* WP/98/113.

Economist Intelligence Unit (1991) *Country Profile: United Arab Emirates, 1991–92*, London.

Economist Intelligence Unit (1992) *Country Report: Kuwait*, No. 1, London.

Eisenbeis, R.A., G.D. Ferrier and S.H. Kwan (1996) 'An Empirical Analysis of the Informativeness of Programming and SFA Efficiency Scores: Efficiency and Bank Performance', Working Paper, University of North Carolina, Chapel Hill, NC, April.

El-Erian, M. and S. Fennell (1997) 'The Economy of the Middle East and North Africa in 1997', International Monetary Fund Pamphlet.

El-Erian, M. , S. Eken, S. Fennell and J. Chauffour (1996) 'Growth and Stability in the Middle East and North Africa', International Monetary Fund Pamphlet.

El-Shazly, A. (2001) 'Incentive-Based Regulations and Bank Restructuring in Egypt', World Bank Conference, May 2001; www.mafhoum.com/press/49E2b.htm'

Eltony, M.N. (2000) *Quantitative Measures of Financial Sector Reform in the Arab Countries*, Arab Planning Institute, Kuwait.

Elyasiani, E. and S. Mehdian (1990) 'A Non-Parametric Approach to Measurement of Efficiency and Technological Change: The Case of Large US Banks', *Journal of Financial Services Research*, 4, 157–68.

Elyasiani, E. and S. Mehdian (1995) 'The Comparative Efficiency Performance of Small and Large US Commercial Banks in the Pre- and Post-Deregulation Eras', *Applied Economics*, 27, 1069–79.

Enders, K., A. Jbili and V. Treichel (1997) 'Financial Sector Reforms in Algeria: Morocco and Tunisia: a Preliminary Assessment', *International Monetary Fund Working Paper* WP 97/81.

Enders, K., V. Fichera, S.P. Horvits and S. Sheibani (1998) *Tunisia: Banking Systems Issues and Statistical Appendix*, International Monetary Fund, Middle Eastern Department, Country Report No. 89/129.

European Commission (1997) *The Single Market Review*, Credit Institutions and Banking, Subseries II: Impact on Services, Vol. 3, Kogan Page, London.

Evanoff, D. and R. Israilevich (1991) 'Productive Efficiency in Banking', Economic Perspective, Federal Reserve of Chicago, 15 (July/August), 11–32.

Evanoff, D. and R. Israilevich (1995) 'Scale Elasticity Versus Scale Efficiency in Banking', *Southern Journal of Economics*, 61, 1036–47.

Fama, E. (1970) 'Efficient Capital Markets: A Review of Theory and Empirical Work', *Journal of Finance*, 25, 383–417.

Fanjul, O. and F. Maravall (1985) 'La eficiencia del sistema bancario Espanol', Research Paper, Alianza University, Madrid.

Farrell, M. (1957) 'The Measurement of Productive Efficiency', *Journal of the Royal Statistical Society*, Series A, CXX, Part 3, 253–90.

Favero, C. and L. Papi (1995) 'Technical Efficiency and Scale Efficiency in the Italian Banking Sector: A Non-Parametric Approach', *Applied Economics*, 27, 385–95.

Ferrier, G., S. Grosskopf, K. Hayes and S. Yaisawarng, (1993) 'Economies of Diversification in Banking Industry: A Frontier Approach', *Journal of Monetary Economics*, 31, 229–49.

Ferrier, G. and C. Lovell (1990) 'Measuring Cost Efficiency in Banking: Econometric and Linear Programming Evidence', *Journal of Econometrics*, 46, 229–45.

Forestieri, G. (1993) 'Economies of Scale and Scope in the Financial Services Industry: A Review of Recent Literature', in: OECD (Ed.). *Financial Conglomerates*, Paris, 63–124.

Fry, M. (1988) *Money, Interest and Banking in Economic Development*, 1st edn, Johns Hopkins University, Baltimore.

Fry, M. (1995) *Money, Interest, and Banking in Economic Development*, 2nd edn, Johns Hopkins University Press, Baltimore.

Fry, M. (1997) 'In Favour of Financial Liberalisation', *The Economic Journal*, 107, 754–70.

Fuentes, R. and M. Vergara (2003) 'Explaining Bank Efficiency: Bank Size or Ownership Structure?', Central Bank of Chile, unpublished paper.

Fukuyama, H. (1993) 'Technical and Scale Efficiency of Japanese Commercial Banks: A Non-Parametric Approach', *Applied Economics*, 25, 1101–12.

Galbis, V. (1994) 'Sequencing of Financial Sector Reforms: A Review', *IMF Working Paper*, 101/94, September 1994.

Gallant, A. (1981) 'On the Bias in Flexible Functional Forms and Essentially Unbiased Form: The Fourier Flexible Form', *Journal of Econometrics*, 15, 211–45.

Gallant, A. (1982) 'Unbiased Determination of Production Technologies', *Journal of Econometrics*, 20, 285–324.

GCC Secretariat General (http://www.gcc-sg.org).

Gilligan, T. and M. Smirlock (1984) 'An Empirical Study of Joint Production and Scale Economies in Commercial Banking', *Journal of Banking & Finance*, 8 (March), 67–77.

Goddard, J., P. Molyneux and J. Wilson (2001) *European Banking: Efficiency, Technology and Growth*, John Wiley, London.

Goldman Sachs and McKinsey & Co. (2001) 'The Future of Corporate Banking in Europe', January 2001, Goldman Sachs and McKinsey & Co., London.

Goldsmith, R. (1969) *Financial Structure and Development*, Yale University Press, New Haven.

Goumiri, M. (1993) *L'Offre de Monnaie en Algérie*, ENAG, Alger.

Gramley, L. (1962) *A Study of Scale Economies in Banking*, Federal Reserve Bank of Kansas City.

Greene, W. (1990) 'A Gamma-Distributed Stochastic Frontier Model', *Journal of Econometrics*, 46, 141–64.

Greene, W. (1993) 'The Econometric Approach to Efficiency Analysis', in Fried, H., C. Lovell and S. Schmidt (Eds.), *The Measurement of Productive Efficiency: Techniques and Applications*, Oxford University Press, New York, 68–119.

Greenwald, B., J. Stiglitz and A. Weiss (1984) 'Informational Imperfections in the Capital Markets and Macro-Economic Fluctuations', *American Economic Review*, 74 (1), 194–9.

Greenwood, J. and B. Jovanovic (1990) 'Financial Development, Growth, and the Distribution of Income', *Journal of Political Economy*, 98 (October), 1076–107.

Gulf Business (1999 to 2002) various editions.

Gulf Business (2002) 'Tightening the Control', August, 12–14.

Hall, P. (2001) 'The Hare and Tortoise: Does Slow and Steady Financial Liberalisation Win the Race? A Tunisian Case Study', *Working Paper* No. 01–19, Development Studies Institute, London School of Economic and Political Science.

Hamdouche, B. (1997) 'Development and the Problems of the Private Sector in Morocco', *Economic Research Forum for the Arab Countries, Iran and Turkey Forum*, vol. 4, no.2.

Handy, H., P. Allum, A. Bisat, J. Daniel, R. Khan, C. Lane, M. Mecagni, J. Mongardini, and A. Subramanian (1998) 'Egypt Beyond Stabilization Toward a Dynamic Market Economy', *International Monetary Fund Occasional Paper* (163/98).

Hao, J., W. Hunter and W. Yang (1999) *Deregulation and Efficiency: The Case of Private Korean Banks*, Federal Reserve Bank of Chicago.

Hasan, I. and K. Marton (2000) 'Development and Efficiency of the Banking Sector in Transitional Economy: Hungarian Experience', Bank of Finland Institute fir Economies in Transition, BOFIT, *Discussion Paper* No. 7.

Heffernan, S. (1996) *Modern Banking In Theory and Practice*, John Wiley & Sons, Chichester, England.

Hellmann, T., K. Murdock and J. Stiglitz (1997) 'Financial Restraint and the Market Enhancing View', 'http://faculty-gsb.stanford.edu/hellmann/pdfs/marketenhancing.pdf'.

Henry, C., and C. Boone (2001) 'Commercial Banking Systems: The Neglected Variable in Political and Economic Developments', University of Texas at Austin, a paper prepared for the 2001 Annual Meeting of the American Political Science Association, Aug.–Sept. 2001.

Hermalin, B. and N. Wallace (1994) 'The Determinants of Efficiency and Solvency in Savings and Loans', *Rand Journal of Economics*, 25, 361–81.

Herring, R.G. and A.M. Santomero (1990) 'The Corporate Structure of Financial Conglomerates', *Journal of Financial Services Research*, 471–97.

Herring, R. and A. Santomero (2000) 'What is Optimal Financial Regulation?', *The Wharton Financial Institution Centre Working Paper* (WP 34/00).

Hughes, J., W. Lang, L. Mester and C. Moon (1995) 'Recovering Banking Technologies When Managers Are Not Risk-Neutral', Conference on Bank Structure and Competition, Federal Reserve Board of Chicago, May, pp. 349–68.

Hughes, J. and L. Mester (1993) 'A Quality and Risk-Adjusted Cost Function for Banks: Evidence on the "Too-Big-to-Fail" Doctrine', *Journal of Productivity Analysis*, 4, 293–315.

Hughes, J., L. Mester, and C. Moon (1996a) 'Efficient Banking under Interstate Branching', *Journal of Money, Credit and Banking*, 28, 1045–71.

Hughes, J., L. Mester and C. Moon (1996b) 'Safety in Numbers? Geographic Diversification and Bank Insolvency Risk', *Federal Reserve Bank of Philadelphia Working Paper* 96–14.

Hughes, J., L. Mester and C. Moon (1997) 'Recovering Risky Technologies Using the Almost Ideal Demand System: An Application to U.S. Banking', *Federal Reserve Bank of Philadelphia Working Paper* 97–8

Hughes, J., L. Mester and C. Moon (2000) 'Are All Scale-Economies in Banking Elusive or Illusive: Evidence Obtained by Incorporating Capital Structure and Risk Taking into Models of Bank Production', *The Wharton School, University of Pennsylvania Working Paper* (WP 33/00).

Humphrey, D. (1985) 'Cost and Scale Economies in Bank Intermediation', in R. Aspinwall and R.A. Eisenbeis (eds), *Handbook for Banking Strategies*, John Wiley, New York.

Humphrey, D.B. (1987) 'Cost Dispersion and the Measurement of Economies in Banking', *Federal Reserve Bank of Richmond Economic Review*, May/June, 24–38.

Humphrey, D.B. (1990) 'Why Do Estimates of Banks Scale Economies Differ', *Federal Reserve Bank of Richmond Economic Review*, 76,38–50.

Humphrey, D. (1991) 'Productivity in Banking and Effects from Deregulation', *Federal Reserve Bank of Richmond Economic Review*, March/April, 16–28.

Humphrey, D.B (1993) 'Cost and technical change: Effects from bank deregulation'. *Journal of Productivity Analysis*, Vol 4, 9–34

Hunter, W. and S. Timme (1986) 'Technical Change, Organizational Form and the Structure of Bank Production', *Journal of Money, Credit and Banking*, 18(2), 152–66.

Hunter, W. and S.G. Timme (1991) 'Technological Change in Large US Banks', *Journal of Business*, 64, 339–62.

Hunter, W., S. Timme and W. Yang (1990) 'An Examination of Cost Sub Additivity and Multiproduct Production in Large U.S. Banks', *Journal of Money, Credit and Banking*, 22(4), 504–25.

Intarachote, T. (2000) 'Financial Liberalisation in Thailand', PhD, University of Wales, Bangor.

International Monetary Fund (1996) *Jordan – Strategy for Adjustment and Growth*, IMF Occasional Paper No. 136, May 20.

International Monetary Fund (1998) *Toward a Framework for Financial Stability*, IMF, Washington DC.

International Monetary Fund (2000) *World Economic Outlook*, IMF, Washington DC.

Iqbal, M., A. Ausaf and K. Tariqullah (1998) *Challenges Facing Islamic Banking*, Occasional Paper No.2, Islamic Research and Training Institute, Islamic Development Bank, Jeddah.

Iqbal, Munawar and David T. Llewellyn, (eds) (2002) *Islamic Banking and Finance: New Perspectives in Profit Sharing and Risk*, Edward Elgar, Cheltenham, UK, and Northampton, MA.

Iradian, G., S. Bazzoni and H. Joly (2000) 'Algeria: Recent Economic Developments', *International Monetary Fund Staff Country Report* No. 00/105.

Isik, I. and K. Hassan (2002) 'Technical, Scale and Allocative Efficiencies of Turkish Banking Industry', *Journal of Banking & Finance*, 26, 719–66.

Ivaldi, M, N. Ladoux, H. Ossard and M. Simioni (1996) 'Comparing Fourier and Translof Specifications of Multiproduct Technology: Evidence from an Uncomplete Panel of French Farmers', *Journal of Applied Economics*, 11, 649–67.

Jackson, P.M. and M.D. Fethi (2000) 'Evaluating the Efficiency of Turkish Commercial Banks: An Application of DEA and Tobit Analysis', presented at the International DEA Symposium, University of Queensland, Brisbane, Australia, 2–4 July 2000.

Jagtiani, J. and A. Khanthavit (1996) 'Scale and Scope Economies at Large Banks: Including Off-Balance Sheet Products and Regulatory Effects (1984–1991), *Journal of Banking and Finance*, 20, 1271–87

Jbili, A., V. Galbis and A. Bisat (1997) *Financial Systems and Reform in the Gulf Cooperation Council Countries*, Middle Eastern Department, International Monetary Fund.

Jondrow, J., C. Lovell, I. Materov and P. Schmidt (1982) 'The Estimation of Technical Inefficiency in the Stochastic Frontier Production Function Model', *Journal of Econometrics*, 19, 233–8.

Kalish, L. and R. Gilbert (1973) 'An Analysis of Efficiency of Scale and Organisation Form in Commercial Banking', *Journal of Industrial Economics*, 21 (July), 293–307.

Kaparakis, E., S. Miller and A. Noulas (1994) 'Short-Run Cost Inefficiency of Commercial Banks: A Flexible Stochastic Frontier Approach', *Journal of Money, Credit, and Banking*, 26, 875–93.

Karasneh, I., P. Cadle and J. Ford (1997) 'Market Structure, Concentration and Performance: Jordanian Banking System, 1980–1993', *University of Birmingham Discussion Paper* 97–12.

Keynes, J. (1936) *General Theory of Employment, Interest and Money*, Macmillan, London.

King, R. and R. Levine (1992) 'Financial Indicators and Growth in a Cross Section of Countries', *World Bank Working Paper* No. 819.

King, R. and R. Levine (1993a) 'Finance, Entrepreneurship, and Growth: Theory and Evidence', *Journal of Monetary Economics*, 32 (December), 513–42.

King, R. and R. Levine (1993b) 'Finance and Growth: Schumpeter Might be Right', *Quarterly Journal of Economics*, 108 (August), 716–37.

Kolari, J. and A. Zardkoohi (1987) *Bank Cost, Structure and Performance*, Lexington Books, Lexington, Mass.

Kraft, E. and D. Tirtiroglu (1998) 'Bank Efficiency in Croatia: A Stochastic-Frontier Analysis', *Journal of Comparative Economics*, 26, 282–300.

Krugman, P. (1998) 'Crises: The Next Generation?', mimeo, presented for the Assaf Razin conference in Tel Aviv.

Kwan, S. H (2002) 'The X-Efficiency of Commercial Banks in Hong Kong', *Federal Reserve Bank of San Francisco Working Paper*, 2002–14.

Kwan, S. and R. Eisenbeis (1995) 'An Analysis of Inefficiencies in Banking: A Stochastic Cost Frontier Approach', *Journal of Banking & Finance*, 19, 733–4.

Landi, A. (1990) *Dimensioni, costi e profitti delle banche italiane*, Il Mulino, Bologna.

Lang, G. and P. Welzel (1996) 'Efficiency and Technical Progress in Banking: Empirical Results for a Panel of German Cooperative Banks', *Journal of Banking & Finance*, 20, 1003–23.

Lawrence, C. and R. Shay (1986) 'Technology and Financial Intermediation in a Multiproduct Banking Firm: An Econometric Study of I.S.S. Banks, 1979–1982', in C. Lawrence and R. Shay (eds), *Technological Innovation, Regulation and the Monetary Economy*, Ballinger, Cambridge, Mass.

Lee, J.K. (2002) 'Financial Liberalisation and Foreign Bank Entry in MENA', a study prepared as a background paper for the MENA trade intensification study, *Financial Sector Strategy and Policy*, World Bank.

Leibenstein, H. (1966) 'Allocative Efficiency vs. X-efficiency', *The American Economic Review*, 56, 392–415.

Leightner, E. and C. Lovell (1998) 'The Impact of Financial Liberalisation on the Performance of Thai Banks', *Journal of Economics and Business*, vol. 50, 115–31.

Levine, R. (1996) 'Foreign Banks, Financial Development, and Economic Growth', in Claude E. Barfield (ed.), *International Financial Markets: Harmonisation Versus Competition*, AEI Press Washington, DC.

Levine, R. (2002) 'Bank-Based or Market-Based Financial Systems: Which Is Better?', *Journal of Financial Intermediation*, 11(4), 398–428.

Levine, R. and A. Demirgüç-Kunt (2000) 'Bank-Based and Market-Based Financial Systems: Cross-Country Comparisons', *World Bank Working Papers – Domestic Finance, Saving, Financial Systems, Stock Markets*. No. 2143.

Maciejewski, E. and A. Mansur (1996) 'Jordan: Strategy for Adjustment and Growth', *International Monetary Fund Occasional Paper* (136).

Mankiw, G. (1994) *Macroeconomics*, Worth Publishers, New York.

Maudos, J., J. Pastor, F. Pérez and J. Quesada (2002) 'Cost and Profit Efficiency in European Banks', *Journal of International Financial Markets, Institutions and Money*, 12, 33–58.

McAllister, R. and D. McManus (1993) 'Resolving the Scale Efficiency Puzzle in Banking', *Journal of Banking & Finance*, 17, 389–405.

McDermott, C. (1996) 'Macroeconomic Environment and Factors Underlying Growth and Investment', in E. Maciejewski and A. Mansur (eds), *Jordan: Strategy for Adjustment and Growth*, IMF, Washington, DC.

McKinnon, R. (1973) *Money and Capital in Economic Development*, Brookings Institution, Washington, DC.

McKinsey and Co. (2001) *Beyond Online*, Spring (McKinsey and Co., London).

MEED (1999) 'A Mixed Year', *Middle East Economic Digest*, 25 June 25 9–11.

Meeusen, W. and J. van den Broeck (1977) 'Efficiency Estimation from Cobb–Douglas Production Functions with Composed Error', *International Economic Review*, 18, 435–44.

Meltzer, A. (1998) 'Financial Structure, Saving and Growth: Safety Nets, Regulation, and Risk Reduction in Global Financial Markets', 'http://www.gsia.cmu.edu/afs/ andrew/gsia/meltzer/financial_structure.pdf'.

Mertens, O. and G. Urga (2001) 'Efficiency, Scale and Scope Economies of the Ukrainian Banking Sector in 1998', *Emerging Markets Review*, 2 , 292–308.

Merton, R. (1995) 'Financial Innovation and the Management and Regulation of Financial Institutions', *Journal of Banking and Finance*, 19, 461–81.

Mester, L. (1987) 'A Multiproduct Cost Study of Savings and Loans', *Journal of Finance*, 42, 423–45.

Mester, L. (1993) 'Efficiency in the Savings and Loan Industry', *Journal of Banking & Finance*, 17, 267–86.

Mester, L. (1994) 'Efficiency of Banks in the Third Federal Reserve District', *The Wharton School*, University of Pennsylvania (WP 13/94).

Mester, L. (1996) 'A Study of Bank Efficiency Taking into Account Risk- Preferences', *Journal of Banking & Finance*, 20, 389–405.

Mester, L. (1997) 'Measuring Efficiency at US Banks: Accounting for Heterogeneity is Important', *European Journal of Operational Research*, 98, 230–43.

Ministry of Planning & CAPMAS of Egypt (1999) *Economic and Financial Indicators/ Egypt*, Central Bank of Egypt.

Mishkin, F. (1998) *The Economics of Money, Banking, and Financial Markets*, Addison Wesley, US.

Mishkin, Frederic S. (2001) 'Financial Policies and the Prevention of Financial Crises in Emerging Market Countries', *NBER Working Paper* No. 8397; and also in Martin Feldstein (ed.), *Economic and Financial Crises in Emerging Market Countries*, University of Chicago Press, Chicago.

Mitchell, K. and N. Onvural (1996) 'Economies of Scale and Scope at Large Commercial Banks: Evidence from the Fourier-Flexible Functional Form', *Journal of Money, Credit and Banking*, 28(2), 178–99.

Mohamed, K.S. (2003) 'The Economics of GCC Bank Efficiency', PhD, University of Wales, Bangor.

Mohammed, Y. (1994) 'Bank Supervision in Jordan', Institute of European Finance, MA, University of Wales, Bangor.

Molyneux, P., Y. Altunbas and E.P.M. Gardener (1996) *Efficiency in European Banking*, John Wiley & Sons, Chichester, England.

Morgan Stanley Dean Witter (2000) *The Internet and Financial Services*, 31 July, Morgan Stanley Dean Witter, London.

Morgan Stanley (2001) *Basel 2: Changing the Banking Landscape*, European Banks, Equity Research Europe, 6 February 2001.

Mullineaux, D. (1975) 'Economies of Scale and of Financial Institutions', *Journal of Monetary Economics*, 1, 233–40.

Mullineaux, D. (1978) 'Economies of Scale and Organisational Efficiency in Banking: A Profit-Function Approach', *Journal of Finance*, 33, 259–80.

Murphy, N. (1972) 'Cost Of Banking Activities: Interaction Between Risk And Operating Cost: A Comment', *Journal of Money, Credit and Banking*, 4 (August), 614–15.

Naas, A. (2003) *Le Système Bancaire Algérien: de la décolonisation léconomie de marché*, Maisonneuve et Larose, Paris.

Nakamura, L. (1994) 'Small Borrowers and the Survival of the Small Bank: Is Mouse Bank Mighty or Mickey?', *Business Review*, issue Nov., 3–15.

Nicholson, W. (1995) *Microeconomic Theory: Basic Principles and Extensions*, The Dryden Press, Texas, US.

Noulas, A., S. Ray and S. Miller (1990) 'Returns to Scale and Input Substitution for Large U.S. Banks', *Journal of Money, Credit and Banking*, 22(1), 94–108.

Okuda, H. and F. Mieno (1999) 'What Happened to the Banks in the Pre-Asian Crisis Period?', *Hitosubushi Journal of Economics*, 40 (2), 97–121.

Oral, M. and R. Yolalan (1990) 'An Empirical Study on Measuring Operating Efficiency and Profitability of Bank Branches', *European Journal of Operational Research*, 46, 282–94.

Pastor, J., F. Pérez, and J. Quesada (1995) 'Efficiency Analysis in Banking Firms: An International Comparison', *Working Paper*, EC 95–18, Istituto Valenciano de Investigaciones Economicas, Valencia, Spain.

Peterson, J. (2001) 'Basel gives banks whip hand', *Euromoney*, March, 48–53.

Porier, D.J. (1976) *The Econometrics of Structural Change with Special Emphasis on Spline Functions*, North-Holland, Amsterdam.

Presley, J.R. (1992) *Banking in the Arab Gulf*, Macmillan, London.

Pulley, L. and D. Humphrey (1993) 'The Role of Fixed Costs and Cost Complementarities in Determining Scope Economies and the Cost of Narrow Banking Proposals', *Journal of Business*, 66(3), 437–62.

Qatar Central Bank (2000) *Executive Instruction Until March 2000*, 2nd edn, Qatar.

Qatar Central Bank (various years) *Annual Reports*.

Qatar Monetary Agency (1992) *The Banking and Financial System in Qatar*, Department of Research and Statistics, Qatar.

Rao, A. (2002) 'Efficiency Analysis of UAE Banks, Finance Working Paper Number 0304011', Economics Working Paper Archive at Washington University St Louis (WUSTL).

Resti, A. (1997) 'Evaluating the Cost-Efficiency of the Italian Banking System: What Can Be Learned from the Joint Application of the Parametric and Non-Parametric Techniques', *Journal of Banking & Finance*, 2, 221–50.

Richmond, J. (1974) 'Estimating the Efficiency of Production', *International Economic Review*, 15, 515–21.

Risk (2001a) 'Basel part two: the jury's verdict', February, 26–29.

Risk (2001b) 'Capital concerns', August, 86–88.

Rodriguez, J.R.O., A.A. Alvarez and P.P. Gomez (1993) 'Scale and Scope Economies in Banking: A Study of Savings Banks in Spain', Universidad De La Laguna, Tenerife, Spain.

Rogers, K. (1998) 'Nontraditional Activities and the Efficiency of US Commercial Banks', *Journal of Banking & Finance*, 22, 467–82.

Rutherford, D. (2000) *Routledge Dictionary of Economics*, Routledge, London.

Saha, A. and T. S. Ravishankar (2000) 'Rating of Indian Commercial banks: A DEA Approach', *European Journal of Operations Research*, 124, 187–203.

Sathye, M. (2001) 'Efficiency of Banks in a Developing Economy: The Case of India', Examining Ten Years of Economic Reforms in India, Conference Proceedings, Australia National University, Canberra, Australia.

Saudi Monetary Agency (various years) *Monthly, Quarterly and Annual Economic Digest* for years 1994–2000.

Saudi Arabia Monetary Agency (2001) *Annual Report*, Kingdom of Saudi Arabia.

Schmidt, P.(1986) 'Frontier Production Functions', *Econometrics Reviews*, 4, 289–328.

Schweiger, S. and J. McGee (1961) 'Chicago Banking', *Journal of Business*, 34(3), 203–366.

Schweitzer, S. (1972) 'Economics of Scale and Holding Company Affiliation in Banking', *Southern Economic Journal*, 39 (October), 258–66.

Sealey, C. and J. Lindley (1977) 'Inputs, Outputs and a Theory of Production and Cost at Depository Financial Institutions', *Journal of Finance*, 32, 1251–66.

Secretariat of the GCC Council (2002) 'Economic Bulletin and other reports', 'http://www.gcc-sg.org'

Shaffer, S. (1991) 'Potential Merger Synergies Among Large Commercial Banks', *Working Paper*, Federal Reserve Bank of Philadelphia, October.

Sharpe, W. (1964) 'Capital Asset Prices: A Theory of Market Equilibrium', *Journal of Finance*, September, 425–442.

Shaw, E. (1973) *Financial Deepening in Economic Development*, Oxford University Press, New York.

Sinkey, J. (1992) *Commercial Bank Financial Management In the Financial-Services Industry*, 4th edn, Macmillan Publishing Company, New York.

Spong, K., R. Sullivan and R. DeYoung (1995) 'What Makes A Bank Efficient? A Look at Financial Characteristics and Bank Management and Ownership Structure', *Financial Industry Perspective*, Federal Reserve Bank of Kansas City.

Srivastava, P. (1999) 'Size, Efficiency and Financial Reforms in Indian Banking', *Indian Council for Research on International Economic Relations*, New Delhi, India July.

Standard and Poor's *Creditweek* (2002) 'Capital Market Trends in The Gulf Cooperation Council Countries', Standard and Poor's *Creditweek*, October 16, London.

Stevenson, R. (1980) 'Likelihood Functions for Generalised Stochastic Frontier Estimation', *Journal of Econometrics*, 13, 57–66.

Stiglitz, J. (1989) 'Financial Markets and Development', *Oxford Review of Economic Policy*, 5(4), 55–68.

Stiglitz, J. (1994) 'The Role of the State in Financial Markets', in *Proceedings of the World Bank Annual Bank Conference on Development Economics 1993*, edited by Michael Bruno and Boris Pleskovic, World Bank, 19–52, Washington.

Stiglitz, J. (1998) 'The Role of Financial System in Development', Presentation at the fourth Annual Bank Conference on Development in Latin America and the Caribbean, The World Bank, San Salvador, El Salvador, June 29, 1998.

Stiglitz, J. E. and A. Weiss (1981) 'Credit Rationing in Markets with Imperfect Information', *American Economic Review*, 71 (3), June, 393–410.

Subramanian, A. (1997) 'The Egyptian Stabilization Experience: An Analytical Retrospective', *International Monetary Fund Working Paper* (WP 105/97).

Taylor, W.R, R.Thompson, R. Thrall and P. Dharmapala (1997) 'DEA/AR Efficiency and Profitability of Mexican Banks – A Total Income Model', *European Journal of Operational Research*, 98, 346–63.

Thakor, A. (1996) 'The Design of Financial Systems: An Overview', *Journal of Banking and Finance*, 20, 917–48.

The World Factbook (2002) (http://www.cia.gov/cia/publications/factbook).

Tobin, J. (1984) 'On the Efficiency of the Financial System', *Lloyds Bank Review*, 153 (July), 1–15.

Tulkens, H. (1993) 'On FHD Efficiency Analysis: Some Methodological Issues and Applications to Retail Banking, Courts and Urban Transit', *Journal of Productivity Analysis*, 4, 183–210.

Turati, G. (2001) 'Cost Efficiency and Profitability in European Commercial Banking', 7th European Workshop on Efficiency and Productivity Analysis, Oviedo (Spain).

UAE Central Bank (2001a) *Annual Report*, Abu Dhabi, UAE.

UAE Central Bank (2001b) 'Dynamic Growth of the UAE Monetary & Banking Sector', http://www.cbuae.gov.ae/DynamicGrowtha.htm.

UNDP (1999) *Human Development Report*, United Nations, New York.

US Commercial Service (2002) 'Countries Commercial Guide (for Jordan, Egypt, Saudi Arabia and Bahrain', www.usatrade.gov/website.

US Embassy Riyadh (2000) 'Saudi Arabia 2000 Economic Trends', http:usembassy.state.gov/riyadh/wwwhet00.html.

Vennet, R. V. (1993) 'Cost Characteristics of Credit Institutions in the EC', Paper presented at the 20th Annual Meeting of the European Finance Association, Copenhagen Business School, 26–28 August, published in section II-D of the Proceedings, 1–38.

Vermeren, P. (2002) *Le Maroc en Transition*, Editions la Decouverte, Paris.

Wachtel, P. (2000) 'Globalization of Banking: Why does it matter?', presente y Futuro del Sistema Financiero en Paises Emergentes, Caracas, Venezuela, October 25–26.

Weill, L. (2001) 'Foreign Ownership and Cost Efficiency: Evidence on Polish and Czech Banks', *LARGE*, University of Robert Schuman, Strasbourg, France.

Weill, L. (2003) 'Banking Efficiency in Transition Economies – The Role of Foreign Ownership', *The Economics of Transition*, 11 (3), September, 569–85.

Whalen, G. (1991) 'A Proportional Hazards Model of Bank Failure: An Examination of Its Usefulness as an Early Warning Tool', *Federal Reserve Bank of Cleveland Economic Review*, Quarter 1, 21–31.

Wheelock, D. and P. Wilson (1995) 'Explaining Bank Failures: Deposit Insurance, Regulation, and Efficiency', *Review of Economics and Statistics*, 77, 689–700.

White,G. (2001) *A Comparative Political Economy of Tunisia and Morocco*, State University of New York Press, Albany.

Wilkenson, B. and A. Atti (1997) *Assessment Report for Bahrain*, UNDP MicroFinance , United Nations, New York.

Williams, J. and E.P.M. Gardener (2000) 'Efficiency and European Regional Banking', University of Wales, Bangor, unpublished.

Williams, J. and T. Intarachote (2002) 'Financial Liberalisation and Profit Efficiency in the Thai Banking System, 1990–1997: The Case of Domestic and Foreign Banks', Working Paper, University of Wales, Bangor.

Williamson, O.E. (1975) 'Markets and Hierarchies: Analysis and Antitrust Implications', 'Costly Monitoring Financial Intermediation, and Equilibrium Credit Rationing', *Journal of Monetary Economics*, 18(2), 159–79.

Wilson, Rodney (ed.) (1990) *Islamic Financial Markets*, Routledge, London.

Wilson, R. and J. Presley (1992) *Banking and Finance in the Arab Middle East*, Macmillan, London.

World Bank (1991) *World Tables 1991*, Johns Hopkins University Press, Baltimore and London.

World Bank (1999) *World Economic and Social Survey*, World Bank, Washington, DC.

World Bank (2000) *World Development Indicators Database*, July 2000.

World Trade Organization (2000) 'Bahrain', 'http://www.wto.org/englishtratop_e/ tpr_e/tp139e.htm'.

Zaim, O. (1995) 'The Effect of Financial Liberalisation on the Efficiency of Turkish Commercial Banks', *Applied Financial Economics*, 5, 257–64.

Zamiti, M. (1998) 'Les Réformes du Sécteur Financier au Maroc: Description et Évaluation', Centre d'Études en Administration Internationale (CETAI), École des Hautes Études Commerciales (HEC), Montréal.

Zeinelabdin, A. (1990) 'World Financial Situation and Islamic Countries', *Journal of Economic Cooperation Among Islamic Countries*, pp. 49–91.

Zeinelabdin, A. (1997) 'A Background Note to the Workshop on Privatisation in the OIC Countries', *Journal of Economic Cooperation Among Islamic Countries*, 1–2(18).

Index